10-Step Evaluation for Training and Performance Improvement

Sara Miller McCune founded SAGE Publishing in 1965 to support the dissemination of usable knowledge and educate a global community. SAGE publishes more than 1000 journals and over 800 new books each year, spanning a wide range of subject areas. Our growing selection of library products includes archives, data, case studies and video. SAGE remains majority owned by our founder and after her lifetime will become owned by a charitable trust that secures the company's continued independence.

Los Angeles | London | New Delhi | Singapore | Washington DC | Melbourne

10-Step Evaluation for Training and Performance Improvement

Seung Youn (Yonnie) Chyung

Boise State University

Los Angeles | London | New Delhi
Singapore | Washington DC | Melbourne

FOR INFORMATION:

SAGE Publications, Inc.
2455 Teller Road
Thousand Oaks, California 91320
Email: order@sagepub.com

SAGE Publications Ltd.
1 Oliver's Yard
55 City Road
London EC1Y 1SP
United Kingdom

SAGE Publications India Pvt. Ltd.
B 1/I 1 Mohan Cooperative Industrial Area
Mathura Road, New Delhi 110 044
India

SAGE Publications Asia-Pacific Pte. Ltd.
3 Church Street
#10-04 Samsung Hub
Singapore 049483

Printed in the United States of America

ISBN: 978-1-5443-2396-1

This book is printed on acid-free paper.

Acquisitions Editor: Helen Salmon
Editorial Assistant: Megan O'Heffernan
e-Learning Editor: Chelsea Neve
Production Editor: Jane Martinez
Copy Editor: Colleen Brennan
Typesetter: C&M Digitals (P) Ltd.
Proofreader: Susan Schon
Cover Designer: Candice Harman
Marketing Manager: Susannah Goldes

RECYCLED
Paper made from recycled material
FSC® C008955

18 19 20 21 22 10 9 8 7 6 5 4 3 2 1

• Contents •

• List of Tables •

• List of Figures •

• List of Exhibits •

• Preface •

Audience for the Book

This book is written for workforce development and performance improvement professionals (or professionals in the making) who need to learn how to conduct program evaluations for their internal or external clients. If you are one of those practitioners, assess your current evaluation-related knowledge and skills by using these five levels—novice, advanced beginner, competent, proficient, and expert. If you fall into the *novice* or *advanced beginner* level, this book is an appropriate one for you to use.

While working in the workforce development and performance improvement capacity in various types of organizations, you may associate yourself with the professional communities of human performance improvement (HPI), human resource development (HRD), and/or training and development (T&D). This book explains how to conduct a program evaluation in the HPI, HRD, or T&D context. Although *workforce development* and *performance improvement* are points of similarity among HPI, HRD, and T&D, it is quite a mouthful to say "program evaluations conducted in the workforce development and performance improvement context." Therefore, in this book, we will treat HPI as a broader concept than HRD and T&D and explain how to conduct program evaluations in the HPI context.

Approaches Used in the Book

It is often said that the best way to learn something new is to do it on your own. This *learning-by-doing* approach is beneficial in many ways—you likely find your learning process more meaningful, retain your knowledge and skills longer, and readily be able to transfer your knowledge and skills to similar situations.

This book is written with the learning-by-doing approach in mind. It helps you learn how to conduct a program evaluation by actually completing a client-based program evaluation. Because it is likely your first full-blown formal program evaluation, you are advised to select a small-scaled evaluation project.

Evaluators use different evaluation designs and approaches depending on the purpose and type of their evaluation, and it would be impossible to explain various evaluation designs in one book. Instead, this book focuses on conducting a program evaluation using a descriptive case study type evaluation design, which you as a novice or advanced beginner level evaluator can easily learn to use and still produce a reasonably comprehensive evaluation project.

This book walks you through the steps to conduct a program evaluation in the HPI context by investigating multiple dimensions of a program, through triangulating multiple data sets, which can be applied to both formative and summative evalua-tions. Once you are familiar with the overall evaluation procedure, you are encouraged to learn more about different evaluation designs, including experimental or ethno-graphic studies. It will enable you to select and apply the most appropriate methodol-ogy for your individual evaluation projects.

Content of the Book

This book explains a 10-step evaluation procedure for conducting a program evaluation:

1. Identify an evaluand.

2. Identify stakeholders and their needs.

3. Identify the purpose of evaluation.

4. Develop a program logic model.

5. Determine dimensions and importance weighting.

6. Determine data collection methods.

7. Develop data collection instruments.

8. Collect data.

9. Analyze data with rubrics.

10. Draw conclusions.

In addition to the micro-level 10 steps listed here, the book explains macro-level tasks to be performed during a program evaluation, including feasibility and risk factor assessments and formative and summative meta-evaluations.

The Introduction describes several evaluation terms and frameworks used in the 10 steps, which are grouped into three phases: identification, planning, and implementation.

Starting with Chapter 1, individual chapters explain the micro-level 10 steps and macro-level tasks to be performed. Chapters 1 and 2 explain the first three steps of the *identification* phase where you identify (or analyze) a program to be evaluated, a.k.a. an evaluand (Step 1), its stakeholders (Step 2), and the purpose of the evaluation (Step 3). As in any projects, it is important to assess feasibility of your evaluation project and risk factors from the beginning of the project. Chapter 3 describes ways to assess fea-sibility and risk factors regarding your evaluation project. The project identification phase will result in writing a statement of work to be submitted to your client, as described in Chapter 4.

Chapters 5 through 8 explain the *planning* phase of your evaluation project. During this phase of your project, you develop a program logic model (Step 4), deter-mine dimensions and importance weighting (Step 5), and determine data collection methods (Step 6). During those steps, you need to revisit Chapter 3 to continue to assess your project feasibility and address risk factors. You also start conducting formative meta-evaluations to ensure that you are using an appropriate evaluation design. The planning phase will result in writing an evaluation proposal that you submit to your client.

Once your evaluation proposal is approved by your client, you follow Chapters 9 through 14 to complete the *implementation* phase of your project and write an evaluation report. During this phase, you need to continue to assess and handle ethical concerns that may arise while collecting data, analyzing data, and reporting results. You conduct formative meta-evaluations to ensure the quality of your data collection instruments and data analysis process. The output of completing all 10 steps is your evaluation report. You conduct a summative meta-evaluation before you share the final report with your client and other stakeholders. Depending on your responsibility and accessibility, you may assist the client and stakeholders to take action on your evaluation findings, such as implementing solutions that you recommended to improve the program quality.

As shown in Figure P-1, the 10 evaluation steps are aligned with the ADDIE process (**A**nalysis, **D**esign, **D**evelopment, **I**mplementation, and **E**valuation), which is commonly used in instructional design and other performance improvement projects.

Use of the Book

This book was originally written as a textbook for a graduate-level evaluation class, but it may be used for an upper-level undergraduate class. Downloadable resources for this book are provided at the SAGE website at **https://study.sagepub.com/chyung.**

If you are an instructor who adopted this book for your evaluation class, you want to design the class to be *project based* rather than totally lecture and discussion oriented, so that your students can actually conduct their own evaluation while learning the content of the individual chapters.

For a 15-week course, you can assign each chapter to each week to facilitate the development of student evaluation projects, as shown in Table P-1. You can use this weekly schedule in a face-to-face, blended, or online course. You may want to ask your students to propose their own evaluation project topics and select several of the most feasible evaluation projects as team projects, rather than having each individual student complete a project.

If you are a student who is taking an evaluation class for which this book is used as a textbook, it is assumed that you are new to program evaluation and do not possess a lot of knowledge in evaluation methodology. You will benefit from working with a couple of classmates to complete a chosen evaluation project as a team project.

If you are a professional who needs guidelines for conducting a program evaluation, you may use this book as a reference, while conducting an evaluation project with your coworkers in your workplace or for your clients.

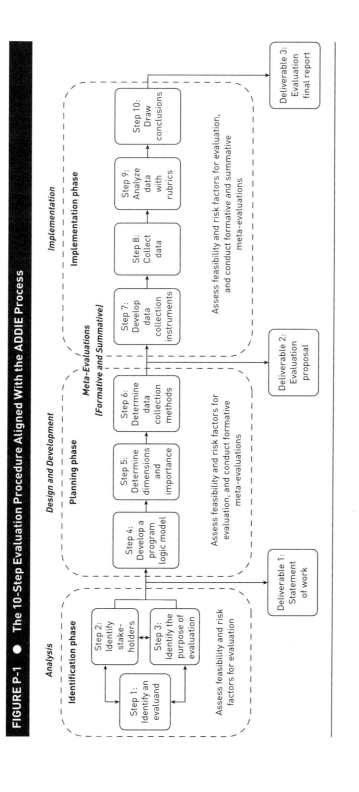

TABLE P-1 ● Use of Book Chapters and Class Activities in a 15-Week Course			
Phase	**Week**	**Chapter**	**Class Activities**
Identification	1–3	Introduction 1. Identify an Evaluand (Step 1) and Its Stakeholders (Step 2) 2. Identify the Purpose of Evaluation (Step 3) 3. Assess Evaluation Feasibility and Risk Factors (macro-level tasks)	• Discuss and complete chapter assignments. • Bring in evaluation topics. • Discuss feasibility and risk factors for individual projects. • Select feasible projects and form evaluation teams (three or four students in each team).
Identification	4	4. Write a Statement of Work (Deliverable 1)	• Present a statement of work (per team).
Planning	5–7	5. Develop a Program Logic Model (Step 4) 6. Determine Dimensions and Importance Weighting (Step 5) 7. Determine Data Collection Methods (Step 6)	• Discuss and complete chapter assignments. • Provide feedback on teams' evaluation steps and outputs as a form of meta-evaluation (macro-level tasks).
Planning	8	8. Write an Evaluation Proposal and Get Approval (Deliverable 2)	• Present a proposal (per team). • Provide feedback on teams' proposals as a form of formative meta-evaluation (macro-level tasks).
Implementation	9–13	9. Develop Data Collection Instruments I: Self-Administered Surveys (Step 7) 10. Develop Data Collection Instruments II: Interviews, Focus Groups, Observations, Extant Data Reviews, and Tests (Step 7) 11. Collect Data (Step 8) 12. Analyze Data With Rubrics (Step 9) 13. Draw Conclusions (Step 10)	• Discuss and complete chapter assignments. • Provide feedback on teams' evaluation steps and outputs as a form of formative meta-evaluation (macro-level tasks).
Implementation	14–15	14. Write a Final Report and Conduct a Summative Meta-Evaluation (macro-level tasks, Deliverable 3)	• Present a final report (per team). • Provide feedback on teams' final reports as a form of summative meta-evaluation.

Acknowledgments

I have been teaching in the Organizational Performance and Workplace Learning (OPWL) department at Boise State University since 1996. OPWL 530 Evaluation has been one of my main teaching assignments. When I started teaching this evaluation class, as most instructors do, I had to provide my own handouts to students to supplement what was missing in the textbook that I chose to use at that time. Several pages of class handouts grew over time, and it became a collection of comprehensive guidelines. Then, in spring 2016, I was awarded a sabbatical leave to focus on converting my guidelines into this book. I came back from my sabbatical with a 300-page manuscript. During the subsequent semesters, I used the manuscript as a textbook in my evaluation class, to refine the content and make it more useful to my students.

Therefore, I thank my students at Boise State University for giving me the reason to write this book. I selected the content of this book largely based on my students' needs. When they asked for more examples, I added more. When they were confused with certain steps, I provided more explanations about the steps. I give special thanks to Ms. Ieva Swanson, an OPWL graduate, who worked as my research assistant and provided thorough editing of the content. Her contributions and feedback helped make the content of this book easy to understand and follow.

In this book, I aimed at presenting an evaluation procedure that is *systematic, systemic,* and *needs-focused,* which are among the fundamental principles of workforce development and performance improvement. I thank the following people for their pioneering work, laying out critical foundations for conducting program evaluations and influencing me to develop the content of this book with those goals in mind. I did not originate the concepts and ideas that go with the 10 steps of evaluation that I present in this book; I give full credit to the pioneers.

First, Michael Scriven's work, especially his Key Evaluation Checklist, was instrumental in developing the systematic 10-step evaluation procedure. Scriven's book *Evaluation Thesaurus* and his numerous articles on evaluation are tremendously valuable to evaluation practitioners. Many of the main concepts and steps explained in this book, such as evaluand, three types of impactees, goal-free evaluation, dimensions, importance weighting, meta-evaluation, and more, are based on Scriven's work. I also found E. Jane Davidson's book *Evaluation Methodology Basics* to be a great source for learning the application of Scriven's Key Evaluation Checklist. Some of the explanations of the concepts provided in this book, such as application of importance weighting, rubric development, and synthesis of dimensional results, were influenced by the content presented in her book.

Second, Robert Brinkerhoff's evaluation approach with a systemic perspective, as illustrated in his book *The Success Case Method,* inspired me to emphasize the use of a system-focused approach during evaluation. Brinkerhoff's training impact model and the W. K. Kellogg Foundation's work on providing guidelines for developing program logic models are also very useful for conducting training evaluations. These logic models are introduced in this book as necessary ingredients for taking a systemic view while designing and implementing an evaluation project step-by-step.

Third, Michael Quinn Patton's utilization-focused evaluation was influential. Along with the use of systematic and systemic approaches to workforce development and performance improvement, another fundamental principle is that interventions should be designed based on the needs of the organization and stakeholders. Patton's notion that evaluation should be designed based on the intended users' needs (i.e., how they intend to use evaluation findings) is clearly aligned with the principle of workforce development and performance improvement, as I point out in this book. Those who are interested in Patton's evaluation approach are encouraged to read his book *Utilization-Focused Evaluation.*

---

xxii 10-Step Evaluation for Training and Performance Improvement

Finally, I cannot thank my friend, colleague, and husband, Don Winiecki, enough for the constant encouragement and emotional support that he has given me throughout the process. It is awesome to have such a smart and patient person near me to bat ideas around.

Seung Youn (Yonnie) Chyung
Boise, Idaho, USA

SAGE and the author would like to gratefully acknowledge the input from the following reviewers:

Bonnie Blakely Alston, *Retired Director of Field Education, Southern University at New Orleans*

Mary Leah Coco, *Associate Director of Technology Transfer at the Louisiana Transportation Research Center*

Bret D. Cormier, *Counseling, Leadership, and Special Education at Missouri State University*

Jennifer Fellabaum-Toston, *University of Missouri*

Charles Moreland, *Barry University*

Evan K. Perrault, *Brian Lamb School of Communication, Purdue University*

Sheila B. Robinson, *University of Rochester*

Sun-Young Shin, *Indiana University*

Sam Vegter, *Western Piedmont Community College*

Greg G. Wang, *University of Texas at Tyler*

• About the Author •

Dr. Seung Youn (Yonnie) Chyung is a professor and associate chair of the Department of Organizational Performance and Workplace Learning in the College of Engineering at Boise State University, Boise, Idaho. She earned a bachelor's degree from Ewha Womans University in Seoul, South Korea, and a doctor of education degree in Instructional Technology from Texas Tech University in Lubbock, Texas. Chyung has expertise in conducting evaluation studies and quantitative research in the learning and performance improvement context. She currently teaches graduate-level courses on program evaluation and quantitative research in organizations. She is the author of *Foundations of Instructional and Performance Technology*, published by HRD Press. During 20+ years of her academic career, Chyung has produced over 150 scholarly works, including research journal publications, professional conference presentations, and grant projects. She also provides pro bono consulting to local nonprofit organizations to perform statistical analysis on their organizational data and conduct program evaluations. She often involves students in her scholarly works and community service projects.

• Companion Website •

The companion website for *10-Step Evaluation for Training and Performance Improvement*, First Edition, is available at **https://study.sagepub.com/chyung**

Instructor Resources include:

- **Chapter quizzes** with pre-written, editable multiple choice and short-answer questions to help assess students' progress and understanding.

- Editable, chapter-specific **Microsoft® PowerPoint® slides** for ease and flexibility in creating a multimedia presentation for your course.

- A **sample syllabus** with a suggested model for structuring your evaluation course using the book.

- All **figures and tables from the book** available for download.

Student Resources include the following **downloadable samples, templates, and worksheets from the book** for use in planning and conducting evaluations:

- A sample **statement of work**

- A sample **evaluation proposal**

- A template for developing a **Gantt chart**

- A template for writing an **evaluation proposal and final report**

- **Worksheets** for developing an evaluation project **(Appendix B)**

• Introduction •

Performance Improvement and Evaluation

You may have been to a performance theater to attend a ballet or modern dance performance, or listen to an orchestra playing classical music. Regardless of the types of performing arts that you have attended, the artists probably went through years of training and practice before they performed in front of the audience. You do not see the behaviors that the artists exhibited during their training process; you only see their performance outcome and applaud for their accomplishments at the end of their performance.

Similarly, performance in the workplace consists of workers' behaviors and their accomplishments (Chyung, 2008; Gilbert, 2007). Workers' behaviors enable their accomplishments. However, organizations value not just workers' behaviors but, more importantly, their accomplishments. For that reason, the phrase *human performance* (or simply *performance*) in the workplace often refers to workers' accomplishments rather than their work behaviors. Competent workers likely produce accomplishments that are valued by not only themselves but also their organization and society. However, workers can become competent and successful only if they are in an appropriate environment (Rummler & Brache, 2012). Thus, performance improvement in the workplace involves finding ways to develop workers' capacity and change environmental factors that contribute to producing valuable performance outcomes.

PERFORMANCE IMPROVEMENT

Human performance improvement (HPI) is a transdisciplinary field of practice that promotes the use of systematic and systemic approaches to engineering work processes (behaviors) and producing desirable outcomes (accomplishments). HPI practitioners find areas to be changed, implement cost-effective solutions, and produce results valuable to the workers, their organization, and the society. Here, we should pay attention to a couple of phrases: a transdisciplinary field of professional practice and systematic and systemic approaches.

HPI AS A TRANSDISCIPLINARY FIELD

HPI is a transdisciplinary field of practice in that it synthesizes knowledge adopted from various disciplines such as psychology, instructional technology, human resource development, management, organizational development, and evaluation. Its synthesized knowledge is applied to various disciplines. Compared to specific disciplines such as nursing or hospitality management (where professionals are educated to acquire a specific branch of knowledge and skills and hold specific job titles with established job responsibilities), HPI is currently a field of professional practice that is not limited to a certain discipline. The existence and development of HPI as a field of practice depends on its assimilation into other disciplines. HPI practitioners work within various industries and organizations in numerous capacities such as instructional designers, trainers, workforce development specialists, human resource specialists, performance improvement professionals, or consultants. HPI can also be an additional professional role or a responsibility that professionals add to their existing job position. For example, nurses or hotel managers may also be educated to apply HPI principles to their daily practice.

Regardless of the type of industries and organizations where HPI practitioners work, they use systematic and systemic approaches to workforce development and performance improvement. **Systematic approaches** follow effective and efficient logical steps that lead to intended outcomes. **Systemic approaches** consider various factors both within and outside the immediate system that may influence the HPI process and outcomes positively or negatively. HPI practice requires a combination of both systematic and systemic approaches, as one often complements the other.

It should be clear by now that the term *HPI practitioner* is not a job title or position, but rather refers to any professional who applies HPI principles (such as systematic and systemic approaches to performance improvement) to any field or industry (i.e., transdisciplinary capacity). The systematic and systemic process of HPI practice is depicted in the human performance technology model (Van Tiem, Moseley, & Dessinger, 2012), comprised of several main phases:

1. Performance analysis, including organizational analysis, environmental analysis, gap analysis, and cause analysis

2. Intervention selection, design, and development

3. Intervention implementation and maintenance

4. Evaluation

5. Change management (which facilitates all previously listed phases)

Each of the five HPI phases is equally important. Evaluation is an essential phase, as it receives information from, and provides information to, the other phases. The information exchange that evaluation facilitates is often critical to the success of the other HPI phases. For example, existing evaluation data may be fed into a performance analysis of related issues, be considered when selecting appropriate solutions, or be used as a benchmark while monitoring performance improvement. Evaluation is conducted not just to improve performance outcomes but to continuously improve the performance improvement process itself.

What Is Evaluation?

So, what exactly is **evaluation**, and how does evaluation contribute to HPI? Although evaluation likely has been part of people's daily lives since early human history, evaluation as a profession emerged only a few decades ago (Stufflebeam & Shinkfield, 2007). As Michael Scriven puts it, "Evaluation is a new discipline but an ancient practice" (Scriven, 1991b, p. 3).

Ralph Tyler's work on the Eight-Year Study in the United States during the 1930s and 1940s is known as one of the pioneering works that facilitated the development of evaluation practice. During the study, new curriculum programs were evaluated to see if they produced expected outcomes as stated in the programs' objectives (Tyler, 1986). Evaluation—a.k.a. program evaluation—emerged as a field of professional practice in the 1960s and 1970s to show accountability when a lot of federal monies were invested to develop and support government programs (Patton, 2008). Evaluation scholars and visionaries at that time also advocated using evaluation as a way to make continuous improvement on programs. Some of the fundamental principles and practices of evaluation such as summative evaluation (seeking accountability) and formative evaluation (seeking improvement) were developed at that time (Scriven, 1967).

The current *Merriam-Webster* dictionary definition of *evaluation* is "to judge the value or condition of (someone or something) in a careful and thoughtful way" ("Evaluation," n.d.). More specifically, Michael Scriven (2013) defines evaluation as "the process of determination of merit, worth, or significance" of someone or something, and is completed when the "value" is declared (p. 3). In fact, according to the *Concise Oxford Dictionary of Etymology,* the word *evaluate* originated from a French word, *évaluer; é-* means 'ex-' or 'out' (i.e., to find) and *valuer* means 'value' ("Evaluate," n.d.). Thus, to evaluate is to find the value of someone or something.

What Is Not Evaluation?

(Adapted from Chyung, 2015)[a]

Evaluation involves value assignment. It means evaluation is not the same as measurement because **measurement** does not include a value judgment. Consider measurement scales such as weight scales or measuring spoons. After you measured someone's weight to be 130 pounds, the weight itself does not tell you if the person is underweight, normal, or overweight. To know it, you need to calculate a body mass index (BMI) and compare it against a set of criteria that define underweight, normal, and overweight conditions. A weight of 130 pounds is normal for a 5'6" tall female adult, but it will put a 4' tall child in an obese category. Similarly, a tablespoon of sugar (measurement) does not tell you if it is too much or too little, until you put it in a context and evaluate it.

MEASUREMENT, ASSESSMENT, AND EVALUATION

Now, consider other measurement methods commonly used in the HPI context such as **survey (self-administered)**, **interview**, **focus group**, **observation**, **extant data review**, and **test**. These are data collection methods that measure people's thoughts, attitudes, or behaviors. Collecting data with these methods is not the same as conducting an evaluation. For example, administering a survey questionnaire to collect employees' attitudes toward their organization's culture is a measurement, not an evaluation. To *evaluate* whether employees have positive or negative attitudes toward their organization's culture, you need to analyze the survey data against standards or criteria (a.k.a. rubrics).

Another term, **assessment**, especially a test form of assessment, is sometimes used to mean evaluation. However, assessments are not evaluations either, unless the assessed results are given a value. A test score of 90 may represent an excellent performance if 60 is set as a passing score. However, it can be a failing score if a score of 95 is required. Think about personality assessments. These assessments are clearly not evaluations, since the assessment results only identify your dominant personality type but do not tell you whether you have a good or bad personality.

---

[a]The content of this section is from the following article with some modifications to make it fit within the chapter content: Chyung, S. Y. (2015). Foundational concepts for conducting program evaluations. *Performance Improvement Quarterly, 27*(4), 77–96. doi:10.1002/piq.21181

Thus, measurement and assessment are not the same as evaluation. However, you will likely perform measurements and assessments while conducting evaluations.

How Does Evaluation Compare With Research?

(Adapted from Chyung, 2015)[a]

To better understand evaluation, it is also important to understand similarities and differences between evaluation and research. First, **research**—especially social science research involving human subjects (which is the usual type of research conducted in the HPI context)—refers to a systematic data collection process concerning a given group of people in order to produce new knowledge about certain phenomena associated with the group. The new knowledge is either generalizable to its population (in quantitative research) or transferable to the understanding of similar groups or contexts (in qualitative research). Some research projects may employ both quantitative and qualitative research methods.

SIMILARITIES AND DIFFERENCES BETWEEN EVALUATION AND RESEARCH

How does evaluation compare with research? The words *evaluation* and *research* are sometimes used interchangeably. Although they hold similar characteristics, they are also different from each other.

Similarities: Both evaluation and research involve an investigation about something, and both are used to answer questions that are valuable to certain groups of people or organizational entities. They both employ data collection methods such as surveys, interviews, focus groups, observations, extant data reviews, or tests. The terms *evaluation* and *research* are often used interchangeably because similar data collection methods are used during evaluation and research. In both cases, the collected data are used as evidence to answer the proposed questions.

Differences: Evaluation is often conducted based on a client's request or approval, whereas most research, whether it is quantitative or qualitative research, is not client based. *Client-based* evaluations are usually reported directly to the clients and the client organizations rather than to the public, whereas research results are often presented in public venues such as research journals or conferences to allow the public as well as other researchers to have access to them.

Evaluation and research are also different in terms of their relationship with the context in which they are conducted. Evaluation activities are often *context-specific* (to investigate what happened in this particular context). In contrast, quantitative research activities are designed to be *context-free* (to ensure generalizability) and qualitative research activities can be characterized as *context-sensitive* (to allow transferability). Most evaluations produce context-specific evaluative conclusions about the quality, value, or significance of the subject being studied, whereas most research intends to produce generalizable or transferrable conclusions about the investigated research questions rather than drawing evaluative conclusions about a specific subject itself.

FIGURE 1 ● The Relationship Between Quantitative Research, Qualitative Research, and Evaluation

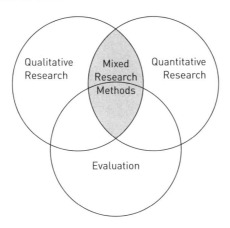

Relationship: Evaluation can be viewed as a subset of research, or vice versa. Evaluation and research can also be viewed as two ending points of a continuum or as overlapping with each other (Mathison, 2008). There is no one right way to define the relationship between evaluation and research. In this book, we will take the view that evaluation and research overlap. Figure 1 shows a Venn diagram illustrating the relationship between evaluation and research. Evaluation may use quantitative research, qualitative research, or mixed research methods, while possessing its own characteristics distinguishing itself from either type of research.

EVALUATION AND RESEARCH OVERLAP

Program Evaluation in the HPI Context

(Adapted from Chyung, 2015)[a]

Earlier, HPI was described as a transdisciplinary field of practice but not a discipline in itself. In contrast, evaluation (as well as research) is a transdisciplinary field of study and is recognized as a discipline (Scriven, 1991b). Evaluation, grown out of mere practice and now developed into its own discipline, crosses disciplinary boundaries aimed at helping to enhance performances of various professions. As illustrated in the examples of HPI application earlier, organizations in various industries would conduct evaluations to make improvements on their practice or products. Evaluation was destined to be included in the HPI practice because evaluation also seeks accountability and improvement of interventions.

EVALUATION AS A TRANSDISCIPLINARY FIELD

When HPI interventions are implemented to improve performance outcomes, the interventions often take the form of new or modified programs (including process-related programs), such as training programs, newly designed work processes, incentive programs, or performance support systems. Therefore, evaluation conducted in the HPI context can be characterized as a type of *program evaluation*. Combining our understanding of HPI and evaluation and largely influenced by Scriven's (1991b) definition of evaluation, we can define **program evaluation** used in the HPI context as the systematic and systemic collection and analysis of information about the process and outcomes of a program in order to make improvements or judgments about the program's quality or value.

• The first part of the definition—"the systematic and systemic collection and analysis of information about the process and outcomes of a program"—describes the *means* used during program evaluation.

• The second part of the definition—"in order to make improvements or judgments about the program's quality or value"—describes the intended *outcomes* of conducting program evaluation.

This definition of program evaluation means that the overall evaluation plan and the data collection and analysis procedure should be executed in a step-by-step fashion (systematic), and the analysis of the information and determination of the program's value should be carried out by considering various interrelated factors and different parts of the organization and its outside community (systemic). In this book, the word *evaluation* refers to program evaluation conducted in the HPI context as defined earlier.

Evaluation Is Often Neglected

As explained earlier, the evaluation phase should interact with each phase of the human performance technology model through an exchange of information. However, despite the important role that evaluation plays in the integrated HPI process, organizations often think of evaluation as a post hoc activity or neglect it altogether. Organizations report that they do not always conduct evaluations after interventions have been implemented, and when they do, they do not produce comprehensive evaluations (Pulichino, 2007).

Let's take a look at the research conducted on training evaluations in particular, as organizations invest a tremendous amount of money on workforce learning and development. For example, in 2011, U.S. organizations spent nearly $156.2 billion on it (American Society for Training & Development, 2012), and in 2015, the average organization spent about 4.3% of payroll on direct learning expenditure, up from 4.0% in 2014 (American Society for Training & Development, 2016). A popular approach to conducting training evaluations is to perform four levels of evaluations: reaction, learning, behavioral changes, and organizational results (Kirkpatrick, 1956, 1996a).

Research has shown that the frequency of evaluating behavioral changes and organizational outcomes has a significantly positive correlation with the trainees' knowledge and skill transfer (Saks & Burke, 2012). Research has also shown that organizations place high value on evaluations of behavioral changes and organizational

PROGRAM EVALUATION DEFINED IN THE HPI CONTEXT

EVALUATION AS A NEGLECTED SPECIES

outcomes (American Society for Training & Development, 2009). However, there seems to be a large gap between such value estimation on evaluation and the actual conduct of evaluation in organizations. It has been reported that although organizations often conduct evaluations to investigate participants' reactions and learning, less than 50% of organizations conduct evaluations on participant's behavioral changes and organizational outcomes (Pulichino, 2007).

Barriers to conducting comprehensive evaluations include environmental factors, such as lack of resources (time and personnel) and lack of managerial support, and personal factors, such as lack of expertise in evaluation methodology (Kennedy, Chyung, Winiecki, & Brinkerhoff, 2014). Thus, you as an evaluator would need to overcome both types of barriers by improving your own evaluation skills while attempting to reduce environmental barriers to conducting evaluations. This book aims to help you develop evaluation-specific skill sets.

BARRIERS TO CONDUCTING COMPREHENSIVE EVALUATIONS

Different Evaluation Designs Used in Program Evaluation

Similar to conducting research, you as an evaluator need to possess a broad range of knowledge and skill sets for planning and executing your evaluation projects with different evaluation designs depending on the type of evaluation questions you need to answer. Among evaluation designs, experimental and descriptive evaluation designs are often used.

When you intend to show a cause-and-effect relationship between an intervention program and its outcomes, you may use an **experimental evaluation design**. You randomly select a sample of participants from the population and randomly assign them to different conditions (e.g., an intervention program used or no intervention program used) to see if the different conditions produce different outcomes. When it is not practical to use a random assignment method, your experimental study becomes a quasi-experiment.

DIFFERENT EVALUATION DESIGNS

The experimental design is considered the most rigorous approach when needing to show a cause-and-effect relationship between the intervention program and its outcomes, that is, if the program indeed caused the observed outcomes. However, to use an experimental design, evaluators need to set up ahead of time a group of people that use an intervention program and a nonintervention group who do not use it. This makes it difficult to use an experimental design in the HPI context because needs for evaluation often arise after intervention programs have been implemented (Wang, 2002).

Alternatively, you may use a **descriptive evaluation design** to study a case without manipulating any variables. The case can be a person, a group of people, or an organization, which is often purposely selected (a.k.a. purposive sampling). By generating descriptive information about the case that you are studying, you gain an in-depth understanding about the case. Although a descriptive evaluation design involves a case (or multiple cases), a case study does not always use a descriptive evaluation design; it may employ an experimental/quasi-experimental design as well. For example, you may conduct a program evaluation within a specific organization (case), where you use a descriptive evaluation design to investigate environmental factors that influence employees' performance. Within the case study type evaluation, you may also use an experimental design with a random sample of employees to investigate the effectiveness of a proposed intervention on their performance outcomes.

Descriptive Case Study Type Evaluation Design

This book will explain to novice or advanced beginner level evaluators how to use a **descriptive case study type evaluation design** to produce a reasonably comprehensive evaluation. For example, consider the following program evaluations you can design with a descriptive case study type evaluation design.

DESCRIPTIVE CASE STUDY TYPE EVALUATION DESIGN USED IN PROGRAM EVALUATION

Example 1: Several years ago, your company implemented a new on-site daycare program to some of the company's branches in the nation, and many employees have been using the program. Your boss asked you to conduct an evaluation of the new on-site daycare program to find out about its value. You identified the overall evaluation question as: *What values does the on-site daycare program provide to the employees?* To answer the evaluation question, you decided to investigate different aspects of the program by answering the following specific questions:

1. Quality of the daycare program curriculum—How well is the daycare program curriculum designed, compared to other programs' curricula?

2. Employee job satisfaction—How does the daycare program influence employees' job satisfaction?

3. Employee turnover—How does the daycare program affect employees' decision to stay or leave the company?

For Question 1, you review the daycare program curriculum and compare it to other programs' curricula. You also observe the daily activities for a few days. To investigate Questions 2 and 3, you use multiple data collection methods. You survey two groups of employees who need a daycare service: those who have participated in the on-site daycare program and those who used an off-site program. You randomly select several employees from the groups and interview them to learn more about benefits and challenges associated with using the on-site versus off-site daycare programs. You also analyze the turnover rates among the employees who have participated in the on-site daycare program and those who have not. You review notes from exit interviews conducted with those who voluntarily resigned or were terminated to see if they indicated daycare-related issues.

Example 2: Animal shelters often get help from volunteers but the volunteers' first-month dropout rate is usually high. You are conducting an evaluation of an animal shelter in your city to find out what can be done to reduce the volunteer dropout rate and improve the quality of the volunteer program. You decide to focus on the following aspects of the volunteer program:

1. Training materials used for new volunteers—How well are the training materials designed?

2. Volunteers' goal achievement—Are volunteers achieving their goals? What are the barriers to achieving their goals?

3. Volunteers' burnout—Do volunteers feel burned out? What causes their burnout feelings?

4. Shelter visitors' satisfaction—How satisfied are visitors toward volunteers' work?

To investigate Questions 1 through 4, you collect data by reviewing existing training materials; surveying and interviewing volunteers, trainers, and visitors; and observing volunteers' training program and actual performance. You collect both quantitative and qualitative data and compare data obtained from multiple sources (volunteers, trainers, and visitors), combine results obtained from multiple aspects of the program in order to draw conclusions and provide recommendations for improvement.

As illustrated in these examples, this book explains how you can conduct a program evaluation by using a descriptive case study type evaluation design. As a novice or advanced beginner level evaluator, you want to start with a small evaluation project for an internal or external client, rather than conducting a high-stakes evaluation. You should continue to develop your evaluation competency level up to competent, proficient, and expert levels by acquiring more knowledge and skills to conduct evaluations using other types of evaluation designs. In addition, while navigating through organizational politics, you need to develop skills for effectively communicating with stakeholders to discover and align their needs with intended and unintended outcomes of the program.

Frameworks for Conducting Evaluations in the HPI Context

Recall that we defined program evaluation conducted in the HPI context as:

> *the systematic and systemic collection and analysis of information about the process and outcomes of a program in order to make improvements or judgments about the program's quality or value.*

Because various types of intervention programs are used for workforce development and performance improvement, HPI practitioners need expertise on conducting evaluations of various types of programs rather than just training programs. In fact, research has shown that only 10.5% of performance improvement interventions are knowledge-improvement programs such as training and education programs

(Gilbert, 1997). Katzell-based Kirkpatrick's four-level training evaluation framework (Kirkpatrick, 1956; Smith, 2008) is designed to help you conduct training evaluation. However, it is not a comprehensive model for conducting evaluations of the remaining 89.5% of nontraining programs. Thus, you need additional frameworks that can be applied to evaluating either training or nontraining interventions.

MULTIPLE
EVALUATION
FRAMEWORKS
AS WELL AS
PROFESSIONAL
STANDARDS AND
PRINCIPLES

There are many evaluation frameworks and approaches to conducting program evaluations. One source lists 26 approaches to evaluation (Stufflebeam & Shinkfield, 2007). There is no one particular evaluation approach that is applicable to all types of evaluations. It is impossible to cover all of the available evaluation frameworks in a book. Therefore, in this book, you will be introduced to the following frameworks (in alphabetic order) that were selected to help you understand the fundamental principles and procedures associated with conducting a program evaluation in the HPI context in a systematic and systemic way (a summary of each is described in Appendix A):

1. Behavior engineering model (Gilbert, 2007)

2. Four levels of training evaluation (Katzell, n.d., as cited in Kirkpatrick, 1956; Kirkpatrick, 1996a)

3. Key Evaluation Checklist (Scriven, 2013)

4. Program logic model guidelines (W. K. Kellogg Foundation, 2004)

5. Success Case Method and training impact model (Brinkerhoff, 2006)

6. Utilization-focused evaluation (M. Q. Patton, 2012)

You will also apply evaluation-specific professional principles and standards, such as the following:

- American Evaluation Association (AEA)'s guiding principles for evaluators (www.eval.org)

- The Joint Committee on Standards for Educational Evaluation (JCSEE)'s program evaluation standards (www.jcsee.org)

Based on these evaluation frameworks and professional standards and principles, we recognize multiple ingredients necessary for conducting a program evaluation (Figure 2).

The 10-Step Evaluation Procedure

The multiple ingredients shown in Figure 2 are incorporated into a 10-step evaluation procedure, which is outlined in Table 1. Michael Scriven's work, especially his **Key Evaluation Checklist** (Scriven, 2013), was instrumental in developing the systematic 10-step evaluation procedure. Many of the main concepts and steps used during the 10-step evaluation procedure, such as evaluand, three types of impactees,

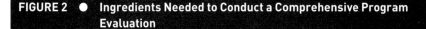

FIGURE 2 ● Ingredients Needed to Conduct a Comprehensive Program Evaluation

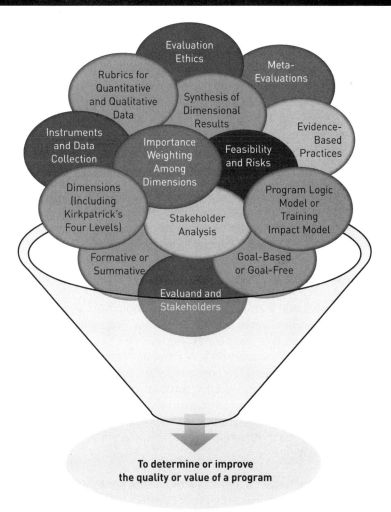

goal-free evaluation, dimensions, importance weighting, synthesis, meta-evaluation, and more, are based on Scriven's work.

The 10 steps are described as *micro*-level steps. You also perform three *macro*-level tasks such as assessments of feasibility, assessments of risk factors, and meta-evaluations. Each of the macro-level tasks is not just a single step to complete but rather an ongoing application throughout the project. As an analogy, the micro-level systematic 10 steps should be immersed in systemic application of the macro-level tasks, as illustrated in Figure 3 (Barkin, Chyung, & Lemke, 2017).

The 10 steps are divided into three phases—identification, planning, and implementation—producing three deliverables (Figure 4). During the **identification phase**, you communicate with your client to identify and clearly understand the program to be evaluated (a.k.a. an evaluand) (Step 1), its stakeholders (Step 2), and the purpose of the evaluation (Step 3). You will likely perform these first three steps simultaneously. You also assess feasibility and risk factors for the evaluation project. If feasible, you prepare the first deliverable to be submitted to your client, which likely takes the form of an agreement or contract regarding the evaluation to be performed. This agreement is called a statement of work (SOW). However, your SOW will not contain detailed information about exactly how you will perform the evaluation. In some cases, where you conduct an evaluation as an internal evaluator or part of your job responsibility, you may proceed to the planning phase without producing a SOW.

During the **planning phase** of your evaluation project, you learn more about the inner workings of the program with a program logic model (Step 4), identify aspects (dimensions) of the program to be investigated (Step 5), and determine the data collection methods you will use (Step 6). You continue to monitor the program feasibility and risk factors. You also start conducting formative meta-evaluations to ensure that you are developing an appropriate evaluation plan. At the end of the planning phase, you are ready to submit your second deliverable to your client—a comprehensive evaluation proposal.

The identification and planning phases of evaluation can also serve as an evaluability assessment stage (Trevisan & Walser, 2015), during which you determine whether or not a program is ready for evaluation, how interested the stakeholders are in conducting the evaluation, and how the stakeholders will use the evaluation results. When the program itself has not quite matured enough to be evaluated for its outcomes, pursuit of an outcome-based evaluation will only yield unreliable results, often showing nonsignificant improvement. In such cases, having an evaluability assessment stage will help you determine whether or not to continue with the evaluation project or recommend postponement until the program develops more and starts producing reliable outcomes.

If the program is determined to be ready for evaluation and your client approves your evaluation proposal, you move on to the **implementation phase**. You develop data collection instruments (Step 7), collect data with the instruments (Step 8), analyze data with rubrics (Step 9), and draw conclusions (Step 10). You perform formative meta-evaluations throughout these steps. At the end of this last phase, you prepare your third deliverable—an evaluation report—and you conduct a summative meta-evaluation. Then, you submit your final report to your client and other stakeholders and assist them in gaining utility and applicability from the findings.

Detailed explanations on how to follow the 10-step evaluation procedure are provided in the rest of this book.

TABLE 1 ●	The 10-Step Evaluation Procedure			
Macro-level	Micro-level	Main Task	During the Step	Deliverable
Assess feasibility, assess risk factors, and conduct meta-evaluations.	1	Identify the program to be evaluated.	Meet with the client to learn what needs to be evaluated.	*Identification phase:* Submit a statement of work (SOW) to the stakeholders and continue with evaluation planning or decline the evaluation request.
	2	Identify stakeholders of the program and their needs.	Understand the program stakeholders' needs.	
	3	Identify the purpose of evaluation based on how the evaluation findings will be used.	Steps 1, 2, and 3 may run in parallel to finalize the purpose of evaluation based on stakeholders' intention to use the findings of the evaluation.	
	4	Develop or review a program logic model for the program.	Involve the client and other stakeholders.	*Planning phase:* Submit an evaluation proposal to the stakeholders and continue with the implementation phase, or forgo/delay it.
	5	Determine dimensions and importance weighting.	Align dimensions with the stakeholders' needs and their intention to use evaluation findings.	
	6	Determine data collection methods.	Plan to use direct measures and multiple data sets whenever possible.	
	7	Develop data collection instruments.	Be sure to develop valid and reliable instruments. Obtain approval from the stakeholders.	
	8	Collect data.	Maintain confidentiality of data and handle human subjects and data ethically.	
	9	Analyze data with rubrics.	Triangulate multiple data sources and check with the stakeholders regarding appropriateness of rubrics.	
	10	Draw conclusions.	Organize findings based on the stakeholders' needs and their intention to use evaluation findings.	*Implementation phase:* Submit an evaluation final report to the stakeholders and assist their use of the evaluation findings.

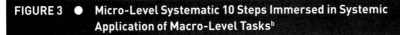

FIGURE 3 ● Micro-Level Systematic 10 Steps Immersed in Systemic Application of Macro-Level Tasks[b]

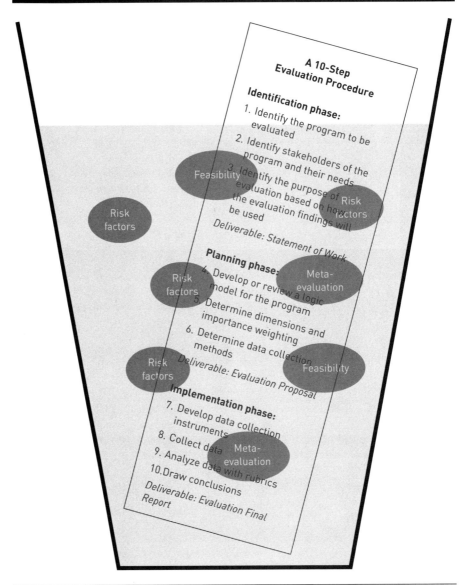

[b] The draft version of this book was the source of the figure cited in the following article: Barkin, J. R., Chyung, S. Y., & Lemke, M. (2017). Following a 10-step procedure to evaluate the administrative services qualification card program. *Performance Improvement, 56*(8), 6–15. doi:10.1002/pfi.21717

FIGURE 4 ● **Three Phases of Evaluation With 10 Micro Steps and Three Macro Tasks to Produce Three Deliverables**

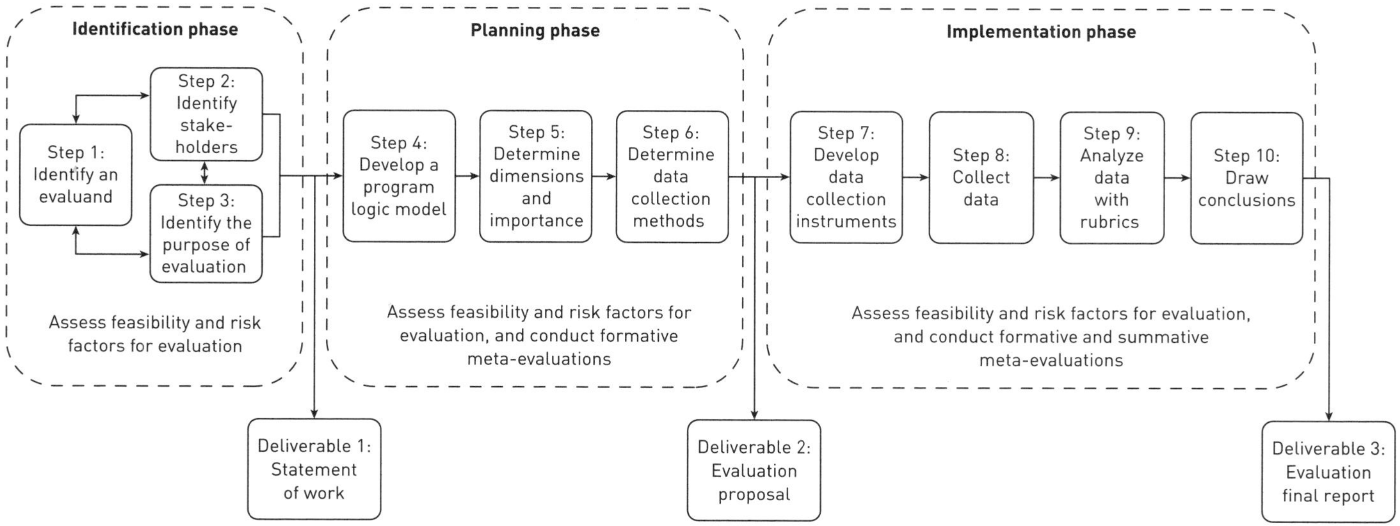

Identification phase

Step 1: Identify an evaluand

Step 2: Identify stakeholders

Step 3: Identify the purpose of evaluation

Assess feasibility and risk factors for evaluation

Deliverable 1: Statement of work

Planning phase

Step 4: Develop a program logic model

Step 5: Determine dimensions and importance

Step 6: Determine data collection methods

Assess feasibility and risk factors for evaluation, and conduct formative meta-evaluations

Deliverable 2: Evaluation proposal

Implementation phase

Step 7: Develop data collection instruments

Step 8: Collect data

Step 9: Analyze data with rubrics

Step 10: Draw conclusions

Assess feasibility and risk factors for evaluation, and conduct formative and summative meta-evaluations

Deliverable 3: Evaluation final report

15

Chapter Summary

- Evaluation, including human performance improvement (HPI), is a transdisciplinary field of practice.

- Evaluation is one of the essential components in the HPI process, and it should interact with each phase of the HPI process.

- Evaluation involves value assignment; thus, evaluation is not the same as measurement or assessment, which does not involve a value judgment.

- Evaluation and research have similarities and differences; they can be described as one being a subset of another, two end points of a continuum, or overlapping with each other.

- Evaluation conducted in the HPI context can be characterized as a type of program evaluation. Program evaluation conducted in the HPI context is defined as the systematic and systemic collection and analysis of information about the process and outcomes of a program in order to make improvements or judgments about the program's quality or value.

- Evaluation can use different evaluation designs, including experimental, quasi-experimental, and descriptive designs.

- Evaluation and research can use various data collection methods, such as self-administered surveys, interviews, focus groups, observations, extant data reviews, and tests.

- Evaluators can conduct program evaluations in the HPI context by using various frameworks derived from the HPI and evaluation fields. In doing so, they should apply evaluation-specific professional standards and principles.

- This book is written for novice or advanced beginner level evaluators to conduct evaluations of instructional or noninstructional programs by using a descriptive case study type evaluation design. To develop evaluation skills to competent, proficient, and expert levels, evaluators should learn to conduct program evaluations with other types of evaluation designs.

- This book explains a 10-step procedure of conducting program evaluations in the HPI context; the 10 steps are divided into three phases—identification, planning, and implementation—producing three deliverables—a statement of work, an evaluation proposal, and an evaluation final report.

Chapter Discussion

1. How good is this apple?

Every day, we perform various evaluations, small or large, informal or formal. For example, you go to a grocery store and may have to decide which apples to buy—your decision depends on whether you are making an apple pie or you want an apple just for munching. Similarly, you may be looking around to buy a car, and your decision will depend on whether it is going to be used as a commuter car for yourself or a family car for your six-member family.

Regardless of what you are evaluating, you go through a similar evaluation process. Let's have a small fun activity with your friends or family members to document the evaluation process.

1. Describe the thing that you want to evaluate: e.g.,

   A bag of apples (based on a sample piece)

2. Describe who will use it: e.g.,

   My family, including two adults and two adolescent children

3. Describe where and why they will use it (context and purpose): e.g.,

   Believing in the saying, "An apple a day keeps the doctor away," family members eat an apple a day as a snack.

4. As shown in the example in Table 2, discuss with the users, and do the following:

   a. List three or four dimensions (aspects) that its users will use to judge its quality.

   b. Rank-order the dimensions in terms of its importance to the users.

   c. Determine a rubric you will use to judge each dimension's quality.

   d. Determine a score for each dimension by measuring it against the rubric.

   e. Determine the overall quality based on the combined results against a final rubric.

   f. Make a data-driven decision.

5. Discuss how this process can be applied to an evaluation of a performance improvement intervention in the HPI context.

2. What individual effort and organizational support are needed to successfully conduct program evaluations in organizations?

Based on your observation at the organization where you currently work or previously worked, how often are performance improvement interventions (programs) evaluated after they are implemented? What are the drivers for and barriers to evaluating performance improvement programs in a systematic and systemic way?

Using Table 3, identify things that you as an individual practitioner and the organization can do to facilitate and support the systematic and systemic evaluation of performance improvement programs.

TABLE 2 ● How Good Is This Apple?				
Dimensions	**Importance Weighting**	**Dimensional Rubrics**	**Dimensional Finding**	**Overall Quality**
List dimensions that its users will use to judge its quality.	Rank-order dimensions in terms of its importance to users: e.g., 1. Important 2. Very important 3. Critical	Develop dimensional rating rubrics with 3-4 levels of descriptions: e.g., 1. Nah 2. OK 3. Awesome	Measure (try the sample piece) and rate each dimension against the dimensional rubric.	Factoring the importance weighting into the dimensional results, develop a final rubric and determine the overall quality. Then, make a final decision.
A. Taste	3. Critical	1. Nah: Bitter tart 2. Not bad: Sweet and a little bit tart 3. Awesome: Really sweet!	It is rated as *Not bad* because it is mostly sweet although it has a little bit of tart taste.	Final rubric: 1. Poor (I would not buy it): If at least one dimension = Nah 2. It's OK (I may buy it if there are no better options): If Critical dimension = Not bad, and other dimensions = Not bad or Awesome 3. Excellent (I will certainly buy it again): If Critical dimension = Awesome, and other dimensions = Not bad or Awesome
B. Size	1. Important	1. Nah: Half of my fist size 2. Not bad: Two thirds of my fist size 3. Awesome: As large as my fist	It is rated as *Awesome* because it is about my fist size.	
C. Texture	2. Very important	1. Nah: Mushy 2. Not bad: Firm 3. Awesome: Crunchy	It is rated as *Not bad* because it is firm enough.	**Overall quality: "It's OK."** **Final decision: I will buy it because there are no better options.**

Adapted from Davidson, 2005, pp. 151–187; Preskill & Russ-Eft, 2005, p. 20.

TABLE 3 ● Identify Individual Effort and Organizational Support Needed for Conducting Systematic and Systemic Evaluation	
Individual effort	**Organizational support**
•	•
•	•
•	•
•	•

Identify an Evaluand (Step 1) and Its Stakeholders (Step 2)

A mong three phases of evaluation (identification, planning, and implementation), you are starting the first phase of your evaluation project—identification. In this book, we will assume that you, as a novice or advanced beginner of evaluation, have located a potential evaluation topic, approached the potential client to discuss the evaluation project, and mutually agreed to pursue the evaluation project. This chapter explains the first two steps—Step 1: Identifying the program to be evaluated and Step 2: Identifying the stakeholders of the program.

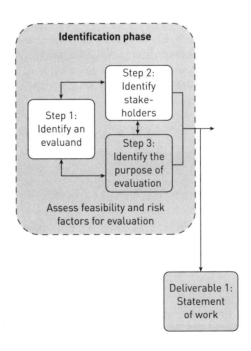

If someone such as your boss has already identified a program to be evaluated and asked you to conduct an evaluation of the program, your role is more to *understand* and/or *analyze* the evaluand than to *identify* one.

Identify a Performance Improvement Intervention as an Evaluand

Throughout this book, you are the **evaluator** (or an evaluation team) who evaluates a performance improvement program. The entity that is being evaluated during a program evaluation is called an **evaluand**, and the person who is being evaluated is called an **evaluee** (Scriven, 1991b). When conducting program evaluations in the human performance improvement (HPI) context, you focus on evaluands rather than on specific evaluees (as in personnel evaluation). However, you may analyze workers' or learners' performance levels as a *dimension* of your evaluation project (you will learn more about dimensions in Chapter 6).

Whether you are conducting an evaluation of a program within your workplace as an internal evaluator or for another organization as an external evaluator, the first thing you should do is to identify a performance improvement intervention as your evaluand. This evaluand identification process starts by communicating with your evaluation client.

An **evaluation client** is the one who asked you (or approved your request) to conduct an evaluation and is the main contact during your evaluation project, providing you with necessary support and approval. A client can be a person or a group of people. In some cases, your evaluation client may be both the one who requested the evaluation (or approved your evaluation request) and the one who is in charge of the program (e.g., a training department manager asks you to evaluate one of the training programs). In other cases, the client who asked you to conduct an evaluation could be the human resources director, while the person in charge of the evaluand is the chief learning officer.

In the HPI context, your evaluand can be, but does not have to be, an instructional intervention. It can be any type of an existing, recently modified, or new performance improvement intervention implemented in an organization, such as:

INSTRUCTIONAL OR NON-INSTRUCTIONAL INTERVENTIONS AS EVALUANDS

- a training program
- a job aid system
- an electronic performance support system
- a coaching or mentoring method
- an incentive program
- an appraisal or feedback system
- a redesigned workflow process
- an employee hiring process

Your evaluand can also be a program provided to the public, such as:

- an online customer service program
- a youth-mentoring program provided by a non-profit organization

- a job placement service program provided by a local government agency
- an organization's website
- an animal shelter program
- a daycare program provided by a church
- a volunteer program that supports girl scouts or boy scouts programs
- a domestic violence victim assistance program

Use the 5W1H Method to Understand the Intervention Program

Suppose you are meeting with your client to find out what the evaluand is. In order to have a clear understanding about the evaluand, you may use a technique similar to the **five Ws and one H (5W1H) method** (Who, When, Where, What, Why, and How) and ask the following questions:

UNDERSTAND YOUR EVALUAND BY USING 5W1H QUESTIONS

- *What* is the program?
- *When* was it first implemented?
- *Where* was it implemented?
- *Why* was it implemented? (Was it based on a needs assessment?)
- *Who* developed and implemented it?
- *Who* is in charge of it now?
- *Who* uses/participates in it?
- *How* does it operate?

Below are a couple of evaluands described in the 5W1H question-answer format.

Evaluand example 1 (based on Chyung, Olachea, Olson, & Davis, 2016):

- What—The evaluand is the College Advisory Program implemented at Total Vision Soccer Club, a nonprofit organization. The organization provides soccer training programs to children and young adults of age 10 to 19. It also offers college recruitment skills through the College Advisory Program. The program aims at helping children and young adults develop to their full potential and enter a college to further their education.
- When—The program was developed in the mid-1980s.
- Where—It was implemented in a mid-size city in the Western United States.
- Why—Youth soccer has been one of the most popular sports in the USA. The organization needed to provide children and young adults with not only the skills and knowledge of the game but also college recruiting resources and exposure to college coaches. There is no record that shows whether the program was initiated based on a needs assessment. However, there were 'felt needs' for the program.

- Who—The soccer club leadership including the President and the Board of Directors decided to develop and implement the program. The Directors of Boys and Girls Coaching are in charge of the program. Soccer players of children and young adults and their parents are the participants of the program.

- How—The program employs college advisors and coaches who provide players and their parents with a yearly seminar and one-on-one advising, and help them network with college coaches.

Evaluand example 2 (based on Chyung, Wisniewski, Inderbitzen, & Campbell, 2013):

- What—The evaluand is the Adventure Scouts Program.

- When—The program was developed in 2008.

- Where—It was implemented in two schools in North Chicago.

- Why—After the Northeast Illinois Council of Boy Scouts of America realized that Scouting was not flourishing in low socio-economic communities, the district leaders decided to begin the Adventure Scouts Program.

- Who—The council members, school administrators, and program designers were involved in the development and implementation of the program. The Vice President of Membership is the evaluation client. The program participants are Hispanic and African American boys, grades 1-5.

- How—Unlike traditional Scouting, in Adventure Scouts, Tigers, Wolves, and Bears run on a three-year rotation. Each boy who participates in the program over the course of three years will have covered all of the requirements for Tiger, Wolf, and Bear.

Ask Why the Intervention Program Was Implemented

An answer to the "why was it implemented?" question is an especially important one for you to find out, because it helps you assess what the intervention program aims at accomplishing (i.e., what are the performance gaps that need to be closed) and if the program goals reflect the performance gaps to be closed (Chyung & Berg, 2009).

While obtaining this information, it is important for you, the evaluator, to have a good understanding about the cyclical process of performance improvement from performance analysis to intervention selection, design, development, implementation, and maintenance, and to evaluation.

Take a look at Figure 5 that illustrates a logical order of performance improvement process toward evaluation (the solid arrows from 1 to 4) and its reverse order for you to take while asking probing questions to retrieve the evaluand's background information (the dotted arrows from 4 to 1).

TRACE BACK THE HISTORY BEHIND THE EVALUAND

While tracing back the history behind the intervention implementation, you may discover information about:

- If the organization detected performance gaps, and if so, what the performance gaps were. A performance gap is understood in terms of:
  - The desired level of performance
  - The current level of performance
  - The gap between the desired and current levels of performance
- If the organization found out several factors that caused the performance gaps, and if so, what the causal factors were.

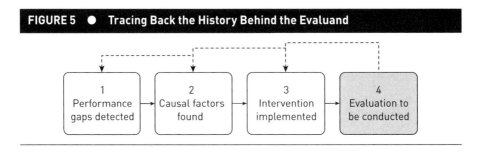

FIGURE 5 ● Tracing Back the History Behind the Evaluand

With such historical information, you have a better understanding about the purpose of (or needs for) the evaluand—i.e., the organization developed and implemented it to close the performance gaps caused by those causal factors. You also have a better understanding about the overall purpose of the evaluation—i.e., it is to see how well the intervention program has been working to close the performance gaps caused by those factors.

USING THE BEHAVIOR ENGINEERING MODEL TO UNDERSTAND THE EVALUAND BACKGROUND

Another way to understand your evaluand's implementation background is to apply Thomas Gilbert's (2007) **behavior engineering model.** The behavior engineering model guides you when assessing probable causes of a performance gap by helping you ask a series of questions regarding three environmental factors (data, instruments, and incentives) and three personal factors (knowledge, capacity, and motives).

When using the behavior engineering model during a cause analysis, you ask the following questions:

1. Do performers receive adequate data and feedback regarding their tasks?
2. Do performers have access to tools they need to complete the tasks?
3. Do performers receive adequate incentives for good performance?
4. Are performers knowledgeable enough to perform the tasks?
5. Are performers physically and cognitively capable of performing the tasks?
6. Are performers motivated to perform the tasks?

Then, you identify the most appropriate interventions to handle the causal factors. Table 4 shows examples of performance improvement interventions by the six categories of the behavior engineering model. For example, you may find out that a one-on-one coaching program was implemented because the root cause of poor performance was a lack of timely feedback. Or, you may find out that a mentoring program was implemented in order to keep new employees motivated to work and to reduce the turnover rate.

TABLE 4 ● Examples of Intervention Programs

	Information	Instrumentation	Motivation
Environmental factors	Data/feedback • Coaching program • Employee evaluation system	Instruments • Learning management system • Work procedure	Incentives • Incentive system • On-site daycare program
Personal factors	Knowledge • Training program • Online or blended learning program	Capacity • Set of hiring criteria • Flexible work schedule	Motives • Job reassignment plan • Mentoring program

Adapted from Gilbert, 2007, Table 3–4 The Behavior Engineering Model.

Any intervention that relates to one of the six factors of the behavior engineering model can be your evaluand, since it was a program implemented to improve organizational and human performance. During your conversation with the client, you can use the behavior engineering model as a job aid to identify which one of the six factors was the main cause of the performance gap. Again, having a clear understanding of the main causal factor of a performance gap helps you identify the needs for the evaluand and the purpose of the evaluation (i.e., it is to investigate how well the intervention program has been working to satisfy the organization's needs). For more information about Gilbert's behavior engineering model, see Appendix A.

Check If Program Goals Are Based on Needs

In an optimal situation, an organization would have conducted a needs assessment before implementing an intervention program, and you would be able to find information about the causal factors associated with the performance gaps that the intervention program intends to close. In reality, however, you may discover different situations when asking the "why was it implemented?" question. Review the following four types of intervention programs and determine which one applies to your evaluand:

1. A performance improvement intervention with clearly stated goals and intended outcomes, developed based on the results of a needs assessment
2. A performance improvement intervention with clearly stated goals and intended outcomes, developed without conducting a needs assessment
3. A performance improvement intervention without clearly stated goals or intended outcomes
4. A performance improvement initiative implemented without a known performance gap

INTERVENTION PROGRAMS IMPLEMENTED WITH OR WITHOUT A NEEDS ASSESSMENT

You can use any one of the four types of intervention programs listed above as your evaluand. Among them, Type #1 and Type #2 have clearly stated goals. These types *may* (although not always) lead you to investigate whether or not the stated goals have been achieved (a.k.a. a goal-based evaluation). In that case, it is worth noting that some evaluation scholars consider a goal- or objective-based approach to be an undesirable way of conducting evaluation—see the following statements by Stufflebeam and Shinkfield (2007):

> Evaluation has been defined in different ways. One of the earliest and still most prominent definitions states that it means determining whether objectives have been achieved. We reject this definition, because following it can cause evaluations to fail. One of its problems is that some objectives are unworthy of achievement. (p. 8)

So, why is a goal-based evaluation considered undesirable? Actually, a better question is, *when* is a goal-based evaluation considered undesirable?

In the HPI context, conducting a needs assessment before implementing a performance improvement intervention is a standard practice. Therefore, conducting a goal-based evaluation in situations described in Type #1 above would not be a concern when the intervention goals were developed based on known needs. However, since needs can change over time, you want to check if the previously identified needs are still applicable.

If you conduct an evaluation in situations where program goals were not developed based on known needs (Type #2) or where the program does not have clearly stated goals and intended outcomes (Type #3), a goal-based evaluation would present a reasonable concern. In such cases, you as an evaluator would have to make sure to investigate stakeholders' needs as part of your evaluation.

Sometimes, you may conduct an evaluation of a performance improvement initiative (Type #4). For example, your organization may have implemented mobile learning (a.k.a. m-learning) as a new way to facilitate learning and knowledge sharing among workers, and now you want to find out how it worked out. In such cases, you may not focus on any specific goals per se, but explore both expected and unexpected outcomes.

Sell Evaluation to the Client

Currently, you are in the first step of your evaluation project, meeting with the client to discuss the program to be evaluated. If the client initiated the evaluation project and asked (or hired) you to conduct the evaluation, you may not have difficulty discussing the evaluation project with the client.

However, evaluation is a tough sell, if you are an internal evaluator who needs to convince your management or your evaluation client to commit resources to conduct program evaluations. The word *evaluation* can be scary to many people. Not knowing exactly what will come out of the evaluation project, the evaluation client may be skeptical about the value of the evaluation project that you are suggesting to conduct.

TALK ABOUT USEFUL OUTPUTS GAINED FROM EVALUATION

Of course, as a strategy, you should point out to the client the importance of conducting an evaluation as part of the continuous performance improvement process. Another strategy you can use is to explain to the client about several specific materials, such as data collection instruments, that you will produce for the program as a result of completing the evaluation project. For example, let's say that you are trying to convince your internal client to evaluate a training program. Review the following elevator speech that you may adopt when talking with your client:

Evaluation client:	"Hey, I'm not against you conducting this evaluation. I'm just not sure what we will get out of this evaluation project. I don't want this to be one of those 'nice things to do' without adding much value. I don't want to waste everyone's time either."
Evaluator:	"Right, we really have to be careful about that. I see this project as not just an evaluation project, but a great opportunity to improve and standardize some of our practice."
Evaluation client:	"What do you mean?"
Evaluator:	"For example, I've talked to you about this before, but you know, right now, different training programs are using their own survey questionnaires. Sometimes, individual trainers use their own surveys even if they are teaching the same topic. So, it's really difficult, actually impossible, to compare the data collected over time or across individual programs."
Evaluation client:	"Yes, I know. That *is* a problem."
Evaluator:	"Here is what I can do. During this project, I will likely have to review the previous survey results anyway. While doing that, I will review the different survey questionnaires and find out what questions we need the most and why. Then, I will propose using a set of questions that apply to different types of programs. So, I think of this project as a great opportunity to develop a standardized survey format. What do you think?"
Evaluation client:	"That sounds like a good idea."
Evaluator:	"Similarly, if I review the content of the training program or observe the program on site, I will develop checklists to check off things that need to be done. I will certainly get your input to develop the checklists to reflect the criteria that you have in mind. These checklists are not only for this project; the instructional designers or trainers can use these checklists as their own job aids too."
Evaluation client:	"Oh, I like that."

During your conversation, you can also talk about the benefit of developing a program logic model or training impact model as one of your evaluation project outputs, which we will cover in Chapter 5. You will be able to use these strategies with confidence once you have completed an evaluation project and witnessed such useful outputs.

Identify Three Groups of Stakeholders

While learning from your client about what it is that you are evaluating (the evaluand), you also need to find out who is involved with the evaluand; i.e., *a stakeholder analysis*.

Stakeholders are literally people who hold a stake in something (such as an organization, a program, or a governing body). Stakeholders can *affect* or *be affected by* it. So, stakeholders in your evaluation project are the ones who affect or are affected by the evaluand. Michael Scriven (2013) explains that there are upstream stakeholders and downstream consumers (see also Davidson, 2005).

- **Upstream stakeholders** (a.k.a. **upstream impactees**) are the ones who were/are involved in the design, development, implementation, and maintenance of the evaluand. They manage the budget and approve of, or make any, changes to be done in the evaluand.

- **Downstream consumers** are the ones who are affected by the evaluand and include two groups:

  - **Direct impactees** (direct consumers), who receive, use, or participate in the evaluand

  - **Indirect impactees** (indirect consumers), who do not use the evaluand, but are impacted via ripple effect (Scriven, 2013)

THREE TYPES OF IMPACTEES AS STAKEHOLDERS

In this book, we will use the term *stakeholders* loosely to refer to all types of impactees (upstream and downstream) (Scriven, 2013). Then, you have three groups of stakeholders: (1) upstream stakeholders/impactees, (2) downstream direct impactees, and (3) downstream indirect impactees.

TABLE 5 ● Examples of Stakeholders

Evaluand	Upstream Stakeholders or Impactees	Direct Impactees	Indirect Impactees
A consulting firm's help desk program that provides technical help desk services to clients	• President of the consulting firm • An outsourced help desk service company	• The consulting firm's client organizations (n = 20) and their employees who use the help desk program (n = approx. 200)	• Employees of the consulting firm (n = approx. 50) • Other employees of the client organizations (n = several thousands)
A training program that teaches volunteers at a kennel to acquire necessary kennel skills	• Executive board • Kennel manager • Volunteer program manager • Volunteer trainers (n = 2)	• New volunteers (n = approx. 30/month)	• Current volunteers (n = approx. 200) • Volunteer mentors (n = 6) • Shelter visitors (n = approx. 50,000/year)
An organization's website that provides customers with information about its products	• Director of Web Strategy, Office of Communications • Director of Marketing • Web design specialists (n = 5)	• Customers who use the website to search for information (n = approx. 300,000/month)	• Customer service representatives (n = approx. 60) • Employees in manufacturing and sales departments of the company (n = approx. 500)
A training program that teaches supervisors at a university to improve their coaching skills	• Senior HR Director • Vice President for Student Affairs • Assistant Vice President for Student Affairs • Instructional designers (n = 3)	• 70 supervisors at the university	• Employees of the supervisors (n = approx. 400) • About 20,000 students who may interact with employees

For example, let's use an onboarding program that many organizations develop and provide to their new employees. The upstream stakeholders/impactees of an onboarding program may include the training manager, the instructional designers, and the trainer, who collectively designed, developed, and implemented the onboarding program. They also make changes to the program as needed. The direct impactees are the new employees who participate in the onboarding program. The indirect impactees are the ones who interact with the new employees who have completed the onboarding program, including the supervisors and coworkers of new employees, the customers that new employees handle, and the families and friends of new employees. Table 5 on the preceding page presents more examples of stakeholders identified in potential evaluation projects.

It is important to clearly identify the three types of stakeholders during the early stage of your evaluation project for a couple of reasons. First, the stakeholder information will help you identify the scope of the evaluation project. Compared to an evaluation project in which there are about 100 direct impactees, another evaluation project involving thousands of direct impactees may mean a high-stakes project. If this is your first formal program evaluation, you want to select a small evaluation project.

WHY IS IT IMPORTANT TO IDENTIFY STAKEHOLDER INFORMATION EARLY?

Second, the stakeholder information helps you clearly understand the program's needs from the stakeholders' standpoint, which will shape the evaluation design. As described in Chapter 2, you want to determine the evaluation purpose largely based on the stakeholders' needs, especially how they want to use the evaluation findings.

Clearly identifying the different groups of stakeholders up front also assists you later during the data collection phase of the project, as stakeholders are likely the main sources of data (evidence) that you will use to determine the quality of the evaluand.

Chapter Summary

Identify an evaluand (Step 1):

- An evaluator is the one who conducts an evaluation. An evaluation client is the one who requests and approves an evaluator to conduct an evaluation.

- An evaluand is the object that is being evaluated (Scriven, 1991b). In the HPI context, various types of performance improvement programs can be evaluands.

- Evaluators can use the five Ws and one H method (Who, When, Where, What, Why, and How) while discussing with the client and other stakeholders to learn about the evaluand.

- While investigating why the performance improvement intervention program (the evaluand) was implemented, evaluators should trace the history behind the program and find out the causal factors associated with the performance gaps that the program intends to close.

  ○ Thomas Gilbert's (2007) behavior engineering model can help evaluators understand what caused the performance improvement programs (as evaluands) to be implemented.

  ○ When the program goals are clearly based on the program stakeholders' needs, evaluators may proceed with conducting a goal-based evaluation because the program goals reflect stakeholders' needs, although evaluators may need to check if stakeholders' needs have changed since the program implementation.

- ○ Otherwise, conducting a goal-based evaluation presents a concern; evaluators should assess and incorporate stakeholders' needs during the evaluation.

- Evaluation is a tough sell. While communicating with the client, evaluators may want to talk about other specific outputs of the evaluation project such as data collection instruments that are useful to the client and the organization.

Identify stakeholders (Step 2):

- While learning about the evaluand, evaluators should conduct a stakeholder analysis to learn about three groups of the program stakeholders—upstream stakeholders/impactees, downstream direct impactees (direct consumers), and downstream indirect impactees (indirect consumers).

- Clear identification of the three groups of stakeholders up front helps evaluators recognize the scope of the evaluation project, determine the purpose of the evaluation based on the stakeholders' needs, and identify potential sources of data to be used during the data collection step.

Chapter Discussion

1. Are the program goals based on needs?

Dan is evaluating a customer service training program delivered to the customer service representatives (CSRs) at a call center. His evaluation client told him that the training program was developed to improve the CSRs' attitudes toward customers and decrease their call time.

Taking that information as the program goals, Dan plans to evaluate how well the program has met its goals—that is, how much the program helped improve customers' attitudes and decrease the average call time.

Is Dan going in the right direction with his evaluation plan? What would you suggest him to do at this point?

2. Who are the program stakeholders?

You have been asked to evaluate a local university's Center for Learning (CLT) website. You are on the phone with the evaluation client, the CLT director, and she is giving you the following information:

- The CLT website provides information about various learning and teaching resources for faculty and students to use.

- Her staff, including a website developer and a graphic designer, developed the website in collaboration with a web communication manager a couple of years ago.

- They also had to comply with the university web design policies and guidelines and adopt the university's website template, all of which are provided by the university's information technology (IT) department.

- The client wants the website to be easy to navigate, be easy to find information, and provide up-to-date and sufficient information to users.

- The client hopes that you will provide information as to what needs to be changed in the CLT website.

Based on the information given, identify the evaluand and its stakeholders (three types). The scenario provides limited information. Thus, imagine that you are still on the phone with the client, and think about what questions you want to ask the client to learn more about the evaluand and its stakeholders.

Now, Your Turn—Identify an Evaluand and Its Stakeholders

Meet with your evaluation client to identify the evaluand and its stakeholders. Use Table B-1 in Appendix B (Evaluation Development Worksheets) as a job aid while discussing with your client. Do not simply email the questions to the client and ask the client to fill in the blanks. It is important to have a personal contact with the client to discuss the project.

When communicating with your client and stakeholders, please avoid using terminology with which they may not be familiar (e.g., evaluand, upstream stakeholders, or direct impactees). Use common language (e.g., What is the program that needs to be evaluated? Who developed the program? Who is in charge of it now? Who needs to complete the program?).

Summarize the information you gathered and fill in Table B-1. See an example in Table 6.

TABLE 6 ● An Example Worksheet for Steps 1 and 2: Identify an Evaluand and Its Stakeholders		
Step	**Question**	**Your Finding**
Identify an evaluand	• What is it?	A blended onboarding program
	• Where is it implemented?	Sawtooth Company in Idaho
	• When was it first implemented?	The onboarding program was initially implemented in 2015, but it was redesigned in September 2017.

(Continued)

TABLE 6 ● (Continued)		
Step	**Question**	**Your Finding**
	• Why was it implemented? What is the program goal? Was it determined based on a needs assessment?	An informal needs assessment based on anecdotal information revealed that the previous 2-day instructor-led onboarding program was insufficient for helping new employees get up to speed. It was redesigned as a 3-day blended learning program, combining instructor-led training and online training. The overall program goal is to help new employees be able to perform their job tasks without assistance 90% of the time.
	• How does it operate?	Day 1 = instructor-led training Days 2 and 3 = four-hour instructor-led training in the morning and three-hour online training in the afternoon.
Identify stakeholders	• Who were/are involved in the design, development, implementation, and maintenance of the evaluand (i.e., upstream stakeholders)? • Briefly describe the role that they play as upstream stakeholders. • Indicate the client for the evaluation.	The following groups of people are upstream stakeholders: • The training manager (evaluation client), who oversees the analysis, design, development, implementation, maintenance, and evaluation of the onboarding program • Two instructional designers, who designed and developed the onboarding program • A trainer, who delivers the onboarding program
	• Who are directly impacted by receiving, using, or participating in the evaluand (i.e., downstream direct impactees)? • Describe an approximate number for each category.[1] • Briefly describe how the direct impactees are impacted by the evaluand.	New employees (n = 10–20 each month) are directly impacted because they are required to complete the blended onboarding program.
	• Who are indirectly affected via ripple effect (i.e., downstream indirect impactees)? • Estimate the size of each group of the indirect impactees.[2] • Briefly explain how they are impacted.	The following groups of people would be indirectly impacted by interacting with direct impactees: • Supervisors and direct coworkers of the new employees (n = approx. 1,000) • Customers that the new employees handle (n = approx. 2,000) • Families and friends of the new employees (n = unknown, likely in hundreds or more per year)

[1] It is important to estimate the size of the direct impactees in order to gauge the size of direct impact of the evaluand.

[2] It is important to estimate the size of the indirect impactees as much as you can, in order to gauge the size of indirect impact of the evaluand.

Identify the Purpose of Evaluation (Step 3)

You are in the identification phase of your evaluation project. During the first couple of steps of your evaluation project, you learn about the program to be evaluated and the program's stakeholders. You also need to learn about the purpose and type of the evaluation.

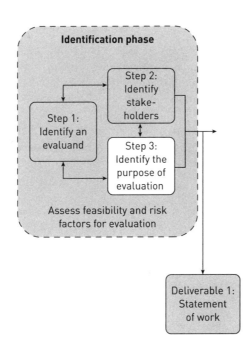

Differentiate Evaluation From Needs Assessment

While determining the purpose and type of your evaluation project, you want to keep in mind that it is an evaluation of a performance improvement intervention rather than a **needs assessment**. There is a fine line between needs assessment and evaluation. One way to describe the relationship between the two is that needs assessment and evaluation are twins separated at birth: They are similar yet different.

Needs assessment and evaluation are similar in that they both address the needs of the organization and stakeholders, use data collected from the stakeholders, and contribute to continuous improvements of the organizational performance.

FRONT-END NEEDS ASSESSMENTS OR BACK-END EVALUATIONS

Then, how are needs assessment and evaluation, especially, program evaluation, different from each other? Here is a simple, but slightly overgeneralized, way to differentiate between the two: In the human performance improvement (HPI) context, needs assessment is conducted *before* an intervention is implemented, and program evaluation (of a performance improvement intervention) is conducted *after* an intervention is implemented. This difference between the two is reflected in their purpose statements.

For example, let's say that a project's purpose is stated this way:

It has been reported that some employees have to make multiple trials on the certification exam before they pass the exam. This project is to find out what percentage of employees pass the certification exam on their first attempt and what needs to be done to help more than 90% of employees pass the certification exam on their first attempt and 99% by their second attempt.

With this purpose statement, you are likely conducting a needs assessment rather than an evaluation of a performance improvement intervention. Here, a performance problem may exist (i.e., some employees are not passing the certification exam on their first attempt), but an intervention has not been implemented. This investigation is conducted to assess organizational needs, and in fact, this needs assessment may end up recommending an intervention to help achieve the desired outcome.

In the HPI context, needs assessment and evaluation are differentiated. Needs assessment (a.k.a. performance analysis) and evaluation are indicated as separate steps in the human performance technology model (as described in the Introduction chapter). However, in the evaluation field, needs assessments are considered as a type of evaluation, which also makes sense because performance improvement is a cyclical process. Even after an intervention has been implemented and an evaluation of that intervention has been completed, another needs assessment can be conducted during the front end of the next performance improvement cycle. Then, another evaluation would be conducted during the back end of the performance improvement cycle.

CIPP MODEL BY STUFFLEBEAM

Daniel Stufflebeam's (2007) context, input, process, product (CIPP) model is a good example that illustrates the relationship between front-end evaluation and back-end evaluation. He presents four types of evaluations and their roles; these four types are **C**ontext evaluation, **I**nput evaluation, **P**rocess evaluation, and **P**roduct evaluation (see Table 7).

Context evaluation and input evaluation would be conducted during the front end of a program where you assess needs, problems, or opportunities to determine interventions or alternative approaches to be implemented. Thus, in this book, we will categorize context and input evaluations as **front-end evaluations**. The employee certification exam example earlier would be a context evaluation.

On the other hand, process evaluation and product evaluation are conducted to assess the effectiveness of implementation process or outcomes after interventions have been implemented. Thus, we will categorize them as **back-end evaluations**.

TABLE 7 ● Front-End Evaluations and Back-End Evaluations				
	Front-End Evaluation		**Back-End Evaluation**	
Type and focus per Stufflebeam's (2007) CIPP model	Context evaluation investigating needs, problems, and opportunities to help determine or refine program goals and outcomes	Input evaluation investigating alternative approaches, proposals, and budgets for meeting identified needs and objectives of a program	Process evaluation investigating the effectiveness of the program implementation and operation process	Product evaluation investigating intended and unintended outcomes of a program
Sample questions to be addressed when evaluating a new employee onboarding program	• How long does it take new employees to get up to speed and perform their job tasks without assistance? How long should it take? • Should the organization provide an onboarding program? If so, what does the onboarding program aim to accomplish? • What other interventions should be provided to help new employees get up to speed within the expected time frame?	• Should the organization develop the onboarding program in-house or outsource it? • Should it be delivered as an instructor-led program or a combination of instructor-led and e-learning programs? • What is the most cost-effective way? What are the initial and ongoing maintenance costs for using a blended learning method?	• How easy or difficult has it been to implement a buddy system during the onboarding program? • Is the blended delivery format working as intended? • Is the length of the program sufficient for delivering the required content? • What level of support does the program receive from the organization? What are the barriers?	• How well did the new employees learn the content? • How confident are they in using their knowledge and skills? • How fast did the new employees get up to speed? • How cost-effective is the program? • What impact, positive or negative, do their performance levels have on other employees and the overall production levels?

Adapted from Chyung, 2015, p. 82, Table 1.

Consider the following revised purpose statement based on the employee certification exam scenario used earlier:

> All employees completed a certification prep program, which aimed to help them pass the certification exam on their first attempt. This project is to find out what percentage of employees pass the certification exam on their first attempt and by their second attempt, and what needs to be done to help them prepare to pass the exam the first time they take it.

This revised statement is written for a back-end evaluation because an intervention program (a certification prep program) has been implemented, and the purpose of the project is to evaluate the effectiveness of the program and find ways to improve the quality of the program.

Although both front-end and back-end evaluations are considered program evaluations, in this book, we will focus on conducting back-end evaluations rather than front-end evaluations (needs assessments), because our focus is to evaluate performance improvement interventions that have been implemented. During your program evaluation, you will likely investigate both the process and outcomes of the program (i.e., a combination of process evaluation and product evaluation). You will find more explanations on this with an application of a gray box evaluation approach when determining dimensions in Chapter 6.

Gather Information About the Evaluation Purpose

Conducting a program evaluation requires you to design the project to obtain appropriate information serving a clear purpose (Tyler, 1991). Therefore, once you have determined your evaluand and its stakeholders, you need to learn more about the client organization's expectations about the evaluation that you will complete. While talking with your client and other stakeholders, you need to determine the overall purpose of the evaluation.

THE OVERALL PURPOSE OF EVALUATION

It is likely that you have already discussed relevant information with your client while asking about the evaluand and its stakeholders. During your conversation with the client, did he or she tell you what the overall purpose of the evaluation was? If so, what was it? If your client did not clearly state the overall purpose of the evaluation, reflect on the information you have gathered so far—what do you think the purpose of the evaluation should be?

Your client is not an evaluator and does not necessarily have evaluation-specific knowledge to articulate the purpose of the evaluation. Therefore, it is not uncommon to hear your client provide a generic purpose statement such as "We want to know how things are going" or a too narrowly focused statement such as "We are interested in finding out if the attendees liked it, would come back, or recommend it to their colleagues." You may also hear statements such as "We just have to do this at least once a year" or "Our funder requires an evaluation."

These statements need to be converted to appropriate purpose statements. It is your job as an evaluator to gather more information to help determine a meaningful and useful evaluation purpose statement. It is rather a collaborative effort between you and your client. In doing so, avoid asking the client a simple question such as "What is the purpose of this evaluation?" Instead, you need to understand *who* will use or benefit from the evaluation findings and *how* they will use the evaluation findings. This information is likely related to the needs of stakeholders (other than the client); therefore, you need to investigate their needs as well, instead of relying on the client's input.

Also recall the previous chapter's discussion that there are some risks in evaluating a program based solely on its stated goals because the program goals may or may not reflect the stakeholders' true needs. Thus, it is important to assess stakeholders' needs for the program especially when you found out that the program was not implemented based on a needs assessment. Even if a needs assessment led to the implementation of the program, stakeholders' needs may change over time, and it is helpful to double-check if the stated needs reflect the current needs.

Assess Stakeholders' Needs for the Program and the Evaluation

When assessing stakeholders' needs for the program as well as the evaluation, you will consult different types of stakeholders—mainly upstream stakeholders and direct impactees. Upstream stakeholders and direct impactees may or may not have the same needs; thus, it is important to consult both groups of stakeholders.

Recall that upstream stakeholders are the ones who were involved in the design, development, and implementation, and are likely responsible for maintaining the program. Due to their roles and responsibilities associated with the program, upstream stakeholders are in a good position to indicate management-oriented needs.

NEEDS OF DIFFERENT TYPES OF STAKEHOLDERS

In contrast, downstream direct impactees are the actual participants and users of the program. They will be able to point out specific needs from consumers' perspectives. Making meaningful judgments of the value of a program based on its consumers' needs is the main focus in Michael Scriven's consumer-oriented approach to evaluation (Stufflebeam & Shinkfield, 2007). It is important to know that Scriven's emphasis is not just on consumers but on consumers' needs.

In some cases, inputs from downstream indirect impactees can be helpful, since they are affected by the performance of direct impactees. They may be able to provide information from a different angle that upstream stakeholders and direct impactees may have failed to perceive.

During your initial talk with the evaluation client (who is likely one of the upstream stakeholders), you discovered some information about why the intervention program was implemented—that is, the needs for the intervention program. In addition to the client's input, now you want to gather data from other stakeholders and incorporate their data into your evaluation design. While assessing their needs for the program, you also find out about their needs for the evaluation—what the stakeholders expect from the evaluation and how they intend to use the evaluation findings. It is an important piece of information that guides shaping your evaluation design later on.

How would you assess stakeholders' needs for the program and the evaluation? To solicit this type of information, it is appropriate to conduct interviews with a small group of different types of stakeholders, using open-ended questions such as the following (these are generic questions and you may customize them as needed):

ASSESS NEEDS FOR THE PROGRAM AND THE EVALUATION

- How familiar with the program are you?

- How much did you get involved when developing and implementing the program? Who else was involved in developing and implementing the program?

- What is your understanding about the purpose of the program?

- Currently, what does it aim to accomplish?

- What *should* it aim to accomplish?

- How is this program supposed to benefit you and the organization?

- What do you hope this evaluation will focus on?

- What do you want to get out of this evaluation?

- What information do you want to see in the final report?

- Which information is "must-have" information and which information is "nice-to-have" information?

- How would you use the information that comes out of this evaluation?

- Other than you, who else will make good use of the evaluation findings?

- What change(s) do you expect to see after you use the evaluation findings?

With the information about stakeholders' needs for the program and the evaluation, you will be able to determine the purpose of the evaluation.

Your interviews at this point are not for soliciting evaluative information about the program from the stakeholders (i.e., how good or bad the program is). You should focus on finding information about what the stakeholders want from the program and how they intend to use the evaluation findings. Especially their input about how they intend to use the evaluation findings will help both you and the stakeholders understand the purpose of the evaluation.

HOW STAKEHOLDERS INTEND TO USE EVALUATION FINDINGS

Read the following script (adapted from an actual interview) and notice what the evaluation client says at the beginning of the conversation with an evaluator and how the client clarifies her evaluation intention after the evaluator has asked additional questions.

Evaluation client: "We recently started this program; just last year. We've run the program twice so far. We conducted this exit survey at the end of the program, but we've never had time to analyze the data. Can you use the data in your evaluation?"

Evaluator:	"Good that you've conducted an exit survey. Yes, the survey data will be useful. What questions did you include in the survey?"
Evaluation client:	"Here are the survey questions [showing a copy of the survey questionnaire]. We were mainly interested in hearing what the participants had to say about the program—if they valued the program activities, if they found them interesting, if they would attend the program again. We want to make sure that they get the most out of the program. We just scanned through the survey data. We also have some anecdotal data."
Evaluator:	"Did you take any actions after you reviewed the survey data or based on the anecdotal data?"
Evaluation client:	"Well, we heard some participants saying that they liked hands-on activities, so we added more hands-on exercises. Some other people said one of the activities was too long, so we shortened it a little bit."
Evaluator:	"So, you *have* made changes to the program based on their input. [The client nods.] Are you willing to make more changes to the program if the evaluation indicates areas for improvement?"
Evaluation client:	"Yes. Like I said, we want to make sure that we provide a good quality program to the participants. We are open to making changes. As we keep making changes to the program, it may look quite different from the first version. And that's OK."
Evaluator:	"Do you intend to use the evaluation results to make administrative or financial decisions? Like deciding whether to continue or discontinue the program? Is there any chance that the evaluation results would influence if or how the program is funded?"
Evaluation client:	"We will continue to offer this program—I don't know until when, but probably for a long time. Currently the program is self-funded. The evaluation results won't impact our decision to self-fund the program. We are seeking external funding sources too, but that's a separate issue."
Evaluator:	"I see. Based on what you've said so far, it looks like the main reason you want to have this evaluation conducted is because you want to see if any areas of the program need to be changed to provide a good quality program to the participants. Is it right? [The client nods.] You want me to include such information in the final report. [The client nods.] Let me ask you this—other than you, who will read the final report and why?"
Evaluation client:	"I work closely with three staff members here. I think I will share the final report with them, because they also need to know what needs to be changed, or if they agree to make those

> changes. Their input is important too. We all worked together to develop the program. But, they are the ones who run the program activities and actually interact with the participants."

Evaluator: "Sounds good. Anybody else from the management level?"

Evaluation client: "No. I don't think they need to see the evaluation report. It's up to us how we run the program. We may just talk to them about the report later."

Evaluator: "OK. I understand. May I also talk with the three staff members?"

Evaluation client: "Of course. Their offices are at the end of the hallway."

USING ONE-ON-ONE OR GROUP INTERVIEWS

As the scenario indicates at the end, you want to interview other stakeholders after discussing with your client. For example, when your evaluand is a training program, you may interview not only the client but also other upstream stakeholders such as trainers or instructional designers and a small group of downstream impactees such as recent program participants and their supervisors.

You may conduct one-on-one interviews with individual stakeholders, or gather multiple stakeholders in one place to conduct a group interview(s). You may conduct a group interview with the same type of stakeholders separately, or a group interview combining stakeholders from different categories (a.k.a. a focus group). There are pros and cons to conducting a group interview with the same type of stakeholders separately and conducting one with different types of stakeholders together; these pros and cons are summarized in Table 8. When it is not feasible to gather multiple people in one place to conduct a group interview, you may conduct one-on-one interviews with individual stakeholders.

Determine If the Evaluation Is a Formative or Summative Type

(Adapted from Chyung, 2015)[a]

With the information obtained from the stakeholders, you will also be able to help them determine the evaluation type. In the previous client–evaluator conversation script, if you (evaluator) had paid attention only to the evaluation client's initial response, you might have assumed that she wanted to find out the overall quality of the program (summative). However, the continued conversation led you to realize that she wanted to find out areas for improvement (formative). The formative and summative distinction is a frequently used dichotomy that helps explain evaluation type. In the 1960s, Michael Scriven (1967) coined the terms *formative evaluation* and *summative evaluation* in relation to curriculum evaluation. At that time, he used the terms to illustrate the *functions* that the evaluation serves (Scriven, 1991a). **Formative evaluations** were designed to support the process of improving curriculum development,

---

[a]The content of this section is from the following article with some modifications to make it fit within the chapter content: Chyung, S. Y. (2015). Foundational concepts for conducting program evaluations. *Performance Improvement Quarterly, 27*(4), 77–96. doi:10.1002/piq.21181

TABLE 8 ● Potential Benefits and Concerns for Conducting a Group Interview With Different Types of Stakeholders, Separately or Together		
	Conducting a separate group interview with each type of stakeholder	**Conducting a group interview with different types of stakeholders**
Benefits	Each group can express their thoughts and concerns freely without worrying about potential ramifications.	Different groups can interact with each other and develop shared needs or uncover hidden agendas.
Concerns	Each group can express its own needs and does not have a good understanding about how its needs may affect the other group's needs, and vice versa.	When Group A has an authoritative relationship with Group B, Group A may lead the discussions, or Group B members may not feel comfortable expressing their thoughts and concerns.

whereas **summative evaluations** were designed and conducted when stakeholders needed evaluative conclusions about the program.

During several decades of usage, the meanings of the terms have evolved and they are now used to distinguish the types of evaluation, which also make a difference in the roles that evaluators play. During formative evaluation, the evaluator would play a constructive role to gather inputs and help make improvements to the program, whereas for summative evaluation, the evaluator would play an end-review role to determine the overall quality and worth of the program.

It is commonly thought that the formative–summative distinction is time specific; that is, formative evaluation is conducted during the program development stage, and summative evaluation is conducted after the program has been developed and implemented. Robert Stake explains the difference well: "When the cook tastes the soup, that's formative evaluation; when the guest tastes it, that's summative evaluation" (as cited in Scriven, 1991a, p. 19).

MAKE AN INTENTION-DRIVEN DECISION

The distinction between formative evaluation and summative evaluation is also intention driven. For example, the typical end-of-course evaluations submitted by the course participants are considered a summative evaluation as the information is intended to be used to judge the quality and worth of the course. However, when the information is used to make changes in the instruction to make improvements on learner perceptions toward the course and their learning outcomes, this change in intention alters the function of the evaluation to a formative one. Using the cook–guest analogy, the cook could use the summative comments on a dish made by guests as formative data to change his or her recipe and to improve future guests' satisfaction levels (Chen, 1996). In this sense, most evaluations have the potential to be used for formative purposes, and it may be why evaluation, compared to research, is sometimes described as being designed to improve, rather than prove, something (Stufflebeam, as cited in Fain, 2005), although this straightforward distinction would not work for all types of evaluation (Mathison, 2008).

FOCUS ON INTENDED USE BY INTENDED USERS

In this book, it is recommended that you use the **intention-driven method** to determine whether your evaluation is a formative or summative type—that is, how the stakeholders intend to use the evaluation findings. Michael Quinn Patton (2012) emphasizes this **utilization-focused evaluation** approach. He asserts that "evaluations should be judged by their utility and actual use" and "the focus in the utilization-focused evaluation is on intended use by intended users" (M. Q. Patton, 2012, p. 4). More specifically in the HPI context,

- It is a summative evaluation if the stakeholders *intend* to use the evaluation findings to produce accountability-related decisions, such as the following:
  - Produce periodic records of the overall quality of the program
  - Assess the quality of the performance outcomes needed to be produced (the amount of performance gap closed)
  - Request additional funding to continue the program
  - Implement similar programs based on lessons learned from this program

- It is a formative evaluation if the stakeholders *intend* to use the evaluation findings to make improvement-related decisions, such as the following:
  - Determine if or how the program content should be redesigned
  - Find if more support from the organization is needed
  - Assess the progress made in producing the needed outcomes (the amount of performance gap to be closed)
  - Determine what methods should be used to monitor the program on an ongoing basis

With that in mind, it is not surprising to find that many program evaluations in the HPI context are formative evaluations because HPI is all about making continuous improvement. Carol Weiss (1972), one of the early pioneers in the development of program evaluation, indicated during the early 1970s that many programs are never "finished" in the sense that curriculum development is finished, and go/no-go decisions in program evaluation are relatively rare. Also, summative evaluation should be conducted when a program is fully implemented and sufficient time has passed to generate observable results. Prematurely conducted summative evaluations will likely reveal that the programs have failed to achieve their intended outcomes.

When conducting a formative evaluation of a program, you will likely need to know how well the program is doing now in order to find out what needs to be improved. This does not mean that you are conducting both summative and formative evaluations all at once. With a formative purpose, you are evaluating how well the program is moving toward achieving the desired outcomes, rather than whether the program has achieved the desired outcomes. So, you want to treat "how well the program is doing now" as part of your formative evaluation rather than as a separate summative evaluation.

However, some evaluations may have a dual purpose: to make managerial decisions and to make continuous improvement. For example, your client may want to ensure that the current training program meets the expected cost–benefit ratio (or return on investment) in order to justify the funding for the program (summative) and to learn how to make the training program more relevant to the employees' needs (formative).

Avoid using terms such as *formative* and *summative evaluation* in questions to your client; clients may not be familiar with these terms. You will be able to identify the type of evaluation while asking how the client and the stakeholders intend to use the evaluation findings.

Determine If the Evaluation Is Goal Based or Goal Free

During Step 1 (identify an evaluand), you learned about why the program was implemented, which likely led you to find out about the program goals. When you evaluate the quality of a program against the program goals that were derived from known needs, it is a **goal-based evaluation** (Scriven, 1991b).

However, program goals sometimes can be stated too narrowly and can fail to reflect other needs that were unknown to the program developer at that time. Or, the stated needs/goals may have changed since the program was developed. So, there may be hidden needs that current stakeholders hope the program will help fulfill. When you evaluate the quality of a program based on the true needs of the current stakeholders (instead of limiting your evaluation criteria to the program goals), you are taking an approach called **goal-free evaluation** (Scriven, 1991b).

Note that goals refer to intended outcomes; therefore, *goal-based evaluation* means evaluating something against its intended outcomes. In doing so, outcomes other than the goal-related ones can be unexamined, or discovered but ignored. A goal-free evaluation approach helps avoid this tunnel vision of the goal-based approach. Instead, *goal-free evaluation* refers to evaluating something's actual outcomes, both anticipated outcomes and side effects, against the needs demonstrated in the context (Scriven, 1991c).

BASED ON INTENDED OUTCOMES OR NOT

So, are you conducting a goal-based or goal-free evaluation? In the HPI context, especially when an intervention was implemented based on a needs assessment, it is likely that you are conducting a goal-based evaluation, or a goal-based evaluation with a goal-free approach, but not often a pure goal-free evaluation. Conducting an entirely goal-free investigation requires experience in evaluation; therefore, you as a novice or advanced beginner level evaluator are recommended to select an evaluation that allows you to use a goal-based evaluation, or you are encouraged to incorporate a goal-free approach within your goal-based evaluation.

For example, let's say you are evaluating the effectiveness of a diversity training program. The goal of the program is to help employees become more tolerant of differences among people. You may conduct a goal-based evaluation, investigating

- how the program has been delivered and perceived, and what needs to be changed to help employees become more tolerant of differences among people (formative), or

- how employees' tolerance toward differences among people has changed as a result of the training program (summative).

You may also incorporate a goal-free approach to uncover if there are other unintended positive and negative side effects that resulted after the program was delivered.

For example, were there any changes in hiring practice or in the employee–supervisor relationship? Adding a goal-free approach to your goal-based evaluation may help you find out systemic impacts of the intervention program.

Determine If the Evaluation Is Merit Focused or Worth Focused

Another set of evaluation-specific concepts that you need to apply when identifying the type of evaluation is *merit* and *worth*.

An evaluand's **merit** refers to its internal quality, which tends to stay the same regardless of where the evaluand is situated (implemented) (Lincoln & Guba, 1980). It is analogous to the quality of diamonds measured by 4Cs (carat, cut, color, and clarity) being stable regardless of their location.

INTERNAL QUALITY OR EXTERNAL VALUE

On the other hand, an evaluand's **worth** refers to its external value, which tends to change depending on the external factors surrounding the evaluand, such as the value of a compass to sailors while sailing (high value) versus its value to bicycle commuters while riding their bicycle (low value).

Although both merit and worth refer to characteristics of a program, merit is a context-independent quality, whereas worth is a context-dependent value, as shown in Table 9.

So, will you focus on the program's merit or worth? Your focus is likely biased toward the program's worth because evaluations conducted in the HPI context are mostly about showing the value of interventions implemented to produce intended outcomes. However, evaluating something's worth usually involves an evaluation of its merit as well, and then its cost factors are added to it. The cost factors are usually viewed as financial factors (e.g., What is the return on investment?), but broadly speaking, cost factors are part of needs (e.g., Is the program satisfying the organization's and stakeholders' needs?).

For example, let's say you are investigating different webinar systems available on the market based on their usability principles. It would be a merit-focused evaluation. However, in the HPI context, you would not stop here. You would be interested in evaluating different webinar systems with a goal of selecting the most appropriate one for your organization. In doing so, you would likely need to compare the internal quality (merit) of the different systems against the budget (cost) or the reasons to use them (needs). Thus, you start by investigating the merit of each webinar system while conducting a worth-focused evaluation.

TABLE 9 ● Merit and Worth		
Degree	**Merit (Context-Independent)**	**Worth (Context-Dependent)**
High	"Wow, that's a new, sophisticated design!"	"Those features are exactly what our employees need to have!"
Low	"Hmm . . . the design is not user-friendly at all."	"We will not need to use most of the features, and it costs too much for us."

Keep in Mind Using
a System-Focused Evaluation Approach

No matter what type of program you evaluate, keep in mind that you should design your evaluation to demonstrate how effectively the organization has used the performance improvement intervention program. Robert Brinkerhoff (2006) emphasizes this in his book *Telling Training's Story*.

Brinkerhoff (2006) explains that conducting an evaluation that focuses only on a training program carries significant risks, such as ignoring the performance system factors that affect the results of training and failing to provide the management with useful feedback to guide performance improvement. Thus, Brinkerhoff emphasizes the importance of shifting the focus from evaluating a training program itself to evaluating how effectively the organization has used the training program. This shifted focus on the system should apply to not only training evaluations but also evaluations of other types of performance improvement interventions. *[SHIFT TO EVALUATION OF HOW THE ORGANIZATION USED THE PROGRAM]*

When you conduct a program evaluation focusing on whether or not a program achieved its goals, you assume that the program itself and alone has full responsibility for its success; HPI practitioners understand that this is often not true. The success or failure of a performance improvement intervention relies on not only the quality of the intervention itself but also the environmental support. For example, an excellent training program can fail miserably in helping workers apply new knowledge after they return to their job if there is no support from the organization, no good reason to use the new knowledge (e.g., lack of incentives), or a barrier in the work environment (e.g., no access to computers when needed).

Recall that HPI practitioners use systematic and systemic approaches to workforce development and performance improvement. You are in the first phase of a *systematic* 10-step approach to evaluation. Including an investigation of environmental factors in your evaluation would make your evaluation more *systemic*. When conducting an evaluation with how the organization used the performance improvement intervention in mind, you likely use a **system-focused evaluation** approach (investigating both the intervention program's effectiveness and the environmental factors that facilitated the program's success) rather than an **intervention-focused evaluation** approach (investigating the intervention program's effectiveness only). A systemic approach to evaluation also helps you discover a program's hidden needs and investigate unintended outcomes. *[SYSTEM-FOCUSED EVALUATION RATHER THAN INTERVENTION-FOCUSED EVALUATION]*

Figure 6 is a visual way to compare a system-focused evaluation approach and an intervention-focused evaluation approach. System-focused evaluation is a more holistic approach than intervention-focused evaluation.

For example, when conducting an evaluation of a training program, it is easy for you to fall into an intervention-focused evaluation approach and focus only on intervention-specific factors such as

- the program's training goals,
- the program's internal training process, and

FIGURE 6 ● System-Focused Evaluation Versus Intervention-Focused Evaluation

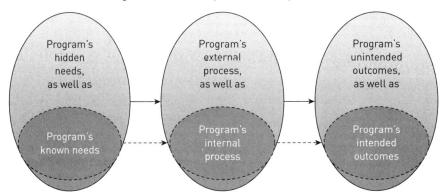

Use a system-focused evaluation approach
(How well the organization used the performance improvement intervention)

Program's hidden needs, as well as

Program's external process, as well as

Program's unintended outcomes, as well as

Program's known needs

Program's internal process

Program's intended outcomes

Rather than an intervention-focused evaluation approach
(How well the intervention produced the intended outcomes)

- the program's intended outcomes (the inner circles and dotted arrows in Figure 6).

In doing so, there is a risk of neglecting systemic factors such as

- the program's hidden and ever-changing consumers' needs,
- the program's external process such as the organizational support and incentives, and
- the program's unintended positive and negative outcomes (the outer circles and solid arrows in Figure 6).

Consequently, you may focus only on investigating how much the training program helped trainees learn, how much it helped them change their behavior, and how much it contributed to increasing organizational results.

With the system-focused evaluation approach in mind, however, you will be able to uncover much more. While assessing the program's known and hidden goals and projected outcomes, you can tell

- what goals/outcomes are currently stated,
- if the goals/outcomes were established based on actual organizational needs,
- what other hidden needs exist,
- if the evaluation should focus on the known goals/outcomes or hidden needs (or both) and why, and
- how the organization intends to use the evaluation findings.

While investigating the quality of process for operating the program, you will see

- how well the program is designed to meet the needs-based goals (internal process), and

- how supportive the environmental factors are in helping the program achieve the goals (external process).

While evaluating the quality of end results generated from the program, you will be able to show

- how well the program has achieved the needs-based goals,

- what other unintended outcomes the program has produced, and

- how the organization can/should use the evaluation findings.

In other words, intervention-focused evaluation is part of system-focused evaluation, as illustrated in Figure 6. System-focused evaluation encompasses both intervention-specific factors and other contributing factors. Without this system view, your evaluation would be narrowly focused.

Write an Evaluation Purpose Statement

After you identify whether your evaluation is formative or summative and goal based or goal free, who the intended users are, and what their intended use of the evaluation findings is, you will be able to formulate a clear purpose statement for the evaluation. As explained in the previous sections of this chapter, you will likely conduct a goal-based evaluation and may incorporate a goal-free approach if desirable, rather than conducting a pure goal-free evaluation. In the HPI context, you are also more likely to conduct a worth-focused evaluation than to focus only on the program's merit. Purpose statements of worth-focused evaluations with a systemic focus would include information about the needs of the organization and/or its stakeholders.

EVALUATION PURPOSE STATEMENT

Here are several examples of an evaluation purpose statement. The following specific information is indicated with superscript numbers:

1. Type of evaluation (formative or summative)

2. Focus of evaluation (to find out or investigate something)

3. Intended users of evaluation findings (specific stakeholders who will use the evaluation findings)

4. Intended use of evaluation findings (how they will use evaluation findings)

5. Organization's and or stakeholders' needs (what is needed for the organization and/or stakeholders; the evaluand's worth)

Example 1: Goal-based, formative evaluation
This formative evaluation[1] is conducted to identify the current status and inner workings of the hospital physician and nurse rounding program.[2] The chief nursing officer

and director of physician relations[3] will use the evaluation findings to make necessary changes to the program and its support system[4] to improve the quality of patient care.[5]

Example 2: Goal-based, summative evaluation

This summative evaluation[1] investigates the overall effectiveness of the revised employee orientation program[2] on preparing new employees for immediate success on the job within the first two months,[5] which will assist the training director[3] in planning for the following year's new employee onboarding methods.[4]

Example 3: Goal-free, summative evaluation

This evaluation has a summative purpose[1] to investigate the impact of new safety regulations and procedures on overall manufacturing operations at XYZ company.[2] Based on the evaluation findings, the chief safety officer[3] intends to develop other guidelines and strategies[4] necessary to maximize quality manufacturing process and outputs.[5]

Chapter Summary

Identify the purpose of evaluation (Step 3):

- Evaluation and needs assessment are twins separated at birth; they are similar yet different.

- Stufflebeam's (2007) CIPP model explains four types of evaluations: context, input, process, and product evaluations. Context and input evaluations are front-end evaluations similar to needs assessments, whereas process and product evaluations are characterized as back-end evaluations. This book focuses on back-end evaluations.

- Evaluators should conduct individual or group interviews with different types of stakeholders (including the client) to assess their needs for the program and for the evaluation, in order to determine the purpose of the evaluation.

- By gathering inputs from stakeholders regarding their needs for the program and for the evaluation, evaluators can determine if the evaluation is

  o formative or summative,

  o goal based or goal free, and

  o merit focused or worth focused.

- Determined based on the stakeholders' intended use of evaluation findings,

  o summative evaluations are conducted to identify the overall effectiveness or make accountability-related decisions, and

  o formative evaluations are conducted to find areas for improvement.

- Evaluations of performance improvement intervention programs are likely goal-based evaluations, or goal-based evaluations with a goal-free evaluation approach, but not often pure goal-free evaluations.

- Evaluations of performance improvement intervention programs likely focus on the programs' worth because of the HPI's emphasis on the value of the interventions to produce outcomes desired by the organization and stakeholders.

- To maximize the impact of evaluation, it is important to use a system-focused evaluation approach (addressing how well the organization used the performance improvement intervention) rather than an intervention-focused evaluation approach (focusing on how well the intervention worked).

- When using a system-focused approach, evaluators will be able to investigate not only the program's known internal needs and intended outcomes but also its hidden needs, external process, and unintended outcomes.

- When evaluating a performance improvement intervention program, the evaluation purpose statement will likely contain information indicating the type and focus of evaluation, intended users and their intended use of evaluation findings, and the organization's and stakeholders' needs.

Chapter Discussion

1. What differences do you expect to see in the scope and impact of intervention-focused and system-focused evaluation approaches?

You are evaluating a training program on chemical lab safety. The training program is designed to teach lab technicians about lab safety rules and standards regarding safe handling, storage, and disposal of chemicals.

Using Table 10, compare the differences in the scope and impact of your evaluation when using two approaches:

- Intervention-focused evaluation

- System-focused evaluation approach

TABLE 10 ● Analyze Differences Between Intervention-Focused and System-Focused Evaluation Approaches			
	What type of needs would you assess?	What type of process would you assess?	What type of outcomes would you assess?
When using an intervention-focused evaluation approach			
When using a system-focused evaluation approach			

2. Are the evaluation purpose statements clearly written?

Two purpose statements are presented (A and B). Identify the following components:

1. Type of evaluation

2. Focus of evaluation

3. Intended users of evaluation findings

4. Intended use of evaluation findings

5. Organization's and stakeholders' needs

Also revise the statement(s) if any of the components are not clearly stated.

A: The purpose of this formative evaluation is to find out strengths and weaknesses of the volunteer training program implemented at the animal shelter. The volunteer manager and trainers will use the evaluation findings to revise the program curriculum and add other necessary support to prepare volunteers to properly handle animals.

B: This evaluation has a summative purpose to determine how successful the e-Girls Camp program is in motivating eighth- and ninth-grade female students to pursue careers in science, technology, engineering, and math (STEM). The evaluation findings will help the camp director and her staff in writing grants to seek future funding and developing engineering education promotion materials to be used at local schools.

Now, Your Turn—Identify the Purpose of Evaluation

Based on your discussion with the client and other stakeholders, identify the purpose of the evaluation. Use Table B-1 in Appendix B (Evaluation Development Worksheets) as a job aid to summarize your finding. Table 11 contains an example.

TABLE 11 ● Example Worksheet for Step 3: Identify the Purpose of Evaluation		
Step	**Question**	**Your Finding**
Identify the purpose of evaluation	• Describe the people with whom you talked, to answer the following questions. List other people with whom you plan to talk in the near future to gather more information about the purpose of evaluation.	I talked with the training manager (the client) and the trainer. I will also talk with a supervisor of new employees who recently completed the program.

Step	Question	Your Finding
	• Who are the intended users of the evaluation findings, and how will they use the evaluation findings?	There are two main groups of intended users of the evaluation findings: 1. The training department staff, including the training manager, instructional designers, and a trainer, will use the information to revise the program content as necessary. 2. The new employees' supervisors will use the information to provide adequate support to new employees during and after the onboarding program.
	• Based on the "intended use" information above, is it a formative evaluation or a summative evaluation, and how so?	It is a formative evaluation because its intention is to find out which areas in the program content and design need to be changed and if more support should be provided.
	• Is it a back-end evaluation, and how so?	It is a back-end evaluation because it evaluates a program that has been implemented as a solution to an existing performance problem.
	• Is it a goal-based evaluation, a goal-based evaluation with a goal-free approach, or a pure goal-free evaluation, and how so?	It is primarily a goal-based evaluation because it investigates the quality of the program against the program goal. The program goal is to prepare new employees to perform their job tasks without assistance 90% of the time. A goal-free approach will also be incorporated in order to find any unexpected results that may have occurred after changing the onboarding program from an instructor-led program to a blended learning program.
	• Combining the above information, write down the evaluation purpose statement for the evaluation. Make sure to include the following: 1. Type of evaluation 2. Focus of evaluation 3. Intended users of evaluation findings 4. Intended use of evaluation findings 5. Organization's and stakeholders' needs	This formative goal-based evaluation will be conducted to find out how well the blended delivery onboarding program is designed and supported to prepare new employees to perform their job tasks without assistance 90% of the time. The evaluation findings will allow the training department staff and supervisors to make necessary changes to the curriculum and performance support to help new employees get up to speed.

Assess Evaluation Feasibility and Risk Factors

During the identification phase of your evaluation, you work with your client and other stakeholders to clearly understand your evaluand, its stakeholders, and the purpose of the evaluation. While doing so, you should also assess feasibility of the evaluation project and identify potential risk factors.

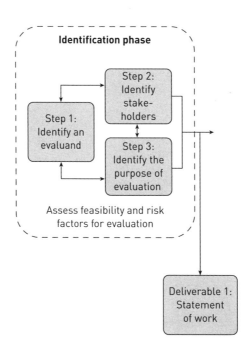

Incorporate Macro-Level Tasks Into Micro-Level Steps

Review Table 1 in the Introduction chapter. Assessments of feasibility and risk factors are not part of the 10 micro-level steps; they are characterized as *macro-level tasks* because you should continue to assess feasibility and risk factors from the outset of your evaluation project and throughout the project.

If you are a novice evaluator, due to a lack of experience, you may use a linear approach during the identification phase, identifying an evaluand, its stakeholders, and the purpose of evaluation, and assessing the feasibility and risk factors of the evaluation, as shown in Figure 7.

However, once you have completed an evaluation project, you would recognize that the first three micro-level steps are intertwined and that assessing feasibility and risk factors is an ongoing process, as illustrated in Figure 8. That is, while identifying an evaluand, you should immediately find out about its stakeholders. Identifying stakeholders and their roles should help you clearly understand the evaluand. Investigating stakeholders' needs will further help you understand the purpose of the evaluation, and vice versa. While identifying the purpose of the evaluation, you will also attain a clear understanding about what you are evaluating.

The macro-level tasks of assessing feasibility and risk factors of the evaluation apply to these intertwined steps. You should keep in mind that not all programs are evaluation-ready due to various reasons. During the initial contact and discussion with your client and other stakeholders, you should assess if it is feasible for you to conduct the evaluation and if the organization is ready for the evaluation.

INTERTWINED STEPS DURING THE IDENTIFICATION PHASE

Assess Feasibility of the Evaluation Project

Feasibility can be assessed based on factors associated with not only the evaluand project itself (a.k.a. *evaluability*) but also the evaluators' capacity.

Following are some broad categories and several questions you can use when assessing feasibility of an evaluation project.

FIGURE 7 ● Linear Approach During the Identification Phase

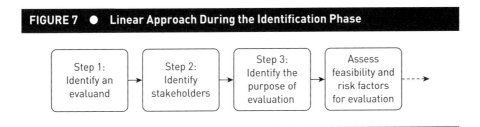

FIGURE 8   ●   Nonlinear Approach During the Identification Phase

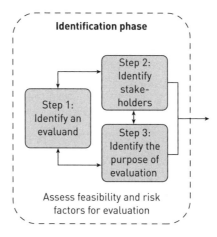

1. Maturity of the evaluand

- Has the evaluand matured enough to be evaluated?

    If you are conducting a formative evaluation, has the evaluand been developed enough to assess whether its process can be improved? If the evaluand exists only in a concept paper, your project may be a front-end evaluation (needs assessment) rather than a back-end evaluation.

    If you are conducting a summative evaluation, has sufficient time passed for the evaluand to produce measurable outcomes? This depends on the type of outcomes to be measured. Workers who have completed a technical training program to learn how to use an upgraded software program may show their learning and behavioral outcomes immediately or within a short time. On the other hand, after managers have completed a leadership training to improve their relationship with employees, it may take several months to recognize perceivable changes in the relationship between the managers and their employees.

2. Scope of the evaluation

- How small or large is the scope of the evaluation? It should not be so small that conducting a comprehensive evaluation would be overkill nor so large that it cannot be completed using the resources that you have.

- Is the client willing to discuss adjusting the scope of the evaluation with you? When a client proposes an evaluation of large scope, is the client open to the possibility of breaking it down to smaller phases and completing a series of evaluation projects?

3. Support for the evaluation

- How does the organization perceive or approach evaluation? Does the client strongly support the evaluation as a way to improve the overall organizational performance? Or, is the evaluation one of the items on the to-do list that the client simply needs to check off?

- How easy or difficult is scheduling meetings to talk with the client and other key stakeholders?

- Will the client be available during the project to answer your questions and to provide you with necessary information in a timely manner?

- Do stakeholders show positive attitudes toward conducting the evaluation? Or, do they show strong reservation toward it?

- Will the stakeholders be available or allowed to participate in surveys, interviews, or observations (as informants) during their work hours?

- Does the organization have records of information that you may need to use, and are you allowed to have access to them? Does the organization require you to sign a nondisclosure agreement form?

- Does the organization require you to get approval from multiple entities to conduct your evaluation? How easy or difficult is it to get approval from them?

4. **Ethical concerns for the evaluation**

- How does the organization *really* intend to use the evaluation results? Are there any signs that indicate that there might be a hidden purpose for conducting the evaluation?

- Are there any signs of ethical problems for conducting the evaluation? Does the organization culture support you to conduct an evaluation in an ethical manner—for example, allowing you to keep confidentiality of data that you collect?

- Are there any organizational politics that would cause serious ramifications for stakeholders who participate in the evaluation?

- What are the benefits for conducting the evaluation? What potential risks, burdens, or harms may the evaluation produce to the stakeholders?

5. **Resources for the evaluation**

- What is the time frame for the evaluation to be completed? Will you be able to meet the timeline? Is there a large enough budget for the project?

- Do you have expertise to conduct the requested evaluation, using the most appropriate evaluation designs?

- Is it beneficial to complete the evaluation with other evaluators as a team? What other expertise should you seek from your team members?

- What is the optimal number of members in your evaluation team to successfully complete the evaluation project within the given time frame?

- Will the evaluation require evaluators to travel to a certain location? If so, will you or your team member be able to do so?

These small or large issues will have an impact on the success of your evaluation project, so it is important to assess feasibility of the evaluation project early during your evaluation identification phase.

If you are a student conducting an evaluation as a class project, you should also pay attention to whether your evaluation can be completed within your class schedule and seek advice from your instructor. Your client organization may require you and your team members sign a nondisclosure agreement. You need to check if the organization's requirements allow you to use your project as a class project and share deliverables in class to obtain feedback from your classmates and instructor.

List Project Assumptions

While assessing the project feasibility during the identification phase, you also need to make a list of assumptions about the project. Project assumptions are things that you expect to see happen during the project, although you cannot guarantee that they will actually happen as assumed.

For a list of assumptions relevant and meaningful to your project, you may think of different categories such as the following:

ASSUMPTIONS ON PEOPLE, PLACE, AND PROCESS

- People
  - Client
  - Stakeholders
  - Evaluation team
- Place
  - Organization
  - Infrastructure
  - Economy
- Process
  - Program operation
  - Budget and other resources
  - Evaluation methodology

For example, you may make the following assumptions during your evaluation project:

- The client supports the project until it is completed.
- The organization stays in business during the project.
- The evaluation team is committed to completing the project.
- The evaluation team uses an appropriate evaluation design.
- Stakeholders provide accurate information during data collection.
- Extant data that the organization provides are accurate.
- The evaluation team has access to available data.
- The evaluation team maintains neutrality during data collection and analysis.

- The client and evaluation team find a workaround through discussion when facing difficulties during the project.

However, as mentioned earlier, project assumptions are not guaranteed to be true. Therefore, you will need to monitor project assumptions throughout the project and incorporate strategies to manage unforeseen factors if they arise.

Estimate Tasks and Time Involving Stakeholders

One of the necessary assumptions during an evaluation project is the involvement of the evaluation client and other stakeholders as informants. However, their lack of time is a common barrier to conducting evaluations. Even if you champion an evaluation project to be conducted, the evaluation client and other stakeholders may feel reserved because they think they have to spend a lot of time to support the evaluation project. Thus, providing the client and other stakeholders with information about estimated numbers of hours that they are asked to spend on the evaluation can help them determine the project feasibility from their perspective and help you get their buy-in.

Table 12 presents a list of steps and tasks that the evaluation client and other stakeholders would likely do during a small evaluation project, suitable for novice and advanced beginner level evaluators to conduct as a class project in a 15-week course. However, the actual number of hours for the individual tasks may vary depending on the situation. For example, during Week 11 through Week 13, the client might end up spending more time than you had estimated to locate and share existing data files with you, simply because the client realized that different versions of files existed and needed to consolidate the data before sharing. Discussing this type of information with the client will also help you assess feasibility of the evaluation project and recognize risk factors associated with the evaluation procedure involving the client and other stakeholders.

ESTIMATED TIME FOR STAKEHOLDERS TO SPEND

Assess Risk Factors for the Evaluation Project

Even seemingly feasible evaluation projects may come with a few risk factors that can negatively impact successful completion of the projects. Also, as mentioned earlier, project assumptions are not guaranteed to be true; therefore, some of the assumptions can become risk factors. Thus, you should identify and manage risk factors to minimize risks and maximize success.

Risk factors are the ones that have potential to cause risks. Many of the feasibility questions you ask yourself should help you identify risk factors.

IDENTIFY RISK FACTORS

For example, suppose that you decided to take on an evaluation project that is a little bit larger in scope than what you normally would take on with your current resources. Or, you have observed ineffective communications with the client and other stakeholders. Those are risk factors that can cause difficulties during your project, such as scheduling problems and delays on completing certain tasks, which would in turn influence the quality of the project outcomes.

TABLE 12 ● Example of Estimated Tasks and Time Involving the Client and Stakeholders During a Small-Scale Evaluation Project to Be Completed in a 15-Week Course

Weeks and Evaluation Steps	The Client's Involvement (Estimated Time)	Other Stakeholders' Involvement (Estimated Time)
Week 1–Week 4 • Step 1 Identify an evaluand. • Step 2 Identify stakeholders and needs. • Step 3 Identify the purpose of evaluation. • Assess feasibility and risk factors. • Write and submit a statement of work (SOW). (Deliverable 1)	• Discuss an evaluation project to be conducted. (30 minutes) • Provide information about the program to be evaluated, its stakeholders, and the evaluation purpose. (30 minutes) • Discuss feasibility and risk factors. (30 minutes) • Review and approve the SOW. (30 minutes)	• A small group of stakeholders who will use the evaluation findings provide their input on needs for the program and needs for the evaluation. (30 minutes–1 hour)
Week 5–Week 8 • Step 4 Develop a program logic model. • Step 5 Determine dimensions and importance weighting. • Step 6 Determine data collection methods. • Write and submit an evaluation proposal. (Deliverable 2)	• Provide information for developing a program logic model; review and approve a finalized program logic model. (1 hour) • Provide information to develop dimensions to be investigated and approve finalized dimensions. (30 minutes) • Provide input as needed while the evaluation team develops data collection methods, and approve the finalized data collection methods. (30 minutes) • Review and approve the evaluation proposal. (30 minutes)	• A small group of stakeholders who will use the evaluation findings (e.g., listed above) provide their input during Steps 4 through 6. (30 minutes–1 hour)
Week 9–Week 10 • Step 7 Develop data collection instruments.	• Approve data collection instruments that the evaluation team developed. (30 minutes)	• A small group of stakeholders may review instruments during a pilot test. (30 minutes)
Week 11–Week 13 • Step 8 Collect data. • Step 9 Analyze data with rubrics.	• Support the data collection process (e.g., providing the evaluation team with existing information to be analyzed and contact info of employees to be surveyed or interviewed), and approve rubrics that the evaluation team developed. (30 minutes)	• Various stakeholders provide data via surveys, interviews, and/or observations. (30 minutes)
Week 14–Week 15 • Step 10 Draw conclusions. • Write an evaluation report, conduct a summative meta-evaluation, and submit the report. (Deliverable 3)	• Review the final report upon its completion and delivery.	• Particular stakeholders review the final report upon its completion and delivery.
Total	5–7 hours	1–3 hours/each person depending on the role and type of informants

You may assess risk levels based on the degrees of damage to the project and its likelihood by using a risk management matrix (Kendrick, 2015; Raydugin, 2013). An example is shown in Table 13. You may modify the number and labels of the rows and columns of the table as needed (e.g., instead of using three levels of likelihood, you may use five levels including *Extremely low, Low, Medium, High, Extremely high*). Risk areas that fall into the light gray cells represent low risk; risk areas that fall into the medium gray cells represent medium risk; risk areas that fall into the dark gray cells indicate high risk.

Risks may vary depending on the type and scope of projects. To illustrate an example, suppose that you have identified several risk areas for your evaluation, which fall into different cells of the table:

RISK LEVELS BASED ON DEGREES OF DAMAGE AND LIKELIHOOD

a. The client returns email or phone messages in 2 or 3 days when it is optimal if the client always returns them in a day. (*Maybe* but *Minor* damage)

b. The evaluator needs more time than what is estimated to complete the project. (*Substantial* damage but *Unlikely*)

c. The evaluator is not able to participate and observe the actual blended onboarding program. (*Likely* and *Moderate* damage)

d. New employees who completed the program are not allowed to spend their work hours to participate in the project. (*Maybe* and *Detrimental* damage)

TABLE 13 ● Risk Assessment Matrix for an Evaluation Project

Damage to Project / Likelihood	Minor	Moderate	Substantial	Detrimental
Unlikely			(b) Schedule slips	
Maybe	(a) Slow communication with the client			(d) No access to data sources
Likely		(c) Indirect data collection		

You may identify "(a) slow communication with the client" as a low-level risk. Although you expect it to happen, you estimate that it would not cause damage to the successful completion of the project unless the project deadline changes to an earlier date. So, it would not change your decision to take on this project.

You may identify "(b) schedule slips" and "(c) indirect data collection" as medium-level risks and continue with the evaluation project while putting forth effort to manage the risks as much as possible. For example, to minimize the impact of schedule slips and to prevent this risk factor from causing serious damage to the project, you want to specify individual deliverable deadlines up front, share the information with the client, and monitor the schedule closely.

Compared to other risk factors, "(d) no access to data sources" presents a high-level risk for successfully completing the project; therefore, you should discuss with the client ways to find a solution before moving on with the project. After finding a workable strategy, you may be able to move this risk factor from *Maybe* to *Unlikely*.

ETHICAL CONCERNS   During your risk assessment, you should pay attention to ethical concerns:

- Common research ethics associated with protecting human participants apply to evaluation as well.

  ○ Evaluation participants' rights should be protected. They should be asked to *voluntarily* participate in your evaluation project and should not be coerced to do so.

  ○ The evaluation purpose should not be disguised or hidden; it should be fully exposed to the participants.

  ○ Confidentiality of the data should be ensured.

- Another ethical concern may have to do with the organization's intention for conducting an evaluation. Suppose that the organization did not fully disclose its intention to conduct an evaluation, and the evaluator later discovered that there was a hidden, undesirable intention, such as using the evaluation findings as a basis for laying off employees. This would pose a serious ethical concern for the evaluator.

- The evaluator's capacity to conduct an evaluation also falls into the ethics category. Especially, novice and advanced beginner level evaluators would face this type of concern. Due to their limited evaluation skills and experience, novice and advanced beginner level evaluators are advised to start with low-risk projects.

Upon careful assessments of feasibility and risk factors associated with your evaluation project, you make a decision whether or not to continue with the project. You would continue with projects that have manageable risks. However, when you find many high-level risk factors, you should clearly document them, discuss ways to minimize their negative impact on the project with the client, and suggest alternatives. As a last resort, you may decline the project.

You should also be aware that risk factors often change over the course of a project. Therefore, risk items should be assessed more than once and as needed during the project. In other words, risk assessment is not a step that you complete and move on; rather, it is an ongoing activity.

Chapter Summary

- While identifying an evaluand, its stakeholders, and the evaluation purpose, evaluators should also assess feasibility and risk factors of the project.

- Evaluators may assess feasibility of the evaluation project using categories such as

   ○ maturity of the evaluand,

   ○ scope of the evaluation,

   ○ support for the evaluation,

   ○ ethical concerns for the evaluation, and

   ○ resources for the evaluation.

- Evaluators can make a list of project assumptions regarding

   ○ people (e.g., the client, stakeholders, and evaluators),

   ○ place (e.g., the organization and infrastructure), and

   ○ process (e.g., the availability of project resources, and use of appropriate evaluation methods).

- Evaluators should provide the client and other stakeholders with estimated tasks and time involving them. It can help determine feasibility and discover risk factors associated with the evaluation procedure involving the client and stakeholders.

- Evaluators should identify risk factors for the evaluation using a risk assessment matrix based on

   ○ the degree of damage to the project that each risk factor will produce, and

   ○ its likelihood of happening.

- Evaluators should discuss with the client ways to handle risk factors and minimize their negative impact on the project.

- Evaluators should decide to continue with the evaluation project or decline the project, based on the findings of the feasibility and risk factor assessments.

Chapter Discussion

1. Feasibility of a summative evaluation

Your organization recently implemented a training program that teaches new sales techniques to sales people. Two weeks ago, all sales people completed the training program. Now, you are asked to conduct a summative evaluation to show the effectiveness of this training program.

How would you rate the feasibility of conducting a summative evaluation now, and why do you think so?

2. Feasibility and risk factors

Read the following scenario:

Betsy is a performance improvement consultant. She recently got a contract with a company to evaluate its company-wide e-learning initiative that was implemented 2 months ago. Bob, the program director, is her evaluation client. During Betsy's first phone conversation with Bob to learn about the evaluation project, he expressed a lot of enthusiasm and support for Betsy's work. He also mentioned that there would be additional evaluation projects in the future that she could be hired to do. A few days later, Betsy had a face-to-face meeting with Bob to learn more about the project. At the end of the meeting, Betsy asked Bob for contact information of several stakeholders that she wants to interview to learn what they want to see from this evaluation project. Bob, while pointing out the importance of an insider's perspective, made a remark that he could represent other stakeholders' perspectives, and it would not be necessary to contact them at this point. (Adapted from Scenario 3 on p. 26 in Chyung, Winiecki, & Downing, 2010, with some modifications)

Put yourself in Betsy's shoes and assess the feasibility and risk factors for this evaluation. Brainstorm potential risk factors and the way you plan to handle the issues, should you take this evaluation project.

Now, Your Turn—Assess Feasibility and Risk Factors

While meeting with your client and other stakeholders to discuss your evaluation project, assess feasibility of the project and risk factors for successfully completing the project. Use the questions presented in Table B-1 in Appendix B (Evaluation Development Worksheets) as a job aid to summarize the information that you have gathered. Table 14 contains an example. Also, see the Assessments of Feasibility and Risk Factors section of the sample evaluation proposal in Chapter 8.

TABLE 14 ● Example Worksheet for Assessing Feasibility and Risk Factors		
Focus	**Question**	**Your Finding**
Assess feasibility and risk factors	• Write down information that you have found about your evaluation project so far in relation to the feasibility categories: 1. Maturity 2. Scope 3. Support 4. Ethical concerns 5. Resources	1. Maturity: The program has been in operation for more than 6 months, and there should be enough data to measure quality of the program. 2. Scope: The project can be completed within the requested time frame, given enough support and resources. 3. Support: The client and other upstream stakeholders have shown enough interest and support for the evaluation. The stakeholders are interested in using the evaluation findings

Focus	Question	Your Finding
		to make improvements on the program. The client has approved giving me full access to the training materials and to groups of new employees and supervisors. I am permitted to gather data by phone and/or via email during their work hours.
		4. Ethical concerns: Although there haven't been any signs that raise ethical concerns, the fact that the lead evaluator is very close to the evaluand is something to keep in mind.
		5. Resources: The project will benefit from having a three-member evaluation team, possessing project management skills, web-based survey design skills, interview skills, and writing skills. The project can be completed within the expected time frame.
	• Make a list of project assumptions.	• The client will provide full support for the project until it is completed, and the evaluation team is committed to completing the project. • As novice-level evaluators, the team will use a descriptive case study type evaluation design for the evaluation project. • The client and the evaluation team will be able to find a workaround through discussion when facing difficulties during the project.
	• Write down your risk assessment findings and describe how you plan to manage the risk factors. • Present a risk assessment matrix.	(See the risk assessment example and Table 13.)

4

Write a Statement of Work

Y ou have completed the identification phase of your evaluation project, including the first three steps—Step 1: Identify an evaluand, Step 2: Identify its stakeholders, and Step 3: Identify the purpose of evaluation. You have also assessed feasibility and risk factors of your evaluation project and concluded that it was a feasible project to complete. The first deliverable of your evaluation project after completing the identification phase is a statement of work.

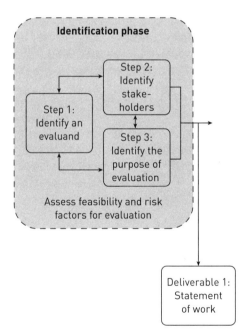

Prepare a Statement of Work for the Evaluation

Whether you are conducting an evaluation as an internal evaluator (e.g., a performance improvement specialist of your organization) or as an external evaluator (i.e., a work-for-hire situation), you use the early stage of an evaluation project (the evaluation *identification* phase) to speak with your client and other stakeholders about the evaluation project and to determine feasibility of the project.

If you determined it to be feasible, you prepare a **statement of work (SOW)** or a contract, which lays out an overall scope of work, budget, and other critical information. Signatures on the SOW by your client as a service requester and you as a service provider indicate mutual agreement to complete the project.

Submitting a SOW for your evaluation project, even at times when it is not necessary for you as an internal evaluator to do so, provides the client with an opportunity to reconnect with important stakeholders of the program and engage in a conversation with them to reassess the needs surrounding the program (Barkin, Chyung, & Lemke, 2017).

If your client has not initiated it yet, you also want to check if the client organization has a nondisclosure agreement that you need to sign.

After your SOW is approved, you continue with the *planning* phase and prepare a more elaborated planning document, which we call an **evaluation proposal** in this book. Having the separate identification and planning phases not only helps you plan for each phase better but also opens opportunities to assess feasibility to move on with the project or forgo the project if you and your client anticipate unreasonable risks or ethical concerns for completing the project.

Determine Sections to Be Included in a Statement of Work

You can use different formats for different SOWs depending on the type and complexity of your projects. In this book, you will use the following sections for writing a SOW:

1. Introduction

2. Background

3. Objectives and deliverables

4. Scope of work and timeline

5. Resources

6. Assumptions and risk factors

7. Acceptance signatures

SECTIONS TO BE PRESENTED IN A SOW

During your first couple of meetings with the client and other stakeholders, you gathered information about the evaluand and its stakeholders, the purpose of the evaluation, and its feasibility and risk factors. Since you have not determined specific evaluation methodology yet, you need to estimate the timeline and resources to be used during the development and implementation of evaluation methodology to your best knowledge. As you gain more experience in conducting evaluations, you will feel more comfortable estimating the time and resources required for individual projects. Some information may be presented as tentative and to be finalized in the evaluation proposal. See Table 15.

TABLE 15 ● Guidelines for Writing a SOW for Conducting an Evaluation	
Section	**Content**
1. **Introduction**	• Briefly describe the purpose of the SOW. Identify the service requester and service provider.

2. **Background**	• Describe the organization, program, stakeholders, and evaluation purpose, based on information that you have gathered so far.
	    ○ Describe the organization's background information, such as its location and history.
	    ○ Explain the needs that caused the organization to develop and implement the program.
	    ○ Describe the program and identify upstream stakeholders and downstream direct impactees.
	    ○ State the purpose of the evaluation by clearly indicating the intended use and users of the evaluation findings.
	    ○ Describe the type of evaluation and any specific evaluation frameworks to be applied.
	
	Note: The information presented in this section will be elaborated and reused in your evaluation proposal and final report.

3. **Objectives and deliverables**	• Describe the main tasks to be accomplished during the evaluation project. • Describe the deliverables of the planning and implementation phases.
4. **Scope of work and timeline**	• Present specific tasks to be completed and stakeholders to be involved during the evaluation. • Present a timeline for the tasks. • Present a Gantt chart.

5. **Resources**	• Present resources required during the project.
	    ○ Personnel
	    ○ Budget
	    ○ Facilities and tools
	    ○ Communication

6. **Assumptions and risk factors**	• Present assumptions and risks associated with the assumptions, as well as currently known risk factors.
7. **Acceptance signatures**	• Provide signature lines for the service requester and the service provider to indicate their acceptance of the SOW.

Develop a Gantt Chart

To illustrate the project timeline in your SOW, you can insert a Gantt chart. A **Gantt chart** is a type of bar graph, originally developed by an American engineer, Henry Gantt, in the 1910s (Gantt, 1919). While studying work performance at manufacturing factories, Gantt used bar graphs—which he called a series of "charts"—to record

FIGURE 9 ● Screenshot of a Gantt Chart Created in Excel

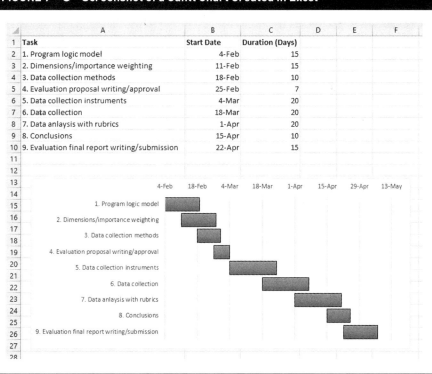

and monitor how long workers spent on their job tasks, how much work they completed, and how training and bonus impacted their work. Since then, such bar graphs showing project timelines have been called Gantt charts and widely used as a project management tool.

You can develop a Gantt chart using Microsoft Excel (Microsoft, 2018). Figure 9 shows a screenshot of an Excel file where a Gantt chart was created based on the data under three columns—Task (a list of tasks to be completed), Start Date (each task's start date), and Duration (the number of days to be spent on each task). You can find several directions on how to create a Gantt chart in Excel on the Web or YouTube.

USING EXCEL TO CREATE A GANTT CHART

Review a Sample Statement of Work

This section provides a sample SOW for a hypothetical evaluation project that you (or your evaluation team) will conduct for an internal client as a class project. A budget section in a work-for-hire situation will present pricing information for completing the tasks specified in the SOW. The budget in this sample will be estimated in terms of your time commitment as an internal evaluator.

STATEMENT OF WORK

An Evaluation of the Blended Onboarding Program at Sawtooth, Inc.

February 5, 2019

1. Introduction

This Statement of Work (SOW) provides an overall understanding of the scope of work, timeline, deliverables, resources, assumptions, and risk factors for evaluating the Blended Onboarding Program at Sawtooth, Inc. The evaluation was requested by the Manager of the Training Department (the Client) and will be provided by the evaluation team of the Performance Improvement and Learning Solutions Department (the Service Provider). The following are the points of contact:

- The Client: Ms. Bobbie Allison, Training Manager, Training Department, Sawtooth Inc., 208-426-000X, BobbieAllison@SawtoothMan.com

- The Service Provider: Ms. Pennie Scully, Evaluation Team Lead, Performance Improvement and Learning Solutions (PILS) Department, Sawtooth Inc., 208-426-000X, EvaluationTeam@SawtoothMan.com

2. Background

The Organization: Sawtooth Inc., a manufacturing company in Boise, Idaho, was founded in 2010. Due to the fast growth of business, the company experienced an increasing number of new hires, which resulted in the implementation of a two-day onboarding program in 2012.

The Program and Stakeholders: The program was initially a face-to-face, instructor-led training program. After a few of years of operating the onboarding program, the company realized that the two-day onboarding program was not sufficient in helping new employees get up to speed. In August 2017, the training department of the company redesigned the program using both in-class and online formats. After operating the blended onboarding program for one and a half years, the training department wanted to have the program evaluated. The evaluation team responded to the request from the Manager of the Training Department (the Client) to conduct an evaluation of the blended onboarding program.

TABLE 1 ● Blended Onboarding Program Schedule

Training Day/Time	Day 1	Day 2	Day 3
Morning (3 hours)	Instructor-led, in classroom	Instructor-led, in classroom	Instructor-led, in classroom
Break (2 hours)	Lunch & Breakout socialization	Lunch & Breakout socialization	Lunch & Breakout socialization
Afternoon (3 hours)	Instructor-led, in classroom	Self-paced, online, in office	Self-paced, online, in office

The current onboarding program is a 3-day blended training program delivered online as well as in the classroom. The overall 3-day training schedule is presented in Table 1.

Although the online curriculum is self-paced, the trainer is still available via email for any questions that new employees may have. The overall goal of the blended onboarding program is to help new employees be able to start performing their job tasks without assistance 90% of the time.

Currently 10 to 20 new employees are hired each month. The blended onboarding program is offered twice a month. The training department, staffed with two instructional designers and a trainer, is open to revising the program content to improve its quality and to help achieve the program goal.

The Evaluation Purpose and Type: Based on the discussion with the training manager, the trainer, and a supervisor of new employees who recently completed the program, the evaluation team discovered that the evaluation findings would be used by (1) the training department staff, including the instructional designers and trainer, to revise and improve the program content; and (2) the new employees' supervisors to provide adequate support to new employees to help them get up to speed as quickly as possible. Because the staff and supervisors intend to use the evaluation findings to recognize areas for improvement, it was determined to conduct a formative goal-based evaluation to find out how well the blended onboarding program is designed and supported to achieve the program goal and what needs to be changed. The evaluation team will also incorporate a goal-free evaluation approach to find out if there have been any unexpected results from the recent change to a blended program.

3. Objectives and Deliverables

The evaluation will be conducted through two phases: planning and implementation. The primary objectives of the evaluation planning phase are to accomplish the following tasks:

1. Identify or develop a program logic model.
2. Determine evaluation dimensions and evaluation questions.
3. Determine data collection methods.

At the end of the planning phase, the evaluation team will deliver to the client an evaluation proposal, which will include descriptions of the program to be evaluated, specific evaluation methodology to be used, and the team's assessment of project feasibility and risk factors to be managed during the implementation phase. The proposal will enable an estimation of the evaluation team's responsibilities and the stakeholders' involvement during the implementation phase. Upon approval of the evaluation proposal, the evaluation team will proceed with the implementation phase. However, if the project feasibility and risks assessments show a significant lack of the organization's readiness for implementing the proposed evaluation plan, the evaluation team and the client may decide to delay or forgo the evaluation project.

The primary objectives of the evaluation implementation phase are to accomplish the following tasks:

1. Develop data collection instruments.
2. Collect data.
3. Analyze data with rubrics.
4. Draw conclusions.

Upon completion of the evaluation, the evaluation team will deliver to the client an evaluation final report, summarizing the findings and evidence-based conclusions. The two deliverables are summarized in Table 2.

TABLE 2 ● Two Deliverables: Evaluation Proposal and Final Report	
Evaluation Proposal	**Evaluation Final Report**
1. Organization	1. Organization
2. Program and Stakeholders	2. Program and Stakeholders
3. Evaluation Methodology	3. Evaluation Methodology
4. Feasibility and Risk Factors	4. Feasibility and Risk Factors
	5. Evaluation Results
	6. Conclusions
	7. Meta-Evaluations and Limitations
	8. Reporting
References	
Appendices	

4. Scope of Work and Timeline

The scope of work, stakeholders to be involved, and tentative duration for each task are described in Table 3. Figure 1 is a Gantt chart illustrating the overall timeline. Any necessary changes will be determined through discussion with the client.

TABLE 3 ● Scope of Work and Timeline		
Task	**Participating Stakeholders**	**Start Date (Duration)**

1. Identify or develop a program logic model for the program.
  ○ The evaluation team will offer a one-hour kick-off workshop to the stakeholders to draft out a program logic model.
  ○ The evaluation team will follow up with stakeholders via telephone and/or email as well as in-person meetings to finalize the model.
	Training manager
	Instructional designer
	Trainer
	Supervisor
		February 4, 2019
		(15 days)

2. Determine three to five evaluation dimensions, specific evaluation questions to be investigated, and relative degrees of importance weighting among dimensions. ○ A one-hour meeting with stakeholders should be scheduled.	Training manager Instructional designer Trainer Supervisor	February 11, 2019 (15 days)
3. Determine specific data collection methods to be used for each dimension. ○ The information can be communicated via email and telephone, as well as in person.	Training manager Supervisor	February 18, 2019 (10 days)

Task	Participating Stakeholders	Start Date (Duration)
4. Prepare an evaluation proposal and submit it to the stakeholders to obtain approval. ○ The stakeholders will provide feedback to make necessary changes, help finalize the evaluation implementation plan, and approve the plan. ○ A significant lack of the organization's readiness for implementing the proposed evaluation plan may cause a decision to delay or forgo the project.	Training manager	February 25, 2019 (7 days)
5. Develop data collection instruments and obtain approval. ○ The evaluation team will develop all required materials to be used to collect data and submit them to the stakeholders for approval.	Training manager	March 4, 2019 (20 days)
6. Collect data. ○ With the stakeholders' support (e.g., granting access to employees and extant data, encouraging employees to participate in the study), the evaluation team will collect data.	Training manager Instructional designers Trainer Trainees Supervisors	March 18, 2019 (20 days)
7. Analyze data with rubrics. ○ The evaluation team will work with the stakeholders to develop rubrics and analyze collected data against the rubrics.	Training manager	April 1, 2019 (20 days)
8. Draw conclusions. ○ The evaluation team will combine dimensional results, draw evidence-based conclusions, and develop recommendations.	Training manager External reviewers	April 15, 2019 (10 days)
9. Prepare an evaluation final report and submit it to the stakeholders. ○ The evaluation team will write an evaluation final report and submit it to the stakeholders via email, and arrange a meeting with the stakeholders for a presentation and Q&A.	Training manager	April 22, 2019 (15 days)

Note: While completing the tasks listed in this table, the evaluation team will conduct internal and external meta-evaluations to ensure credibility of the methods used and conclusions drawn from the collected data.

(Continued)

(Continued)

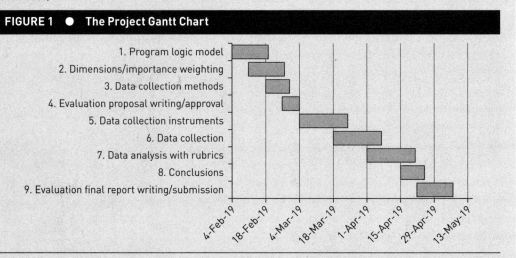

FIGURE 1 ● The Project Gantt Chart

5. Resources

To successfully complete the evaluation, the following resources are needed:

- Personnel
  - The evaluation team's expertise
  - The evaluation client's commitment

- Time
  - The evaluation team's time (approximately 100 hours collectively)
  - The evaluation client's time for communication (6–8 hours)
  - Other stakeholders' time to participate in evaluation activities (1–2 hours/each person)

- Facility and tools
  - The face-to-face meetings will be held in the training department conference room, equipped with a whiteboard, a computer projector, and a flipchart.
  - Other formal and informal face-to-face discussions may occur in the stakeholders' offices.
  - Other tools that are needed during discussions will be supplied by the evaluation team.

- Communication
  - In addition to the face-to-face meetings with stakeholders, telephone, email, and/or videoconference meetings will be held to gather information from stakeholders necessary to complete the evaluation.

6. Assumptions and Risk Factors

To successfully complete the project, it is critical to have the client's support and stakeholders' active participation. Thus, the following assumptions are made:

- The client provides full support for the project until it is completed, and the evaluation team is committed to completing the project.

- The stakeholders are allowed to participate in in-person meetings and engage in telephone and online communications during their work hours.

- When communicating with stakeholders via email and phone, all messages are returned within two working days.

The currently known risk factors are presented in Table 4. The evaluation team and the client will continue to monitor the risk factors and find ways to minimize the negative impact. Failing to do so may jeopardize successfully completing the evaluation project, and result in rescheduling or canceling the project.

TABLE 4 ● A Risk Assessment Matrix

Damage to Project / Likelihood	Minor	Moderate	Substantial	Detrimental
Unlikely	–	Scope creep and schedule slips	–	–
Maybe	Employee turnover (changes in program stakeholders)	–	Lack of stakeholders' participation resulting in missing data from surveys	–
Likely	–	Slow communication between evaluation team and stakeholders	–	–

7. Acceptance Signatures

The Client

Ms. Bobbie Allison, Training Manager

Sawtooth, Inc.

Signature:

Date:

The Service Provider

Ms. Pennie Scully, Evaluation Team, PILS

Sawtooth, Inc.

Signature:

Date:

Now, Your Turn—Write a Statement of Work

Please prepare a SOW for your evaluation project to be submitted to your client. You may adopt some of the content presented in the sample SOW if it applies to your evaluation project.

A sample SOW and a Gantt chart template are available for download at **https://study.sagepub.com/chyung**

5

Develop a Program Logic Model (Step 4)

There are three phases of evaluation: identification, planning, and implementation. You have completed the identification phase and submitted a statement of work (SOW) to your client. After you and your client agree on the SOW, you move forward with the planning phase of your evaluation project. The first step in the planning phase is to review the program logic model for the program that you are evaluating. If the program does not have a program logic model, you will develop one.

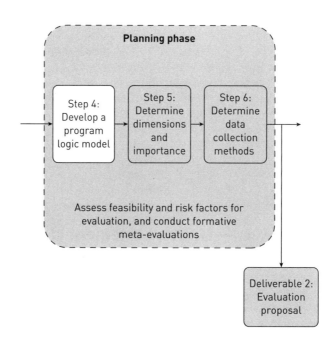

Apply a Theory-Based, If–Then Logic to Developing a Program

A new social program is purposely developed based on a theory of change that explains what the program will do and how it will lead to a desired change in outcomes. The program developer uses a hypothesis that *if* the program uses certain resources and completes specific activities, *then* it is expected to achieve its desired outcomes (i.e., goals) (McLaughlin & Jordan, 2004).

An initiative or intervention program used in the human performance improvement (HPI) context should also be developed based on its own theory of change, although it may not be always formally documented. More commonly, needs assessments are performed to reveal probable causes of a performance gap, based on which a set of interventions is generated to help close that performance gap. An implicit program theory here is that *if* this set of interventions is successfully implemented (means), *then* there will be a desired change in closing the performance gap (ends) (Kaufman, 2000). This theory-based approach is applied not only when developing programs but also when producing evidence to support the causal model of intervention (Weiss, 1995).

A model that illustrates the *if–then* relationship among key elements of a program is called a **program logic model**, and it serves as a road map to develop, maintain, and evaluate a program (W. K. Kellogg Foundation, 2004). The concept of program logic modeling was developed by several pioneers and theorists of program evaluation in the 1970s through the 1980s. For example, Joseph Wholey, in his book *Evaluation: Promise and Performance* (1979), used the term *logic model* to present the logic of causal linkage among the inputs, activities, and objectives that a program intended to use and produce (Wholey, 1979).

PIONEERS OF PROGRAM LOGIC MODELS

There are several ways to develop program logic models, using slightly different components and labels to indicate program logic. Among the early theorists and adopters were United Way of America, who published *Measuring Program Outcomes: A Practical Approach* in 1996 describing its program outcome model (United Way of America, 1996), and the W. K. Kellogg Foundation, who published its *Evaluation Handbook* and *Logic Model Development Guide* in 1998 (W. K. Kellogg Foundation, 1998, 2004). An evaluation model widely used in the training and development community is Katzell-based Kirkpatrick's four-level training evaluation framework (Kirkpatrick, 1956, 1996a; Smith, 2008; Thalheimer, 2018) (see Appendix A). Brinkerhoff's training impact model, included in his book *Telling Training's Story* published in 2006, provides a similar framework specifically for evaluating training programs (Brinkerhoff, 2006). Let's have an overview of each of those models.

Review United Way's Program Outcome Model

In *Measuring Program Outcomes*, United Way of America (1996) emphasized adopting a program outcome model, which includes not only the three major components presented in the traditional service program model—inputs, activities, and outputs—but also a fourth level, outcomes:

1. Inputs—Resources dedicated to or consumed by the program

2. Activities—What the program does with the inputs to fulfill its mission

3. Outputs—Direct products of program activities, such as materials developed and the number of participants served

4. Outcomes—Benefits or changes in knowledge, skills, attitudes, behaviors, values, condition, status, and other attributes of individuals during or after participating in program activities, grouped into initial short-term, intermediate, and longer-term outcomes

Examples of outcomes provided in the book, *Measuring Program Outcomes* (United Way of America, 1996), include the following:

- Children demonstrating age-appropriate physical, mental, and verbal skills (a childcare program)

- Homeless people coming off the street and using a shelter (a shelter program)

- Seniors experiencing a decrease in social and health problems (a congregate meals program for senior citizens)

It is clearly indicated in the book that participant satisfaction with a program is generally not an outcome of the program, because it does not indicate whether the participants' condition has improved as a result of the program service. Table 16 is a hypothetical example of a program outcome model for a nonprofit organization's healthy cooking program. Inputs and activities are means; outputs and outcomes are end results.

TABLE 16 ● Program Outcome Model for Healthy Cooking Classes for Kids

Inputs	Activities	Outputs	Outcomes		
			Short-Term	Intermediate	Long-Term
• Staff time • Volunteer time • Donated cooking materials • Grant funding • Healthy cooking recipes • Website	• Develop a class • Offer the class at local middle schools • Hand out recipes to participants • Provide supporting materials on website • Survey participants via email	• 70+% of local middle schools participate in the program • Students at participating schools attend the class • Participants bring recipes to their homes • Participants respond to a survey	Participants: • Become aware of importance of eating healthy food • Develop ability to cook simple and healthy meals at home • Gain an interest in learning more about healthy recipes	Participants: • Cook healthy meals for themselves and their families • Purchase healthy meals and snacks • Encourage family and friends to choose a healthy lifestyle	Participants and their family members: • Maintain a healthy lifestyle • Improve self-esteem • Make positive changes for their family • Reduce healthcare costs

Review Kellogg Foundation's Program Logic Model

The W. K. Kellogg Foundation (1998) developed a similar framework, primarily for project directors who have direct responsibility for conducting evaluation of projects funded by the foundation. As presented in the W. K. Kellogg Foundation's *Program Logic Model Development Guide* (2004), Kellogg's program logic model is composed of five components:

1. Resources—What does the program need to use (including personnel, funding, organizational support, and community support)?

2. Activities—What does the program do with the program resources?

3. Outputs—What products are immediately generated (or what services are delivered) by the program activities?

4. Outcomes—What specific changes do program participants make as a result of the program activities?

5. Impact—What intended or unintended changes happen to the organization, community, and system as a result of the program activities?

FIVE ELEMENTS IN KELLOGG FOUNDATION'S MODEL

The first four components in United Way's program outcome model and Kellogg's program logic model are virtually the same. The Kellogg's program logic model includes *impact* as a fifth level, to differentiate lasting impact of the program on the system other than the participants themselves. Some long-term outcomes in United Way's program outcome model could align with the impact component in Kellogg's program logic model. Table 17 and Table 18 are hypothetical examples based on Kellogg's program logic model structure.

TABLE 17 ● Program Logic Model for a Municipal Recycle Promotion Program

Resources	Activities	Outputs	Outcomes	Impact
• Staff time • Funding • Written materials on recycling • Town meeting place • Resident addresses • Organization addresses	• Prepare a talk about recycling at town meetings • Invite local news media to report the recycling agenda at town meetings • Mail a "how to recycle" job aid to residents and organizations	• Residents and organization representatives participate in town meetings • Local news covers the talk on recycling at town meetings and broadcasts a documentary on recycling • Residents and organizations receive a job aid in mail	• People are aware of importance of recycling • People are motivated to have a recycling bin in their house • People recycle more often at home and workplace • People request local shops to have recycling bins for customer use	• The amount of landfill garbage is reduced • The amount of recycled materials is increased • Risk for groundwater contamination is reduced

TABLE 18 ● Program Logic Model for the "Reduce Plastic Microbeads" App				
Resources	**Activities**	**Outputs**	**Outcomes**	**Impact**
• Researchers • Volunteers • App developers • App website • Website developer • Access to social media	• Develop an app that scans for inclusion of plastic microbeads in products • Develop and maintain a website to promote the app • Announce the app via social media • Update the app	• An app that scans products for plastic microbeads • A website promoting the app • Number of social media users who have access to the app announcement	• The public is aware of the problems associated with using plastic microbeads in products • The public uses the app • The public avoids purchasing products with microbeads	• Companies stop using plastic microbeads in their products • Companies put less pollution in the water

Inspired by the Beat the Microbead project, http://www.beatthemicrobead.org.

Review Brinkerhoff's Training Impact Model Compared to the Four-Level Training Evaluation Framework

Whereas United Way's program outcome model and Kellogg's program logic model can be used for any type of program, Brinkerhoff's (2006) training impact model is specifically for *training* programs. It is composed of four categories, which are end results of a training program:

1. Program capabilities—What capabilities should the trainee acquire?

2. Critical actions—What behaviors should the trainee demonstrate on the job as a result of training?

3. Key results—What job results should the trainee leave behind?

4. Business goals—To what organizational goals would the training program contribute?

FOUR ELEMENTS IN BRINKERHOFF'S MODEL COMPARED TO THE FOUR-LEVEL EVALUATION FRAMEWORK

The four categories of Brinkerhoff's training impact model can be compared to Katzell-based Kirkpatrick's four-level training evaluation framework (Kirkpatrick, 1996a):

1. Reaction—Are the participants satisfied with the training program?

2. Learning—Did the participants learn what they were supposed to learn?

3. Behavior—Did the participants change their job behavior?

4. Results—Did the organization gain the expected results?

In comparing Brinkerhoff's categories and the four levels, it is important to recognize that the four categories of Brinkerhoff's training impact model address outcomes of a training program. However, Level 1 (reaction) often measures trainees' satisfaction toward resources and activities used during the program, which may not be a true outcome of a program, as indicated in United Way's program outcome model (see United Way of America, 1996, p. 19). Thus, we will exclude Level 1 from the outcome-specific comparison.

Then, think about how Brinkerhoff's four outcome-based categories are aligned with Level 2 (learning), Level 3 (behavior), and Level 4 (results).

- Program capabilities are related to trainees' learned capacity, such as knowledge, skills, and attitudes (KSAs), which are Level 2 (learning) outcomes.

- Critical actions refer to trainees' job behavior, which is Level 3 (behavior).

- Key results and business goals are aligned with Level 4 (results).

Table 19 is a hypothetical example showing how different elements of Brinkerhoff's model align with the levels of learning, behavior, and results.

Here, it is worth revisiting the meaning of KSAs as learning outcomes. Brinkerhoff (2006) describes the program capabilities category of the training impact model as "the skills and knowledge that the training targets" (p. 78). Since instruction (training or education) can also change learners' attitudes, we can include attitudes in the program capabilities category, which makes KSAs. Kirkpatrick (1996a) also explains that Level 2 learning outcomes are measured by changed "knowledge, skills, and/or attitudes" (p. 44).

KNOWLEDGE, SKILLS, AND ATTITUDES (KSAS) PER BLOOM'S THREE DOMAINS OF EDUCATIONAL OBJECTIVES

The three types of learning outcomes (KSAs) are also supported by the three domains of educational objectives that Benjamin Bloom and a group of educational psychologists developed in the 1950s (Bloom, Engelhart, Furst, Hill, & Krathwohl, 1956):

- Cognitive domain (knowledge)

- Psychomotor domain (skills)

- Affective domain (attitudes)

TABLE 19 ● Training Program for New Volunteers at a Dog Shelter			
Learning (KSAs)	**Behavior**	**Results**	
Program Capabilities	**Critical Actions**	**Key Results**	**Business Goals**
Volunteers know: • when to put a leash or a harness on dogs • how to put a harness on dogs • how to handle aggressive dogs • how to recognize sick dogs based on symptoms • how to train dogs to follow basic commands (e.g., sit, stay, heel, etc.)	Volunteers do: • walk small, medium, and large dogs on a leash or harness • safely handle dogs without causing injuries on dogs or volunteers themselves • report sick dogs • train dogs to follow basic commands	The shelter gets: • no injuries among volunteers • healthy dogs • more adoptable dogs • visitors being able to walk dogs with or without help of volunteers	The shelter achieves: • satisfaction among visitors • increased number of adoptions • satisfaction among volunteers • increased number of volunteers

Also known as *Bloom's taxonomy*, the main purpose of developing the taxonomy was to help educators clearly state educational objectives and design necessary instructional content and assessment methods congruently. Each domain has several hierarchical levels of intended behaviors that learners should be able to exhibit as a result of learning. Bloom's taxonomy has been used widely in instructional design.

The A in KSAs in some work situations (e.g., in hiring) refers to "abilities." However, from an instructional design standpoint, it may not be clear exactly what "abilities" entail. It could mean natural talent, aptitudes, or a combination of knowledge and skills. Abilities based on natural talent and aptitudes are difficult to change through training programs. If abilities indicate knowledge and skills, it is redundant to list abilities next to knowledge and skills. Thus, in this book, the A in KSAs refers to attitudes.

Compare Elements Used in Different Frameworks

As described previously, each evaluation model is composed of slightly different elements (labels). The structures used in United Way's program outcome model and Kellogg's program logic model are similar. United Way's model and Kellogg's model have been widely used in various organizations, including nonprofit and government agencies. On the other hand, the four-level training evaluation framework and Brinkerhoff's training impact model are usually applied to industry training programs.

SIMILARITIES AND DIFFERENCES AMONG DIFFERENT MODELS

Table 20 presents a comparison of elements used in these different models, showing how the categories of end results in different models can be aligned with each other.

In the following section, we will explore more about developing a program logic model based on Kellogg's guide and developing a training impact model introduced with Brinkerhoff's Success Case Method.

Developing and using a program logic model or training impact model during an evaluation project helps you, the evaluator, as well as the program stakeholders recognize the *systematic* aspect of program operation in terms of how the program should be designed and

TABLE 20 ● Comparing Elements Used in Different Models

Model \ Category	Means		Ends					
United Way	Inputs	Activities	Outputs	Outcomes (initial, intermediate, long-term)				
Kellogg	Resources	Activities	Outputs	Outcomes			Impact	
Kirkpatrick	Reaction		–	Learning	Behavior	Results		–
Brinkerhoff	–		–	Capabilities	Critical actions	Key results	Business goals	–

Adapted from Chyung, 2015, p. 88, Table 4.

executed, in order to produce necessary outputs, desirable outcomes, and positive impact. It also helps you and the stakeholders have a *systemic* perspective on the program as it portrays the overall picture of how the different elements of the program influence each other to work toward common goals and explains the important role that each element plays.

Develop a Program Logic Model

In W. K. Kellogg's program logic model (2004), the resources and activities categories are means, and the outputs, outcomes, and impact categories are end results (see Figure 10). The program needs to use the resources and perform the activities in order to produce the intended end results of outputs and outcomes, which may create a long-lasting impact on organizations and communities.

Another way to understand the structure of a program logic model is to think about the relationship between the 'if you use and do' part (the means; your planned work) and the 'then you get' part (the ends; your intended results) (Knowlton & Phillips, 2009), as shown at the bottom of Figure 10. If you use the resources and do those planned activities, you will get outputs, outcomes, and impact as intended.

MEANS (IF) AND ENDS (THEN) IN PROGRAM LOGIC MODEL

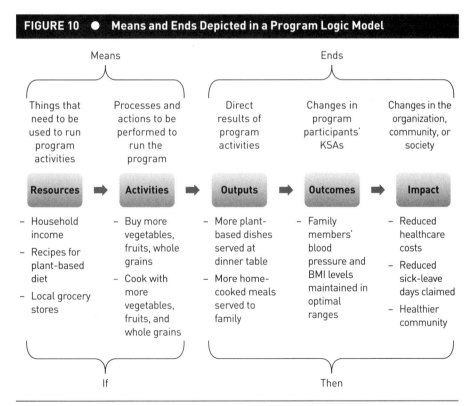

FIGURE 10 ●   Means and Ends Depicted in a Program Logic Model

Adapted from Knowlton & Phillips, 2009; W. K. Kellogg Foundation, 2004.

Check with your client if a logic model was developed as a planning tool for the eval-uand. If a program logic model exists, you need to review it and discuss with the client if information in the logic model is current, if necessary elements are logically (systemati-cally) illustrated, and if any information needs to be revised. It would not be surprising if you found out that a logic model had not been developed for the evaluand. Then, you will work with your client and other stakeholders to develop one. Below are steps to follow.

Step 1. It is best if you have a face-to-face meeting with your client and stakeholders to collect information to develop a program logic model. During the meeting, you might want to use Post-it notes to brainstorm with them to develop elements to be included in the program logic model. You may use a videoconferencing system if it is difficult to gather people in one place. If you have to talk with them over the phone, instead of having a face-to-face meeting, jot down their information, draft out a logic model based on their input, email the information to them to get their feedback, and revise it as needed. You will continue to communi-cate with your client and other stakeholders, and you can revise the logic model later as you gather more information that needs to be incorporated into the logic model.

Step 2. Discuss with the client and stakeholders how specific types of stakeholders are aligned with specific categories of their program logic model. A program logic model serves as a road map for a program to produce its intended outcomes for different types of stakeholders. Therefore, one way to better understand and identify the five categories of a program logic model is to think about how three types of stakeholders are associated with each category.

Upstream stakeholders are involved in the design, development, and/or implemen-tation of the program. Thus, they are closely associated with the selection, design, and implementation of the items that fall under the resources, activities, and outputs cate-gories of the program logic model. For example, the sales department director, training manager, and instructional designers, as part of the program's upstream stakeholders, may have determined what resources and activities to use to produce and deliver a sales technique training program.

Downstream direct impactees are the ones who participate in the program and produce outcomes. Direct impactees are related mostly with program outcomes (e.g., learning outcomes or behavioral changes that salespeople produce upon completion of the program), which in turn influence the program impact. To produce program outcomes, direct impactees are also directly associated with some of the program activ-ities and outputs (e.g., salespeople are asked to complete a sales training program that has been revised with scenario-based instruction).

Downstream indirect impactees in the organization and the community are affected by the results that direct impactees produce. Therefore, indirect impactees are often asso-ciated with program impact. For example, customers interacting with more capable sales-people (who successfully learned sales techniques from the training program) may feel satisfied and may be more likely to return. Increased sales could also have some impact on other departments in the organization, such as the manufacturing department (pro-duction increase) or human resources department (hiring increase). Therefore, custom-ers, as well as any indirectly impacted employees in other departments, are indirect impactees. However, in a systemic sense, upstream stakeholders and direct impactees, as well as indirect impactees (i.e., all three types of stakeholders), would be affected by the program's long-lasting impact, directly or indirectly.

Figure 11 illustrates the association between logic model elements and three groups of stakeholders.

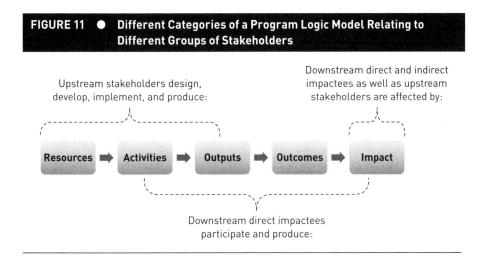

FIGURE 11 ● Different Categories of a Program Logic Model Relating to Different Groups of Stakeholders

Upstream stakeholders design, develop, implement, and produce:

Downstream direct and indirect impactees as well as upstream stakeholders are affected by:

Resources ➡ Activities ➡ Outputs ➡ Outcomes ➡ Impact

Downstream direct impactees participate and produce:

Step 3. List outcomes that the direct impactees are expected to produce, instead of developing means (resources and activities) right away. Write outcomes as specific and measureable as possible (W. K. Kellogg Foundation, 2004). For example,

- *Trainees' job performance* ← This is not specific or measurable enough.
- *100% of trainees are able to submit the form on time* ← This is written in a specific and measurable format.

It may not be always possible to describe outcomes in quantity. For example, following examples are still specific and measurable:

- *Employees' improved job commitment* ← You can still measure how much employees have improved their job commitment levels as long as you have a baseline to compare to.
- *Reduced healthcare costs* ← This could be sufficient if you cannot specify the reduced amount with a certain percentage (e.g., reduced healthcare costs by 20%), as long as you have a baseline to compare to.
- *Positive customer satisfaction levels* ← This can be sufficient as long as the organization has a standard or rubric to identify what "positive" means.

You may describe outcomes in full sentences or in phrases. When using phrases, do not start an item with a verb, which makes it sound more like an *action* item than an end result; for example,

- *Increase* number of emergency room (ER)/physician referrals ← "Increase" is an action, not a result.

- *Increased* number of ER/physician referrals ← "Increased" implies an end result.

Step 4. Discuss the impact that the outcomes would have on all types of stakeholders. Program impact can also be made on the program organization itself—add such program impact as well. Reflect if the listed outcomes would create any negative impact.

Step 5. Identify specific outputs that the program should produce in order to enable the direct impactees of the program to produce their outcomes.

Step 6. Identify what resources are needed and what activities should be performed in order to produce those outputs. Do not forget to include environmental factors that influence the program's outputs.

Remember that a program logic model describes how a program *should* work, rather than how a program is being operated now. Therefore, you should describe the desirable status of the elements under each column, instead of the current status, which may or may not be the desirable level.

EXAMPLES OF PROGRAM LOGIC MODEL

Program logic models may be developed in a diagram or table format. Use the format that works best for you and your client organization. It may be easier to list items in a table format first, and, if desirable, you can convert the information to a diagram format later. As an example, Table 21 is a program logic model developed for a new tech support ticketing and tracking system.

Develop a Training Impact Model

If your evaluand is a training program, you can use Brinkerhoff's (2006) method to develop a **training impact model** for the training program instead of a program logic model based on W. K. Kellogg's (2004) logic model structure. However, note that all four categories of the training impact model refer to end results. This means that when presenting a training impact model with those four categories, you are not presenting any information about the means to be used, such as the resources and activities used in Kellogg's guide.

To provide a complete structure of means and end results, you will add two means-related categories (resources and activities) to your training impact model, which makes a total of six categories:

ADD RESOURCES AND ACTIVITIES TO A TRAINING IMPACT MODEL

- Resources—What resources should be used to run the training program?
- Activities—What activities should be used to run the training program?
- Program capabilities—What capabilities (KSAs) should the trainees acquire?
- Critical actions—What behaviors should the trainees demonstrate on the job as a result of training?
- Key results—What job results should the trainees leave behind?
- Business goals—To what organizational goals would the training program contribute?

TABLE 21 ● Program Logic Model for a New Tech Support Ticketing and Tracking System				
Resources	**Activities**	**Outputs**	**Outcomes**	**Impact**
What resources should be used to run the program?	What activities should be performed to run the program?	What products should be produced to support the intended outcomes?	What changes in the stakeholders should be made in the next three months (short-term) or a year (long-term)?	What changes in the organization and its society are expected in two or three years due to the outcomes?
• Technical support specialists • Software engineer • Student workers • Web portal • System software (purchased from a vendor and already installed) • Server • Annual budget	• Announce the launch of a new tech support ticketing and tracking system to users • Post job aids to web portal • Redirect users' requests from phone, email, or drop-in to the new system • Monitor ticketing and tracking process • Survey users about their experience	• A new tech support ticketing and tracking system • Repeated email announcements to users • Percentage of requests through the new system • Percentage of requests through other types of communication • User feedback	Short-term: • More than 80% of users are aware of the new system • More than 30% of requests come in through the new system • All tech support specialists are comfortable in using the new system Long-term: • More than 70% of requests come in through the new system • Users are confident in using the new system • Users are satisfied with tech support received	• Tech support office prevents increasing costs for personnel • Tech support office is able to analyze trends of issues and trouble-shooting methods • Relationship between tech support office and users improves • Users have more reliable technologies, less technology-caused downtime • Users are more productive

Similar to the way you develop a program logic model, you should start by identifying the key results and business goals categories, and move on to the critical actions and program capabilities, before developing resources and activities of the program. You should describe the desirable (but not necessarily optimal) status of the elements under each column instead of the current status, which may or may not be the desirable level. For example, if the training department hopes to conduct four-level training evaluations as part of the program activities, such information should be listed under the activities category whether such activities are currently performed well or not.

Table 22 is a training impact model for an operations manager training program aimed at reducing violations of operations-related compliance. Make sure that you think of activities from a project management perspective and refer to things that the organization needs to do to develop, operate, and maintain a training program. Do not think of activities as lesson activities that learners complete during a training program, and do not think of them as evaluation activities.

TABLE 22 ● Training Impact Model for an Operations Manager Training Program					
Resources	**Activities**	**Program Capabilities**	**Critical Actions**	**Key Results**	**Business Goals**
What resources should be used to run the training program?	What activities should be performed to run the training program?	What capabilities (KSAs) should the trainees acquire?	What behaviors should the trainees demonstrate on the job?	What job results should the trainees leave behind?	To what organizational goals would the training program contribute?
• Instructional designers • Trainers • Operations managers to be trained • Existing training materials • Changed compliance policies and procedures • Audit criteria • Budget for traveling • Training facilities • Learning management system	• Revise training materials to reflect changes in compliance policies and procedures • Analyze the number of operations managers to be trained • Schedule training sessions • Enroll all operations managers to be trained in the program • Track program completion rate	• Knowledge of operations-related policies • Knowledge of equipment and facilities inspection procedures • Confidence in completing operations-related management tasks • Knowledge of audit criteria	• Correctly complete operations-related tasks • Inspect equipment and facilities • Supervise employees to prevent compliance violations during operations • Complete pre-audit reports • Assist during on-site audit • Complete post-audit reports	• Increased operations compliance • Decreased operations-related policy violations • Pre-audit documents without errors • Post-audit reports addressing deficiencies • Improved compliance audit scores	• Increased profit in stores • Decreased number of stores to be closed due to violation of operations-related compliance • Decreased turnover among operations managers

Chapter Summary

Develop a program logic model (Step 4):

- The first step in the planning phase of an evaluation project is to develop a (or revise an existing) program logic model.

- Several frameworks such as United Way of America's program outcome model, Kellogg Foundation's program logic model, and Brinkerhoff's training impact model can be used to develop a logic model for a program.
  - o United Way of America's program outcome model is composed of four components—inputs, activities, outputs, and outcomes.
  - o Kellogg Foundation's program logic model is composed of five components—resources, activities, outputs, outcomes, and impact.
  - o Brinkerhoff's training impact model is composed of four categories that indicate end results of a training program—program capabilities, critical actions, key results, and business goals.

- Katzell-based Kirkpatrick's four levels of training evaluation—reaction, learning, behavior, and results—can be compared to Brinkerhoff's four categories of training impact model.

- Three groups of stakeholders are involved in different categories of the program logic model:
  - o Upstream stakeholders are involved in the design, development, and implementation of the items listed in the resources, activities, and outputs categories.
  - o Direct impactees are associated with mostly outcomes and some of the activities and outputs categories.
  - o Indirect impactees as well as direct impactees and upstream stakeholders would be affected by the program impact, directly or indirectly.

Chapter Discussion

1. Program logic model categories and elements

You are evaluating an e-learning program that new call center agents complete as part of their new employee orientation program. Working with a group of stakeholders, you are developing a program logic model for the program. The stakeholders have brainstormed several important aspects of the program, three of which are listed in the second column of Table 23. Please match each item in the second column of the table with the most appropriate category of program logic model listed in the first column, and explain why.

TABLE 23 ● Match Program Logic Model Categories	
Categories of the Program Logic Model	**Important Aspects of the Program**
• Resources • Activities • Outputs • Outcomes • Impact	• Call center agents' successful use of techniques learned from e-learning courses • The number of e-learning courses developed • Callers' satisfaction levels

2. Brinkerhoff's training impact model and training evaluation

You are evaluating a leadership training program implemented in your client organization. You developed a training impact model to lay out the systematic and systemic relationship among the different levels of expected end results of the training program. You will be evaluating three aspects of the program, selected from different categories of the training impact model:

1. One selected from the program capabilities category

2. One selected from the critical actions category

3. One selected from the key results category

The client agreed with the plan but asked you, "My boss is familiar with the four-level training evaluation framework, and she will ask me if we are evaluating Level 3. Are we?"

What is the most appropriate answer to this question?

Now, Your Turn—Develop a Program Logic Model or a Training Impact Model

Work with your client and other stakeholders and develop either a program logic model or a training impact model for your evaluation project (or revise an existing one). Use Table B-2 or Table B-3 in Appendix B (Evaluation Development Worksheets) as a job aid.

While developing a program logic model or training impact model with program stakeholders, you may want to have a conversation with them about what parts of the program need to be evaluated. You and the program stakeholders should be able to identify several important items listed in the program logic model as the ones to be evaluated. In doing so, you also need to recall the overall purpose and type of the evaluation that you helped them identify (i.e., formative or summative). For example, for a formative evaluation, you may focus more on elements relating to resources, activities, and outputs rather than outcomes or impact. Conversely, a summative evaluation may focus more on the elements listed in the end result categories.

In addition to referring to the formative/summative label, also think about the intended use of the evaluation findings (Patton, 2008). Knowing specifically how the evaluation findings will be used helps you determine which elements of the program logic model need to be investigated. For example, if the stakeholders hope to know what needs to be changed to improve new employees' ramp-up time during their onboarding process, the focus is not the end results but the means (what to be changed). So, you would focus more on what part of the resources and activities used during the onboarding process needs to be changed.

Those elements that you decide to investigate in your evaluation are program dimensions, and in the following chapter, we will discuss more about how to determine dimensions.

Determine Dimensions and Importance Weighting (Step 5)

With a program logic model (or training impact model) of the program (Chapter 5), you have a better understanding about what resources and activities the program uses, how the program operates, and what end results the program intends to produce. The next step is to determine which parts—or dimensions—of the program to investigate.

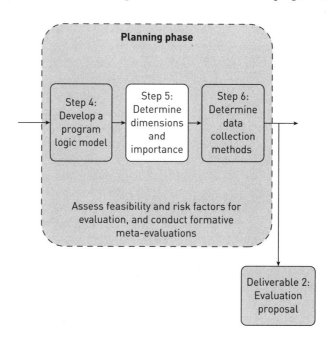

Think About Dimensions of the Evaluand to Investigate

Recall the "How good is this apple?" activity that you did at the end of the Introduction chapter (Table 2). You evaluated an apple based on several aspects or dimensions of apple, such as taste, size, and texture.

Michael Scriven (2013) describes **dimensions** as "the characteristics of the evaluand" pertaining to the evaluand's merit, significance, or worth (p. 3). However, recall that in the human performance improvement (HPI) context, you should evaluate how the organization uses the program rather than how good the program itself is (Brinkerhoff, 2006). Also, review Figure 6 in Chapter 2 that illustrates the difference between a system-focused evaluation approach and an intervention-focused evaluation approach. It is recommended that you take a system-focused evaluation approach (investigating both the intervention program's effectiveness and the environmental factors that facilitated the program's success) rather than an intervention-focused evaluation approach (investigating the intervention program's effectiveness only).

Therefore, in this book, we will use a broader definition of the word *dimensions* (of an intervention program that you are using as your evaluand), referring to not only the program's internal characteristics but also the environmental factors that influence the program operation and results.

You will describe a dimension in a word or a short phrase that represents the focus of your evaluation among the internal characteristics and environmental factors of the program. Then, you will convert the dimension to a **dimensional evaluation question**. For example, let's say that you are evaluating a safety training program, and you decide to investigate the quality of the training materials as one of the program dimensions. Then, you might identify this dimension and its evaluation question as follows:

DIMENSIONS AND
DIMENSIONAL
EVALUATION
QUESTIONS

- Dimension—Training materials

- Dimensional evaluation question—How well are the training materials designed to support industry expectations and standards?

To investigate if there has been sufficient support from the management to make the program successful, you might use another dimension and question, for example:

- Dimension—Managerial support

- Dimensional evaluation question—How much support does the management provide for the training program?

When conducting a comprehensive program evaluation, you will likely investigate multiple dimensions of the program. Some dimensions may address means (e.g., the quality of the training content and implementation process used), and some dimensions may address end results (e.g., trainees' knowledge test scores or number of sales).

Adding to the dimension examples provided previously, a formative evaluation of a safety training program may include investigations of the following dimensions, addressing both means and end results:

1. **Training materials**—How well are the training materials designed to support industry expectations and standards?

2. **Managerial support**—How much support does the management provide for the training program?

3. **Incidents monitoring**—How well has the organization been monitoring safety-related incidents?

4. **Safety culture**—How comfortable are workers in following safety rules and procedures and reporting incidents, and how confident are they in doing so?

5. **Preventative incidents**—In the past few years, how many preventative incidents occurred to the workers who had completed the training program, and what can be done to prevent similar incidents from happening again?

So, how should you determine dimensions for your evaluation project? What sources should you use to identify dimensions? Among various sources available, consider the following as the main sources:

- Stakeholders' needs (reflected in the evaluation purpose statement)

- Program logic model (relating to the evaluation purpose statement)

- Theoretical frameworks

- Professional and ethical standards

Start With the Stakeholders' Needs

DIMENSIONS SELECTED BASED ON STAKEHOLDERS' NEEDS

During the identification phase of your project, it was emphasized that the purpose for evaluating a program should be determined based on stakeholders' needs that the program intends to satisfy. For the same reason, when determining which dimensions of a program to investigate, you should check stakeholders' needs associated with the program.

If the organization has recently conducted a needs assessment, check if the needs assessment results are reflected in the program's goal statements. Also, find out if the specific objectives of the program were developed based on known needs. The goals and objectives of the program will help you select dimensions to investigate. Examining goal-based dimensions will lead you to conduct a goal-based evaluation or a goal-based evaluation with some goal-free approach.

If no needs assessment information is available, you should solicit as much needs-specific information as possible from the stakeholders. You did this while determining the purpose of the evaluation. Existing program goals are not always the same as the direct impactees' needs. Understanding direct impactees' needs will help you and your client determine needs-based dimensions.

Relate the Purpose of Evaluation to the Program Logic Model Elements

When determining needs-based dimensions, the program's logic model is an important source to use, because the program logic model—when carefully and comprehensively developed—reflects the stakeholders' needs and helps you identify the stakeholders' intended use of your evaluation findings. You already know whether your evaluation is a formative or summative evaluation; the type of evaluation guides you to determine the type of dimensions to focus on.

DIMENSIONS SELECTED BASED ON PROGRAM LOGIC MODEL

While determining dimensions with your stakeholders, ask them:

- How they want to use your evaluation findings (again)
- Which elements in the program logic model are aligned with their intended use of your evaluation findings

Using the municipal recycling promotion program example presented in Table 17 in the previous chapter, let's say that the program goal was to increase the community's recycling rate, which is reflected in the program logic model. Then, the purpose of the evaluation is to determine the effectiveness of the program on helping residents recycle more, and the stakeholders will use the evaluation findings to submit a grant proposal to request more funding for the program. Based on this information, it will likely be a summative evaluation, and most dimensions to be investigated should come from the outcomes category of the program logic model, as shown in Table 24.

TABLE 24 ● Sample Dimensions Derived From Outcomes	
Outcomes	**Dimensions**
• People are aware of importance of recycling	• Awareness of the importance of recycling
• People are motivated to have a recycling bin in their house • People recycle more often at home	• Behavioral change in recycling
• People request local shops to have recycling bins in their shops for their customers to use	• Changes in local shops' recycling practice

TABLE 25 ● Sample Dimensions Derived From Activities and Outputs		
Activities	**Outputs**	**Dimensions**
• Prepare a talk about recycling at town meetings	• Residents and organization representatives participate in town meetings	• Number of people who participate in the meeting • Participants' reaction to the town meeting
• Invite local news to report the recycling agenda at town meetings	• Local news covers the talk on recycling at town meetings and broadcasts a documentary on recycling	• TV program ratings • People's knowledge on how to recycle
• Mail a "how to recycle" job aid to residents and organizations	• Residents and organizations receive a job aid in the mail	

On the other hand, the evaluation could be a formative evaluation, with the client intending to use the evaluation results to find out how well the promotion activities worked out during the first attempt (so the program could perform the activities more effectively during the subsequent attempts). Then, you would focus on investigating dimensions based on the activities and outputs categories, as the stakeholders would likely intend to use the evaluation results to make improvements in the means that lead to improvements in end results. See Table 25.

Incorporate Relevant Theoretical Frameworks and Professional Standards

You may also consult theories and models relevant to the program while selecting dimensions. For example, if you are evaluating a training program, it may be helpful to refer to training evaluation frameworks (e.g., Holton, 1996; Kirkpatrick, 1996a). The taxonomies used in such frameworks can be adopted as dimensions, for example, trainees' motivation levels, management support, trainees' reaction to training, trainees' motivation to transfer their new skills, environmental factors that influence skill transfer, and so forth. However, chances are that those elements may have already been indicated in the program logic model.

DIMENSIONS SELECTED BASED ON TRAINING EVALUATION FRAMEWORKS

Recall Table 20 in the previous chapter that compares categories used in different models. When you apply Katzell-based Kirkpatrick's four-level training evaluation framework, you should be aware that Level 1 evaluation is about trainees' reaction toward what was used during the training program and how the training program was conducted, which fall into the resources and activities categories. Levels 2, 3, and 4 are evaluations of the program's end results, which fall into the outcomes and impact categories. See Table 26.

You should not include certain dimensions just because they are suggested by an evaluation model or framework. As emphasized earlier, selection of dimensions should be based on the purpose of the evaluation. If you end up including all four levels (reaction, learning, behavior, results) as the dimensions of your evaluation, it is likely because you are conducting a goal-based summative evaluation to focus on intended results of the program. If you are conducting a formative evaluation, you will have a different set of dimensions than the four levels.

TABLE 26 ● Dimensions Developed Based on the Four-Level Training Evaluation Framework and Program Logic Model Categories	
Dimension and Dimensional Question	**Category**
• **Participants' reaction to training program (Level 1)**—How satisfied are the trainees with the program?	Resources Activities
• **Learning outcomes (Level 2)**—How well did they learn the content?	Outcomes
• **Behavioral change (Level 3)**—How well did they perform the tasks on the job?	
• **Results (Level 4)**—Has the organizational goal been achieved?	Impact

Even if you are conducting a summative evaluation, you do not have to include all four levels in your evaluation. Again, selection of dimensions depends on how stakeholders intend to use the evaluation findings. In some cases, you may conduct Level 2 and Level 3 only, or Level 3 and Level 4 only.

If your evaluand is not a training program, it would not be appropriate to apply the four-level training evaluation framework that includes reaction to training and learning outcomes. You should not claim that you used the four-level training evaluation framework just because you evaluated the participants' reaction to a nontraining program such as a hiring process.

Other theories and models developed in the fields of learning and organizational psychology as well as HPI can help you shape dimensions.

DIMENSIONS SELECTED BASED ON THEORIES AND MODELS

- Use lesson design models such as Robert Gagné's (Gagné, Briggs, & Wager, 1992) nine events of instruction, David Merrill's (2013) *First Principles of Instruction*, or Bloom's *Taxonomy of Educational Objectives* (Bloom et al., 1956) or the revised version of the cognitive domain (Anderson & Krathwohl, 2001) when developing dimensions specific to instructional design.

- Use John Keller's (1987) ARCS model as a framework to evaluate how interesting, challenging, relevant, and satisfying the instructional materials are to the target audience.

- Use a set of e-learning design principles generated by Richard Mayer's (2003) research (such as multimedia, contiguity, modality, redundancy, coherence, and personalization principles) to evaluate e-learning content.

- Refer to Frederick Herzberg's (1968) motivation-hygiene (two factor) theory when investigating job satisfaction/dissatisfaction levels.

- Take a system-focused approach and refer to three levels of performance (organization, process, and performer) and three dimensions of performance (goals, design, and management) (a.k.a. the nine boxes model by Rummler and Brache [2012]) when needing to evaluate different levels and types of organizational support and outcomes.

These examples are presented in Table 27.

TABLE 27 ● Examples of Dimensions Addressed by Certain Theoretical Frameworks	
Dimension and Dimensional Question	**Category**
• **Quality of lessons**—How well are the lessons designed when compared to Gagné's nine events of instruction?	Activities Outputs
• **Instructional sequence**—How effectively is the instructional sequence designed (per Merrill's *First Principles of Instruction*, including activation, demonstration, application, and integration)?	Activities Outputs
• **Motivational instructional materials**—How motivational, in terms of Keller's ARCS factors, are the instructional materials?	Activities Outputs
• **Congruence in instructional design**—How well are instructional objectives, strategies, and assessments aligned (per Bloom's taxonomy)?	Activities Outputs
• **E-Learning design**—How well is the e-learning content designed to satisfy e-learning principles as suggested by Mayer's research?	Activities Outputs
• **Job satisfaction/dissatisfaction**—How satisfied or dissatisfied are employees with their job (per Herzberg's two-factor theory)?	Outcomes
• **Performance support**—How much support is provided at the performer level, process level, and organizational level (per Rummler and Brache's nine boxes model)?	Activities Outputs

DIMENSIONS SELECTED BASED ON PROFESSIONAL STANDARDS

Certain programs may need to adhere to professional standards, which can be another source for determining evaluative dimensions for the program. Here are some examples:

- To evaluate a safety-related intervention, the Occupational Safety and Health Administration (OSHA) regulations may be relevant (https://www.osha.gov/).

- To identify which instructional design aspects of a training program need to be evaluated, the standards developed by the International Board of Standards for Training, Performance, and Instruction (IBSTPI) may be used (http://ibstpi.org/).

- To address ethical concerns, gender equity could be included as a dimension for programs that tend to be biased toward a gender group.

However, complying with professional standards such as OSHA regulations may have been recognized as one of the important elements in the program logic model. Therefore, you may have already selected a relevant dimension regarding the program needing to comply with professional standards.

Write Dimensional Evaluation Questions

While selecting a set of dimensions and writing down a short phrase that indicates each dimension, also prepare an evaluation question for each dimension. How would you develop dimensional evaluation questions? Here are some tips.

Start with "how well"—When writing dimensional evaluation questions, keep in mind that you are evaluating "how good" things are. So, it is helpful to start the dimensional evaluation questions with the word *how* if possible. For example, compare the following two dimensional evaluation questions and see how they would help you report the findings:

TIPS FOR WRITING
DIMENSIONAL
EVALUATION
QUESTIONS

1. *Question*: Is the curriculum designed to support industry expectations and standards?

    Findings: Yes, it is, or No, it is not.

2. *Question*: How well is the curriculum designed to support industry expectations and standards?

    Findings: Very well, Pretty well, Not well, or Poorly.

The second type of question is more suitable in most evaluation cases because it helps you develop meaningful rubrics for determining quality of the dimension.

Combine similar dimensions—If there are similar dimensions, think about if they can be combined into one dimension. For example, two dimensions such as instructional strategies and length of lessons can be combined into a dimension called instructional design.

Align dimensions with program logic model categories—If you developed specific dimensions mainly based on the program logic model, it is likely that you are conducting a goal-based evaluation. In doing so, indicate the category (or categories) from the program logic model that relates to each dimension as shown in Table 28 and Table 29.

Add a dimension(s) about environmental factors when applicable— Make sure to use a system-focused approach, rather than an intervention-focused approach, and think about whether it is important to investigate the quality of environmental support as well.

Add a dimension to use a goal-free approach if applicable—It is possible to add a goal-free approach to your goal-based evaluation. Adding a goal-free approach to a goal-based evaluation would mean that while investigating expected goal-related process and outcomes, you are also investigating other unexpected outcomes that could have resulted from the program. To do so, you can add another dimension labeled as "other outcomes" as shown in Table 29 to investigate goal-free outcomes.

TABLE 28 ● **Example of Dimensions and Dimensional Evaluation Questions (Formative Evaluation)**

Dimension and Dimensional Question	Category
1. **E-learning design**—How well does the e-learning program employ appropriate instructional strategies, and how appropriate is the length of each lesson?	Resources Activities[a]
2. **Tracking data from learners**—How well is the e-learning program designed to track learners' completion data and store the data in the learning management system (LMS)?	Resources Activities Outputs[b]
3. **Cost for e-learning development**—How much does it cost to develop each e-learning lesson?	Resources
4. **Number of errors during job performance**—After completing the e-learning program, how many errors do employees make in their reports?	Short-term outcomes

[a]The e-learning design dimension falls into the resources and activities categories because it aims at finding areas in existing e-learning content (resources) that need to be revised (activities).

[b]The tracking data from the learners dimension falls into the resources, activities, and outputs categories because it is about using the existing LMS (resources), checking/revising how the e-learning content is designed to track data (activities), and examining the tracked data (outputs).

TABLE 29 ● **Example of Dimensions and Dimensional Evaluation Questions (Summative Evaluation)**

Dimension and Dimensional Question	Category
1. **Curriculum design**—How well is the curriculum designed to support industry expectations and standards?	Resources Activities[c]
2. **Online learning environment**—Does the online delivery technology provide a positive learning environment?	Resources Outputs[d]
3. **Students' professional accomplishments**—How does the program help students achieve professional accomplishments such as landing a new job, being promoted, receiving awards, and presenting or publishing papers?	Outcomes
4. **Graduation rate**—What is the program's 3-year graduation rate? How does it compare to the university's expectations?	Impact
5. **Other outcomes**—What other positive and negative, tangible and intangible outcomes have students and graduates experienced during, and after completing, the program?	Outcomes

[c]The curriculum design dimension falls into the resources category because existing information about industry expectations and standards is being used, and it also falls into the activities category because it investigates if/how faculty members develop their instructional materials to reflect industry expectations and standards.

[d]The online learning environment dimension falls into the resources category because the department is using an existing system as its delivery media and also falls into the outputs category because the media environment is set up and presented/delivered to learners.

Determine Importance Weighting
Based on Usage of Dimensional Findings

While you narrow down and finalize the list of dimensions for your evaluation, you also need to determine relative importance of each dimension compared to others (Davidson, 2005). The **importance weighting** should be determined based on the prioritized intended usage of the dimensional evaluation findings—that is, which dimension's findings will be immediately, more widely, or more critically used? Consider the four dimensions presented in Table 28:

1. E-learning design, including instructional strategies used and length of each lesson

2. Tracking data from learners

3. Cost for e-learning development

4. Number of errors during job performance

If you simply ask your stakeholders which dimension is the most important one, they may think automatically of the organization's goal and say that the fourth dimension about reducing the number of errors during job performance is the most important dimension because it is the ultimate goal to achieve.

However, remind them that the purpose of conducting this formative evaluation is to improve the quality of the program and ask them to think about which dimension's results will be most useful for the purpose of improvement. Because they want to revise the e-learning content with better instructional strategies while maintaining a certain length of each lesson, they might say that the first dimension will generate the most useful information for that purpose. If so, then, the first dimension is the most important dimension of all.

Involve several stakeholders among the intended users of the evaluation findings, instead of using the client's input only. When asking the stakeholders to rank-order the dimensions based on the degree of usefulness of the dimensional findings, you may use a sequence of questions such as these:

DIMENSIONAL WEIGHTING BASED ON USEFULNESS OF EVALUATION FINDINGS

1. Which dimension will generate *the most useful* information? How so? You can select multiple dimensions if you think they will generate equally useful information.

2. Which dimension will generate *the next most useful* information? How so? You can select multiple dimensions if you think they will generate equally useful information.

Repeat the second question until you have weighted all dimensions. The number of levels of importance weighting will range between one level (when all dimensions are equally important) and the total number of dimensions (when each dimension is assigned a different weight). You may assign qualitative or quantitative values to the ranks. See examples in Table 30. Be aware that "Not important" or "Not useful" cannot be an option because if a dimension were not important or not useful, you would have not selected it as a dimension.

TABLE 30 ● Examples of Dimensions With Different Levels of Importance Weighting				
	Importance Weighting (IW) Examples			
Dimension and Dimensional Question	**Four Levels**	**Three Levels**	**Two Levels**	**One Level**
1. **Curriculum design**—How well is the curriculum designed to support industry expectations and standards?	Fairly important (2)	Very important (2)	Important (1)	Important (1)
2. **Online learning environment**—Does the online delivery technology provide a positive learning environment?	Very important (3)	Very important (2)	More Important (2)	Important (1)
3. **Students' professional accomplishments**—How does the program help students achieve professional accomplishments?	Important (1)	Somewhat important (1)	Important (1)	Important (1)
4. **Graduation rate**—What is the program's 3-year graduation rate? How does it compare to the university's expectations?	Most important (4)	Extremely important (3)	More Important (2)	Important (1)

USE OF IMPORTANCE WEIGHTING DURING THE PROJECT

Rank-ordering dimensions based on importance of usage helps you and your stakeholders in various ways:

1. It helps you and stakeholders have another opportunity to discuss the purpose of conducting the evaluation, that is, who intends to use the evaluation findings and how the evaluation findings will be used.

2. It helps you decide how much attention you should pay to individual dimensions during the data collection and analysis phase. You would want to ensure allocation of sufficient resources and use comprehensive evaluation activities to investigate the more important dimensions.

3. It helps you prioritize a list of recommendations generated upon completion of data analysis.

Recognize a Black Box, Gray Box, or Clear Box Evaluation

While finalizing the selection of dimensions, you will recognize whether you are conducting a black box, gray box, or clear box evaluation. Let's explore what those types of evaluations are. The concepts come from types of software testing.

In software testing, there are three types of testing—clear box testing, black box testing, and gray box testing (R. Patton, 2006). Clear box testing involves testing of internal structures of software at the coding level, whereas black box testing focuses on the application and functionality of the software without looking at its programming codes. Gray box testing uses positive aspects of clear and black box testing; it looks at the architectural structure of software as well as its functionality.

For example, testing of a website by exploring the webpages is an example of black box testing. Additional reviews of some of the HTML behind the webpages make it gray box testing. Additional thorough reviews of the programming codes used in interactive and dynamic features make it clear box testing.

These methods of software testing can be applied to evaluation, as Michael Scriven (1999) labeled three types of outcome evaluation:

- In a clear box evaluation, you study the inner workings of the program fully.

- In a black box evaluation, you investigate the end results of the program without studying how the program works.

- In a gray box evaluation, you investigate both the end results and the components of the program, although you do not evaluate the operation principles in detail. Often, your evaluations may fall into the gray box evaluation category.

GRAY BOX
EVALUATION AS
AN ALTERNATIVE
TO CLEAR BOX
OR BLACK BOX
EVALUATION

Figure 12 illustrates black box evaluation and clear box evaluation in terms of how you would select dimensions from a program logic model.

Being analogous to the clear box software testing done at the source code level, **clear box evaluation** involves careful investigations of specific resources and individual activities that the program used to produce outputs. Comprehensive formative evaluations may adopt clear box evaluation techniques. However, in some cases, clear box evaluation can be an unrealistic option because it is both time-consuming and expensive.

Summative evaluation, also referred to as *outcome evaluation*, can be a form of **black box evaluation**, as it focuses on evaluating the quality of program outcomes. You may conduct a black box type of summative evaluation because of the client's request or due to a limited budget. You may exclude any means-related dimensions from your summative evaluation, because a recent evaluation has already investigated means-related dimensions or because another evaluation team (internal) is conducting evaluation using means-related dimensions while you as an external evaluation team have been invited to conduct a summative evaluation on the end results.

FIGURE 12 ● Dimensions Investigated in Black Box Evaluation and Clear Box Evaluation

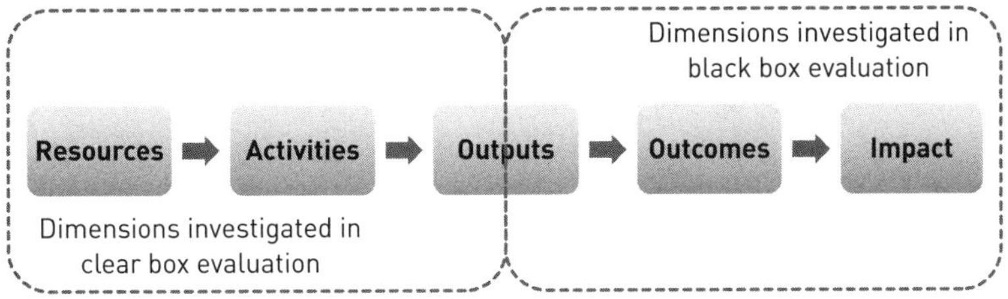

Other than these cases, some evaluation scholars recommend against using a black box evaluation approach, noting that focusing only on outcomes (end results) without looking at the process (means) is not considered a best practice.

> Evaluations to determine merit and worth often examine whether the program is successful in achieving its goals or objectives. Thus, there tends to be a focus on outcomes. . . . Most evaluators would consider it bad practice to study program outcomes without some sense of what is being delivered. Such studies are contemptuously called "black box" studies—outcomes are described without any sense of what went on in the "box." (Fitzpatrick, Christie, & Mark, 2009, p. 20)

Black box evaluation—because it does not include an investigation of how the program works—does not provide you with information to explain what caused positive or negative end results.

As an alternative to the clear box and black box approaches, you may conduct a **gray box evaluation** that includes both means-related and results-related dimensions.

DIMENSIONS FOR A GRAY-BOX TYPE, FORMATIVE EVALUATION
A gray-box type of formative evaluation may include more dimensions from the resources, activities, and outputs categories than the outcomes or impact categories as illustrated in Figure 13. Also, the dimensions that fall into the resources, activities, and outputs categories would have higher levels of importance weighting because stakeholders intend to use the results of these dimensions to improve the quality of the program.

The focus is on finding out how well the program is doing toward achieving the intended outcomes and how well it is handling factors outside the program. It aims at providing recommendations on changing those means and improving the quality of the early end results, which will in turn help improve the quality of other results in the outcomes and impact categories.

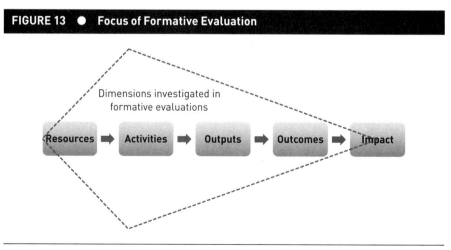

FIGURE 13 ● Focus of Formative Evaluation

Adapted from W. K. Kellogg Foundation, 2004.

For example, imagine you are conducting a formative evaluation to improve the effectiveness of the physician/nurse rounding process implemented at a hospital. Among the following five dimensions used, the first three dimensions are means related and the other two dimensions are results related (adapted from Qarterman & Shaerrer, 2011):

1. **Rounding frequency**—How frequently has physician/nurse rounding been performed (quantity)?

    a. Program logic model category: Activities

    b. Importance weighting: *Important*

2. **Rounding reporting**—How well has physician/nurse rounding been tracked? How well is reporting integrated in their daily routine?

    a. Program logic model category: Activities

    b. Importance weighting: *Very important*

3. **Removal of rounding obstacles**—What are the obstacles to physician/nurse rounding, and how well are these obstacles being handled (minimized)?

    a. Program logic model category: Resources and Activities

    b. Importance weighting: *Extremely important*

4. **Clinician perceptions of rounding**—How much do the physicians and nurses value the rounding process, and how can their perceptions be improved?

    a. Program logic model category: Outcomes

    b. Importance weighting: *Very important*

5. **Patient perceptions of rounding**—What are the patients' perceptions of the rounding process, and how can their perceptions be improved?

    a. Program logic model category: Outcomes

    b. Importance weighting: *Somewhat important*

DIMENSIONS FOR A GRAY-BOX TYPE, SUMMATIVE EVALUATION

On the other hand, the main purpose of summative evaluation is to determine the overall quality of the program and performance outcomes rather than making continuous improvement on the means used during the program. Therefore, when conducting a gray-box type of summative evaluation, you would focus more on dimensions from the outputs, outcomes, and impact categories than resources and activities categories, as illustrated in Figure 14. Among the selected dimensions, the dimensions that fall into the end results categories would have higher degrees of importance weighting than other dimensions that fall into the means categories.

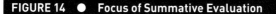

FIGURE 14 ● Focus of Summative Evaluation

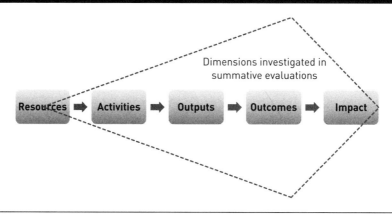

Dimensions investigated in summative evaluations

Resources ➡ Activities ➡ Outputs ➡ Outcomes ➡ Impact

Adapted from W. K. Kellogg Foundation, 2004.

For example, imagine that you have been asked to conduct a summative evaluation to determine the effectiveness of a youth science and engineering summer camp program designed to encourage students (in Grades 8–9) to pursue science and engineering programs in college. You may decide to use the following five dimensions (adapted from Denton, Eisele, & Swanson, 2015).

1. **Content alignment**—How well are the camp activities aligned with the program objectives?

   a. Program logic model category: Activities

   b. Importance weighting: *Somewhat important*

2. **Participation rate**—How many children in Grades 8 and 9 have participated in the program?

   a. Program logic model category: Outputs

   b. Importance weighting: *Somewhat important*

3. **Continuing contact**—How closely is the program keeping contact with the participants until they enter a college?

   a. Program logic model category: Outcomes

   b. Importance weighting: *Very important*

4. **Growing interest**—How interested are the participants in pursuing a science or engineering program in college?

   a. Program logic model category: Outcomes

   b. Importance weighting: *Very important*

5. **College enrollment rate**—How many former campers have enrolled in a science or engineering program in college?

   a. Program logic model category: Outcomes

   b. Importance weighting: *Extremely important*

You designed it as a gray-box type of summative evaluation in which you focus on investigating results-related dimensions with high levels of important weighting, while you also assess the program content alignment and participation rate.

Finalize the Number of Dimensions

You have made a list of dimensions to investigate. Before you finalize the dimensions, you want to check again if any dimensions are so similar to each other that you can combine them into one dimension. For example, let's say you initially listed five dimensions, two of which are the following:

COMBINE SIMILAR DIMENSIONS INTO ONE

- **Trainees' motivation to transfer**—How motivated are the trainees to use new skills after they go back to their job?

- **Trainees' confidence**—How confident are the trainees in using new skills on the job?

It is not wrong to list them as two separate dimensions; however, it is also possible to combine them into a dimension. While making a decision, you want to think about the data sources that you will likely use to evaluate the two items. If the same data sources will be used to evaluate the two items (e.g., surveys with trainees, interviews with selected trainees, interviews with trainers, interviews with supervisors), you may consider using one combined dimension:

- **Trainees' motivation and confidence in skill transfer**—How motivated and confident are the trainees in using new skills on the job?

Conversely, you want to check if any dimension needs to be split into multiple dimensions. For example, consider the following dimension developed to evaluate a university website:

SPLIT A DIMENSION INTO MULTIPLE DIMENSIONS

- **Website navigation and application process**—How easy or difficult is the website to navigate and complete the application process?

Both items are website usability issues, and you can certainly use this dimension to look at the website usability and application process together. You can also separate the overall website navigation and the application process and write two dimensions:

- **Website navigation**—How easy or difficult is the website to navigate and find information?

- **Application process**—How clearly is the application process laid out, and how easy or difficult is it to follow and complete the process?

While doing some necessary adjustment on the initial list of dimensions, you also want to double-check if you have an adequate number of dimensions. How many dimensions should you include in your evaluation? It depends on the scope and budget of the evaluation project.

DETERMINE AN APPROPRIATE NUMBER OF DIMENSIONS

Comprehensive evaluation projects dealing with complex programs may include many dimensions about the program in order to reveal in-depth information and carefully determine the overall quality of the program and performance outcomes. However, more is *not* always better. You also need to assess feasibility of the evaluation here again. Often because of limited resources, evaluators may not be able to investigate a long list of dimensions. You have to choose the most important dimensions.

Dimensions of a program are analogous to pieces of a jigsaw puzzle. Selecting important dimensions to investigate is like finding several crucial pieces of a jigsaw puzzle. Imagine you are looking at many small pieces of a jigsaw puzzle. Although it is necessary to have all of those pieces to complete the picture, some of the pieces can give you enough of a clue to estimate what the overall picture should be.

In conducting a program evaluation, the selected dimensions are those *crucial* pieces of a jigsaw puzzle that allow you to estimate the overall picture of the program. You do not have to investigate all possible characteristics (i.e., dimensions) of a program to make a reasonably accurate estimation about the quality of the program. It may be sufficient to use a short list of *crucial* dimensions. For a small-scale evaluation project, it would be adequate to use three or four dimensions. Again, these dimensions should be linked to how the stakeholders intend to use the evaluation findings.

Chapter Summary

Determine dimensions and importance weighting (Step 5).

- Dimensions are important internal and external aspects of the program to be investigated.

- To select dimensions, evaluators and stakeholders may use various sources:
  o Stakeholders' needs
  o Program logic model
  o Theoretical frameworks
  o Professional and ethical standards

- Evaluators and stakeholders need to determine the degrees of importance among individual dimensions based on the prioritized intended usage of dimensional evaluation findings. The importance weighting information will help evaluators determine appropriate data collection methods to be used for individual dimensions and prioritize among a list of recommendations.

- Conducting a clear box evaluation can be time-consuming, whereas a black box evaluation focuses only on outcomes (thus, it is also known as outcome evaluation). In many cases, it may be helpful to conduct a gray box evaluation as it involves an investigation of multiple dimensions across means and end results with partial knowledge of the inner workings of the program.

- Formative evaluations tend to focus on ways to improve the quality of items listed in the resources, activities, and outputs categories, whereas summative evaluations tend to focus on evaluating end results such as the items listed in the outputs, outcomes, and impact categories.

- The total number of dimensions to be investigated in an evaluation project depends on the scope of and budget for each evaluation project. Similar to how you can recognize the entire picture of a jigsaw puzzle based on several crucial pieces, you may be able to draw conclusions by using a short list of crucial dimensions.

Chapter Discussion

1. Dimensions for a clear box, gray box, or black box evaluation

Your organization developed a new performance assessment tool and implemented it in one of the departments as a pilot study. You are conducting an evaluation to identify areas for improvement before the tool is rolled out to all other departments. You plan to investigate the following three dimensions.

1. **Quality of the tool**—How well is the new performance assessment tool designed? When is it not working, and why? (Resources and Activities)

2. **Organizational support**—What type of organizational support exists to facilitate implementation of the tool? What are the barriers? How is the organization handling the barriers? (Resources and Activities)

3. **User adoption**—How well is the tool adopted by the users? What do they think about using it? Does it satisfy their needs? Would they accept this change? (Resources, Activities, and Outputs)

Based on the descriptions of the dimensions, would you characterize this evaluation as a clear box, gray box, or black box evaluation, and how so?

2. Dimensions for a formative or summative evaluation

A consulting company runs a help desk program for its client organizations to use when they need administrative and tech support. By offering the help desk service to the client organizations, the consulting company hopes to free consultants from handling the clients' administrative tasks and technical problems, so that the consultants can focus on consulting tasks and meet deadlines. The company also hopes that this will lead to a high level of client satisfaction.

An evaluation has been conducted to reveal how well the help desk program is meeting the program goals, by investigating four dimensions. Based on stakeholders' needs (both the consultants and clients) and reflecting on the program logic model, the four dimensions have three different levels of importance weighting (Important, More important, and Most important), as presented in Table 31.

Would you characterize this evaluation as a formative or summative evaluation, and how so?

TABLE 31 ● Identify Evaluation Type Based on Dimensions, Program Logic Model Categories, and Importance Weighting

Dimension and Dimensional Question	Category in Program Logic Model	Importance Weighting
1. **Agent expertise**—Are the help desk agents knowledgeable and prepared to respond to the client questions?	Resources Activities	Important
2. **Process**—Are the help desk requests ticketed, prioritized, and resolved in a timely manner?	Activities	More important

(Continued)

TABLE 31 ● (Continued)		
Dimension and Dimensional Question	**Category in Program Logic Model**	**Importance Weighting**
3. **Time saving for consultants**—Does the help desk program save consultants' time?	Outcomes	Most important
4. **Client satisfaction**—Are clients satisfied with the help desk support?	Outcomes	Most important

Adapted from Peeterse, Catcott, & Yandell, 2011.

Now, Your Turn—Determine Dimensions and Importance Weighting

Discuss with your client and other stakeholders and determine dimensions and importance weighting of individual dimensions. Use Table B-4 in Appendix B (Evaluation Development Worksheets) to summarize how you determined a list of dimensions and importance weighting. Double-check the usefulness of the dimensions against the intended use of the evaluation. Table 32 presents an example for evaluating a graduate degree program, using the sample dimensions presented in Table 29 and Table 30 in this chapter.

Next chapter is about determining data collection methods. If you can, brainstorm and start drafting out data collection methods using Table B-5 in Appendix B (Evaluation Development Worksheets).

TABLE 32 ● Example Worksheet for Step 5: Process for Determining Dimensions and Importance Weighting	
Question	**Your Finding**
• How did you determine the dimensions? Briefly describe specific sources you used (among the following four options), the process you followed, and the people whom you involved during the decision:	Four dimensions were selected: 1. Curriculum design 2. Online learning environment 3. Students' professional accomplishments 4. Graduation rate

Question	Your Finding
a) Stakeholders' needs b) Program logic model c) Theoretical frameworks d) Professional and ethical standards	The decision was based on the following sources: a) Stakeholders' needs and purpose of evaluation—Based on discussions with the client and the department chair, it was decided to conduct a summative evaluation, which puts more emphasis on investigating quality of end results. b) Program logic model—With that in mind, the evaluation team asked the client and the department chair to list several areas to investigate, and then verified their items using the program logic model. c) Theoretical frameworks—The Success Case Method will be used to investigate success and nonsuccess cases of students who produced presentations or publications.
• How did you determine the relative degree of importance weighting among dimensions? Briefly describe who were involved in the decision and how you involved them during the decision.	The department faculty and staff members are intended users of the evaluation. They plan to use the evaluation findings as part of their internal self-study to ensure quality education. During a face-to-face meeting, the evaluation team asked the client and the department chair (as representatives of the intended users) to explain how they would use the findings of each dimension, which dimension(s) would be the most useful for them, and why. Based on their responses, it was determined that the most important dimension was to understand if they are graduating enough students, as maintaining a high graduation rate is their priority. Second, the department hopes to help students produce many accomplishments while pursuing the degree program and as a result of completing the degree. The stakeholders want to learn more from success cases in order to assist other students. They also want to know if the program is providing students with a good quality curriculum, which will enable students to produce accomplishments outside their classroom. They want to learn strengths and weaknesses of their online curriculum. Third, the stakeholders want to know if the online environment using the learning management system is working well for faculty and students. However, the learning management system has been selected by the university; therefore, the department cannot change the system. They can only implement strategies to overcome the weaknesses of the current system, if there are any. Therefore, it was listed as the least important dimension among all.

(Continued)

TABLE 32 ● (Continued)

Question	Your Finding
• List dimensions and dimensional questions, and indicate the category of the program logic model or training impact model under which each dimension falls. Also indicate the degree of importance weighting for each dimension.	1. Curriculum design—How well is the curriculum designed to support industry expectations and standards? PLM: Resources and Activities IW: Very important 2. Online learning environment—Does the online delivery technology provide a positive learning environment? PLM: Resources and Activities IW: Somewhat important 3. Students' professional accomplishments—How does the program help students achieve professional accomplishments? PLM: Outcomes IW: Very important 4. Graduation rate—What is the program's 3-year graduation rate? How does it compare to the university's expectations? PLM: Impact IW: Extremely important
• Think about the intended usage of your evaluation findings again. Who among the stakeholders will make use of the evaluation results (directly or indirectly), for what purpose (formative or summative), and in what way? Will the dimensions generate information useful for them?	It is projected that using the evaluation findings on the four dimensions in order of importance weighting, the stakeholders would be able to: 1. Understand if the program is meeting the university expectation of graduation rate, and use the information to lay out its next 5-year plan. 2. Use lessons learned from success/nonsuccess cases of students (in terms of their accomplishments outside the classroom) to generate ideas that will encourage and assist more students to accomplish outside the classroom. 3. Highlight the strengths of the program in marketing, while improving areas that show weaknesses. 4. Use the information regarding the quality of the program curriculum and online environment while advising new/current students. Most of the intended usage of the evaluation findings listed in this table is clearly associated with the summative purpose of the evaluation.

IW, Importance weighting; *PLM*, program logic model.

Determine Data Collection Methods (Step 6)

You have selected multiple dimensions to be investigated (Chapter 6), and now you need to decide how to collect data to investigate those dimensions. When

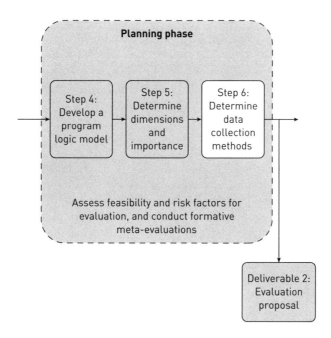

determining data collection methods, you first need to review each dimensional evaluation question and determine the overall evaluation design to be applied to each dimension (e.g., experimental or descriptive case study type evaluation design). However, as stated earlier, we will focus on using a descriptive case study type evaluation design in this book. With that in mind, you will identify the most feasible data collection methods by doing the following:

1. Selecting the most direct data sources that help answer individual dimensional evaluation questions (e.g., employees, supervisors, database records, etc.)

2. Selecting the most feasible data collection methods (e.g., by conducting self-administered survey questionnaires, by conducting interviews or focus groups, through observations, by reviewing existing data, or by administering written or performance tests)

3. Making a plan on how to triangulate data obtained from multiple sources

You also want to continue to assess feasibility and risk factors for the project and conduct formative meta-evaluations before you produce your second deliverable, the evaluation proposal.

Determine Evaluation Designs for Dimensional Evaluations

Recall different types of evaluation design described in the Introduction chapter—experimental and descriptive case study type evaluation designs. Ideally, evaluators would determine a separate evaluation design for each dimension, and they would make the determination largely based on the purpose of the evaluation project (formative or summative) and the intention to investigate each dimension. The experimental design is considered the most rigorous approach, especially when conducting summative evaluations. However, it is not always the most cost-effective or feasible option, especially in the HPI context.

EXPERIMENTAL OR DESCRIPTIVE CASE STUDY TYPE EVALUATION DESIGN

An alternative is to use a descriptive case study type evaluation design, which helps you uncover how things are going, what happened, and/or why and how things happened. You study the phenomena in a natural setting where the intervention has been implemented, using the whole population if it is fairly small or using a purposively selected sample case (e.g., night shift workers). You investigate each dimension of a program by triangulating multiple sets of data. You use both quantitative and qualitative data to gather sufficient evidence to answer individual dimensional questions. For quantitative data, you may report *descriptive statistics* such as total scores, average scores, percentages, and standard deviation values. Qualitative data also enable you to understand the quality of the case itself and to provide recommendations for making necessary decisions. Table 33 compares the characteristics of an experimental or quasi-experimental design and a descriptive case study type design.

It is possible to use a mix of experimental and descriptive case study type evaluation designs in an evaluation project, as shown in Option 1 in Table 34, based on the example presented in Table 28 in the previous chapter.

Evaluation Design Option 1 in Table 34 uses experimental/quasi-experimental designs for Dimensions 1 and 4 and a descriptive case study design for Dimensions 2 and 3. Experimental designs using *inferential statistics* can be used when

- the population size (in this case, the number of employees who use the e-learning program) is large enough that it makes sense to study with a sample of the population instead of the whole population,
- it is possible to use a sample randomly selected from the population, and
- it is feasible to randomly assign the sample participants into the intervention and nonintervention groups (if this condition cannot be met, it is a quasi-experimental study).

TABLE 33 ● Comparison of Characteristics of Experimental and Descriptive Case Study Type Evaluation Designs

Characteristic / Evaluation Design	Experimental Study	Descriptive Case Study
Participants involved	Randomly selected from a population and randomly assigned to intervention and nonintervention groups	A small population or a purposively selected sample/case
Data type collected	Typically quantitative data	Both quantitative and qualitative data
Statistics used	Inferential statistics as well as descriptive statistics	Descriptive statistics
Evidence tested	Hypotheses are tested to show a cause-and-effect relationship	Multiple sets of data are triangulated to describe and explain observed phenomena

TABLE 34 ● Different Evaluation Design Options

Dimension	Option 1	Option 2
1. **E-learning design**—How well does the e-learning program employ appropriate instructional strategies, and how appropriate is the length of each lesson?	An experimental/quasi-experimental design to compare two groups (one that uses an e-learning program with specific instructional strategies and another one that uses an e-learning program without the instructional strategies) and to show which group is more favorable	A descriptive case study design involving multiple stakeholders such as the e-learning program developers and a group of employees that use the e-learning program to show how they felt about the e-learning design
2. **Tracking data from learners**—How well is the e-learning program designed to track learners' completion data and store the data in the learning management system (LMS)? 3. **Cost for e-learning development (per lesson)**—How much does it cost to develop each e-learning lesson?	A descriptive case study design involving multiple stakeholders such as the e-learning program developers, the LMS administrator, and a group of employees that use the e-learning program	A descriptive case study design involving multiple stakeholders such as the e-learning program developers, the LMS administrator, and a group of employees that use the e-learning program
4. **Number of errors during job performance**—After completing the e-learning program, how many errors do employees make in their reports?	An experimental/quasi-experimental design to compare two groups (one that uses an e-learning program with specific instructional strategies and another one that uses an e-learning program without the instructional strategies) and to show which group makes fewer errors in reports	A descriptive case study design involving a group of employees that use the e-learning program and their supervisors to describe errors made in reports after they complete the e-learning program

However, because this hypothetical evaluation is meant to be a formative evaluation, it may be premature or overkill to conduct experimental studies. In this case, Option 2, which uses descriptive evaluation designs for all dimensions, can still achieve rigor by *triangulating* multiple sources of data, as explained later in this chapter.

Some program evaluations may need to be conducted as descriptive case studies, because it makes sense to answer the overall evaluation question and the dimensional questions with qualitative data and descriptive statistics rather than quantitative data with inferential statistics. The example used in Table 29 in the previous chapter (which is also used in Table 35 in this chapter) is one such case. In this example, it would not make sense to manipulate variables in the program to collect data to investigate individual dimensions. As shown in Table 35, sufficient evidence to answer the individual dimensional questions can be obtained by involving multiple groups of stakeholders and using descriptive statistics of quantitative data as well as qualitative data.

TABLE 35 ● Program Evaluation Conducted With a Descriptive Case Study Design	
Dimension	**Descriptive Case Study Design Involving Multiple Stakeholders**
1. **Curriculum design**—How well is the curriculum designed to support industry expectations and standards?	The program instructors, students, and current/potential employers in the industry to show how they feel about the curriculum design
2. **Online learning environment**—Does the online delivery technology provide a positive learning environment?	The program instructors and students to show how they feel about the online learning environment
3. **Students' professional accomplishments**—How does the program help students achieve professional accomplishments such as landing a new job, being promoted, receiving awards, and presenting or publishing papers?	The program instructors and students to reveal the quantity and quality of professional accomplishments that students produced and to understand the process they took to produce such accomplishments
4. **Graduation rate**—What is the program's 3-year graduation rate? How does it compare to the university's expectations?	The program administrators and staff to reveal the current graduation rate, compared to the program's graduation rate in the past and the university's goal (also using the industry average if the information is available) The program staff, instructors, and students to investigate reasons for course dropouts and program dropouts
5. **Other outcomes**—What other positive and negative, tangible and intangible outcomes have students and graduates experienced during, and after completing, the program?	The program instructors, students, graduates, and their employers to uncover other outcomes

Select Data Collection Methods That Allow Direct Measures of Dimensions

After you have determined appropriate evaluation designs for individual dimensions, you need to identify the most direct sources of data and the most appropriate **data collection methods** to use.

When you conduct an experimental study, you typically use survey questionnaires with closed-ended questions, objective tests, and types of observations and extant data reviews that generate *quantitative* data, rather than interviews, focus groups, and observations, which generate *qualitative* data.

When conducting a descriptive case study, you are open to all types of data collection methods. While selecting appropriate data collection methods, you should consider advantages and disadvantages of different types of data collection methods, as shown in Table 36.

It should be noted that a survey can mean either type of the following data collection methods:

- Informants complete a survey questionnaire on their own (a.k.a. a self-administered survey).

- An interviewer collects information from each informant by asking questions (a.k.a. a one-on-one interview).

However, in this book, we will refer to the self-administered survey method as a *survey*, and refer to the interviewer-led survey method as an *interview*.

Among various options, you need to select the most direct and feasible data collection methods for measuring each dimension of your evaluation project, instead of using the methods with which you feel most comfortable. Ask yourself: *Am I using valid (appropriate) data collection methods for answering each dimensional evaluation question?* In answering the question, you need to think about what you will measure and how you will measure it.

USE DIRECT MEASUREMENTS WHENEVER POSSIBLE

Let's say, you are investigating employees' behavioral changes after they have completed a workshop. What would be the most appropriate way to measure behavioral changes? Possible methods include a direct observation or a review of records that tracked their behavioral changes. Thus, you should go after this type of data first. If not available, you can consider asking the employees to self-assess or ask supervisors to provide assessments of their employees, which would be done by surveys and/or interviews. Always go after *direct* measurements first before you decide to employ an alternative, indirect method.

However, direct sources do not always contain perfect or complete information. Sometimes, direct sources such as performance records showing employees' changed behavior may contain erroneous information. For that reason, it is helpful to collect data from more than one source and verify accuracy of the information (a.k.a. triangulation). If you have to rely on indirect measures, it makes it more important to do so. While triangulating multiple sources of data, you apply the critical multiplism strategy.

TABLE 36 ● Advantages and Disadvantages of Different Data Collection Methods		
Method	**Advantages (Strengths)**	**Disadvantages (Weaknesses)**
Self-administered survey — On site (in person, as a group, using written questionnaires)	• Can administer it to a group of people at once • Can handle participants' questions in person immediately	• Costly to print out copies of the questionnaire • Necessary to use a survey administrator for each site • Time-consuming to enter data into an electronic file
Via mail	• Can administer it to a large number of people in different locations • Participants can complete it during their preferred time	• Costly to print out and mail copies of the questionnaire • Notoriously low survey return rates • Time-consuming to enter data into an electronic file
Online	• Can administer it to a large number of people in different locations • Participants can complete it during their preferred time • Data are already stored in an electronic file, ready for statistical analysis	• Notoriously low survey return rates • Survey administrators and participants must have access to technology
One-on-one interview — In person	• Can observe interviewees' body language • Can retrieve detailed information[a]	• Interviewers and interviewees need to be in the same location • Costly and time-consuming to complete multiple interviews[a]
By telephone	• Interviewers and interviewees do not need to be in the same location • Most people have access to telephone	• Cannot observe interviewees' body language • Interviewers and interviewees must have access to telephone
Via video conferencing	• Interviewers and interviewees do not need to be in the same location • Can observe interviewees' body language	• Interviewers and interviewees must have access to video conferencing technology
Focus group — In person	• Participants' body language provides additional data • Can retrieve information from a group of people at once[b] • Participants can learn other people's views and generate group opinions on a chosen topic through discussions[b]	• Discussions can be influenced by the physical environment (e.g., room setup, sitting arrangement) • All participants must be in the same location at the same time • Time-consuming to monitor and record participants' responses[b]
By telephone conferencing	• Participants do not need to be in the same location	• Cannot observe participants' body language

Method		Advantages (Strengths)	Disadvantages (Weaknesses)
Observation	Via video conferencing	• Participants do not need to be in the same location	• Difficult to observe participants' body language or reaction to other participants' responses • Participants must have access to technology
	On-site (participant observation)	• Can understand phenomena in natural settings • Can retrieve additional information for better contextual understanding when observers interact with participants • Can be used to verify self-reported data	• Participants may behave differently than usual due to the presence of observers (a.k.a. the Hawthorne effect) • Time-consuming for the observers to become accepted as part of the natural settings • Costly to use a large number of spot observations through random sampling
	Video-recorded (nonparticipant observation)	• Can obtain information unobtrusively as observers are not present at the setting • No/little interruption to the participants and setting • Can be used to verify self-reported data • Can be replayed for careful analysis	• Limiting to rely on recorded information • Lacking opportunity to interact with participants to obtain contextual information • Costly to use a large number of spot observations through random sampling
Extant data review	In print	• Can reveal actual historical information[c] • Can be used to verify self-reported data[c]	• Not easy to share collected data with other members of the evaluation team (compared to electronic files) • Time-consuming to enter data into an electronic file when needed
	In electronic files	• Can share and access easily • Can readily conduct statistical analysis on some quantitative data	• Time-consuming to analyze large amounts of information • Difficult to detect errors in information without comparing it to other sources[c]
Test	Written (on site or online)	• Can reveal actual knowledge • Can be used to verify self-assessed knowledge or confidence levels	• Difficult to measure knowledge • Unreliable results potentially caused by participants' test anxiety
	Performance	• See Observation	• See Observation

[a]Common to all types of one-on-one interviews.

[b]Common to all types of focus groups.

[c]Common to all types of extant data review.

Apply Critical Multiplism

POSTEXPERIMENTAL
PERSPECTIVE

According to 19th-century positivists, who assumed that an objective reality exists, experimental research is considered to be the best approach to revealing true knowledge by establishing causality between variables. Then, in the 1960s and 1970s, applied social scientists started acknowledging the limitations associated with empirical studies and emphasizing that a single measure is not perfect and multiple measures are recommended (Cook, 1985). This postexperimental view of *multiplism* was developed by Thomas Cook and his colleagues in the 1980s (Chen, 1990). Thomas Cook (1985) describes the multiplist approach this way:

> The fundamental postulate of multiplism is that when it is not clear which of several options for question generation or method choice is "correct," all of them should be selected so as to "triangulate" on the most useful or the most likely to be true. If practical constraints prevent the use of multiple alternatives, then at least more than one should be chosen, preferably as many as span the full range of plausible alternative interpretations of what constitutes a useful question or a true answer. (p. 38)

USE MULTIPLE
METHODS THAT
COMPLEMENT
STRENGTHS AND
WEAKNESSES

Various forms of multiplism applied to evaluation practice include involving multiple stakeholders when developing evaluation questions, evaluating multiple dimensions of a phenomenon, and collecting data with multiple measurement methods. However, applying the multiplist approach to measurement methods is not about selecting *any* multiple measures. Based on the notion that individual measurement methods are imperfect, it is important to apply **critical multiplism** and use different types of measurement methods to balance their strengths and weaknesses (Shadish, 1993). Applying critical multiplism to the selection of data collection methods requires knowledge of strengths and weaknesses among different justifiable methods in order to select multiple methods that complement each other's limitations (Houts, Cook, & Shadish, 1986).

Compare strengths and weaknesses of the various data collection methods presented in Table 36. Although self-administered surveys are convenient and helpful in collecting data from a large number of people at once (strength), they do not generate in-depth information and they are notorious for low return rates (weakness). On the other hand, although it is costly to conduct interviews with many people (weakness), interviews help you uncover hidden factors that you normally cannot learn from surveys (strength). In some cases, observations may give you a better opportunity to understand the circumstances (strength) compared to interviewing people to ask them to describe the situation based on their recollection (weakness).

Triangulate Multiple Sets of Data

Application of critical multiplism to data collection in your evaluation project involves **triangulation** of the multiple sets of data you collected, during which you verify what one source tells you with what the other sources say. Different evaluation theorists have suggested slightly different methods to triangulate (e.g., Denzin, 2009; Scriven, 1991b). Largely based on their methods, we will emphasize using different sources, methods, time frames, and investigators.

- Data sources—A 360-degree performance evaluation method is an example of triangulating data obtained from multiple sources, such as the performers themselves, their supervisors, and their subordinates.

- Data collection methods—Selecting multiple data collection methods with critical multiplism in mind allows you to use different methods that complement each other.

- Data collection time frames—Repeated measures of the same issue over time can be triangulated to check reliability.

- Investigators—Multiple evaluators analyze the data and compare their analyzed results, in order to reach conclusions. Working with other evaluators as a team allows you to use this investigator triangulation method.

TRIANGULATE DIFFERENT SOURCES, METHODS, TIME FRAMES, AND INVESTIGATORS

Both critical multiplism and triangulation help increase the credibility of the conclusions that you will draw for your dimensions. For example, when investigating employees' job performance, it would be better to use both the employees' self-assessments and their supervisors' observation-based assessments, and then triangulate the multiple sources of data. Here, you are using two different *sources* (employees and their supervisors). Next, you need to decide the *type of data* you intend to gather (e.g., survey data, interview data, observation data, etc.). You may gather the same type of data from the two sources (e.g., surveys with both employees and their supervisors). Or, you may gather different types of data from the two sources (e.g., survey data from employees and interview data from their supervisors).

The point here is that you should not rely on one source or one type of data. Whenever possible and appropriate, you want to triangulate multiple sources and/ or types of data. If employees said this, what did their supervisors say about that? Employees responded to survey questions this way, but what did they say when they had an opportunity to speak out during a one-on-one interview or focus group? By connecting the dots, you get a better picture of the situation.

When triangulating multiple sets of data, you should not assume that the different sets of data will support each other. It is not always the case that data sets will converge. You should expect to find various results such as the following:

TRIANGULATED RESULTS

- The multiple sets of data support each other (consistency).

- The multiple sets of data contradict each other (contradiction).

- The multiple sets of data support each other in some parts but contradict each other in other parts (inconsistency). (Mathison, 1988)

Then, you will need to think about how to interpret the results and find ways to make use of the triangulated results. See Table 37 for examples.

TABLE 37 ● Examples of Various Results of Triangulation				
Dimension	**Data Set 1**	**Data Set 2**	**Triangulation Result**	**Interpretation and Action**
Use of new skills—How well are trainees using their new skills?	Trainees who responded to a web-based survey indicate that they are able to use their new skills to complete their job tasks.	During one-on-one structured interviews, several supervisors of trainees indicated that they observed trainees performing job tasks well.	Consistent: Both trainees and their supervisors agree that trainees are able to use new skills to complete their job tasks.	Because the trainees' supervisors closely work with the trainees, the supervisors' observation-based input coupled with the trainees' self-assessment seems sufficient to draw a credible conclusion.
Length of e-learning lesson—Is the length of the e-learning lesson adequate?	A web-based survey revealed that on average, e-learners spent 41 minutes to complete the lesson, and 20% of them felt it was too long.	The LMS's learner data show that on average, e-learners spent 27 minutes to complete the lesson (std. dev. = 3.7).	Inconsistent: There were several outliers in the survey responses, which increased the average length of completion time. Without the outliers, their self-assessed information is close to the LMS's data.	The company's e-learning guidelines recommend each lesson be completed within 30 minutes. Based on the LMS data and survey data without outliers, the length is within the company's guideline recommendation. Interview outliers to investigate their experience (e.g., any distractors).
Communication—How effectively are mentors and mentees communicating with each other?	During interviews, mentees indicated that they did not have effective communications with their mentors.	During interviews, mentors indicated that they had effective communications with their mentees regularly once a week.	Contradicting: Mentees' and mentors' perceptions differ. However, other information obtained from interviews with mentees indicates that they prefer receiving more frequent one-on-one coaching to only once-a-week meetings.	The different perceptions seem to come from different expectations. Discuss with mentors about adding one-on-one coaching opportunities to once-a-week meetings.

Select Appropriate Methods When Using the Four-Level Training Evaluation Model

If you are evaluating a training program, you may have developed dimensions by incorporating the **four levels of training evaluation**. If so, how would you collect data for each level?

To measure a Level 1 reaction, it is common to conduct self-administered surveys; however, surveys are not the only way to do so. You can also use one-on-one interviews, focus groups, or observations.

When you conduct a Level 2 evaluation (learning outcomes), a direct measure of trainees' knowledge and skill acquisition is a written test. You can also use an observation to measure acquisition of knowledge and skills in a learning context. Differentiate an actual knowledge test from a survey that asks participants how much they think they have learned from the instruction. A survey is a self-assessment rather than a direct test of knowledge. However, tests being direct measures of knowledge and skills do not mean that they are *perfect* measures of learning outcomes—for example, multiple-choice questions used in a test may have measured learners' comprehension-level knowledge but may not have fully captured learners' application skills and analytic and synthesized knowledge that they gained from instruction. So, keep in mind critical multiplism again. Considering limitations associated with written tests in measuring knowledge and skills, you may also decide to use other types of data, such as results from interviews with trainers, trainees' supervisors, or their coworkers to solicit their thoughts on trainees' increased knowledge and skills.

Similarly, a direct measure of a Level 3 evaluation (behavioral change) is an observation of behavior on the job or a review of records that indicate changed behaviors. Again, asking the trainees how much *they think* they have changed their behavior since they completed the instruction is a self-assessment rather than a direct observation of their behavioral changes. However, because observations are a costly method, practitioners often end up using a one-time observation or a small number of observations of a convenience sample (a sample chosen because they are accessible), which can result in biased results. Record reviews are not perfect measures either, considering a possibility of erroneous information recorded and limited data available. Therefore, whether you use direct or indirect measures of behavioral changes, you should consider adding other sources of data to strengthen the evidence, such as coworkers' or supervisors' assessments of the trainees' behavioral changes.

Table 38 presents examples of various data collection methods for each level of Katzell-based Kirkpatrick's four-level training evaluation framework.

DIRECT MEASURES VS. SELF-ASSESSMENTS

Select Appropriate Methods When Using Brinkerhoff's Success Case Method

Brinkerhoff's (2006) **Success Case Method** (SCM) is another evaluation method that you can incorporate in your data collection methods. He explains the SCM's data collection sequence as follows:

1. Identify success and nonsuccess cases among performers, usually by conducting a self-administered survey (the survey participants' names must be requested).

2. Conduct in-depth interviews with selected success and nonsuccess cases to learn about factors that contributed to the results.

TABLE 38 ● Examples of Various Data Collection Methods for Four Levels of Training Evaluation				
Level Method	1. Reaction	2. Learning	3. Behavioral Change	4. Results
Self-administered surveys	• Survey trainees' reaction (a.k.a. smiley sheet) at the end of a program. • Survey trainers about their experience with trainees.	• Survey trainees to self-assess their learning. • Survey trainers about their experience with trainees.	• Survey trainees to self-assess their behavioral change. • Survey trainees' coworkers or supervisors about their experience with trainees.	• Survey trainees and other stakeholders, and have them self-assess organizational results. • Survey customers about quality of organizational service provided to them.
Interviews and focus groups	• Interview trainees individually or as a group. • Interview trainers about their experience with trainees.	• Interview trainees to self-assess their learning. • Interview trainers, coworkers, or supervisors about their experience with trainees.	• Interview trainees to self-assess their behavioral change. • Interview trainees' coworkers or supervisors about their experience with trainees.	• Interview trainees and other stakeholders, and have them self-assess organizational results. • Interview customers about quality of organizational service provided to them.
Observations (including performance tests via observations)	• Observe trainees' reaction during the program (participant observation).	• Observe trainees' new knowledge and skills during the learning process.	• Observe trainees' on-the-job behaviors (pre vs. post). • Compare trainees' on-the-job behaviors to those of people who did not complete the training.	• Observe organizational results such as customers' reactions.
Extant data reviews	• Review existing data that documented trainees' thoughts about the program quality.	• Review existing data that documented trainees' learning outcomes.	• Review existing data that documented trainees' job performance.	• Review existing data that documented organizational results. • Compare organizational results obtained from the group that participated in training with results obtained from a group that did not participate in training.

Level / Method	1. Reaction	2. Learning	3. Behavioral Change	4. Results
Written tests	–	• Test trainees' new knowledge at the end of training and compare with pretraining knowledge. • Compare test results obtained from trainees to the test results obtained from people who did not complete the training.	–	–

First, to identify success and nonsuccess cases among performers, you will conduct a survey with performers. Be aware that you cannot use an anonymous survey when using the SCM. You need to ask for respondents' names in the survey, in order to identify success and nonsuccess cases.

Success/nonsuccess cases are determined based on Level 3 behavioral change (i.e., "I have or have not tried the new knowledge/skills") and Level 4 organizational results (i.e., "I have or have not produced desirable results"), which are aligned with the critical actions and key results categories in the training impact model, respectively.

To design SCM survey questions, write a statement about performing a task, likely from the critical action category of a training impact model; for example, "Apply the new sales techniques." Then, develop a response scale that reflects the key results category, such as the following, suggested in Brinkerhoff's (2006) book, *Telling Training's Story*:

1. Tried this and achieved a concrete and worthwhile result
2. Tried this, but have not noticed any results
3. Tried this, but did not work
4. Have not tried this yet (p. 93)

Because the survey results are self-assessed information, it would be better if you can also gather data from other sources such as supervisors' assessments or actual performance records to verify their self-assessment. Instead of using a survey, you may also select success/nonsuccess cases by reviewing performance records (e.g., sales records, document errors, and customer satisfaction levels).

The unit of analysis for selecting success and nonsuccess cases does not always have to be trainees. It could be branch offices. For example, when evaluating a sales training provided to multiple branches of a bank, you could identify branch offices

SURVEY IDENTIFYING SUCCESS & NONSUCCESS CASES BASED ON LEVEL 3 AND LEVEL 4

that increased sales the most versus the least as the success and nonsuccess cases (R. Brinkerhoff, personal communication, December 17, 2017).

After you identify success and nonsuccess cases, you will interview success and nonsuccess cases. The contributing factors that you may find from using the SCM's follow-up interviews could fall into various types of environmental and personal factors (per Gilbert's behavior engineering model).

INTERVIEWS
SHOWING
ENVIRONMENTAL
AND PERSONAL
FACTORS

For example, interviews with success cases may reveal that they thought that not only the training program itself but also the job aids provided after the training program helped them perform better (environmental factor), or that high levels of job commitment helped them engage during the training program and transfer their new skills on the job (personal factor). Or, nonsuccess cases may reveal that managerial support was lacking and they did not receive help with their skill transfer (environmental factor).

Most of these findings from the interviews indicate the quality of *means*. It is also possible to learn about other unintended outcomes of the program from interviews with success and nonsuccess cases (e.g., "When I used the new techniques I learned from the training program, I did not necessarily reduce errors, but it took me less time to complete the task").

In other words, you will use the SCM survey to measure critical actions and/or key results (end results) related dimensions and conduct the SCM interviews with success and nonsuccess cases to measure resources, activities, and program capabilities related dimensions and potentially to reveal unintended, positive or negative outcomes. This is summarized in Table 39.

TABLE 39 ● How the SCM's Survey and Interviews Can Be Used as Part of Data Collection Methods for Different Dimensions

Dimension	Category	Data Source
1. **Training materials:** How well are the training materials designed to help the employees practice new skills?	Resources Activities Program Capabilities	SCM interviews
2. **Managerial support:** How much incentive and support from management did the employees receive for using new skills?	Activities	SCM interviews
3. **On-the-job application:** How well did the employees use their newly learned skills on the job?	Critical Actions (Level 3)	SCM survey
4. **Customers' reaction:** How did the customers react to the new approach?	Key Results (Level 4)	SCM survey
5. **Unintended positive or negative outcomes:** What other unintended outcomes did the employees experience from using their new skills?	Program Capabilities (Level 2) Critical Actions Key Results	SCM interviews

When deciding whether to use the SCM or not, please remember that just because you are using a survey and follow-up interviews does not mean that you are using the SCM. The SCM's data collection techniques include conducting a survey where participants indicate their names, followed by interviews with success or nonsuccess cases identified based on the survey data.

Review an Example of Data Collection Methods

What would an appropriate data collection plan for an evaluation project look like? Table 40 presents a simple example of a data collection plan for conducting a goal-based summative evaluation of an online master's degree program. Four dimensions are investigated: (1) curriculum design, (2) online learning environment, (3) students' professional accomplishments, and (4) graduation rate.

When describing data collection methods, think about the sources of data and how you will collect data from the sources. When you describe human sources, please be specific about who they are (e.g., titles) and how many of them you will use as informants. Add time frame information when appropriate. For example, in Table 40, to investigate Dimension 2 (online learning environment), you plan on gathering data via telephone interviews not only from six full-time faculty members and 50% of part-time faculty members, but also via a web-based survey from current students and alumni who took online courses using the new LMS between fall 2016 and fall 2018.

BE SPECIFIC WHEN DESCRIBING DATA COLLECTION METHODS

Here are more examples of data source descriptions:

- Survey trainees who completed the program between January 2018 and March 2018 (n = approximately 200)

- Observe 10 randomly selected employees during their calls

- Interview employees' supervisors (n = 6)

- Review customers' feedback collected during 2017

- Test usability of the system with five operators

Be aware that the more dimensions you have, the more complicated the overall data collection methods will be. If this is your first comprehensive evaluation project, think about an appropriate number of dimensions that you can manage with the resources available. If you do not have sufficient resources, it is better to investigate a small number of dimensions with multiple data collection methods for each dimension (so you can apply critical multiplism and triangulation in each dimension) than investigating a large number of dimensions with only a single data collection method for each dimension.

TABLE 40 ● Example A: Four Dimensions With Multiple Data Collection Methods

Dimension, PLM, and IW	Data Collection Method	Instrument to Be Developed	Rationale for Using Multiple Sets of Data (Critical Multiplism and Triangulation)
1. **Curriculum design**—How well is the curriculum designed to support industry expectations and standards?	1-1. Record review of the curriculum by evaluators—all required courses and current elective courses will be reviewed.	1-1. Document review checklist	If data collection is based only on the documented materials, the evaluators may not be able to fully recognize exactly how the department (individual faculty members) intended to meet the industry expectations and standards. This detailed information is obtained from the semi-structured telephone interviews with the faculty members.
PLM: Resources and Activities IW: Very important	1-2. Interview in person with six full-time faculty members and via telephone with at least 50% of current part-time faculty members (five or more)	1-2. Semi-structured telephone interview instrument for faculty, including an interview solicitation email message, an informed consent form, and interview questions	
2. **Online learning environment**—Does the online delivery technology provide a positive learning environment?	2-1. Web-based survey with current students and alumni who took online courses via the new LMS between fall 2016 and fall 2018	2-1. Structured survey questionnaire uploaded to a web-based survey system and a survey invitation email message	Current and former students' inputs on this dimension are triangulated with the faculty members' inputs (e.g., the type of learning experiences the faculty members intended to provide to students and the ways the students have experienced the environment). A web-based survey is efficient to reach out to a large number of students; interviews help reveal detailed information from faculty members (the course developers).
PLM: Resources and Activities IW: Somewhat important	2-2. Interview in person with six full-time faculty members and via telephone with at least 50% of current part-time faculty members (five or more)	Included in 1-2 (1-2, 2-2, and 3-3 are completed in the same interviews)	
3. **Students' professional accomplishments**—How does the program help students achieve professional accomplishments such as landing a new job, being promoted, receiving awards, and presenting or publishing papers?	3-1. Record review by evaluators (dept. record provided by the department); compare with other programs' student accomplishments.	3-1. Document review checklist	The record review is a direct measure of this dimension. However, in-depth interviews with success/nonsuccess cases of students and faculty members will provide much more information about the process that produced their accomplishments, including:

Dimension, PLM, and IW	Data Collection Method	Instrument to Be Developed	Rationale for Using Multiple Sets of Data (Critical Multiplism and Triangulation)
PLM: Outcomes IW: Very important	3-2. In-depth interview via telephone (due to different locations) with selected students (success cases vs. nonsuccess cases—about five cases each)	3-2. Semi-structured telephone interview instrument for students, including an interview solicitation email message, an informed consent form, and interview questions	• motivators and barriers during the process, and • tangible/intangible, and short-term/long-term benefits associated with each type of accomplishments.
	3-3. Interview in person with six full-time faculty members	Included in 1-2	
4. **Graduation rate**—What is the program's 3-year graduation rate? How does it compare to the university's expectations? PLM: Impact IW: Extremely important	4-1. Record review by evaluators (record provided by the department), compared to the university expectations and other available data from other universities	4-1. Document review checklist	In addition to reviewing the current graduation record (direct measure), interviews with the dean, department chair, and associate program developer will provide a better understanding of the departmental goals and strategies used, the university's expectations, and the trends during the recent past years.
	4-2. Interview in person with the dean, dept. chair, and associate program developer	4-2. Semi-structured telephone interview instrument for the dean, department chair, and associate program developer, including an interview solicitation email message, an informed consent form, and interview questions	

In summary, the following instruments need to be developed:

- Three document review checklists
- One web-based structured survey questionnaire
- Three semi-structured telephone interview instruments for three different groups

IW, Importance weighting; *PLM*, program logic model.

Use an Iterative Design Approach

After you entered the planning phase of your evaluation project, you followed a step-by-step procedure to develop a program logic model and determined a set of dimensions and degrees of importance weighting among dimensions. Now, you are designing data collection methods. Following a systematic procedure does not mean that you complete each step only once. While following the systematic procedure of evaluation planning, you are likely to use an **iterative design approach**.

As you learn more about your evaluation project, you will likely revisit previous steps and modify your plan with new information. For example, when finalizing your data collection methods, you want to revisit several areas.

- Double-check with your stakeholders about the initially determined list of dimensions and the degrees of importance weighting among the dimensions. Adjust the dimensions and importance weighting if necessary.

- Investigate each dimension with comprehensive data collection methods that allow you to draw credible conclusions about the quality of the dimension. If you receive pushback from your stakeholders about your plan to use certain data collection methods, help them understand how necessary and critical it is to have access to appropriate types of information in order to produce useful findings from the evaluation project.

- Check again if similar dimensions can be combined into one dimension. If you designed multiple dimensions with exactly the same data collection methods, think about whether the multiple dimensions are distinct dimensions or similar enough to be combined into one dimension.

- Check if you selected dimensions that are so narrowly focused that they are actually measurement questions rather than dimensions. This issue is somewhat related to combining multiple similar dimensions into one dimension. For example, review the following dimensions:

  - Ease of use: How easy is it to use the job aid?
  - Up to date: Is the job aid up to date?
  - Use of images: How effective are the images inserted in the job aid?

  These are measurement questions rather than dimensional questions. You can combine these three aspects into a general dimension called job aid design (How well is the job aid designed?) and repurpose the original three questions as survey or interview questions to measure the quality of the job aid design.

Assess Feasibility and Risk Factors Again

During the evaluation planning phase, you should continue to assess feasibility and risk factors for your evaluation project. Whether you are conducting an evaluation as an internal evaluator or an external evaluator, you understand that not all requested evaluation projects are feasible and that virtually all evaluation projects come with some risk factors. Earlier, the following broad categories were suggested for assessing feasibility of an evaluation project:

1. Maturity of the evaluand

2. Scope of the evaluation

3. Support for the evaluation

4. Ethical concerns for the evaluation

5. Resources for the evaluation

During the first couple of steps of your evaluation project (the identification phase), you gained a good understanding of the project feasibility in terms of the maturity of the evaluand and the scope of the evaluation. Then, while determining evaluation methodology (the planning phase), you should continue to assess the level of organizational support, ethical concerns, and resources for the evaluation.

Support for the evaluation—You may find out that despite the client's intent to conduct an evaluation, there is a lack of stakeholder interest and support. You may also find out that the client lacks availability to continue effective communication. These issues can jeopardize successful completion of the project.

Ethical concerns—You may discover ethical concerns regarding the evaluation project such as the following:

CONTINUE TO CHECK ORGANIZATIONAL SUPPORT, ETHICS, AND RESOURCES

- Conflicts of interest

- The organization's hidden motives for conducting the evaluation

- The organization's unethical data collection practice

- Potential misuse of the evaluation data causing harm to stakeholders

If such ethical issues arise, you need to assess if you will be able to successfully resolve the issues and make a decision as to whether you should or should not continue with the evaluation project.

Evaluation resources—Although you know which methodology you should use to generate useful information, you may recognize a lack of time and budget to carry out the desirable evaluation methodology. For example, the evaluation project requires a comprehensive benchmarking study, but there is not enough time and money to conduct such a study. In some cases, it may be possible to use an alternative evaluation methodology to a certain extent. In other cases, using an alternative methodology could dramatically reduce the quality of the evaluation results to the point where it may be better to forgo the project.

A related issue is the evaluator's knowledge, skills, and attitudes for completing the evaluation project. You as an evaluator may realize that you lack experience in performing specific evaluation methodology that is required for the project (e.g., a need to conduct an experimental study for a summative evaluation). Again, in some cases, it is possible to use an alternative evaluation methodology without sacrificing the quality of the project too much. In other cases, it might jeopardize the success of the project to such a degree that it would be better to pass on the opportunity. However, this issue can be resolved by completing the evaluation project with a team of evaluators who possess different sets of knowledge and skills.

When handling a large-scale project, it may be helpful to complete it in several phases and to propose each phase of evaluation separately. Doing so not only helps you better manage unpredictable factors during the lengthy duration of an entire project, but it also allows you to work with different personnel (team members) who possess appropriate types of expertise to complete each phase of the project.

Based on the project feasibility and risk factor assessments, you may find a significant lack of readiness on the part of the organization to implement the proposed evaluation plan. For example, you may find out that because of the recent merger and layoffs, it would be extremely difficult for the employees who completed the program to become informants for your evaluation and that your client's workload has substantially increased, which is negatively affecting her or his availability to support the evaluation project. That is, the level of damage to the project could be detrimental or substantial and the likelihood of its happening may be likely (see Table 13. A Risk Assessment Matrix as an example). In such cases, you and your client will need to discuss and make a decision as to whether it is still feasible to continue the project or whether it would be better to delay or forgo it.

Conduct Formative Meta-Evaluations

To increase credibility of your evaluation process and conclusions, you are advised to conduct an evaluation of the quality of your own evaluation project. An evaluation of an evaluation is called a **meta-evaluation** (Scriven, 2005). The Joint Committee on Standards for Educational Evaluation (JCSEE) suggests that you conduct internal and external meta-evaluations (see Evaluation Accountability Standards in the JCSEE at http://www.jcsee.org/program-evaluation-standards-statements).

A meta-evaluation is often listed as a step to be completed after the evaluation has been completed to assess how well the evaluation has been conducted, which implies a summative purpose. However, meta-evaluations can be conducted formatively as well as summatively (Scriven, 1991b). In fact, it would be helpful for novice evaluators to conduct a series of formative meta-evaluations to improve the quality of the evaluation design and execution process during their project. In this book, you are advised to conduct both formative and summative meta-evaluations.

For example, you should conduct internal and external formative meta-evaluations while finalizing the data collection methods to be used in your evaluation project. The formative meta-evaluations will help you ensure that you select a feasible evaluation project, collect sufficient information to design the overall evaluation methodology, and select appropriate data collection methods to answer the overall evaluation questions.

CONDUCT INTERNAL AND EXTERNAL META-EVALUATIONS

An *internal* meta-evaluation can be conducted by the evaluators themselves (Scriven, 1991b) or by someone internal to the organization that hosts the evaluand (Yarbrough, Shulha, Hopson, & Caruthers, 2011). You should conduct an internal formative meta-evaluation by reflecting on whether you followed appropriate steps during the project and double-checking if sufficient data sources are used for each dimension. You may also evaluate your own evaluation against professional evaluation standards such as the JCSEE's (2017) program evaluation standards or the American Evaluation Association's (2004) guiding principles for evaluators. Comparing your evaluation practice against professional standards is another type of ethical conduct of evaluators.

You may also conduct an *external* formative meta-evaluation by having an evaluation expert review your evaluation plan (Davidson, 2005). Before doing so, you want to check with the client about sharing evaluation-related information with an external meta-evaluator, especially if you signed a nondisclosure agreement. The expert should be familiar with systematic, systemic, and ethical conduct of evaluation, and examine appropriateness of the evaluation purpose and the scope of your evaluation plan. You will revise your evaluation plan based on the expert's feedback and finalize all information to be included in your evaluation proposal.

Chapter Summary

Determine data collection methods (Step 6):

- There are different types of evaluation design. Experimental/quasi-experimental and descriptive case study types are often used in program evaluations.

- Evaluators need to select an appropriate evaluation design for each dimension:
  - Use an experimental/quasi-experimental design with a randomly selected sample to assert a cause-and-effect relationship among variables using inferential statistics.
  - Use a descriptive case study design with a purposively selected sample to explain observed phenomena by triangulating multiple data sets (quantitative and/or qualitative).

- There are different types of data collection methods—self-administered survey, interview, focus group, observation, extant data review, and test.

- Evaluators should select data collection methods that directly measure the study variables and appropriately answer the individual dimensional evaluation questions whenever possible.
  - When using the four-level training evaluation framework, a direct way to measure Level 2 learning outcomes is to actually test learners' knowledge. A survey of learners' confidence in their knowledge is an indirect, and often unreliable, measurement.
  - When using the Success Case Method, it is appropriate to use a survey questionnaire to have performers self-assess their performance levels. As an alternative, it is also appropriate to review extant data showing the records of performance levels.

- Even direct sources of data may contain incomplete or erroneous information; thus, evaluators should use multiple data sources and apply critical multiplism and triangulation methods to increase credibility of conclusions.

- Evaluators should use an iterative design approach during the evaluation process; evaluators should revisit previous evaluation steps and modify the plan as needed, based on new information they have uncovered.

- Evaluators should continue to check feasibility and risk factors of their evaluation plan.

- Evaluators should conduct internal and external formative meta-evaluations to ensure the quality of the evaluation plan.

Chapter Discussion

1. Triangulation methods

You and your evaluation team members are selecting multiple data collection methods, so you can triangulate the data from the multiple sources. Below are several options you put on the table. Which ones are reasonable triangulation methods and why? If one of them is not a reasonable triangulation method, why do you think so?

a. Using interview data collected from the employees who completed the program and their supervisors

b. Using data collected from three different observers who observed trainees' work performance

c. Using data collected from a web-based survey conducted with 30 different trainees who completed the program

2. Evaluation dimensions with the four-level training evaluation framework in mind

A consulting company is delivering a three-hour training program to its 20 employees (consultants) to teach them how to use new consulting techniques. An intern, Jane, was asked to conduct an evaluation of this training program. To design the evaluation, Jane has been working with her internship supervisor and other stakeholders, including the program curriculum developer, the trainer, and some of the training participants.

   Jane is proposing to her internship supervisor to include three dimensions and data collection methods (time frame), as shown in Table 41. The supervisor, who is familiar with Katzell-based Kirkpatrick's evaluation model, asks Jane if this proposed evaluation plan includes an evaluation of a Level 3 outcome. What should Jane's answer to the supervisor be?

TABLE 41 ● Identify Level 3 Evaluation Based on Dimensions and Data Collection Methods	
Dimension and Evaluation Question	**Data Collection Method (Time Frame)**
1. Training methods—Do trainees perceive that the training methods such as role play and peer evaluation used during the training session were appropriate for learning the new consulting techniques?	• Survey 20 trainees (at the end of training). • Interview the instructional designer and the trainer (after training, the same day).
2. Task confidence—As a result of the training program, how confident do the trainees feel in using the new consulting techniques?	• Survey 20 trainees (at the end of training). • Interview the trainer (after training, the same day).
3. Value expectation—Upon completion of the training program, how much do the trainees value the new consulting techniques in terms of improving their communication with clients?	• Survey 20 trainees (at the end of training). • Interview five most confident and five least confident trainees who are selected based on the survey results (after training, the same day).

Now, Your Turn—Determine Data Collection Methods

Develop data collection methods for your evaluation project by using Table B-5 in Appendix B (Evaluation Development Worksheets) as a template. Refer to Table 40 for an example of a table summarizing data collection methods. Table 42 is another example.

While developing data collection methods, revise the dimensions, dimensional evaluation questions, and categories in your program logic model (or training impact model) as needed.

When describing data collection methods, make sure to provide specific information, including the following:

- Type of data collection methods

- Number of participants, if interviews or surveys are used

- Source of information, if extant data reviews are used

- Observation context and observers, if observations are used

Describe the rationale for using multiple sets of data in terms of critical multiplism and triangulation techniques. This column helps you double-check if you are using the best options. You may or may not present this information to your client.

Before finalizing your data collection methods, check with your client about feasibility of your plan and if you need to get approval from someone other than the client.

Assess and document feasibility and risk factors for completing the project again, based on additional information that you have gathered since you wrote the statement of work (SOW).

After you conduct your own formative meta-evaluation on your data collection plan, and before you finalize your data collection methods, ask an evaluation expert to review and provide feedback.

TABLE 42 ● An Example Worksheet for Step 6: Determine Data Collection Methods (for a New Tech Support Ticketing and Tracking System)			
Dimension, PLM, and IW	**Data Collection Method**	**Instrument to Be Developed**	**Rationale for Using Multiple Sets of Data (Critical Multiplism and Triangulation)**
1. **User-friendliness of system interface**—How user-friendly is the system interface? Which parts need job aids? PLM: Resources IW: Important	1-1. Observe five users while using the system, using a think-aloud method.	1-1. Observation solicitation email message, informed consent form, and observation checklist	Conducting usability testing with actual users is a direct way to measure user-friendliness of the system interface. Additional information can be obtained from the tech support specialists and software engineer regarding their experience in using and supporting users. The combination of the two sources will help identify areas that need more support such as providing clearly written job aids to users.
	1-2. Conduct face-to-face interviews with three technical support specialists and a software engineer.	1-2. Interview solicitation email message, informed consent form, and semi-structured interview questions	

(Continued)

TABLE 42 ● (Continued)

Dimension, PLM, and IW	Data Collection Method	Instrument to Be Developed	Rationale for Using Multiple Sets of Data (Critical Multiplism and Triangulation)
2. **Efficiency in ticketing and tracking process**—How efficiently are the ticketing and tracking process handled? Which steps are delayed, and for what reasons? PLM: Activities IW: Most important	2-1. Observe three technical support specialists while using the system, using a think-aloud method.	2-1. Observation solicitation email message, informed consent form, and observation checklist	It is important to gather data from both tech support staff and users to understand the process that they need to go through while using the system. Their data will be compared with the system log.
	2-2. Conduct face-to-face interviews with three technical support specialists and a software engineer.	Included in 1-2	
	2-3. Conduct face-to-face or telephone interviews with 7 to 10 users.	2-3. Interview solicitation email message, informed consent form, and semi-structured interview questions	
	2-4. Review system logs.	2-4. Document review checklist	
3. **User satisfaction**—How satisfied are the users with the tech support they received via the system? PLM: Outcomes IW: Very important	3-1. Conduct a web-based survey with all users.	3-1. Email solicitation message, and an anonymous semi-structured web-based survey instrument	The web-based survey with all users will provide users' overall reaction to the system. Since a low survey return rate is expected, additional interviews with selected users will provide information about factors that influence their satisfaction. Data obtained from the users will be compared with data obtained from interviews with tech support staff.
	3-2. Conduct face-to-face or telephone interviews with 7 to 10 users.	Included in 2-3	
	3-3. Conduct face-to-face interviews with three technical support specialists.	Included in 1-2	

IW, Importance weighting; *PLM*, program logic model.

8

Write an Evaluation Proposal and Get Approval

Recall that an evaluation project consists of identification, planning, and implementation phases. You are at the end of the planning phase now. During the planning phase, you worked closely with your client and other stakeholders to gather information necessary to develop your evaluation methodology. Now you need to propose your evaluation implementation plan and get approval from the client before you implement it.

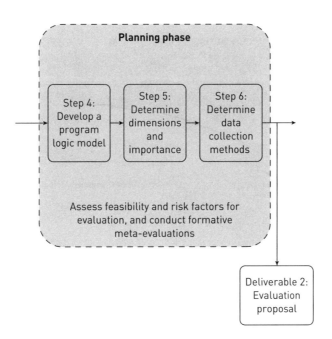

Determine Sections to Be Included in an Evaluation Proposal

There are different formats you can use for writing an evaluation proposal and a final report. One way is to use the sections presented in Table 43. This format is designed to minimize your time and effort during your evaluation project, by writing your evaluation proposal in a way that the content will be reused in your final report. Then, while writing your final report, you will make minor revisions to the evaluation plan and complete the remaining sections.

Table 44 provides specific information about what is expected in each section of an evaluation proposal. To improve the flow of information, you may present some information in a different section. Use your best judgment.

The overall structure of the sections to be included in the evaluation proposal, as shown in Table 44, is generic enough to support the use of various evaluation frameworks, including the following:

A GENERIC STRUCTURE TO INCORPORATE VARIOUS EVALUATION FRAMEWORKS

- Four levels of training evaluation (Katzell, as cited in Kirkpatrick, 1956; Kirkpatrick, 1996a)

- Program logic model (W. K. Kellogg Foundation, 2004)

- Utilization-focused evaluation approach (Patton, 2008)

- Key Evaluation Checklist (Scriven, 2013)

- Success Case Method (Brinkerhoff, 2006)

TABLE 43 ● Sections to Be Included in an Evaluation Proposal and Final Report	
Evaluation Proposal	**Final Report**
1. Organization	1. Organization
2. Program and Stakeholders	2. Program and Stakeholders
3. Evaluation Methodology	3. Evaluation Methodology
4. Feasibility and Risk Factors	4. Feasibility and Risk Factors
	5. Evaluation Results
	6. Conclusions
	7. Meta-Evaluations and Limitations
	8. Reporting
References	
Appendices	

TABLE 44 ● Information to Be Presented in an Evaluation Proposal	
Section	**Content**
1. Organization	• Present the organization's background information, such as its location and history. • Explain the needs that caused the organization to develop and implement the program. • Present other supporting information, if any, in an appendix.
2. Program and stakeholders	• Provide a detailed description of the program so that readers have a good understanding about how the program operates. Do not assume that your evaluation client is the only reader of the evaluation proposal. The document can be accessed by others, during or after the evaluation project, who may or may not be familiar with the program. • Present any figures or tables that help readers better understand the program (e.g., a room setting, a flowchart of a work process, or a workshop procedure). • List different categories of stakeholders (upstream stakeholders, direct impactees, and indirect impactees) with descriptive information to help readers understand how the stakeholders belong to each category. Describe the size of each stakeholder group, which helps readers understand the scope of the program and the evaluation project. • Present a program logic model or training impact model. • Present other supporting information, if any, in an appendix (e.g., a sample lesson plan).
3. Evaluation methodology	• State the purpose of the evaluation. Clearly describe the intended users and their intended use of evaluation findings. • Describe the type of evaluation (e.g., formative or summative, and goal-based or goal-free) and evaluation frameworks you applied. • Present a list of dimensions to be investigated along with specific dimensional evaluation questions, and explain how you determined the dimensions and their importance weighting values (i.e., whom you involved during the decision and how you facilitated the decision process). • Describe the overall data collection procedure and timeline. • Present specific and feasible data collection methods in a table format, in either this section or an appendix.
4. Feasibility and risk factors	• Describe feasibility of the evaluation implementation phase, regarding the scope of the project, the expected timeline for completion, and other relevant factors. • Assess risk factors based on the degrees of damage to the project and its likelihood, and describe how you plan to manage the risk factors.
References	• List references that you cited in the document.
Appendices	• Present appendices, as needed. • Make sure to refer to each appendix in your descriptions in the main sections.

Review a Sample Evaluation Proposal

The following section provides a sample evaluation proposal for a hypothetical situation in which a team of students is conducting a formative evaluation of a leadership skills training program as a class project.

A FORMATIVE EVALUATION OF TAMRACK LEADERSHIP SKILLS TRAINING PROGRAM

Evaluation Team: Jane Doe, John Doe, and Janie Doe

March 2019

Table of Contents

1. Tamrack, Inc.

Tamrack, Inc. (a pseudonym) provides cleaning supplies to hospitals and nursing homes. The company was founded in 2001, and it recently expanded its business from a regional company to a national corporation. In addition to its headquarters located in Boise, Idaho, the company now has branches across 10 states of the United States.

The recent expansion of the business created an immediate need for providing more structured training to its leaders to improve their competencies in leadership. A mid-tier management training program already exists in the company. However, it was designed with generic information, and it is no longer helpful for the mid-tier managers of this fast-expanding company, which requires a lot of cross-branch operations and virtual teamwork.

The Learning and Performance Solutions (LPS) department, located in the company headquarters, was in charge of revising the existing mid-tier management training program and deploying a new Leadership Skills Training Program at all branches. The growing needs for providing training to an increasing number of employees at multiple branches has been a challenge for the LPS department. Although the company has considered incorporating e-learning strategies into their training solutions, the current limited resources prohibit the LPS department from implementing them. The LPS department has used several training programs purchased from vendors. However, the LPS department realized that it would be best to develop the new Leadership Skills Training Program in-house, since the department can design the instruction tailored to the specific and constantly changing needs of the employees and the company.

The LPS department developed the new Leadership Skills Training Program for mid-tier managers using data from multiple sources, including the annual performance review, annual employee engagement survey data, and interviews with a sample of mid-tier managers and their direct reports. The data helped the LPS department identify gaps between desired and actual competencies of mid-tier managers and design the training program to close those gaps.

The Leadership Skills Training Program was launched in January 2019. During the first two months, the program was delivered to 60 participants at 2 of the 10 company sites. The program is scheduled to be delivered at the remaining sites by the end of 2019. Informal feedback received from the participants has been positive. In March 2019, Mr. Berg,[1] the LPS director, requested the evaluation team to conduct a formal evaluation of the Leadership Skills Training Program. He serves as the client for this evaluation.

2. Leadership Skills Program and Stakeholders

2.1. Instructor-Led Leadership Skills Training Program

The leadership skills program is an instructor-led, three half-day, face-to-face training program that teaches participants about different leadership styles and coaching skills. The program is designed with

---

[1]All personnel names presented in this document are pseudonyms.

some lecture-style components followed by interactive group activities. The program's daily activities are outlined in Table 1.

In addition to the main goal of helping participants increase their knowledge, skills, and attitudes about effective leadership skills, another intended outcome of the Leadership Skills Training Program is to help participants develop a network for sharing information such as lessons learned and provide support for handling challenges and conflicts that may arise in the workplace.

Through communication with the client, the evaluation team helped develop a training impact model for the Leadership Skills Training Program. Table 2 is the training impact model (TIM), outlining the means and end results of the program.

- Resources: Facilities, tools, materials, data, personnel, etc. that the program will use
- Activities: Process that the program will execute
- Program Capabilities: Knowledge, skills, and attitudes that participants will acquire
- Critical Actions: Job-specific behaviors that participants will exhibit
- Key Results: Job-specific outcomes that participants will leave behind as a result of their job behaviors
- Business Goals: Organizational outcomes to which the program will contribute

2.2. Stakeholders

There are three types of stakeholders for the Leadership Skills Training Program.

Upstream Stakeholders

Several stakeholders played a role in deciding to provide a new Leadership Skills Training Program and performing the actual design, development, and delivery of the program. The key upstream stakeholders are the following:

- Ms. Gibson, the human resources (HR) director
- Mr. Berg, the LPS director
- Three instructional designers
- Two trainers

TABLE 1 ● Daily Activities of the Leadership Skills Training Program		
Day 1	**Day 2**	**Day 3**
• Introduction • Tamrack Leadership Model • Different leadership styles—When/where, what, why, and how • Group activities—Effective leadership and communication	• Coaching—What is effective coaching, and how do you know when it is effective? • Coaching models • Effective communication • Group activities—Role-play on active listening	• Performance evaluation methods • 360-degree feedback • Ways to increase employee engagement • Group activities—Action plan for coaching and performance evaluation

(Continued)

(Continued)

TABLE 2 ● Leadership Skills Training Impact Model					
Resources	**Activities**	**Program Capabilities**	**Critical Actions**	**Key Results**	**Business Goals**
By using the following resources: • Organizational goals • Customer feedback • Annual engagement survey data obtained from different branches • Mid-tier managers and their direct reports • Director of the Learning and Performance Solutions Department • Instructional designers • Trainers • Training facility • Materials of the existing Leadership Skills Training Program • New training resources about different leadership styles and coaching models	By completing the following steps: • Review existing Leadership Skills Training Programs • Conduct performance gap analysis and learner analysis with mid-tier leaders and their direct reports • Develop a new leadership training program to close the mid-tier leaders' performance gap • Enroll mid-tier leaders into the program • Conduct Levels 1 and 2 evaluations at the end of program • Conduct Level 3 evaluation 3 months after program • Conduct Level 4 evaluation 6 months after program	Mid-tier managers should acquire: • Knowledge of Tamrack Leadership Model • Knowledge of different leadership styles • Knowledge of the importance of using different leadership styles for different purposes • Knowledge of types of listening (the difference between active and inactive listening) • Skills required for active listening • Skills of effective coaching • Willingness to make personal bonds with employees • Willingness to provide feedback	Mid-tier managers should be able to perform the following tasks: • Diagnose work situations where leadership is needed • Use an appropriate leadership style depending on the context • Provide effective strategies to handle conflict • Provide timely coaching to employees • Use strategies that facilitate collaboration among employees	Mid-tier managers' work performance should produce the following observable on-the-job results: • Positive relationships between leaders and direct reports • Effective change and conflict management results • Improved team capacity • Organizational culture where leaders network, share new knowledge, and apply new shared knowledge with one other	The training program will contribute to achieving the following organizational goals: • Provide consistent and excellent services to customers • Increase the company revenue • Become a sustainable organization • Make a transition from national operations to international operations

Direct Impactees

The past and future participants of the Leadership Skills Training Program are the direct impactees of the program. They are all mid-tier management level employees in 10 branches.

- At the time of writing this proposal, 60 managers have completed the program.
- About 200 managers will complete it within the next few months.
- Thus, a total of approximately 260 managers fall into this direct recipients group.

Indirect Impactees

Success or failure of the Leadership Skills Training Program would have an impact on not only the immediate recipients of the program (mid-tier managers), but also other groups of people.

- Direct reports
- Employee colleagues of impacted direct reports
- External customers who interact with impacted managers, impacted direct reports, and impacted colleagues

The primary indirect impactees of the program are direct reports of the mid-tier managers who complete the program. This includes the approximately 1,000 employees.

The secondary indirect impactees of the program are approximately 4,500 employees who closely interact with the direct reports of the managers who complete the program.

External customers will also be affected by the quality of the products that they receive, which is indirectly impacted by the organizational leadership and culture that this leadership training program aims at improving.

3. Evaluation Methodology

3.1. Evaluation Purpose and Type

Based on discussions with Mr. Berg (the evaluation client), Ms. Swanson (an instructional designer), and Ms. Kennedy (a trainer), the evaluation team learned that their primary intent for conducting this evaluation is to assess areas for improvements in the program. The three stakeholders want the evaluation team to assist the LPS department in revising the program and changing the relevant support system for the remaining sites. Thus, it was decided to conduct a formative evaluation of the Leadership Skills Training Program, with the overall evaluation purpose being to *find areas of the Leadership Skills Training Program and its support system that need to be improved in order to produce more positive outcomes.*

This formative evaluation aims at assessing how well the program is designed to have a positive impact on improving mid-tier managers' knowledge of, skills for, and attitudes toward using effective leadership to help achieve organizational goals. Therefore, it is a goal-based evaluation, focusing on the program's worth. The evaluation results will be used to make necessary improvements to close gaps in expected outcomes.

3.2. Evaluation Dimensions, Questions, and Importance Weighting

Through initial communication with the client (Mr. Berg) and based on the training impact model for the Leadership Skills Training Program (see Table 2 in the previous section), the evaluation team began to develop a list of specific program dimensions to investigate. Two additional upstream stakeholders (an instructional designer and a trainer) reviewed and provided their input on the draft list of dimensions via email.

Based on the three key stakeholders' input, the evaluation team proposed several dimensions and met with the three stakeholders to finalize key dimensions to investigate. During the meeting, the stakeholders

(Continued)

(Continued)

and the evaluation team consulted the program's training impact model together. They finally agreed on investigating four dimensions of the program. Once the dimensions were established, the evaluation team discussed with the three key stakeholders how they intended to make use of the evaluation findings. Based on their input, the evaluation team helped them identify the relative degrees of importance weighting (IW) among the dimensions. Results are shown below (also see the first column of Table 3):

1. Curriculum alignment (Critical)
2. Program implementation (Important)
3. Leadership application (Very important)
4. Leaders' network (Important)

3.3. Data Collection Procedure and Methods

As the overall approach to this evaluation, the evaluation team is following Chyung's (2019) 10-step evaluation procedure. The 10-step procedure assists the evaluation team to design an evaluation based on the stakeholders' needs and the stakeholders' use of the evaluation findings. The evaluation team is also using multiple levels of the four-level training evaluation framework (Kirkpatrick, 1996) for evaluating the four dimensions:

1. Curriculum alignment (Level 1 Reaction, based on participants' inputs about how well the curriculum is designed to help close their performance gaps)

2. Program implementation (Level 1 Reaction, based on participants' inputs about how adequate the overall program schedule was)

3. Leadership application (Level 3 Behavioral Change, based on participants' self-assessment of their behavior and environmental support, and their direct reports' assessment on their manager's behavior and environmental support)

4. Leaders' network (Level 4 Results, based on participants' self-assessment of their behavior and their direct reports' assessment of their manager's behavior)

The evaluation team will also apply Brinkerhoff's (2006) Success Case Method while evaluating Dimensions 3 and 4, to investigate factors that influence leaders' successful and nonsuccessful application of their knowledge and skills and their networking with other leaders.

While incorporating these frameworks, the evaluation team will use multiple sources of data, including the LPS director, instructional designers, managers (program participants), and direct reports of the managers. Additionally, the evaluation team will use multiple types of data collection methods:

• Survey—Web-based survey questionnaires will be administered.

• Interview—Semi-structured telephone interviews will be conducted.

• Extant data review—Existing Level 1 and Level 2 evaluation data will be reviewed.

• Observation—Web conferencing among leaders will be observed.

The multiple types of data collection methods are selected to complement strengths and weaknesses of each method, and the data collected from multiple types/sources will be triangulated to draw credible conclusions. Three evaluation team members will also compare their analysis and interpretation of extant data to avoid drawing biased conclusions. Data collection methods are summarized in Table 3.

The following is a tentative timeline for the implementation phase to be completed in 2019:

- Data collection instrument development—March 4 through March 24
- Data collection—March 18 through April 14
- Data analysis—April 1 through April 21
- Preparation of a final report—April 15 and 30
- Delivery of a final report to the client—April 31

TABLE 3 ● Data Collection Methods

Dimension	Data Collection Method	Instrument to Be Developed and Used	Rationale for Using Multiple Sets of data (Critical Multiplism and Triangulation)
1. Curriculum alignment: How well is the curriculum designed to help close the managers' performance gaps? TIM: Resources and Activities IW: Critical	1-1. Record review of the curriculum 1-2. Record review of Level 1 evaluation data obtained from previous training sessions 1-3. Semi-structured telephone interview with the LPS director, three instructional designers, two trainers, and a sample of managers (n = 6)	1-1. Document review checklist 1-2. Document review checklist 1-3. Interview solicitation email message, informed consent form, and interview questions	This is a critical dimension; thus, it is important to obtain comprehensive information. Two types of document reviews will help identify gaps in the alignment between the content and the expected performance outcomes. This information will be compared to the key upstream stakeholders' perspectives on how the content is designed to facilitate performance improvement.
2. Program implementation: How adequate is the overall program implementation process? TIM: Activities IW: Important	2-1. Record review of the training schedule and other relevant information, including Level 1 evaluation data 2-2. Web-based survey with all managers who completed the program (n = 60+)	2-1. Document review checklist 2-2. Web-based survey questionnaire; survey respondents' names will be asked but will be kept confidential	The document review will help identify factors that facilitate or hinder the success of program implementation. This information will be compared to the actual participants' (managers) perspectives. At least a 50% survey return rate should be obtained.

(Continued)

(Continued)

Dimension	Data Collection Method	Instrument to Be Developed and Used	Rationale for Using Multiple Sets of data (Critical Multiplism and Triangulation)
	2-3. Interview with the LPS director, three instructional designers, two trainers, and a sample of managers (n = 6)	Added to 1-3 (1-3 and 2-3 are completed in the same interviews)	More information about various factors is expected to be revealed from the interviews, which will be compared to other types of data for consistency.
3. Leadership application: How well are the managers applying their new leadership knowledge and skills? How supportive is the work environment for them to use their new skills? TIM: Critical actions (and Resources and Activities for improvement) IW: Very important	3-1. Web-based survey with all managers who completed the program	Added to 2-2 (2-2, 3-1, and 4-1 are completed in the same survey)	This is a very important dimension. Information will be obtained from both managers and their direct reports, and the two sets of information will be triangulated. The in-depth interviews will also help identify various factors that may influence the success and nonsuccess of performance outcomes, which the surveys may not reveal.
	3-2. Semi-structured telephone interview with three or four success and three or four nonsuccess cases of managers who completed the program	3-2. Interview solicitation email message, informed consent form, and interview questions	
	3-3. Anonymous web-based survey with all direct reports of the managers who completed the program	3-3. Anonymous web-based survey questionnaire	
4. Leaders' network: How and how well are the mid-tier leaders using their network? What other support do they need to effectively network with each other? TIM: Key results (and Resources and Activities for improvement) IW: Important	4-1. Web-based survey with all managers who completed the program	Added to 2-2 (2-2, 3-1, and 4-1 are completed in the same survey)	Survey, interview, and observation methods will help assess the type of network that managers have established and the quality of the network from different angles. The interviews will again help identify various factors that may influence the success and nonsuccess of performance outcomes.
	4-2. Semi-structured telephone interview with three or four success and three or four nonsuccess cases of managers who completed the program	Added to 3-2 (3-2 and 4-2 are completed in the same interviews)	
	4-3. Observation during web conferencing among managers who network with others	4-3. Observation checklist and informed consent form	

Dimension	Data Collection Method	Instrument to Be Developed and Used	Rationale for Using Multiple Sets of data (Critical Multiplism and Triangulation)

In summary, the following instruments will be developed:

- Three document review checklists (1-1, 1-2, and 2-1)
- Two web-based survey questionnaires (2-2/3-1/4-1, and 3-3)
- Two interview instruments (1-3/2-3, and 3-2/4-2)
- One observation checklist (4-3)
- Informant solicitation emails and informed consent forms as needed

IW, Information weighting; *LPS*, Learning and Performance Solutions (department); *TIM*, training impact model.

4. Feasibility and Risk Factors

4.1. Feasibility

The following is a summary of the evaluation team's assessment on project feasibility:

1. *Maturity*. The program has been implemented in two branches, which can provide enough information about what went well and what should be continued, and what did not go well and what should be changed.

2. *Scope*. The project can be completed within the requested time frame (8 weeks upon an approved proposal), given enough support and resources for the project.

3. *Support*. The client and other upstream stakeholders with whom the evaluation team has communicated so far have shown enough interest and support for the evaluation. The stakeholders are interested in using the evaluation findings to make improvement on the program. The client has approved giving the team full access to the training materials and groups of new employees and supervisors. The team is permitted to gather data by phone and/or via email during the employee work hours.

4. *Ethical concerns*. Although there have not been any signs that raise ethical concerns, the fact that the evaluation team is composed of external evaluators is something to keep in mind since it may prevent the team from having access to the necessary data in a timely manner. The evaluation team will also ensure confidentiality of data. In particular, the data collected from using the Success Case Method can be sensitive.

5. *Resources*. The following resources will be used during this evaluation:

   - Expertise/capacity
     - The evaluator's expertise in conducting program evaluations (level: developing). The project will benefit from having this three-member evaluation team, possessing project management skills, web-based survey design skills, interview skills, and writing skills.
     - The university instructor who supervises the project (level: expert)
   - Funds
     - No additional financial costs are imposed to the client/organization.

(Continued)

(Continued)

- Time
    - The evaluation team has committed their time during 8 weeks to implement the approved evaluation plan and submit a final evaluation report.
    - The client and stakeholders are expected to commit their time to provide necessary data and communicate with the evaluation team.
- Facilities/communication
    - Most interactions between the evaluator and the client/stakeholders will be done via email, web conference, and/or telephone. Some interactions may occur face-to-face, likely at the client site.

Based on the evaluation team's assessments on project feasibility, the team has concluded that it is a feasible project to complete within the expected time frame and given resources.

4.2. Risk Factors

To complete the evaluation project successfully, the evaluation team will monitor the following risk factors and collaborate with the program stakeholders to implement strategies to manage the risk factors as needed:

A. Ineffective communication among the evaluation team members—The three members of the evaluation team will communicate in person, by phone, via email, or through a conferencing system on a daily basis. All members of this evaluation team are familiar with virtual communication methods and are committed to successful completion of the project. Thus, it is unlikely that the project would be jeopardized by this risk factor.

B. Failing to meet the time frame for project completion—The client has a specific time frame (8 weeks) for the evaluation project to be completed. To meet the expectation, it is critical that all communications between the evaluation team and the program stakeholders (including the evaluation client) be done efficiently. Some delays in meeting project milestones may occur; however, there is adequate time built into the project timeline to make up short-term schedule slips.

C. Lack of time for stakeholders to participate in evaluation—To help stakeholders participate in data collection, it is important that they be allowed to spend time during their work hours to complete surveys and interviews. With the client organization's support, this arrangement can be easily made.

D. Stakeholders' lack of motivation in participating in surveys and interviews—It is critical to have full participation of the stakeholders, especially the managers, during data collection. The evaluation team and the upstream stakeholders need to use effective strategies to motivate the managers to participate in data collection since many of them may suffer from survey fatigue. It is essential to receive support from the client organization to achieve a high survey return rate and obtain interview volunteers.

E. Ineffective communication between the evaluation team and the stakeholders—Most of the communications between the evaluation team and the program stakeholders will be via email or by phone, which raises a concern for potential communication breakdown. Although the client and upstream stakeholders have shown high commitment to the project so far, failure to have effective communication between the two parties would result in detrimental damage to the project. The evaluation team will be responsive to the stakeholders' requests by returning emails or phone calls within 24 hours and ask for clarification whenever needed. The team requests the stakeholders to do the same.

Table 4 summarizes the risk assessment results. Overall, it is the evaluation team's opinion that the potential costs for dealing with consequences after implementing the program at the remaining branches without having an opportunity to conduct an evaluation and to improve the program quality are greater than costs for completing the evaluation project with the identified risks and unknown risks that may be discovered during the project.

TABLE 4 ● Risk Assessment Matrix				
Damage to Project / Likelihood	Minor	Moderate	Substantial	Detrimental
Unlikely			A. Ineffective communication among evaluation team members	E. Ineffective communication between evaluation team and stakeholders
Maybe		B. Failing to meet time frame for project completion	D. Stakeholders' lack of motivation in participating in surveys and interviews	
Likely		C. Lack of time for stakeholders to participate in evaluation		

References

Brinkerhoff, R. O. (2006). *Telling training's story: Evaluation made simple, credible, and effective*. San Francisco, CA: Berrett-Koehler.

Chyung, S. Y. (2019). *10-step evaluation for training and performance improvement*. Thousand Oaks, CA: Sage.

Kirkpatrick, D. (1996). *Evaluating training programs: The four levels*. San Francisco, CA: Berrett-Koehler.

Now, Your Turn—Write an Evaluation Proposal

Now it is time to write an evaluation proposal, submit it to your client, and get approval to proceed with the implementation phase. You have been interacting with the client and other stakeholders throughout the identification and planning phases, so the client should not be surprised by the information that you present in your proposal.

Your client may have some feedback on your proposal. Revise your plan as needed, before you move onto the next phase of your evaluation project, which is implementation.

A sample evaluation proposal is available for download at **https://study.sagepub.com/chyung**

9

Develop Data Collection Instruments I
Self-Administered Surveys (Step 7)

You have completed the planning phase of your evaluation project and obtained approval on your evaluation proposal from your client. Now you are starting the implementation phase of your evaluation project by developing the data collection instruments that you proposed to use.

This chapter presents information on how to develop instruments for conducting self-administered surveys. Chapter 10 presents information on how to develop instruments for administering one-on-one interviews, focus groups, observations, extant data reviews, and tests.

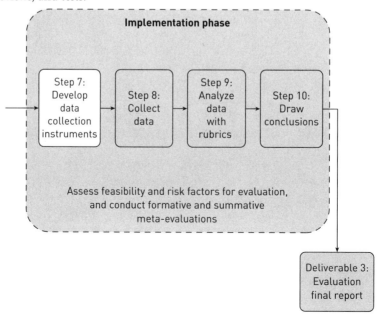

Comply With IRB Requirements

You can use various data collection methods during your evaluation project, such as surveys, interviews, focus groups, observations, extant data reviews, and tests (see Table 36. Advantages and Disadvantages of Different Data Collection Methods in Chapter 7).

When collecting data through surveys, interviews, focus groups, observations, and tests, you handle **human subjects**. When using extant data, you also collect data *about* human subjects quite often. When collecting data from or about human subjects, your work falls into the *human subject research* category, and you must follow professional guidelines for ethically handling human subjects.

You should also follow institutional or organizational requirements. Which requirements you need to follow may depend on several factors:

FOLLOW GUIDELINES AND REQUIREMENTS FOR COLLECTING DATA FROM OR ABOUT HUMAN SUBJECTS

- Whether you are conducting an evaluation as a class project

- If you and your client intend to disseminate your evaluation results through a publication or presentation

- If your client organization has an entity such as a legal department or a research ethics board by which you need to run your evaluation project

If you are conducting an evaluation as a class project, and if you and your client intend to disseminate a summary of the evaluation project through a publication or presentation, your educational institution will likely treat your evaluation project as a type of research and require you to comply with its **institutional review board** (IRB) requirements. The IRB is a committee that reviews procedures and materials researchers will use during their research to ensure that researchers take appropriate steps to protect the rights and well-being of human subjects involved in the research. In this case, you are likely subject to your educational institution's IRB requirements and approval. However, if you and your client do not plan to disseminate a summary of the evaluation project through a publication or presentation, you should follow your instructor's advice to see if the IRB will waive its requirements.

Whether you are conducting an evaluation as a class project or not, you also need to find out if the client organization has an entity that governs ethical conduct of data collection activities using human subjects. The entity may be a legal department of the organization, or it may be called a research ethics board. If the client organization has such an entity, you will likely need to comply with its requirements—you should discuss it with your client. Or, you may find that the client organization does not have such an entity, and your client has full authority to approve all of your data collection activities.

In all situations, you should also follow evaluation-specific professional guidelines, which are described in Chapter 11 (e.g., the American Evaluation Association's guiding principles for evaluators, and the Joint Committee on Standards for Educational Evaluation's program evaluation standards). These professional guidelines are often reflected in IRB requirements. Thus, even if you are not required to comply with the IRB requirements of your educational institution or the requirements of your client organization's ethics board, you likely use similar evaluation practice as you follow

TABLE 45 ● Comply With IRB Requirements, Client Organization's Requirements, and/or Professional Guidelines		
When the client organization \\ When you are conducting an evaluation	As a class project with intention to disseminate results	As a class project with no intention to disseminate results, or not as a class project
Has an entity that governs evaluation activities	You comply with: • the educational institution's IRB requirements • the client organization's requirements • professional guidelines	You comply with: • the client organization's requirements • professional guidelines
Does not have such an entity	You comply with: • the educational institution's IRB requirements • professional guidelines	You comply with: • the client's requests • professional guidelines

IRB, Institutional review board.

evaluation-specific professional guidelines. Table 45 summarizes the different situations described earlier.

Regardless of your situation, you need to adhere to some main principles:

- Fully inform participants of the purpose for collecting data.

- Allow voluntary participation; allow participants to quit participating in data collection any time for any reason.

- Give no penalty or disadvantage for nonparticipation.

- Cause no mental, emotional, or physical harm to participants.

- Protect participants' privacy and human rights.

In this chapter and the next chapter, you will find information about how to prepare to comply with an educational institution's IRB requirements, including the use of informed consent forms.

Use Informed Consent Forms

If you are asked to comply with an educational institution's IRB requirements, you likely need to provide participants with an informed consent form that describes your evaluation project and seeks participants' consent to become **informants**. If you are not required to use informed consent forms by an educational institution's IRB or the client organization, you may prepare a less formal type of cover letter.

An **informed consent form** is a document that typically contains the following information (be aware that the IRB would treat your evaluation as a type of research; thus the word *research* is used in the list):

- Title of the research
- Researcher name, position, organization, and contact information
- Sponsor name, position, and organization (if applicable)
- Purpose of the research
- Procedure of the research
- Risks associated with the research
- Benefits associated with the research
- Participants' rights and methods for protecting confidentiality of data
- Contact information for participants to use to ask questions
- Statement that participation is voluntary
- Participant's consent signature line (if a printed form is used)
- If applicable, proof of approval obtained from the IRB or a legal department of the organization for conducting the research

TYPICAL CONTENT
OF AN INFORMED
CONSENT FORM

Samples of basic informed consent forms are presented in this chapter and the next chapter (Chapter 10).

- Exhibit 4. Sample informed consent form for conducting a survey
- Exhibit 7. Sample informed consent form for conducting an interview
- Exhibit 12. Sample informed consent form for conducting a survey and a follow-up interview
- Exhibit 14. Sample informed consent form for conducting an observation

These samples are provided only to explain the overall structure and required materials. Conventionally, participants would sign a printed informed consent form. The samples provided in this book are written in a way that participants' consent is obtained via an electronic checkbox (in web-based surveys) or in an audio recording (during interviews). Each educational institution's IRB likely provides its own templates and requirements (e.g., see Boise State University, Office of Research Compliance, 2017). When preparing informed consent forms, you want to follow the recommendations provided by your educational institution's IRB. If your client organization's IRB-equivalent entity has its own requirements, you may need to incorporate both requirements in developing your informed consent forms.

Determine Materials to Be Developed for Different Data Collection Methods

If you are asked to submit an IRB application to get IRB approval, in the application package, you will typically need to include a copy of your data collection instruments, informed consent forms, and other supporting materials such as participation solicitation letters and specific directions for using the instruments. For example, to prepare to conduct a web-based survey with employees of an organization, you would need to develop the following:

- An email message to be sent to the employees to solicit their participation in the survey

- An informed consent form

- A survey questionnaire including directions for completing the web-based survey and survey questions

Table 46 summarizes materials that you may need to develop to seek IRB approval for conducting evaluation. Again, if you are not required to comply with an educational institution's IRB requirements, you may adjust the materials and procedure as you see fit.

Distinguish Anonymity From Confidentiality

While preparing informed consent forms to be used with individual data collection instruments, you will likely use the words *anonymity* and/or *confidentiality*. In doing so, you should clearly understand the difference between these two terms.

You can ensure **anonymity** of data by not asking informants, especially survey participants, to provide their names or other identifiable information. Then, you obtain anonymous data. If you collect identifiable information, it is no longer anonymous data. In some cases, you may need to collect informants' names—for example,

- when using the SCM and needing to identify success and nonsuccess cases based on survey respondents' data, and

- when comparing program participants' data (e.g., test scores) before and after they completed the program (you need to match their pre- and post-data).

Unless your evaluation design requires informants' names and other identifiable information, you should not collect such data.

Even if you obtained anonymous data, it may be still possible to guess the informants based on the data content. Therefore, after you collect data—whether anonymous or identifiable—you should keep **confidentiality** of data by not sharing with other people any data that contains personal or other identifiable information. You should also present composite data (instead of raw data) in your final report and other presentations, so that others cannot match specific data with individual informants. Figure 15 illustrates the difference between anonymity and confidentiality.

TABLE 46 ● Materials Needed for Collecting Data

Method		How Will You Solicit Participation?	Need to Provide an Informed Consent Form?	Directions to Be Used With The Instrument	Measurement Instrument

Self-administered survey	On site	• Verbally request participants to complete and submit the enclosed survey	• Yes, if it is an identifiable survey
			• Obtaining participants' signature (indicating their voluntary participation in evaluation) may be waived if it is an anonymous survey; check with the IRB
				• Survey directions that:
				  ○ describe the survey purpose and the expected time for survey completion
				  ○ explain participants' rights (refer to the informed consent form if provided)
				  ○ indicate the evaluator(s) contact information
					• Survey questions in print

	Via mail	• Include a cover letter in the mail, requesting participants to complete and return the enclosed survey			• Survey questions in print
	Via the web	• Send a survey invitation email message to participants, requesting them to complete a web-based survey			• Survey questions uploaded to a web-based survey system

One-on-one interview	In person
	
	By phone
	
	Via video call
		• Verbally request, send a cover letter in mail, or send an email message, asking participants to:
		  ○ review the consent form
		  ○ decide whether they would participate in an interview
		  ○ if participating, reply to schedule an interview
			• All interviewees are identified during interviews; therefore, an informed consent form should be provided
			• When conducting in-person interviews, interviewees can sign the consent form before the interview starts
				• An opening script that the interviewer will use to:
				  ○ describe the interview purpose and interviewee's rights as described in the consent form
				  ○ ask participants to confirm their consent to participate in an interview (and allow them to cancel the interview)
				  ○ assign a pseudonym to each interviewee to protect confidentiality
				  ○ ask for permission to audio-record it (if desirable to do so)
					• Interview questions

TABLE 46 ● (Continued)

Method		How Will You Solicit Participation?	Need to Provide an Informed Consent Form?	Directions to Be Used With The Instrument	Measurement Instrument

Focus group	In person
	
	By telephone conferencing
	
	By video-conferencing
		• Verbally request, send a cover letter in mail, or send an email message, asking participants to:
		
		  ○ review the consent form
		
		  ○ decide whether they would participate in a focus group
		
		  ○ if participating, reply to the message, indicating their available date/time among the suggested options
			• All participants are identified during the focus group; therefore, an informed consent form should be provided
			
			• When conducting an in-person focus group, participants can sign the consent form before the focus group starts
				• An opening script that the focus group facilitator will use to:
				
				  ○ describe the focus group purpose and participants' rights as described in the consent form
				
				  ○ ask participants to confirm their consent to participate in a focus group (and allow them to leave if they decide not to participate)
				
				  ○ ask participants to keep confidentiality of information shared during the focus group
				
				  ○ ask for permission to audio/video-record it (if desirable to do so)
					• Focus group facilitation questions

Observation	On site (participant observation)	• Verbally request, send a cover letter in mail, or send an email message, asking participants to:
		
		  ○ review the consent form
		
		  ○ decide whether to allow an observation
		
		  ○ reply to schedule observation
			• All participants are identified during observation; therefore, an informed consent form should be provided	• An opening script that the observer will use to:
				
				  ○ describe the observation purpose and participants' rights as described in the consent form
				
				  ○ ask participants to confirm their consent to be observed (and allow them to cancel the observation)
				
				  ○ assign a pseudonym to each participant to protect confidentiality
				
				  ○ ask for permission to video-record it (if desirable to do so)
					• Observation checklist

Method		How Will You Solicit Participation?	Need to Provide an Informed Consent Form?	Directions to Be Used With The Instrument	Measurement Instrument
Extant data review	Video-recorded (non-participant observation)		• If you ask the client to video-record the site and give the recoding to you, you may need to prepare all materials needed for on-site observations and provide them to the client. • If the client organization gave you an existing video-recording and ask you to analyze the recording, discuss with the client whether you can treat it as an extant data review and if there are any ethical issues associated with using the recorded video.		
	In print In electronic files		• You will likely obtain the existing information from the client. Discuss with the client about following certain guidelines for protecting the privacy of human subjects when sharing their information with you: e.g., Family Educational Rights and Privacy Act (FERPA)[1] and Health Insurance Portability and Accountability Act (HIPAA).[2] In some cases, the client may need to remove identifiable information in an extant data file before handing it over to you.		• Document review checklist

Test	Written	• The client organization may administer the test as part of their official activity	• Not applicable—also see the directions provided in the Extant Data Review section	• Test directions
				When administering the test as part of their official activity:
				  – describe the purpose of the test
				  – explain the expected time for test completion
				If not, also:
				  – explain participants' rights (refer to the informed consent form if provided)
				  – indicate the evaluator(s) contact information
					• Test questions

	Written (on site)	• Verbally request participants to complete and submit the enclosed test	• Yes, if it is an identifiable test • It can be waived if it is an anonymous test; check with the IRB		
	Written (online)	• Send an email message, requesting that participants complete a web-based test			
	Performance	• See Observation			

[1] For more about the FERPA, see https://www2.ed.gov/policy/gen/guid/fpco/ferpa/index.html

[2] For more about the HIPAA, see https://www.hhs.gov/hipaa

155

FIGURE 15 ● Anonymity Versus Confidentiality

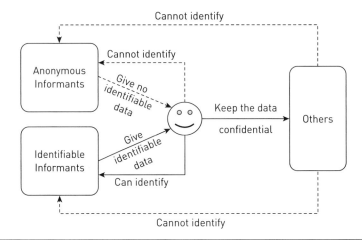

Detailed explanations about materials you need to develop for using surveys, interviews, focus groups, observations, extant data reviews, and tests are presented in the following sections of this chapter and in Chapter 10.

Develop Materials for Conducting Self-Administered Surveys

Imagine that you are conducting a formative evaluation of a mentoring program provided at NECE, Inc. (pseudonym). Two of the dimensions you decide to investigate are mentoring activities and program short-term benefits. You decide to conduct a self-administered survey with program participants to collect data about these two dimensions.

You may conduct the survey on paper (on site or by mail) or via the web. In this section, we will discuss recruitment of survey participants via email and administration of a web-based survey using a web-based survey system. If you are conducting surveys on site or by mail, you can modify the materials presented in this section in a way that will work in your particular situation.

FOR A WEB-BASED SURVEY   To recruit survey participants via email and conduct a web-based survey, you need to develop the following:

1. A recruitment script to be sent via email

2. An informed consent form

3. A survey questionnaire to be uploaded to a web-based survey system

The following sections explain how to prepare those materials.

Develop an Email Script to Be Sent to Recruit Survey Participants

Exhibit 1, Exhibit 2, and Exhibit 3 are samples of a survey recruitment email message to be used when conducting a web-based survey. The messages are written depending on whether the evaluator (or evaluation team) is internal or external to the organization and who is sending out the message—the evaluator (or evaluation team) or an internal sponsor (e.g., the client).

If you are an evaluator internal to the client organization, and if the recipients of your survey recruitment email message are familiar with your name and job title, they may find your recruitment email message to be less intrusive than when they receive a message from an external evaluator (i.e., a stranger). More trust can be gained when the survey link contains the organization's domain. The email recipients will read the attached informed consent form to decide whether to complete the survey or not. Clicking on the URL link inserted in the email message will open a survey questionnaire on a web browser. See Exhibit 1.

If you are conducting a survey as a class team project, and if none of your team members work in the client organization where the survey is conducted, you may want to provide specific information about your team as well as the name and title of your client or another upstream stakeholder (as a sponsor) in the message. Then, the

EXHIBIT 1 ● Sample Email Message Sent by an Internal Evaluator, Recruiting Survey Participants

To: Recipient@neceurl.org

Subject: Survey regarding the mentoring program

Hi [name],

I am Jane Doe, Performance Improvement Specialist at NECE, Inc. I am working on an evaluation project regarding the mentoring program provided at NECE to find out how helpful the program was and what can be changed to improve the mentor–mentee experience for future participants. I am conducting a survey as part of the evaluation project, and I am inviting you to participate in the survey since you recently completed the program. A detailed description of the project is provided in the attached informed consent form.

Please click the link below to start the survey:

http://www.surveyurl.org/yoursurvey.htm

Thanks for your participation!

Jane Doe

Performance Improvement Specialist, NECE, Inc.

Phone: (123) 456-7890

Email: JaneDoe@neceurl.org

Attachment: InformedConsentFormForSurvey.pdf

recipients will understand that their organization supports the survey that is being conducted by your team. See Exhibit 2.

In some cases, a survey recruitment email message can be sent by the organizational sponsor on your behalf, especially if you are external to the organization. This method can improve the survey response rate if the sponsor is well known to the recipients of the survey recruitment email message (as compared to when the recipients receive an email message from a stranger). See Exhibit 3.

Develop an Informed Consent Form to Be Provided to Survey Participants

The informed consent form should help the survey participants understand the investigators, the purpose of the evaluation, the evaluation procedure, potential risks and benefits for participating in the evaluation project, a clear explanation that their participation in the evaluation project is totally voluntary, and the IRB approval status. The informed consent form should enable the participants to make an informed decision as to whether or not to participate in the evaluation project.

Exhibit 4 is a sample informed consent form to be provided to survey participants. It is written for conducting an identifiable survey (i.e., the survey questionnaire asks for participants' names). If you are conducting an anonymous survey, you need to revise the content accordingly. You may also want to clearly state that it is an

---

EXHIBIT 2 ● Sample Email Message Sent by an External Evaluation Team, Recruiting Survey Participants

To: Recipient@neceurl.org

Subject: Survey regarding the mentoring program

Hi [name],

Sponsored by Mr. James Doe, Director of Learning and Performance Improvement of NECE, Inc., we, a team of graduate students from BBB University, are working on an evaluation project regarding the mentoring program provided at NECE to find out how helpful the program was and what can be changed to improve the mentor–mentee experience for future participants. We are conducting a survey as part of the evaluation project, and we are inviting you to participate in the survey since you recently completed the program. A detailed description of the evaluation project is provided in the attached informed consent form.

Please click the link below to start the survey:

http://www.surveyurl.org/yoursurvey.htm

Thanks for your participation!

Jane Doe, Steve Martin, and Mary Kim

Evaluation Team, BBB University

Phone: (123) 456-7890

Email: JaneDoe@bbb.edu

Attachment: InformedConsentFormForSurvey.pdf

EXHIBIT 3 ● Sample Email Message Sent by an Internal Sponsor of an External Evaluation Team, Recruiting Survey Participants

To: Recipient@neceurl.org

Subject: Survey regarding the mentoring program

Hi [name],

I am sponsoring a team of graduate students from BBB University to conduct an evaluation of the mentoring program provided at NECE to find out how helpful the program was and what can be changed to improve the mentor–mentee experience for future participants. I am inviting you to participate in a survey since you recently completed the program. A detailed description of the evaluation project is provided in the attached informed consent form.

Please click the link below to start the survey:

http://www.surveyurl.org/yoursurvey.htm

Thanks for your participation!

James Doe

Director of Learning and Performance Improvement, NECE, Inc.

Phone: (123) 456-7890

Email: JamesDoe@neceurl.org

Attachment: InformedConsentFormForSurvey.pdf

EXHIBIT 4 ● Sample Informed Consent Form for Conducting a Survey

Informed Consent

Title: Evaluation of the Effectiveness of the Mentoring Program

Investigator: Jane Doe, Performance Improvement Specialist, NECE, Inc.

Sponsor: James Doe, Director of Learning and Performance Improvement, NECE, Inc.

Approval: This evaluation project has been approved by the legal department of NECE, Inc.

Purpose: The mentoring program at NECE, Inc. has been in operation since 2017. I am conducting a formative evaluation to understand how effective the mentoring program has been and what needs to be changed to produce better outcomes. I am conducting a survey to gather information needed for the evaluation project.

Procedure: You have received a link to the web-based survey questionnaire. It will take about 5 minutes to complete the survey.

Confidentiality: I will do my best to keep any identifiable information confidential. Only a summary of data will be presented in a report, and your name will not be used in any written or oral reports.

Risks: There are minimal risks associated with this survey. If you do not feel comfortable answering particular questions presented in the survey, you can skip those questions or stop completing the survey at any time by closing your web browser.

Benefits: By submitting your data, you are sharing information that helps improve the quality of the program.

(Continued)

EXHIBIT 4 ● **(Continued)**

Questions: If you have any questions or concerns about participation in this evaluation project, please contact me at (123) 456-7890 or janedoe@neceurl.com. If you have questions about your rights as a participant, you may contact the NECE's legal department at legaldept@neceurl.com.

Voluntary Participation: Your participation in the evaluation project is voluntary. If you decide to participate, you will be asked to click a checkbox on the survey questionnaire to confirm your consent to become a survey participant for the evaluation project before you proceed with the survey questionnaire. If you decide not to participate, simply close this form and the web browser showing the survey questionnaire.

anonymous survey, as it can help motivate the survey participants to complete the survey questions with their honest responses.

Develop a Survey Questionnaire to Be Self-Administered

Imagine that the recipients of your survey recruitment email message click on the URL link inserted in the email message to open the survey questionnaire on a web browser. On the first webpage, especially if you are collecting the participants' names in the survey, you can ask the survey participants to confirm their consent to participate in the evaluation project by clicking a checkbox before they proceed with the survey questions, as shown in Exhibit 5. Then, you can show the survey questionnaire containing a survey title, directions, questions, and closing statements in the subsequent webpage(s).

The survey questionnaire shown in Exhibit 5 is designed as an identifiable survey. If you conduct an anonymous survey, you do not ask them to enter their name. You also want to avoid asking other demographic information unless it is necessary. By asking many demographic questions (e.g., gender, department, and job title), you can guess the person who submitted the data.

Among the survey questions presented in Exhibit 5:

- Questions 1 and 2 intend to provide supporting information (nonevaluative data).

- Questions 9 through 12 measure the activities dimension.

- Questions 3 through 8 and Question 13 measure the program short-term benefits dimension.

EXHIBIT 5 ● **Sample Identifiable Survey Questionnaire**

Survey for the Mentoring Program

If you decide to participate in the evaluation project as described in the informed consent form below,

InformedConsentFormForSurvey.pdf

☐ please select this checkbox to confirm your consent to participate in the evaluation project, before you click the Next button below. If you decide not to participate in the evaluation project, you may close the web browser.

Next ⇨

Survey for the Mentoring Program

Directions: This survey is designed to measure your experience with the mentoring program. Please think about the mentoring program that you completed while responding to each question.

   Your participation in the survey is voluntary, and you may decide not to complete the survey questionnaire at any time simply by closing the web browser. If you do not feel comfortable answering particular questions presented in the survey questionnaire, you can skip those questions. If you have any questions about the survey, please contact the evaluator, Jane Doe, at (123) 456-7890 or JaneDoe@neceurl.org.

Please write your name: _____

1. When did you participate in the mentoring program?

   ○ Fall 2017 ○ Spring 2018 ○ Summer 2018

2. Why did you choose to participate in the mentoring program? Please describe:

   _____

   For Questions 3 through 8, please select the option that best represents your experience.

3. The program helped me get up to speed with my job tasks.

   ○ Strongly disagree ○ Somewhat disagree ○ Neutral ○ Somewhat agree ○ Strongly agree

4. The program helped me improve the interpersonal skills I need in the workplace.

   ○ Strongly disagree ○ Somewhat disagree ○ Neutral ○ Somewhat agree ○ Strongly agree

5. My mentor helped me develop achievable professional goals.

   ○ Strongly disagree ○ Somewhat disagree ○ Neutral ○ Somewhat agree ○ Strongly agree

6. Based on my mentor's feedback, I was able to make positive changes in how I do my job.

   ○ Strongly disagree ○ Somewhat disagree ○ Neutral ○ Somewhat agree ○ Strongly agree

7. After completing the program, I became a more competent worker than before.

   ○ Strongly disagree ○ Somewhat disagree ○ Neutral ○ Somewhat agree ○ Strongly agree

8. After completing the program, I became more committed to my job than before.

   ○ Strongly disagree ○ Somewhat disagree ○ Neutral ○ Somewhat agree ○ Strongly agree

9. Was the once-a-week meeting schedule appropriate for you?

   ○ Yes ○ No

   If you selected No, please explain why and provide suggestions:

   _____

10. Was the length of the program (3 months) appropriate for you?

    ○ Yes ○ No

(Continued)

EXHIBIT 5 ● **(Continued)**

If you selected No, please explain why and provide suggestions:

_____

11. Did you have trouble in fully engaging in the mentoring program? If so, please describe:

_____

12. What was the best part about the mentoring program? Please describe:

_____

13. Would you recommend the mentoring program to other employees?

   O Yes O No

Please explain why and add any other comments about the program:

_____

Thanks for completing the survey questions! Please click the Submit button below.

Submit

Data obtained from the questions that collect supporting information (including demographic information) can be analyzed to reveal other useful information. For example, using the data obtained from Question 1, you may compare the three groups of data (FA17, SP18, and SU18) to check whether the data were consistent or fluctuated over time.

Similarly, if you want to find out if the mentoring program was beneficial to both gender groups, you would add a question asking the respondents' gender (female vs. male) and compare the two gender groups' data.

In the following sections, we will talk more about how to design survey questionnaires. While developing data collection instruments, it is also helpful to think about rubrics to be used. See Chapter 12 to learn how to develop rubrics.

Determine Whether to Use Closed-Ended Questions, Open-Ended Questions, or Both

You can design survey questionnaires using closed-ended questions (structured), open-ended questions (unstructured), or a mix of closed- and open-ended questions (semi-structured), depending on the type of respondents' data that you need to gather. Exhibit 5 (presented in the previous section) included both closed- and open-ended survey items.

Table 47 compares the three types of survey questionnaires to be self-administered. In the following sections, we will discuss methods for developing closed-ended survey items.

TABLE 47 ● Structured, Semi-Structured, and Unstructured Survey Questionnaires to Be Self-Administered			
	Structured	**Semi-Structured**	**Unstructured**
Design	Designed mostly with closed-ended questions so that respondents choose from response options	Designed with a mix of closed- and open-ended questions as needed	Designed mostly with open-ended questions so that respondents are allowed to provide information in their own words
Example	The program content was relevant to my job. • Strongly disagree • Disagree • Agree • Strongly agree Which topics were relevant to your job? Select all that apply: • Topic 1 • Topic 2 • Topic 3	Indicate the quality of the service and explain how so: Topic 1 Poor 1 2 3 4 5 Great Explain why: _____ Topic 2 Poor 1 2 3 4 5 Great Explain why: _____	With which aspects of the program are you satisfied? _____ With which aspects of the program are you dissatisfied? _____ What suggestions do you have for the program? _____
Pros and cons	• Easy to compile and analyze data • Difficult to understand reasons behind the responses	• Can have closed-ended and open-ended questions as needed • Respondents may complete closed-ended questions but not open-ended questions	• Able to understand respondents' experience better • Time-consuming to analyze data

Ask Specific Questions That Measure the Quality of a Dimension

When developing survey items, you should remember that you are conducting an evaluation to solicit respondents' perceptions about the quality of a dimension or ways to improve the quality. Thus, you should develop survey items that will generate data that can be used to answer your dimensional evaluation questions.

For example, let's say you are evaluating a job aid system that was developed in-house to support the use of a new human resources management system (HRMS). You may use the following specific questions in a survey questionnaire to determine the quality of the job aid system—note that the five closed-ended survey items use a *question* format (ending with a question mark), and each survey question is paired with a different **response scale**.

1. How relevant are the job aids to your job tasks?

   ○ All of them are irrelevant

   ○ Many of them are irrelevant

   ○ Some of them are irrelevant, and some are relevant

   ○ Many of them are relevant

   ○ All of them are relevant

2. How clearly are the job aids written?

   ○ All parts are confusing

   ○ Many parts are confusing

   ○ Some parts are confusing, and some parts are clear

   ○ Many parts are clear

   ○ All parts are clear

3. How easy is it to retrieve the job aids from the system?

   ○ Very difficult

   ○ Somewhat difficult

   ○ Pretty easy

   ○ Very easy

4. Overall, how effective is it to use job aids to support your performance?

   ○ Very ineffective

   ○ Somewhat ineffective

   ○ Somewhat effective

   ○ Very effective

5. Would you recommend this job aid system to your coworkers?

   ○ Yes ○ No

Design Survey Items Using a Question or Statement Format

You can convert the *question* format used in the five questions to a *statement* format (ending with a period) and use the same response scale (e.g., the Likert scale) for all survey items, as shown in Questions 6 through 10.

6. The job ads are relevant to my job tasks.

   ○ Strongly disagree ○ Disagree ○ Neutral ○ Agree ○ Strongly agree

7. The job aids are clearly written.

 ○ Strongly disagree ○ Disagree ○ Neutral ○ Agree ○ Strongly agree

8. It is easy to retrieve the job aids from the system.

 ○ Strongly disagree ○ Disagree ○ Neutral ○ Agree ○ Strongly agree

9. Overall, I think the job aids are effective in supporting my performance.

 ○ Strongly disagree ○ Disagree ○ Neutral ○ Agree ○ Strongly agree

10. I would recommend this job aid system to my coworkers.

 ○ Strongly disagree ○ Disagree ○ Neutral ○ Agree ○ Strongly agree

PROS AND CONS OF QUESTION AND STATEMENT FORMATS

There are pros and cons of using a question format with different response scales as shown in Questions 1 through 5 and a statement format with the same response scale as shown in Questions 6 through 10.

Questions 1 through 5 in the previous section may provide more detailed data than Questions 6 through 10. For example, compare the following hypothetical results obtained from Questions 1 and 6:

- Question 1 result: 80% of respondents indicated that many of the job aids were irrelevant to their job tasks.

- Question 6 result: 80% of respondents somewhat disagreed that the job aids were relevant to their job tasks.

The Question 1 result is a bit more specific than the Question 6 result. However, Questions 6 through 10 make it easier to combine data, present an average score, or run other statistical tests. On the other hand, note that Questions 1 through 5 use different types of response scales: Question 5 uses a 2-point scale, Questions 3 and 4 use 4-point scales, and Questions 1 and 2 use 5-point scales. The use of different response scales prevents you from combining data from the multiple questions to calculate an average score.

Here, you also want to think about how you will analyze the survey data with a rubric later. For example, if you used Questions 6 through 10, you may plan to use the following rubric based on the group average score:

- Met expectations: $4.0 \leq$ average score ≤ 5.0

- Some improvement needed: $3.0 \leq$ average score ≤ 3.9

- Major improvement needed: $1.0 \leq$ average score ≤ 2.9

If you use Questions 1 through 5, your rubric will look lengthy and complicated because individual questions used different response scales (Chapter 12 provides more information about developing rubrics).

For more information, see Appendix D, which provides a sample survey questionnaire, designed with a mix of closed-ended and open-ended questions. The sample questionnaire presented in Appendix D also illustrates how you can organize survey items to measure two dimensions. Note that the same 7-point response scale is used in the closed-ended questions. Also, see the sample rubrics for analyzing data for the two dimensions.

Recognize Nominal, Ordinal, Interval, and Ratio Scales

To better understand how to choose from different types of response scales, you need to be able to recognize the differences among nominal, ordinal, interval, and ratio scales.

Stanley Smith Stevens, a professor of psychology at Harvard University, was a notable scholar who conceptualized four different types of measurement scales: nominal, ordinal, interval, and ratio (S. S. Stevens, 1946).

FOUR TYPES OF MEASUREMENT SCALES *Nominal scales* label members in a group or category with names or labels without any assumed rank-orders among the names or labels. For example,

Indicate your job title:

○ Instructional designer ○ Trainer ○ E-Learning developer ○ Other

Ordinal scales contain a group of rank-ordered levels, but the distance between a set of two consecutive levels is different from the distance between another set of two consecutive levels. An example is:

How helpful was the simulation?

○ Not helpful at all ○ A little bit helpful ○ Quite helpful ○ Very helpful

Interval scales contain a group of rank-ordered levels like ordinal scales, but the distance between a set of two consecutive levels is the same as the distance between another set of two consecutive levels. Therefore, you can describe the distance between the first level and the third level as twice as much as the distance between the first level and the second level, or the distance between the second level and the third level. However, there is no absolute zero value in interval scales. Any zero values used in interval scales are arbitrary zero values. For example, an opinion of being neither dissatisfied nor satisfied (i.e., neutral) can be expressed with an arbitrary zero value in the following response scale:

How satisfied are you with the product?

Very dissatisfied   –5   –4   –3   –2   –1   0   +1   +2   +3   +4   +5   Very satisfied

It is an arbitrary zero value because the response scale can be converted to the following scale, in which an opinion of being neither dissatisfied nor satisfied is now expressed with 5 instead:

How satisfied are you with the product?

Very dissatisfied   0   1   2   3   4   5   6   7   8   9   10   Very satisfied

Ratio scales have an equal distance between intervals. Examples are age, length, weight, height, income, and time. They have an absolute zero value, which indicates the absence of the attribute measured (e.g., a zero income means no income at all; zero time spent on a job task means no time was spent on it). The following are examples of survey questions measured with ratio type response scales:

For how many years have you worked as a manager? ___ years

Write your current annual income: $_____

However, if you ask the first question with the following response scales, the data you gather from them are no longer ratio type data, but ordinal data (a) or nominal data (b):

a. For how many years have you worked as a manager?

    O 0–1 year O 2–4 years O 5–7 years O 8 or more years

b. Have you worked as a manager?

    O Yes O No

A benefit of using higher-level scales (ratio or interval) is that you can convert the data to lower-level type data if needed. For example, after you collect annual income levels in dollar values (ratio), you can group the values in several or two categories (interval, ordinal, or nominal). However, you cannot convert lower-level type data ("I *have* worked as a manager") to higher-level type data ("I *have* worked as a manager for *five* years"). Figure 16 depicts the relationship among the four types of measurement scales, where a higher level possesses the characteristics of its lower level(s).

Decide Whether to Include or Omit a Midpoint in the Likert Scale

The Likert scale is often used in survey questionnaires. Rensis Likert (1932), an American social psychologist, developed the Likert scale in the 1930s. The wording

FIGURE 16 ● The Relationship Among Four Types of Measurement Scales

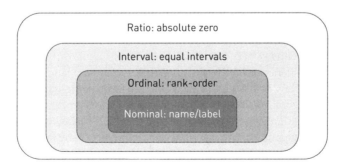

he originally used in the Likert scale was *Strongly disapprove, Disapprove, Undecided, Approve,* and *Strongly approve.* Over time, the wording changed from *Disapprove* and *Approve* to *Disagree* and *Agree,* and different wording *Neutral* or *Neither agree nor disagree* is used as a midpoint. Sometimes, the midpoint is omitted.

**4-POINT AND
5-POINT LIKERT
SCALES—AN
ORDINAL OR
INTERVAL SCALE?**

Consider the following two survey items, one using a 4-point Likert scale without a midpoint and another one using a 5-point Likert scale with a midpoint. Are the 4- and 5-point Likert scales an ordinal scale or an interval scale?

I would recommend this program to my coworkers.

O Strongly disagree O Disagree O Agree O Strongly agree

I would recommend this program to my coworkers.

O Strongly disagree O Disagree O Neutral O Agree O Strongly agree

The 4-point Likert scale without a midpoint is considered an ordinal scale. Why? Consider the distance between the two consecutive levels:

- Distance between *Strongly disagree* and *Disagree*

- Distance between *Disagree* and *Agree*

- Distance between *Agree* and *Strongly agree*

It would be difficult to argue that all three distances are the same. The scale has ordered levels, but the intervals between two consecutive levels are not the same. Thus, it is an ordinal scale.

Then, by adding a midpoint, would a 5-point Likert scale become an interval scale? For the 5-point Likert scale to function as an interval scale, survey respondents should also perceive the five anchors to be aligned with numerical values of –2, –1, 0, +1, and +2, indicating that there is an approximately equal distance between any set of two consecutive points on the scale (Tuckman, 1994).

Interestingly enough, research has shown that survey respondents perceive the 5-point Likert scale to be an ordinal scale (Worcester & Burns, 1975). As shown in Figure 17, the survey respondents' perceptions on *Disagree* and *Agree* are not perfectly aligned with numerical values, –1 and 1, respectively. The respondents perceived *Disagree* to be a little bit toward *Strongly disagree* (and *Agree* toward *Strongly agree*). However, the researchers found out that when a modifier such as *Slightly* was added to *Disagree* and *Agree*, survey respondents perceived *Disagree slightly* or *Agree slightly* to be moderate, thus moving closer to –1 or +1, respectively, as shown in Figure 17. Based on this research evidence, it is recommended that you use the modified phrases of the second and fourth anchors when using a 5-point Likert scale (i.e., *Strongly disagree, Slightly disagree, Neutral, Slightly agree, Strongly agree;* or *Strongly disagree, Somewhat disagree, Neutral, Somewhat agree, Strongly agree*).

**A MIDPOINT AS A
DUMPING GROUND**

The perceived meaning of a midpoint is another aspect of the Likert scale to which you need to pay attention. Whether it is *Neutral* or *Neither agree nor disagree,* a midpoint should indicate the respondents' opinion being in the middle of the scale. However,

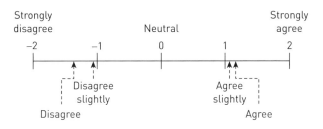

FIGURE 17 ● Changed Perceptions After Adding a Modifier *Slightly* to *Disagree* and *Agree* on the Likert Scale

Adapted from Worcester & Burns, 1975.

research (e.g., Garland, 1991; Raaijmakers, van Hoof, 't Hart, Verbogt, & Vollebergh, 2000) has shown that some respondents choose a midpoint when they are not familiar with the survey topic or do not want to express their opinion, especially if they think it is not viewed favorably by others (a.k.a. *social desirability bias*). These behaviors would threaten the accuracy of your data.

For that reason, you may be inclined to remove the midpoint and use a 4-point Likert scale (Johns, 2005). However, omitting the midpoint may create another problem, because survey respondents who indeed have a neutral opinion, as well as those who do not want to express their opinion, are now forced to choose a side, likely giving you inaccurate data. You may also see more missing data if some survey respondents were not ready to respond or decided not to respond than to be forced to respond to the survey items.

A strategy to mitigate these problems is to provide another option such as *I don't know*, *It depends*, or *Not applicable* whether you use a 4- or 5-point Likert scale (Kulas & Stachowski, 2013; Nadler, Weston, & Voyles, 2015). See the following example. When you include such an additional option, you report the *I don't know*, *It depends*, or *Not applicable* responses separately.

PROVIDE "DON'T KNOW" OR "N/A" OPTIONS

My organization supports informal learning activities.

○ Strongly disagree ○ Slightly disagree ○ Neutral ○ Slightly agree
○ Strongly agree ○ Don't know

The information in this section should be helpful when you decide to use a 4-point ordinal Likert scale or how to set a 5-point scale as close to an interval scale. You should also be aware that if you plan to perform statistical tests with the data, you need to collect a certain type of data that supports the statistical tests. You need to collect interval or ratio data if you plan to use arithmetic interpretations (such as average scores) of the data or certain statistical procedures that require interval or ratio data. On the other hand, if you have ordinal or nominal data, you want to look at frequencies or percentages of the data that fall into each scale point:

- Strongly disagree (5%), Slightly disagree (10%), Slightly agree (25%), Strongly agree (60%)

- Never (1%), Seldom (11%), Sometimes (35%), Often (48%), Always (5%)

- Yes (85%), No (15%)

For a collection of research evidence and research-based recommendations on the use of a midpoint in the Likert scale, see Chyung, Roberts, Swanson, and Hankinson (2017).

Decide Whether to Use Ascending or Descending Order of the Likert Scale Options

In addition to the decision on inclusion or exclusion of a midpoint in the Likert scale, you want to think about whether to present the Likert scale options in ascending or descending order, when presenting them horizontally.

- Horizontal ascending order: *Strongly disagree, Disagree, Neutral, Agree, Strongly agree* (or *Definitely disagree, Mostly disagree, Neither agree nor disagree, Mostly agree, Definitely agree*)

- Horizontal descending order: *Strongly agree, Agree, Neutral, Disagree, Strongly disagree* (or *Definitely agree, Mostly agree, Neither agree nor disagree, Mostly disagree, Definitely disagree*)

BE AWARE OF LEFT-SIDE SELECTION BIAS
While making a decision, it is important to be aware that survey respondents who are familiar with reading from left to right tend to select an option on the left side more often than an option on the right side of a scale (a.k.a. *left-side selection bias*). Survey respondents may also show a yea-saying tendency (a.k.a. *acquiescence bias*) and a satisficing behavior (i.e., quickly select the one that appears to be satisfactory rather than spending time to find an optimal option). Likely because of these behaviors combined, when survey respondents use the Likert scale in descending order, their scores tend to be higher, compared to when they use ascending order (Maeda, 2015; Nicholls, Orr, Okubo, & Loftus, 2006).

These response selection biases (from using descending order) may not be a big issue if you are comparing multiple groups based on the survey results (i.e., relative judgment), since all groups would be influenced by these biases. They become an issue if you are using survey results to make absolute judgment on quality, since you may get inflated results (Maeda, 2015).

In this book, we will support the use of response scale options in horizontal ascending order to avoid the potential response selection biases and inflated data. If you prefer using horizontal descending order, one way to control the left-side selection bias is to have half of respondents complete a survey with ascending order of the Likert scale levels, and another half with descending order, and use combined, averaged results (Nicholls et al., 2006). For a summary of research evidence and research-based recommendations on the use of ascending and descending order of Likert-type scale options, see Chyung, Kennedy, and Campbell (in press).

You can also present response scale options vertically:

- Vertical ascending order:
  - Strongly disagree
  - Disagree
  - Neutral
  - Agree
  - Strongly agree

- Vertical descending order:
  - Strongly agree
  - Agree
  - Neutral
  - Disagree
  - Strongly disagree

Interestingly, research did not find an *up-down selection bias* from the use of a vertical layout (Maeda, 2015). Thus, a vertical layout may be a preferred choice. However, the research also revealed that survey respondents spent more time and made more clicks when using a vertical layout of response options compared to when using a horizontal layout. This raises a concern regarding respondents becoming fatigue and careless. For that reason, you may be inclined to use a horizontal layout. However, you also need to be aware that a horizontal layout does not work well if survey respondents use mobile devices to complete the survey.

Therefore, you need to consider the overall length of your survey instrument and the survey medium used as well as the research findings discussed earlier to determine whether to use a horizontal or vertical layout.

NO UP-DOWN SELECTION BIAS

Follow Other Guidelines for Developing Survey Items

The previous sections provided research-based recommendations on the use of the Likert scale. The following are 10 additional guidelines for developing survey items.

TEN ADDITIONAL GUIDELINES

1. **Use one thought in each statement** (avoid double-barreled statements).

Here is an example of a double-barreled statement:

- The *handouts* and *role-plays* helped me understand the content and the way the steps are applied.

It is possible that respondents think that the handouts were helpful but the role-plays were not, or vice versa. Then, they would have difficulty choosing only one option from the response scale—they may choose a midpoint! You should measure each aspect in a separate question. For example,

- The *handouts* helped me understand the content.

- The *role-plays* helped me understand how I could apply the steps.

2. **Use active voice, and write in first person.**

Compare the following statements:

- I liked the workshop. (This statement uses active voice.)

- The workshop was well received. (This statement uses passive voice.)

- The attendees liked the workshop. (This statement asks for group consensus.)

You conduct surveys to collect information about respondents' individual thoughts and opinions. Thus, you should ask respondents what *they* think or feel about the issue by using active voice. Do not ask them how the issue was *viewed* by using passive voice. Do not ask how a group of people thought about it because a single respondent cannot represent others' thoughts.

3. **Use positively worded statements** (rather than mixing them with negatively worded statements).

Here are a positively worded statement and a negatively worded statement:

- The *handouts* helped me understand the content.

- The *role-plays* did not help me understand how I could apply the steps.

When you present a mix of positively and negatively worded statements in a survey questionnaire, uninterested, careless, or fatigued survey respondents may overlook or misinterpret negatively worded statements as positively worded ones (Merritt, 2012). The result is you receive inaccurate data.

Some survey questionnaires may have to use negatively worded statements because the survey topic itself deals with negative aspects such as depression. Otherwise, it is recommended that you use positively worded statements only.

If you need to mix positively and negatively worded statements, provide clear directions before presenting negatively worded statements. For more information on this topic, see Chyung, Barkin, and Shamsy (2018).

4. **Avoid double-negatives.**

It is difficult to select an option from a response scale after reading double-negatives such as:

- The quality of the video was *not bad*.

Present a positive statement:

- The quality of the video was *good*.

5. **Present survey items in the order in which things happened.**

Presenting survey items in chronological order helps survey respondents feel more comfortable answering the questions. For example, you may design survey items based on the following chronologically ordered experiences:

a. Experience with the online registration process before attending the workshop

b. Experience with handouts received during the workshop

c. Experience with the length of the workshop after completing it

6. **Avoid presenting text in all capital letters.**

IT TENDS TO TAKE A LITTLE MORE TIME TO READ AND COMPREHEND TEXT WRITTEN IN ALL CAPS; also, text written in all caps looks like YOU ARE SHOUTING AT THE READER! If you need to emphasize certain text, present the text in **bold** instead.

7. **Use clearly defined terms.**

Let's say you are evaluating a train-the-trainers program, where there is a trainer who provided the instruction, but learners are also trainers by title/profession. Imagine that you presented the following questions in your survey questionnaire:

*   The trainer was well prepared.

*   The program content was relevant to the trainers.

*   The trainer provided constructive feedback to the trainees.

It can be confusing. You want to revise the statements this way:

*   My trainer was well prepared.

*   The program content was relevant to my needs.

*   My trainer provided constructive feedback on my performance when I asked.

8. **Provide balanced options to choose from.**

Think about the following response scale:

○ Poor ○ Good ○ Very good ○ Excellent

There are more positive options than negative options in this scale, which will naturally generate positively biased results. It may be appropriate to use this type of unbalanced scales if you know that most survey respondents have positive attitudes toward the topic and if you want to see more variance in data by avoiding *the ceiling effect* (i.e., most respondents select the top option of the scale). Otherwise, it would be better to use a scale that balances an equal number of positive and negative options, such as:

○ Poor ○ Mediocre ○ Good ○ Excellent

9. **Provide mutually exclusive options to choose from.**

The following scale is designed to measure frequency. Is there something wrong with this scale?

○ Less than 5 times

○ Between 5 and 10 times

○ Between 10 and 20 times

○ Between 20 and 30 times

○ More than 30 times

The numbers 10 and 20 are included in the multiple options; that is, the options are not mutually exclusive. This type of error in scales will generate unreliable data. The scale can be revised this way:

○ Up to 4 times

○ Between 5 and 9 times

○ Between 10 and 19 times

○ Between 20 and 29 times

○ 30 times or more

10. Spell out acronyms.

Do not assume that all survey respondents are familiar with the acronyms that you present in the survey. To avoid misunderstanding, spell out all acronyms at least once when you first introduce them.

To put the previously discussed principles to practice, see the survey instrument makeover example presented in Appendix C.

Develop Survey Items That Measure a Construct

CONSTRUCTS =
ABSTRACT
CONCEPTS

While investigating a dimension, you may need to develop a structured survey instrument to measure a certain abstract concept or idea, called a **construct**, which you cannot directly observe, such as job commitment, learner motivation, or job satisfaction. To measure a construct, you develop survey items that measure *indicators* of the construct.

For example, how would you measure happiness? You need to come up with multiple items that indicate happiness, that is, indicators. Using a medical analogy, think of happiness as a medical condition and think about its symptoms. When you have a sore throat, have a runny nose, sneeze, and cough, they can be symptoms of a cold (diagnosis). Doctors may measure those symptoms to diagnose whether you have a cold or not. Using Miller's analogy format (**A** is to **B** as **C** is to **D**):

Diagnosis is to **Symptoms** as **Construct** is to **Indicators**

Apply the medical analogy to measuring happiness. When people are happy (construct), they tend to smile, laugh, and talk with others, and tend not to argue with other people or cry (indicators). If these five behaviors are valid and reliable indicators for happiness, you can design survey questions that measure those indicators to determine how happy individuals are.

Similarly, when you measure employee *job satisfaction*, you want to develop survey questions based on various aspects and symptoms that indicate satisfaction with their jobs, such as recognition, incentives, relationship with bosses and coworkers, job security, and so on. That is, employees tend to feel satisfied with their job (construct) when they are recognized for good performance, are satisfied with their salary, have good relationships with their bosses and coworkers, and have a secure job (indicators).

Measuring job satisfaction with only one question such as the following one does not capture various aspects (indicators) of the construct, job satisfaction:

Please indicate how satisfied with your job you are on a 5-point scale:

○ Extremely dissatisfied

○ Somewhat dissatisfied

○ Neutral

○ Somewhat satisfied

○ Extremely satisfied

Instead, you want to use multiple survey items addressing various indicators, such as the following items, and you may use the same response scale for all of them:

1. I feel recognized for my good performance.

2. My current salary is adequate for my performance.

3. I have a good relationship with my boss.

4. I have a good relationship with my coworkers.

5. I have a secure job.

After you develop a survey instrument to measure a construct, you need to test for validity and reliability of the instrument. If you are using an existing survey instrument, you want to find out if it has been tested for validity and reliability.

Test Validity and Reliability of a Survey Instrument

Testing validity of your survey instrument is to check if the multiple survey items that you developed indeed measure what you intend to measure. As a simple analogy, a valid instrument to use when measuring your weight is a bathroom scale, not a ruler. So, ask yourself: Is my survey questionnaire a valid instrument?

The **validity** of a survey instrument can be checked through different types of testing. You want to start by focusing on the instrument's face validity and content validity.

Face validity is tested by asking people—such as coworkers, users, or decision makers—to assess appropriateness of the instrument. You are asking them to check if the survey questions seem to measure what you intend to measure. Checking face validity of your survey instrument is a starting point but not a rigorous method.

Content validity is similar to face validity, but it is examined by subject matter experts who can provide a systematic examination—often based on theoretical frameworks relevant to the survey topic—to judge if the survey questions sufficiently cover the content domain to be measured (DeVellis, 2012). For example, if you develop a survey instrument to measure employees' job satisfaction, experts who are familiar with theories and research on job satisfaction can examine the survey questions

VALIDITY
TESTING

you include in your survey instrument. The experts may use Herzberg's motivation-hygiene theory and research findings to check if the survey questions cover sufficient aspects of job satisfaction.

You can test a survey instrument's *construct validity* to check if the multiple items in the survey instrument are designed to measure a single construct or independent multiple constructs. For example, if you hope to measure if employees perceive their organization as a learning organization, you may use the Dimensions of the Learning Organization Questionnaire (Marsick & Watkins, 2003). It is a 43-item survey instrument designed to measure seven dimensions (constructs) of a learning organization. Because this instrument has been tested for validity (Yang, Watkins, & Marsick, 2004), you have high confidence that the survey data indeed measure seven distinct dimensions of a learning organization.

If you developed a multi-item survey instrument to measure a construct (e.g., employee engagement), in addition to conducting face validity and content validity on your survey instrument, you may run a statistical analysis to test if the multi-items measure a single factor (construct). However, it is beyond the scope of this book to provide detailed explanations, and you are advised to look up other sources (e.g., Brown, 2015; Fabrigar & Wegener, 2012).

RELIABILITY TESTING

When you are using a multi-item survey instrument to measure a construct, you also need to test internal consistency among the multiple items; this is about instrument **reliability**. Reliability testing involves using a statistical analysis tool such as SPSS. It is also beyond the scope of this book to provide detailed explanations about reliability testing of a survey instrument. Instead, Appendix E provides a simple example of running reliability testing with SPSS and interpreting outputs.

You should keep in mind that not all dimensions in your evaluation project require that you use multiple survey items. For example, if one of your dimensions is called employee turnover rate, you may collect fact-based data showing employee turnover rates over the past couple of years.

Conduct Formative Meta-Evaluations

You conducted formative meta-evaluations during Step 6 while determining data collection methods (Chapter 7). You conducted formative meta-evaluations at that time to ensure that you made an adequate data collection plan.

Now you are in Step 7 to develop data collection instruments, and you need to conduct internal and external formative meta-evaluations on the survey instruments and other materials that you have developed.

Here are several techniques you can use:

FORMATIVE META-EVALUATION TECHNIQUES

- Use the face validity method to check if the survey instruments are developed clearly and appropriately.

- Ask an expert on survey design to review and provide feedback on your survey design.

- Ask your client or other stakeholders to review your survey instruments and other materials and ask for feedback on areas to be changed.

- Reflect and discuss with your team members and client to ensure ethical conduct during the data collection procedure.

You also need to start designing rubrics you will use to analyze the data obtained from your instruments (see Chapter 12 for rubric development). Your formative meta-evaluations during Step 7 (Develop data collection instruments) should include checking if your instruments would generate appropriate types of data to be analyzed with the rubrics that you plan to use.

Failing to conduct formative meta-evaluations on your instruments and other materials can result in using inappropriate or unethical data collection methods and procedures, obtaining incomplete or irrelevant (useless) data, and jeopardizing the quality of your evaluation.

Chapter Summary

Develop data collection instruments—self-administered surveys (Step 7):

- Evaluators can use various data collection methods, including self-administered surveys, one-on-one interviews, focus groups, observations, extant data reviews, and tests.

- Evaluators may be required to comply with IRB requirements and use informed consent forms to provide evaluation participants with a sufficient explanation of the evaluation project to help them make an informed decision as to whether or not to participate in the evaluation as informants.

- Evaluators should develop data collection instruments and procedures in a way that allows anonymity of data whenever possible and protects confidentiality of data.

- When using a self-administered survey, evaluators need to develop not only the survey questionnaire but also an informed consent form (or a cover letter) and a script to be used for recruiting survey participants.

- Evaluators may use a structured (using closed-ended items), unstructured (using open-ended items), or semi-structured (a mix of both types) survey questionnaire. Survey items should measure specific areas of the dimension that is being investigated.

- When developing closed-ended survey items, evaluators can use a question or statement format. To be able to calculate an average score of data obtained from multiple survey items, it is often helpful to use a statement format with the same response scale.

- When selecting a response scale, evaluators should be able to distinguish four different types of scales—nominal, ordinal, interval, and ratio scales.

- A 4-point Likert scale without a midpoint is an ordinal scale, and it is appropriate to report the data obtained from a 4-point Likert scale with frequencies or percentages of the data that fell into each scale point.

- A 5-point Likert scale with a midpoint is also an ordinal scale; however, it may be treated as an interval scale, especially by adding a modifier such as *Slightly* before *Disagree* and *Agree*— for example, *Strongly disagree, Slightly disagree, Neutral, Slightly agree, Strongly agree*—enabling evaluators to report an average score and use statistical tests that require interval data.

- To prevent survey respondents from using a midpoint as a dumping ground, which threatens the accuracy of data, it is recommended to provide another option such as *I don't know*, *It depends*, or *Not applicable*.

- Evaluators should be aware of various response selection biases, such as the left-side selection bias, acquiescence bias, and satisficing, associated with Likert-type response scales. Due to the response selection biases, survey respondents may choose more positive options when they use response scale options displayed in horizontal descending order.

- Additional guidelines for developing survey items include using one thought per item, using active voice and first person writing, using positively worded statements, avoiding double-negatives, presenting items in chronological order, avoiding using all capital letters, using clearly defined terms, using balanced options in response scales, using mutually exclusive options in response scales, and spelling out acronyms.

- When using a structured survey instrument to measure a construct, evaluators need to test for the instrument's validity and reliability.

- Evaluators should conduct internal and external formative meta-evaluations on survey instruments and other materials that they developed. It is particularly important to ensure that the instruments generate appropriate types of data to be analyzed with the rubrics that evaluators plan to use.

- Evaluators should get approval from the client for using the survey instruments they developed.

Chapter Discussion

1. Anonymity versus confidentiality of data

In your evaluation project, you are conducting a web-based survey in order to use the Success Case Method. You included a field that asks for the respondent's name, because you plan to identify success and nonsuccess cases based on the survey data and contact them for follow-up interviews.

You plan to recruit survey participants via email, so you developed a recruitment email script. In that script, you included the following paragraph:

> Your participation in this survey is voluntary and you will remain anonymous. Your response to the survey will also be kept confidential, and only a summary of the survey responses will be presented in the report.

Are the words *anonymous* and *confidential* used appropriately in the script? How so?

2. Extreme makeover—Survey edition

You were recently hired as a trainer at a company. You found out that the previous trainer, before he left, had drafted out the following questions to be used in the end-of-course survey questionnaire. The survey questionnaire has not been used yet, and the training manager asks you to make any changes to make it better before you start using the survey. The manager also says she wants this survey questionnaire to generate an average score of multiple survey items that indicates the overall quality of a training course.

Based on the evidence-based survey design recommendations you learned in this chapter, discuss the parts that you want to change and the reasons why. Produce a revised version. Also see the survey instrument makeover example presented in Appendix C.

1. Was the content of the course relevant to you?

   O Yes O No

2. What do you think about the quality of the trainer?

   O Excellent O Good O Not bad O Not good O Poor

3. How was the training pace?

   O Too slow O Slow O Fine O Fast O Too fast

4. Was the training facility:

   O Comfortable but too small for the group

   O Adequate

   O Needs remodeling

5. Was the course interesting and interactive enough for you?

   O Strongly agree O Agree O Disagree O Strongly disagree

6. Overall, how would you rate the course?

   O Excellent

   O Very Good

   O Neither Good nor Bad

   O Poor

   O Total waste of my time

7. If you would change one thing about the course, what would it be?

8. If you would keep one thing about the course, what would it be?

9. How much information of this course do you think you will be able to use?

   O None O Some O Half O A lot O All of it

10. The amount of practice provided during the course was just right.

    O Strongly agree O Agree O Kinda O Disagree O Strongly disagree

Now, Your Turn—Develop Survey Instruments

In your evaluation proposal, you included a table describing your plan for using certain data collection methods. Convert the table to an instruments and rubrics development worksheet, as shown in Table B-6 in Appendix B (Evaluation Development Worksheets). Then, develop recruitment scripts and informed consent forms as well the measurement instruments in separate documents.

10

Develop Data Collection Instruments II

Interviews, Focus Groups, Observations, Extant Data Reviews, and Tests (Step 7)

Y ou are still working on Step 7 to develop data collection instruments. The previous chapter focused on how to develop self-administered survey instruments; this chapter provides information about how to develop instruments for interviews, focus groups, observations, extant data reviews, and tests. The previous chapter's

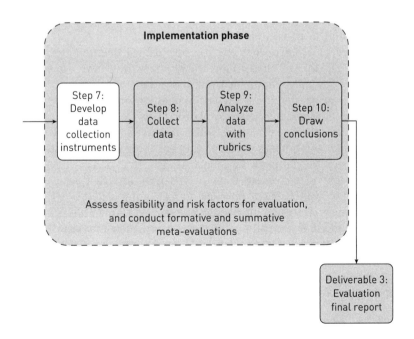

sections—"Comply With IRB Requirements," "Use Informed Consent Forms," and "Distinguish Anonymity From Confidentiality"—apply to this chapter as well.

Determine Whether to Use a Structured, Unstructured, or Semi-Structured Interview

One-on-one interviews involve private conversations between an interviewer and an interviewee where the interviewee is provided with an opportunity to express his or her knowledge, thoughts, or opinions about specific topics. Interviews can be conducted in person, via telephone, or via video call. Interviews generate qualitative data and some quantitative data as well. During any type of interview, you as an interviewer have an opportunity to observe interviewees' behavioral or auditory cues during conversations, which are also a type of data.

One-on-one interviews can be structured, unstructured, or semi-structured. You (the interviewer) use structured interview questions when you know what you do not know and ask specific questions to uncover the information that you intend to find out. On the other hand, you use unstructured questions when you do not know what you do not know and ask the interviewees to tell you what you need to know (Lincoln & Guba, 1985).

STRUCTURED, UNSTRUCTURED, OR SEMI-STRUCTURED INTERVIEWS

During *structured interviews*, you should use an interview guide that remains the same for all interviewees, ensuring consistency during questioning. You do not make spontaneous changes in the set of questions to ask; you ask prepared interview questions in a certain order. You may use closed-ended questions to record interviewees' responses on a response scale, which allows easy comparison of data obtained from multiple interviewees. For this reason, you may think of structured interviews as similar to structured self-administered surveys. A difference is how it is administered—self-administered or administered by an interviewer. During interviews, you can clarify questions if interviewees have difficulty understanding any questions. If you are asking questions via email and having people respond via email, this interaction is not an interview; it is rather a self-administered survey via email.

During *unstructured interviews*, you use open-ended questions to allow interviewees to tell their stories. You as an interviewer allow interviewees to express their thoughts, experiences, and opinions in detail, and you ask follow-up questions tailored to their responses rather than using prescribed questions in a preset order. To obtain detailed information from interviewees, you need to develop good rapport with them first. If you are conducting an evaluation with a goal-free approach, you will likely use unstructured interviews or focus groups to find out about unknown issues. A downside of using unstructured interviews, compared with structured interviews, is that it may take longer for you to complete your analysis of the interview data.

You may use a *semi-structured interview* format, using a mix of structured and unstructured formats. You as an interviewer are prepared with a list of specific closed-ended questions to ask in a certain order, but you also allow interviewees to provide detailed explanations by asking open-ended, follow-up questions, which may not be prescribed. A pitfall is that during your analysis, it may be easy to focus more on the numerical values collected from closed-ended questions, no matter what the interviewees say in their explanations. Table 48 compares the three types of one-on-one interviews.

TABLE 48 ● Structured, Semi-Structured, and Unstructured One-on-One Interviews		
	Structured	**Semi-Structured**	**Unstructured**
Design	• It uses an interview guide that remains the same for each interviewee, where the questions and their order are fixed. • It records interview responses on a scale while collecting other qualitative information as well.	• It is designed with a mix of structured and unstructured formats.	• It uses an interview guide that allows spontaneous changes or follow-up questions based on individual responses. • It uses open-ended questions to allow interviewees to provide information in their own words.
Example	How often do you see an error sign when you click the links? Would you say, ○ Every time, ○ 75% of the time, ○ 50% of the time, ○ 25% of the time, or ○ Never? Whom do you contact for help first? ○ A coworker, ○ The help desk, or ○ Others? (If so, whom?)	What makes you feel motivated to come to work every day? (Probe into various contributing factors.) On a 5-point scale where 1 is very dissatisfied and 5 is very satisfied, how would you rate your experience with the organization culture, and why? ○1 ○2 ○3 ○4 ○5	Tell me a situation where you felt extremely dissatisfied while using the system: _____ Tell me a situation where you felt extremely satisfied while using the system: _____
Pros and cons	• Important but not critical for the interviewer to develop rapport with interviewees • Easy to compile and analyze data obtained from multiple interviewees by multiple interviewers • No intention to make spontaneous changes or follow-up questions to uncover the reasons behind interviewees' responses	• Able to use closed-ended and open-ended questions, as needed • Able to use both planned and unplanned follow-up questions • Quantitative data may overpower qualitative data during analysis (i.e., no matter what they said in their explanations, the numerical values become more important)	• Acceptable to change the order or type of questions based on interviewee's response • Able to understand respondents' experience better • Requires rapport with interviewees to obtain detailed information • Time-consuming to analyze data

Compared to one-on-one interviews, *focus groups* involve group conversations in which you are there to facilitate (and not to direct) the participants' conversations, to help them reveal their knowledge, thoughts, and opinions about specific topics. It is recommended that you keep the size of a focus group to no more than 10 to 12 people (O'Sullivan, 2004). Focus group participants are often asked to respond to open-ended questions (i.e., unstructured), resulting in mostly qualitative data.

Develop Materials for Conducting Interviews or Focus Groups

Chapter 9 explains how to prepare survey materials when you need to comply with an educational institution's institutional review board (IRB) requirements. Similarly, this chapter provides information about materials needed for conducting interviews, focus groups, observations, extant data reviews, and tests, with an assumption that you are asked to comply with an educational institution's IRB requirements. If you are not required to comply with IRB requirements, you may adjust the information and procedure as you see fit.

To prepare to conduct a one-on-one interview or focus group, you would need to develop the following materials:

1. A recruitment script

2. An informed consent form

3. An interview protocol, including an opening script, interview questions, and a closing script

Develop a Recruitment Script and Informed Consent Form to Be Sent to Recruit Interview or Focus Group Participants

For interviews (including focus groups), you purposely select the participants and you see them and/or hear them talking during interviews. Because all participants' identities are exposed to you, it is not possible to conduct anonymous interviews, although you can certainly code their identities with pseudonyms to protect confidentiality of their data.

You may recruit interview or focus group participants via email, and you can present an informed consent form in your email message. Exhibit 6 is a sample recruitment email message based on the previously used mentoring program example. You attach an informed consent form to the email message. A sample informed consent form is shown in Exhibit 7. You want to find out if the IRB or legal department of your client organization requires you to use a certain format and/or content in your informed consent form.

EXHIBIT 6 ● Sample Email Message Sent by an Internal Evaluator, Recruiting Interview Participants

To: Recipient@neceurl.org

Subject: Interview regarding the mentoring program

Hi [name],

I am Jane Doe, Performance Improvement Specialist at NECE, Inc. I am working on an evaluation project regarding the mentoring program provided at NECE to find out how helpful the program was and what can be changed to improve the mentor–mentee experience for future participants. I am conducting a series of interviews as part of the evaluation project, and I am inviting you to participate in an interview since you recently completed the program.

The attached informed consent document provides additional information requesting your consent to participate in the interview.

If you are willing to participate in this interview, please reply to this email. Then, I will contact you to schedule a day/time for the interview. If you have any questions regarding this interview, feel free to contact me via email or phone.

Thanks for your participation!

Jane Doe

Performance Improvement Specialist, NECE, Inc.

Phone: (123) 456-7890

Email: JaneDoe@neceurl.org

* Attachment: InformedConsentForInterview.pdf

EXHIBIT 7 ● Sample Informed Consent Form for Conducting an Interview

Informed Consent Form

Title: Evaluation of the Effectiveness of the Mentoring Program

Investigator: Jane Doe, Performance Improvement Specialist, NECE, Inc.

Sponsor: James Doe, Director of Learning and Performance Improvement, NECE, Inc.

Approval: This evaluation project has been approved by the legal department of NECE, Inc.

Purpose: The mentoring program at NECE, Inc. has been in operation since 2017. I am conducting a formative evaluation to understand how effective the mentoring program has been and what needs to be changed to produce better outcomes. I am conducting interviews to gather information needed for the evaluation project.

Procedure: I will contact you via email to schedule an interview date and time. The interview will be conducted via telephone and will last for about 30 minutes. With your permission, I will audio-record the interview for transcription only, and then I will destroy the audio file after the transcript is complete.

(Continued)

EXHIBIT 7 ● (Continued)

Confidentiality: I will do my best to keep any identifiable information confidential. During the interview, you will be assigned to a pseudonym and will be referred to as such. Only a summary of data will be presented in a report, and your name will not be used in any written or oral reports.

Risks: There are minimal risks associated with this interview. If you do not feel comfortable answering particular questions during the interview, you can skip those questions or stop participating in the interview at any time.

Benefits: By submitting your input, you are sharing information that helps improve the quality of the program.

Questions: If you have any questions or concerns about participation in this evaluation project, please contact me at (123) 456-7890 or janedoe@neceurl.com. If you have questions about your rights as a participant, you may contact the legal department at NECE, Inc. at legaldept@neceurl.com.

Voluntary Participation: Your participation in the evaluation project is voluntary. If you decide to participate, please reply to the email message to which this document was attached. I will contact you to schedule for an interview date and time.

Develop an Interview Protocol

An interview protocol includes an opening script, interview questions, and a closing script.

OPENING SCRIPT   It is important to start an interview with a well-prepared *opening script*. By providing explanations up front about what the interview is for and what rights the interviewees have, you can put interviewees at ease and build trust with them. Especially when you use multiple independent interviewers, having a written opening script also helps all interviewers provide consistent information to all interviewees.

As part of the opening script, you want to inform interviewees of their rights as participants—or remind them of their rights if you have already provided them with an informed consent form via email. Even though you received their email reply showing their agreement to participate in the interview, there are times when you also want to obtain their written signature on a printed informed consent form, especially if you are conducting an on-site, face-to-face interview. For example, the IRB or legal department may require that you obtain a written signature from participants on an informed consent form before you begin your interview. In such cases, you need to add that request to the opening script.

You may also ask for permission from interviewees about audio-recording their responses if it is difficult for you to write down all of the information they provide. To protect their identity, you can assign a pseudonym to each interviewee before you start your interview and use the pseudonym during the interview. That way, the pseudonym is used in your written notes and captured in the audio file.

INTERVIEW   After the opening script, you start asking your *interview questions*. While question-
QUESTIONS   ing, you should observe the interviewee's body language and tone of voice as another type of data. If you notice that the interviewee feels uncomfortable answering questions, you should allow him or her to express concerns, and ask if you should skip

questions or stop the interview. You should also manage time to complete the interview within the scheduled time frame.

It is also important to provide a formal *closing script*, announcing the end of the interview, thanking the interviewee for participation, and allowing the interviewee to ask questions. Abrupt ending of an interview can leave the interviewee with a negative impression toward the interview experience.

CLOSING SCRIPT

Exhibit 8 is a sample interview protocol that you can adopt, modify, and use. In the sample protocol, it is assumed that during your recruitment, you have already obtained participants' electronic signature or received their email reply indicating their agreement to participate in the interview. This sample contains semi-structured interview questions.

EXHIBIT 8 ● Sample Interview Protocol

Opening:

Hi, I am [introduce yourself]. First, thank you for agreeing to participate in this interview.

As you read in the informed consent form that you received via email, the purpose of this interview is to better understand how effective the mentoring program has been and what needs to be changed to produce better outcomes. It will take about 30 minutes to complete this interview. Your participation is voluntary, and you can skip any question or stop the interview any time for any reason. Do I have your consent to conduct this interview? [Wait for a response.]

Thank you. In order to protect your privacy, I would like to use a pseudonym to refer to you during the interview. May I call you [Bob] instead of your real name? [Wait for an answer.]

Thanks, Bob. I would also like to record the interview because it is difficult for me to write down all of the information that you will share with me. I will destroy the audio file as soon as I finish transcribing it. Do I have your permission to record this session? [Wait for an answer.]

OK. Before we begin our interview, do you have any questions? [Answer questions if any.] Thank you. I will start recording now. [Start the recording.]

Semi-structured interview questions:

1. [Bob], when did you participate in the mentoring program?

    ○ Fall 2017 ○ Spring 2018 ○ Summer 2018

2. How did you decide to participate in the program? Was it recommended by someone else, or did you decide to do it on your own? What did you want to get out of the program?

3. [Bob], tell me about the initial procedure that you and your mentor used during the first couple of weeks to start the program. On a scale of 1 to 5, one being *it didn't work well at all* and five being *it worked very well*, how would you rate the effectiveness of the startup procedure?

    ○ 1 ○ 2 ○ 3 ○ 4 ○ 5

    Why? Did it get better? How?

(Continued)

EXHIBIT 8   ●   (Continued)

4. What was the overall procedure that you and your mentor used during the remaining weeks of the program?

    (If anything changed) Who initiated the change? How did it work out for you?

5. [Bob], earlier, you described what you wanted to get out of the program. Did you gain those things from the program?

    (If so) How are you different now after having completed the program?

    (If not) What prevented you from achieving your goals?

6. What would you say was the best part of the program?

7. Knowing what you know now from your experience, if you did this again, what would you do differently? How would it make a difference in terms of your experience and outcomes?

8. If you have an opportunity to provide suggestions to other employees who are going to enroll in the program soon, what would you tell them?

9. Lastly, how would you rate the overall quality of the program, using a 5-point scale, *Poor, Mediocre, Fair, Good, or Excellent*?

    O Poor O Mediocre O Fair O Good O Excellent

    What is the main reason for your rating?

Closing:

It is time to close our interview. Do you have any questions or comments to add? [Wait for the response.]

[Bob], thank you very much for participating in the interview. If you have any questions about the interview you participated in today, please feel free to contact me. The contact information is listed on the email message that I sent to you. [Stop the recording.]

Develop a Focus Group Protocol

FOCUS GROUP WITH OPEN-ENDED QUESTIONS

Because focus groups are used to generate discussions among multiple participants, open-ended questions are often used.

Exhibit 9 is a sample focus group protocol, including an opening script, open-ended questions, and a closing script. In this sample, it is assumed that during your recruitment, you have already obtained participants' electronic signatures on an informed consent form or received their email reply indicating their agreement to participate in the focus group. If written signatures are required, you will need to add this step during the opening phase.

While developing interview or focus group questions, you want to think about a rubric to be used to analyze the data, in order to ensure that you are collecting adequate and sufficient data to get analyzed against a rubric. The following is an example of rubrics to be used to analyze interview data:

*   Met expectations: Comments are mostly positive about the program procedure and how the program met their needs; suggestions are for minor changes that can be easily implemented.

EXHIBIT 9 • Sample Focus Group Protocol

Opening:

Hi, everyone! Thank you for coming here today to talk about the employee childcare program. My name is Jane Doe, Performance Improvement Specialist at NECE, Inc., and I will be the facilitator for the focus group.

We started this childcare program for the NECE employees a couple of years ago. We invited you to this focus group because you have used or are currently using the employee childcare program.

So, the purpose of this focus group is to listen to your experience with the childcare program and to get your feedback about how we can better serve NECE employees with children, like yourselves, who need to use a childcare program during their work hours. We want to hear from you how the program worked out for you, what did not work well, and what can be changed, so we can better serve you and your children, and future employees and their children, and ultimately better support the company's goals.

The focus group will last for an hour. The information that you will share during the focus group will be valuable for improving the quality of the program. As we explained in the informed consent form, we will audio-record the discussion to make sure that we capture the information accurately. We will destroy the audio file as soon as we complete our transcripts. We will do our best to protect your privacy, and all transcripts will be coded with pseudonyms. We also ask you not to talk about what other participants shared during the focus group with people outside this group. Do we have your permission to audio-record the session, or does anyone have any concerns? [Wait for the response.]

Your participation in this focus group is voluntary. You can skip any question or stop participating in the focus group by leaving the room any time for any reason.

Do you have any questions before we begin? [Wait for questions.]

OK, we will start our audio-recording now. [Start the recording.]

Focus group discussion:

1. To begin, we want to ask each of you to introduce yourself to the group, and talk about how you heard about the employee childcare program and how long you have been using the program. Let's start with you here. [Listen to their introductions and explanations.]

2. OK. Now, I will ask the group some questions. Think back to when you first heard about the program. What were your thoughts? Did you want to enroll your children in the program right away, did you need to look for more information before you made a decision, or did you not want to use the program at all, and why? [Provide follow-up questions if "why" information is lacking.]

3. When you were looking for a childcare program, what criteria did you use? Does the employee childcare program meet your criteria? Which criteria does the program not meet? [Provide follow-up questions to solicit information about how the program meets or does not meet their criteria.]

4. Had anyone used a different childcare program before you switched to our company's employee childcare program? What were the reasons for your decision?

5. Has anyone thought about switching from this employee childcare program to a different program but decided not to? What were the reasons that caused you to think about switching to a different program, and what were the reasons for your decision to stay with this employee childcare program?

(Continued)

EXHIBIT 9 ● (Continued)

6. What improvements in the program have you observed over time? [If necessary, ask them to clarify specific areas for improvement and time frames involved.]

7. Let's talk about a couple of things more specifically. What do you think about the program center? The building, the rooms, the décor, the furniture, the playground, etc. What do you think about the program curriculum? Tell us your child's age first.

8. What do you want the program to continue to do?

9. What sort of things do you think the program can change without adding costs?

10. What sort of things do you want the program to change or add even if those changes result in an additional fee, paid out of your pocket?

Closing:

It's time to close our discussion. Are there any other comments, concerns, or questions that you have today? [Wait for comments.]

Thanks for participating in the focus group today. We've received a lot of good information from you. If you have any questions about the focus group you participated in today, please feel free to contact us. The contact information is listed on the informed consent form. [Stop the recording.]

- Some improvement needed: A mix of positive and negative comments are made about the program procedure and how the program met or did not meet their needs; suggestions are for making some minor and some important changes.

- Major improvement needed: Many negative comments are expressed about the program procedure and how the program did not meet their needs; suggestions are for making substantial and important changes.

The preceding rubric designed for interview or focus group data uses three rubric levels (*Met expectations, Some improvement needed,* and *Major improvement needed*). You can use a different number of rubric levels (e.g., four levels) and different labels for the rubric levels (e.g., *Excellent, Good, Mediocre,* and *Poor*). However, within the same evaluation project, you want to use the same number of rubric levels and the same labels for rubric levels for all types of data across dimensions. Only the rubric definitions are tailored to the types of data. This consistency in rubric levels and labeling will help you combine the results obtained from multiple data sources (e.g., results from surveys, interviews, extant data reviews, etc.). Recall the "How good is this apple?" activity you did at the end of the Introduction chapter (Table 2). Chapter 12 provides more information about developing rubrics.

Solicit Interview Volunteers at the End of a Self-Administered Web-Based Survey

INTERVIEW VOLUNTEERS FROM AN IDENTIFIABLE SURVEY

In some cases, you may solicit interview volunteers among self-administered survey respondents. The survey can be an anonymous survey or an identifiable survey.

If it is an identifiable survey, you can simply insert a question at the end of the survey questionnaire to ask respondents to volunteer to participate in a follow-up interview, as shown in Exhibit 10. You have collected their names from the survey questionnaire, so you know who volunteered to participate in a follow-up interview.

Be aware that when you are using the Success Case Model (SCM), it is not appropriate to use the method presented in Exhibit 10, because you do not know who are success and nonsuccess cases yet. You need to analyze the survey data first in order to identify success and nonsuccess cases and then contact selected success and nonsuccess cases separately.

If you use an anonymous survey, you cannot simply add a question as shown in Exhibit 10 because you do not know who responded to the interview solicitation question. You cannot ask for participants' names in the same anonymous survey questionnaire either, because it must remain an anonymous survey.

INTERVIEW VOLUNTEERS FROM AN ANONYMOUS SURVEY

One way to handle this situation is to develop a separate survey questionnaire in which you ask for voluntary participation in a follow-up interview and ask for name and contact information. To do so, the design of your anonymous survey questionnaire will remain the same, except that you will design it so that after respondents click the Submit button, they will be taken to another survey form where they are asked to voluntarily participate in a follow-up interview, as shown in Exhibit 11. That way, the data collected from the first anonymous survey questionnaire will be stored in a data file separate from the data to be collected from the second interview-solicitation survey form. You may present an informed consent form for the interview in the second interview-solicitation survey.

Or, you may describe both a self-administered survey and a follow-up interview in the same informed consent form as shown in Exhibit 12, whether you are soliciting interview volunteers among participants of an identifiable or anonymous survey. That is, you are combining the information presented in Exhibit 4 for conducting a self-administered survey and the information presented in Exhibit 7 for conducting an interview in one informed consent form. You can present this combined informed consent form when you recruit survey respondents, informing them that they will also be asked to voluntarily participate in a follow-up interview.

EXHIBIT 10 ● Method for Soliciting Interview Volunteers at the End of an Identifiable Web-Based Survey

Thank you for completing the survey questions above!

We'd love to hear from a small group of survey respondents to learn more about their experience with the program by conducting a follow-up interview. Detailed information is presented in the informed consent form attached below:

InformedConsentForInterview.pdf

May we contact you to schedule for a 30-minute follow-up telephone interview? If so, please checkmark the box below and let us know how you prefer to be contacted.

☐ Yes, I will participate in a follow-up interview. To schedule a follow-up interview, please contact me:

○ via email; my email address is _____.

○ by telephone; my phone number is _____.

Please click the Submit button below.

Submit

EXHIBIT 11 ● Method for Soliciting Interview Volunteers After an Anonymous Web-Based Survey

Thank you for completing the survey questions! Please click the Submit button below.

| Submit |

(A new webpage)

Thank you. Your data has been successfully stored in a database.

We'd love to hear from a small group of survey respondents to learn more about their experience with the program by conducting a follow-up interview. Detailed information is presented in the informed consent form attached below:

InformedConsentForInterview.pdf

May we contact you to schedule for a 30-minute follow-up telephone interview? If so, please checkmark the box below and let us know how you prefer to be contacted and your name. This is a separate form; the personal information you provide below will not be linked to the survey responses you have submitted.

☐ Yes, I will participate in a follow-up interview. To schedule a follow-up interview, please contact me:

○ via email; my email address is _____.

○ by telephone; my phone number is _____.

My name is: _____.

| Submit |

EXHIBIT 12 ● Sample Informed Consent Form for Conducting a Survey and a Follow-Up Interview

Informed Consent Form

Title: Evaluation of the Effectiveness of the Mentoring Program

Investigator: Jane Doe, Performance Improvement Specialist, NECE, Inc.

Sponsor: James Doe, Director of Learning and Performance Improvement, NECE, Inc.

Approval: This evaluation project has been approved by the legal department of NECE, Inc.

Purpose: The mentoring program at NECE, Inc. has been in operation since 2017. I am conducting a formative evaluation to understand how effective the mentoring program has been and what needs to be changed to produce better outcomes. I am conducting a web-based survey and a follow-up phone interview to gather information needed for the evaluation project.

Procedure: You have received a link to the web-based survey questionnaire. It will take about 5 minutes to complete the survey. At the end of the survey, you will be asked if you would also participate in a 30-minute follow-up phone interview.

Confidentiality: I will do my best to keep any identifiable information confidential. Only a summary of data will be presented in a report, and your name will not be used in any written or oral reports.

Risks: There are minimal risks associated with the survey and interview. If you do not feel comfortable answering particular questions presented in the survey or during the interview, you can skip those questions or stop completing the survey or participating in the interview at any time.

Benefits: By submitting your data, you are sharing information that helps improve the quality of the program.

Questions: If you have any questions or concerns about participation in this evaluation project, please contact me at (123) 456-7890 or janedoe@neceurl.com. If you have questions about your rights as a participant, you may contact the legal department at NECE, Inc. at legaldept@neceurl.com.

Voluntary Participation: Your participation in the evaluation project is voluntary. You may participate in only the web-based survey or in both the web-based survey and the follow-up phone interview. If you decide to participate in the web-based survey, please return to the survey questionnaire and click the checkbox to confirm your consent and proceed with the survey questionnaire. At the end of the survey, you will be asked if you would also participate in a follow-up interview, which you can decide at that time.

Develop Materials for Conducting Observations

Preparation of data collection instruments for on-site observations is similar to preparation for interviews; you need to develop the following materials:

1. A recruitment script

2. An informed consent form

3. An observation checklist

Prepare an Observee Recruitment Script and an Informed Consent Form

The identity of the observee (the performer to be observed) is revealed during recruitment and observation, and you need to attach an informed consent form to your recruitment script. See Exhibit 13 and Exhibit 14.

Develop Checklists for Observations

When you observe people's behavior on site or from a videotape, you likely need to use a checklist. The checklist will look different depending on what you are observing and why you are observing it. You might plan to observe the *quantity* of a behavior (e.g., how many times a call center agent interrupts customers' talking) or the *quality* of a behavior (e.g., how friendly a call center agent sounds).

EXHIBIT 13 ● Sample Observation Recruitment Script

To: Recipient@neceurl.org

Subject: Observing your use of the new HRMS

Hi [name],

I am Jane Doe, Performance Improvement Specialist at NECE, Inc. I am working on an evaluation project to find out the effectiveness of the training program that was designed to help employees make a smooth transition to using the new human resources management system (HRMS). You recently completed the training program, and I would like to observe your use of the new HRMS to see how much the training program helped and what should be changed in the program to produce better outcomes.

Please see the attached informed consent document that provides detailed information about the observation, requesting your consent to allow my observation.

If you are willing to allow me to observe your use of the HRMS, please reply to this email. Then, I will contact you to schedule a day/time for the observation. If you have any questions regarding this observation, feel free to contact me via email or phone.

Thanks for your participation!

Jane Doe

Performance Improvement Specialist, NECE, Inc.

Phone: (123) 456-7890

Email: JaneDoe@neceurl.org

* Attachment: InformedConsentForObservation.pdf

EXHIBIT 14 ● Sample Informed Consent Form for Conducting an Observation

Informed Consent Form

Title: Evaluation of the New HRMS Training Program

Investigator: Jane Doe, Performance Improvement Specialist, NECE, Inc.

Sponsor: James Doe, Director of Learning and Performance Improvement, NECE, Inc.

Approval: This evaluation project has been approved by the legal department of NECE, Inc.

Purpose: The rollout of a new HRMS is expected to be completed in the next 6 months. A training program has been made available to employees to make a smooth transition to the HRMS. I am conducting a formative evaluation to find out how well the training program helps employees use the system and what needs to be changed in the program. An observation of your use of the system is needed to gather information for the evaluation project.

Procedure: I will contact you via email to schedule an observation date and time. The observation will take place in your office for 30 minutes. You will be asked to think aloud while completing several tasks using the system. Duration for completing each task will be measured.

Confidentiality: I will do my best to keep any identified information confidential. During the observation, you will be assigned to a pseudonym and will be referred to as such. Only a summary of data will be presented in a report, and your name will not be used in any written or oral reports.

Risks: There are minimal risks associated with this interview. If you do not feel comfortable being observed during your use of the system, you can stop or cancel the observation session at any time.

Benefits: By allowing an observation of your use of the system, you are sharing information that helps improve the quality of the training program for future participants and develop other performance support tools if needed.

Questions: If you have any questions or concerns about participation in this evaluation project, please contact me at (123) 456-7890 or janedoe@neceurl.com. If you have questions about your rights as a participant, you may contact the legal department at NECE, Inc. at legaldept@neceurl.com.

Voluntary Participation: Your participation in the evaluation project is voluntary. If you decide to participate, please reply to the email message to which this document was attached. I will contact you to schedule for an observation date and time.

EXHIBIT 15 ● Checklist for Observation—Sample 1

User#:	Task:	Time spent (min.):
Click#	**Clicked location**	**Comments**
1	__Menu: __Button: __Text link: __Other:	
2	__Menu: __Button: __Text link: __Other:	
3	__Menu: __Button: __Text link: __Other:	
4	__Menu:	

In the example of the HRMS user observation as described in the recruitment script (Exhibit 13) and the informed consent form (Exhibit 14), you plan to use a *think-aloud protocol* during your observation, which is a usability testing method to ask computer system users to verbalize what goes through their mind while performing tasks (Lewis & Rieman, 1994). Let's say, you intend to measure how many clicks users make and how long it takes for users to navigate through the steps to complete each task, where they get confused, or if they get lost and are unable to complete the task. Then, you may use a checklist such as the one shown in Exhibit 15 to record where on the screen users clicked to complete a given task and how long it took for each user to complete the task.

CHECKLIST WHEN USING A THINK-ALOUD PROTOCOL

#	Behavior	Did not do it well (0)	Did it well (1)	Comments
1	Demonstrates a positive attitude toward the applicant			
2	Engages the applicant through small talk			
3				
9				
10	Maintains appropriate eye contact with the applicant			

EXHIBIT 16 ● Checklist for Observation—Sample 2

CHECKLIST TO OBSERVE JOB INTERVIEW BEHAVIOR

Consider another situation where you are observing a supervisor's interview skills during a job applicant interview. This supervisor has completed a training program on interview skills, and the supervisor is supposed to exhibit a couple of specific behaviors during an interview. As with survey data, you should also think carefully about the type of data you need to collect and the way you want to analyze the data (i.e., what the rubric would look like; see Chapter 12), and use the most appropriate scale in your checklist. You may use a checklist like the one shown in Exhibit 16 to record the quality of each behavior.

A MIX OF QUANTITATIVE AND QUALITATIVE DATA FROM OBSERVATIONS

Use of observation checklists may generate a mix of quantitative and qualitative data, similar to what semi-structured survey questionnaires would do. Again, think about the rubrics you will use to analyze the data generated from your checklists. (Chapter 12 provides more information about developing rubrics.) For example, if you observed five supervisors' interview skills using the checklist shown in Exhibit 16, you might use a rubric such as the following based on a group average of individual supervisors' scores (quantitative data) and the comments describing specific aspects of each behavior (qualitative data). When there are 10 behavioral criteria, each supervisor would get a score of zero to 10. Thus, a group average would also fall between zero and 10.

- Met expectations: $9.0 \leq$ average score ≤ 10.0, and there are no unexpected negative interview behaviors.

- Some improvement needed: $8.0 \leq$ average score ≤ 8.9, and the interview behaviors that are lacking do not present serious consequences.

- Major improvement needed: $0 \leq$ average score ≤ 7.9, and the interview behaviors that are lacking present serious consequences.

Develop Materials for
Conducting Extant Data Reviews

To perform extant data reviews, you need permission from the organization to review existing data. Often, you will receive data from the client, or the client may connect you to a person who will provide data.

PROTECT
CONFIDENTIALITY
AND SECURITY OF
EXTANT DATA

Types of extant data vary. Some may be considered public information and be readily available (e.g., information posted on websites). Some information, even though not public, can be shared without much caution. Other data may be proprietary, protected, or sensitive, and you must pay special attention to protect confidentiality and security of the data. Examples include people's names, addresses, birth dates, medical records, and education records. You should also be aware of laws and regulations on handling such data, for example, the Health Insurance Portability and Accountability Act (HIPAA) and the Family Educational Rights and Privacy Act (FERPA) of 1974.

In some cases, for analysis purposes, you may need identification information such as names, employee numbers, or gender. You must check if it is *must-have* information or *nice-to-have* information. You should ask for the minimum information necessary to complete your evaluation project. An alternative is to request a summary of data, instead of raw data, from the client organization.

You also need a checklist when reviewing extant data, whether you are the actual reviewer or you are asking someone else (e.g., a subject matter expert) to review the data. For example, let's say that you are reviewing a website to check for its accessibility by using the *Web Content Accessibility Guidelines* (WCAG; https://www.w3.org/TR/WCAG/). Your checklist could be designed based on the guidelines as shown in Exhibit 17.

CHECKLIST FOR
REVIEWING
EXTANT DATA

For another example, let's say that there are 10 lessons in the training program that you are reviewing here and that all 10 lessons are supposed to be designed to teach not only knowledge- and comprehension-level but also application-level skills per the cognitive domain of Bloom's taxonomy (Bloom et al., 1956). You might use a checklist as shown in Exhibit 18.

EXHIBIT 17 ● Checklist for Extant Data Review—Sample 1

WCAG 2.1 Guidelines	Not applicable	All pages violate (0)	Many pages violate, some support (1)	Some pages violate, many support (2)	All pages support (3)	Comments
1.1 Text alternatives						
1.2 Time-based media						

	EXHIBIT 18 ● **Checklist for Extant Data Review—Sample 2**			
Lesson	**Knowledge Level (1)**	**Comprehension Level (2)**	**Application Level (3)**	**Comments**
1				
2				
3				
4				
9				
10				

A MIX OF QUANTITATIVE AND QUALITATIVE DATA FROM EXTANT DATA REVIEWS

While developing checklists for extant data reviews, again, think about what your rubrics may look like. Rubrics for analyzing data generated by extant data review checklists will be similar to the ones used for observation data, since the extant data review checklists often generate a mix of quantitative and qualitative data. For example, the following rubric may be used for analyzing data obtained by using a checklist shown in Exhibit 18. (Chapter 12 provides more information about developing rubrics.)

- Met expectations: Nine or 10 out of the 10 lessons address application-level skills, and no comments indicate major improvement needed.

- Some improvement needed: Six to eight out of the 10 lessons address application-level skills, and a few comments indicate some minor improvement needed.

- Major improvement needed: Zero to five out of the 10 lessons address application-level skills, and many comments indicate serious improvement needed.

Develop Materials for Administering Tests

Knowledge test instruments, whether they are administered in a print or electronic form, may use various types of questions such as true/false, multiple choice, fill-in-the-blank, short answer, or essay questions.

EXISTING OR NEW TESTS

If you are using a knowledge test during your evaluation project, your situation may fall into one of the following possibilities:

- You need to develop a new set of knowledge test questions and administer the test. In this case, you may likely be recruiting a group of testees for your evaluation, so you need to develop a recruitment script and an informed consent form, as well as the knowledge test questions.

- You are collecting data by using an existing knowledge test. If so, you may need to develop an informed consent form to obtain permission to collect and use the test data for your evaluation project.

- If the client organization is already planning to administer the existing knowledge test as part of their organizational practice without needing to involve you in the process, discuss with your client if you can treat this as an extant data review.

- A knowledge test had been administered before you started your evaluation project, and you are analyzing existing test scores. Then, you should characterize this data source as an extant data review instead.

If objective test questions are used, you would not need a checklist. Rather, you will get a score by coding a correct answer with 1 and an incorrect answer with 0. If essay questions are used, you will need to prepare a checklist to evaluate and score the test results, similar to the checklists you would use during extant data reviews.

Conduct Formative Meta-Evaluations

As you do with survey instruments, you should conduct internal and external formative meta-evaluations on the instruments that you use for interviews, focus groups, observations, extant data reviews, and tests. Here are several techniques you can use:

- Use the face validity and content validity techniques to ensure that all instruments are adequately designed to produce the data that you need to use.

- Reflect and discuss with your team members and client to ensure ethical conduct during the data collection procedure.

- One-on-one interviews, focus groups, and observations are qualitative data collection methods. Ask an expert on qualitative research to review and provide feedback on your instruments and procedures that you plan to use during interviews, focus groups, or observations.

- As part of formative meta-evaluation activities, you should ask your client to review your instruments and give feedback on areas to be changed before the client gives you approval.

Again, your formative meta-evaluations during Step 7 (Develop data collection instruments) should include checking if your instruments would generate appropriate types of data to be analyzed with the rubrics that you plan to use.

Keep in mind that failure to detect errors in data collection instruments will result in incomplete or irrelevant (useless) data and jeopardize the quality of your evaluation.

Chapter Summary

Develop data collection instruments—interviews, focus groups, observations, extant data reviews, and tests (Step 7):

- Evaluators may use structured, unstructured, or semi-structured interviews. Focus groups use mostly open-ended questions.

- To conduct a one-on-one interview or focus group, evaluators need to develop a script to be used for recruiting participants, an informed consent form, and an interview or focus group protocol.

- Evaluators may solicit interview volunteers at the end of a self-administered survey questionnaire.

- To conduct an observation, evaluators need to develop a script to be used for recruiting observees, an informed consent form, and an observation checklist.

- To perform an extant data review, evaluators may receive data from the client. In some cases, evaluators may need to prepare a letter to request permission from informants for using their data. Evaluators would need to develop a data review checklist.

- To administer a test, evaluators may need to develop a script to be used for recruiting testees, an informed consent form, and a set of test questions.

- While developing data collection instruments, evaluators should think about rubrics to be used to analyze the data obtained from the instruments (Chapter 12) and adjust the instruments as needed.

- Evaluators should conduct internal and external formative meta-evaluations on all instruments that they develop. It is particularly important to ensure that the instruments generate appropriate types of data to be analyzed with the rubrics that evaluators plan to use.

- Evaluators should get approval from the client for using all instruments they develop.

Chapter Discussion

1. Email-based interviews or surveys?

Tom is evaluating a chemical lab safety training program provided to newly hired technicians in his company. He was planning to conduct one-on-one telephone interviews with two trainers as well as 10 technicians randomly selected from those who recently completed the training program. Each interview should take about 20 minutes. However, he was experiencing difficulty scheduling individual interviews. So, he decided to send out the interview questions to the 12 people via email and ask them to reply with their responses to the questions.

Tom is now wondering if he is conducting an interview or a self-administered survey with each person, and asks you about it.

Determine whether it is an interview or a self-administered survey and clearly explain how you came to that conclusion. Discuss pros and cons of the method that Tom is using.

2. Observations through a video camera

As part of his evaluation project, Tom is also planning to observe several new technicians to see how well they are doing in the lab and if they are following the company safety rules that they learned from the training program.

He does not want to disrupt their work by observing them in the lab. So, he wants to videotape their lab performance and review the videotape instead.

In planning this, Tom wonders if he needs to inform the technicians about videotaping them in the lab or if he can bypass it because it is done during their work hours. He asks you about it. What would be your response to him?

Now, Your Turn—Develop Instruments for Conducting Interviews, Focus Groups, Observations, Extant Data Reviews, and Tests

In the previous chapter, you were asked to convert the data collection methods table you included in your evaluation proposal to an instruments/rubrics development worksheet, as shown in Table B-6 in Appendix B (Evaluation Development Worksheets). Based on the instruments and rubrics development worksheet, develop recruitment scripts and informed consent forms as well the measurement instruments in separate documents.

Combining your work from the previous chapter (developing materials for administering surveys) and this chapter (developing materials for conducting interviews, focus groups, observations, extant data reviews, and/or tests), you now have a complete set of instruments and supporting materials to be used to collect data.

Collect Data (Step 8)

After you receive approval from your client to use the data collection instruments you developed and after you obtain IRB approval (if applicable), you can start collecting data.

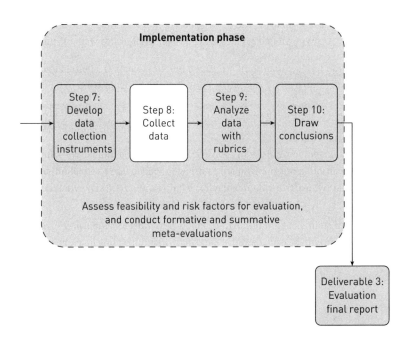

Follow Professional and Ethical Guidelines

Evaluation, as all other types of research activities should, must be planned and executed in an ethical manner. During Step 7 (Chapter 9 and Chapter 10), you carefully designed data collection instruments to ensure ethical conduct of data collection. You developed informed consent forms (or cover letters) to allow informants to make an informed decision on whether to participate in your evaluation project or not. You developed instruments to protect their privacy as much as you can. During Step 8 (this chapter), you should execute the use of the data collection instruments and other materials that you developed as planned and as ethically as possible.

When it comes to ethical conduct during your professional work, you likely apply the professional code of ethics provided by the professional communities in which you participate as well as your own personal code of ethics. Examples of professional codes of ethics in fields related to human performance improvement (HPI) include the following:

- Academy of Human Resource Development (AHRD)'s standards on ethics and integrity (www.ahrd.org/standards)

- International Society for Performance Improvement (ISPI)'s code of ethics (www.ispi.org/ISPI/Credentials/ISPI_Code_of_Ethics.aspx)

For your evaluation project, you should also consult evaluation-specific guiding principles and standards such as these:

- American Evaluation Association's (AEA) guiding principles for evaluators

- Joint Committee on Standards for Educational Evaluation's (JCSEE) program evaluation standards

The AEA's guiding principles for evaluators consist of the following five categories of principles (for the full text, see the AEA guiding principles for evaluators on the AEA website; at the time of writing this book, the AEA is preparing an updated version): **AEA'S GUIDING PRINCIPLES FOR EVALUATORS**

A. **Systematic inquiry**: Evaluators conduct systematic, data-based inquiries.

B. **Competence**: Evaluators provide competent performance for stakeholders.

C. **Integrity/honesty**: Evaluators display honesty and integrity in their own behavior, and attempt to ensure the honesty and integrity of the entire evaluation process.

D. **Respect for people**: Evaluators respect the security, dignity, and self-worth of respondents, program participants, clients, and other evaluation stakeholders.

E. **Responsibilities for general and public welfare**: Evaluators articulate and take into account the diversity of general and public interests and values that may be related to the evaluation. (AEA, 2004)

The JCSEE's program evaluation standards are five types of standards to follow when conducting program evaluations, as summarized here (for descriptions of individual standards, see the JCSEE website): **JCSEE'S PROGRAM EVALUATION STANDARDS**

1. **The utility standards** are intended to increase the extent to which program stakeholders find evaluation processes and products valuable in meeting their needs.

2. **The feasibility standards** are intended to increase evaluation effectiveness and efficiency.

3. **The propriety standards** support what is proper, fair, legal, right, and just in evaluations.

4. **The accuracy standards** are intended to increase the dependability and truthfulness of evaluation representations, propositions, and findings, especially those that support interpretations and judgments about quality.

5. **The evaluation accountability standards** encourage adequate documentation of evaluations and a meta-evaluative perspective focused on improvement and accountability for evaluation processes and products. (JCSEE, 2017; Yarbrough et al., 2011)

ETHICAL VS. UNETHICAL EVALUATION BEHAVIORS

All of these sources emphasize fair, safe, and respectful treatment of human subjects. You should use these sources as checkpoints while developing your data collection instruments and procedures. For example, let's compare the two sets of practice presented in Table 49 to see which one is ethically done, which one is not, and why. Also, compare them to your own conduct during your evaluation project.

The behaviors listed in the Evaluation Conduct 1 column are ethical ones, whereas the behaviors listed in the Evaluation Conduct 2 column raise a red flag. The actions described in Evaluation Conduct 2 violate ethical guidelines associated with displaying integrity and honesty, securing respect for people, and ensuring welfare and confidentiality of people in particular. You as an evaluator must carefully reflect on your own actions and do your best to avoid unethical evaluation conduct from occurring.

For example, let's think about Action 1 under Evaluation Conduct 2. Self-administered surveys are notorious for low return rates. A way to influence informants to submit their survey data is to involve their leaders to use their power. However, there are different types of power. While *reward power* involves the use of something tangible or intangible (gift cards, bonuses, paid time off, or praise) that is valuable to the recipients, *coercive power* involves the use of performance penalties or punishments (Johnson, 2012). For example, intentionally administering an identifiable survey when participants' names are not needed for data analysis, only to call on or discipline nonparticipants could be problematic. Such coercive tactics can cause damage to the relationship between the informants and their leaders. When informants are forced to participate in data collection to avoid negative consequences, there also is a risk that they provide information that they think the leaders want to hear instead of offering their true opinion, thus threatening the quality of collected data.

Instead, consider using a motivator such as providing a clear explanation about how important it is to obtain employees' input and how their input will benefit themselves in the future. Collecting data anonymously whenever possible and ensuring confidentiality of collected data not only are ethical procedures for conducting evaluations but also help you obtain honest data from your informants. Your ethical conduct during evaluation can help you earn the trust of your informants.

Action	Evaluation Conduct 1	Evaluation Conduct 2
	TABLE 49 • Ethical Conduct Versus Unethical Conduct During Evaluation	
1	I will allow participants to voluntarily choose to participate in my evaluation. I will allow them to stop participating in my evaluation at any time for any reason.	To achieve a high level of participation, I will require participants to participate in my evaluation by using a form of coercive power.
2	I will provide the participants with sufficient information about the purpose of my evaluation so that they can make an informed decision about whether or not to participate in my evaluation.	I will hide some of the information about the purpose of my evaluation from the participants for fear that they may decide not to participate in my evaluation if they know about it.
3	I am testing the effectiveness of a new intervention, and the intervention will not cause any physical or psychological harm to the participants. I will allow them to quit immediately if they present distress due to participating in my evaluation.	I am testing the effectiveness of a new intervention program, and participating in the program can cause some psychological harm to the participants since they will be asked to recall some of their painful memories. Even if they present distress due to participating in my evaluation, I will have them complete the program because they agreed to participate in the evaluation.
4	I am comparing two groups of participants with different types of intervention, and both groups will receive similar benefits. One group that does not receive the benefit during the intervention will receive it after completing the intervention.	I am comparing two groups of participants with different types of intervention, and one group will benefit from participating whereas the other group will not. They are randomly assigned to one of the two groups, and there is nothing I can do about it.
5	As I promised to participants, I will not share their names or any other identifiable information in my written or oral presentations without their permission, to protect their privacy.	It is OK for me to discuss with the client and others any information that individual informants submitted to me, as long as I do not publish such identifiable information in my report.

What Would You Do?

Even with a perfect plan, things can go wrong. Even after you develop an ethically sensitive evaluation plan, you may encounter ethical dilemmas while executing your data collection plan. In fact, it is safe to assume that every single step and decision to be made during evaluation has to do with ethics to some degree.

For example, think about Pat's situation.

PAT'S SITUATION

Pat, a corporate trainer in the sales department, is collecting data from 150 salespeople via a web-based survey to measure the value of a new sales technique that they recently learned from a training program. To allow her to identify how much the training program helped them improve their productivity, she administered an identifiable web-based survey questionnaire before the training program, and now she is conducting it again 2 months after the training program. A week has passed since she invited them to submit the post-training survey questionnaire, but she has received responses from only 10% of the participants. So, she sent out a reminder message to those who had not submitted the survey, emphasizing the importance of getting their responses. She also discussed this situation with Bob, the director of the sales department. Bob responded to Pat by saying, "I can help you. Please give me a list of people who have not submitted the survey yet. I will send out a message or talk to each of them myself and ask them to submit it. I'm sure they will do it if I ask them to do it."

Pat understands that Bob has good intentions to help with the low survey return rate problem. However, it puts Pat in a situation where she has to determine whether it is ethical to release such information to Bob. At the same time, Bob is also Pat's boss. What would you do, if you were Pat?

Analyze Pat's situation against your personal code of ethics and professional standards. Pat's situation is particularly related to:

- AEA's respect for people principle

- JCSEE's propriety standards

Especially, take a look at AEA's (2004) second guideline under its respect for people principle:

Evaluators should abide by current professional ethics, standards, and regulations regarding risks, harms, and burdens that might befall those participating in the evaluation; regarding informed consent for participation in evaluation; and regarding informing participants and clients about the scope and limits of confidentiality. (p. 3)

It is important that Pat protect confidentiality of potential informants. One way to handle the situation is to discuss the following points with Bob:

- She clearly indicated to the employees in her informed consent form that she was asking them to voluntarily participate in the survey.

- She also promised to them that she would keep any of the data confidential.

- There should not be any ramifications for their decision not to participate in the survey.

Reminding Bob of her obligation as an evaluator can help him understand why it is not appropriate (not ethical) for her to share such information with him and gear the discussion toward other strategies to improve the survey return rate. Openly discussing ethical issues with supervisors and coworkers will also raise awareness of ethical conduct during the current and future evaluation projects. Pat may suggest Bob send out an email message to the entire pool of survey participants to explain the importance of achieving a high return rate and express a strong support for the survey.

Let's review another scenario, Terry's story. Think about if Terry is engaged in ethical conduct during his evaluation.

Terry is a performance improvement specialist at a hospital. He was recently assigned to evaluate workflow efficiency at the hospital. Key stakeholders include administrators, internal caregivers (hospital physicians, nurses, and physician assistants), and external caregivers (external physicians). The total number of key stakeholders adds up to 180 people. Terry's boss suggested that Terry form an advisory board that represents the key stakeholders, and get input and guidance from the advisory board during the evaluation design process. Taking the suggestion, Terry assembled an advisory board with two people from each of the five groups (administrators, internal physicians, internal nurses, internal physician assistants, and external physicians). Terry ran his data collection plan by the advisory board before finalizing the plan to conduct a survey with all stakeholders. Now, Terry is expected to complete his evaluation project in 2 weeks. He feels he does not have enough time to gather data from all 180 stakeholders. He wants to find a way to gather stakeholders' input quickly. Because he has established a good working relationship with the advisory board and already has their contact information, he decides to gather data only from the 10 members of the advisory board since they represent the stakeholders, although the original plan was to collect data from all stakeholders. Terry completes the survey with the 10 advisory board members and writes a final report based on their data (Adapted from Scenario 2 on p. 25 in Chyung et al., 2010, with some modifications).

TERRY'S SITUATION

Using the following 4-point scale, how would you rate Terry's decision to conduct the evaluation based on the data obtained from the 10 advisory board members, and why do you think so? Put yourself in Terry's shoes; what would you do in his situation?

1. Definitely ethically problematic
2. Probably ethically problematic
3. Probably not ethically problematic
4. Definitely not ethically problematic

Terry's situation is related to:

- AEA's systematic inquiry principle
- JCSEE's accuracy standards

The above standards or principles are related to each other; they refer to the use of appropriate evaluation methodology to produce accurate information. For example, review two specific guidelines under the AEA's (2004) systematic inquiry principle:

1. To ensure the accuracy and credibility of the evaluative information they produce, evaluators should adhere to the highest technical standards appropriate to the methods they use.

2. Evaluators should explore with the client the shortcomings and strengths both of the various evaluation questions and the various approaches that might be used for answering those questions. (p. 2)

Evaluators may not think of competent evaluation practice as an ethical issue; however, both AEA's guiding principles for evaluators and JCSEE's standards clearly include *systematic inquiry* and *competent practice* as important parts of evaluators' professional and ethical conduct (Chyung et al., 2010). Thus, it is important that you be aware that using appropriate data collection methods and ensuring data accuracy are part of ethical conduct during your evaluation project.

In Terry's case, when substantially changing the survey sampling method and sample size, he failed to realize that he would compromise the validity and reliability of data. It would be better for Terry to negotiate with the client to extend the deadline for completing the evaluation project so that Terry can conduct the survey with all stakeholders.

Use Strategies to Collect Data Successfully and Ethically

This section provides tips for collecting data with your instruments.

Think About What's in It for Them

First, regardless of the type of data collection methods you are using, it is important to remind informants about how you intend to use the data they will provide and how the data may affect them in the future. This "what's in it for me" information can encourage them to decide to remain as informants during your data collection process, which can help reduce the chances of gathering incomplete data.

Be Aware of Vulnerable Populations

WHEN HANDLING VULNERABLE POPULATIONS

Vulnerable populations include minors, prisoners, and pregnant women (including fetuses and neonates) (U.S. Department of Health & Human Services, Office for Human Research Protections, 2010). When involving these vulnerable populations in your evaluation activities, you must give special care to minimize the risk for causing physical or psychological harm to them and the risk of breach of privacy and confidentiality.

For example, when conducting evaluation with minors, you should obtain parental permission to contact their children for evaluation purposes and obtain minors' assent as to whether or not they agree to participate in evaluation. Discuss with the client organization whether it is appropriate to use *active consent* (parents confirm their permission in writing) or *passive consent* (their permission is assumed unless parents return a signed opt-out or withdrawal form).

Students and employees are also vulnerable to coercion or undue influence. Also, when involving the following groups of people in your data collection activities, you should consider additional safeguards to protect their rights and welfare:

- Mentally disabled persons (may not be able to provide consent for themselves)

- Economically disadvantaged persons (may be easily coerced with incentives)

- Educationally disadvantaged persons (may have difficulty understanding written informed consent or directions)

Store Data in a Secure Place

Regardless of the type of data collection methods you used, make sure to store the data you collected in a secure place to which only you (or your evaluation team) have access. Strategies include storing paper-based data inside a locked cabinet in a locked office, adding a password to electronic files, and storing data on a password-protected computer (or a password-protected cloud system).

Use Strategies When Collecting Data From Self-Administered Surveys

Self-administered surveys are a convenient way to obtain data; however, it is common to experience a low return rate. A large amount of missing data causes a serious validity issue. There are various methods you can use to increase a survey response rate.

When administering a web-based survey or mailed survey:

- **Test the web-based survey system**: Especially, if you are an external evaluator, you should test out the web-based survey system to ensure that you have no difficulty accessing survey participants via the system. Your email invitation messages with attachments or embedded URLs coming from the outside of the organization can be blocked by the organization's firewall. Your email invitation messages may be sent to their spam folder.

- **Indicate the sponsor**: If you are an outsider to the survey participants, they may not be highly responsive to your survey invitation message or cover letter, as you are a stranger. If they are familiar with the client of your evaluation project, with the client's permission, you may want to indicate him or her as the sponsor of the evaluation in your invitation message. Or, the client can send out an email message to the survey participants prior to your invitation message, informing them that they will receive a message from you and that the client is supporting you to conduct the survey.

- **Email from a known address**: You may ask the client or someone in the organization with whom they are familiar to send out the survey invitation message on behalf of you or your evaluation team, by using the organization's internal survey system.

TIPS FOR WEB-BASED OR MAILED SURVEYS

- **Spell out the deadline**: In the survey invitation message, you want to indicate the deadline to complete the survey.

- **Send out a reminder message(s)**: You may send out one or two reminder messages. Send the first reminder message a few days after the initial invitation message, and send another reminder message a few days after the first reminder message.

- **Use an anonymous survey**: To encourage participants to freely express their thoughts, use an anonymous survey, unless you have a clear reason to collect their names, such as conducting a Success Case Method (SCM) survey where it is necessary to collect the names of survey participants, or planning to compare pre- and post-measures.

- **Offer the participants an incentive**: You can use monetary or nonmonetary incentives to motivate participants to submit their data. An example of nonmonetary incentives is to announce to participants in the beginning of the survey that when participants complete the survey, they will be taken to a website where they see information useful to them.

When administering an on-site survey (a pencil-and-paper version):

TIPS FOR ON-SITE SURVEYS

- **Take advantage of an existing gathering event**: Find out if there is an official event where survey participants gather together (e.g., a department meeting). Administer the survey during the event.

- **Bring pencils (or pens)**: Make sure that all survey participants have access to pencils (or pens) to complete their surveys. When using anonymous surveys, providing all survey participants with the same type of pencils (or pens) helps secure anonymity of their data (i.e., not being recognized by the color or type of the pen they used).

- **Consider pros and cons of using open-ended questions in anonymous surveys**: Open-ended questions allow survey participants to explain their thoughts in detail. However, they have to leave their comments in handwriting, which can reveal their identity and therefore may discourage them from completing open-ended questions. Therefore, consider pros and cons of using open-ended questions in anonymous surveys while developing the survey instruments.

- **Ask a third party to compile survey data that contain open-ended questions**: If you want to eliminate any chance to recognize survey respondents' identity by their handwriting, ask a third-party person to enter the data into an electronic file for you, while keeping the raw data in a secure place.

Use Strategies When Collecting Data From Interviews and Focus Groups

You chose to conduct interviews or focus groups because you need to obtain in-depth information about certain topics.

When conducting interviews or focus groups:

- **Audio-record conversations**: There will be a lot of information to record during each interview. For that reason, it is usually helpful to audio-record conversations whether you are conducting interviews face-to-face, by telephone, or through a video-conferencing system, so that you can focus on conversations during interviews, and listen to the audio files during your analysis later. Do not have interviewees wait while you are jotting down or typing notes. Be respectful of their time. For similar reasons, you would likely need to audio-record discussions during a focus group.

- **Have multiple interviewers present when audio-recording is not allowed**: With multiple interviewers present during an interview, one of the interviewers may lead the conversations while other interviewers write down interview responses. It is usually more efficient to hand-write than to type; also, typing sound can be distracting. Immediately after each interview session, the multiple interviewers should discuss what they heard or observed during the interview, compare and verify the accuracy of their notes, and record other information that they could not write down during the interview.

- **Use a written interview protocol**: Whether one interviewer or multiple interviewers are present during interviews, using a written interview protocol ensures that each interviewer uses the same language and procedure to conduct the interviews.

- **Monitor the interview time**: You should complete the interview within the expected time frame. Using more time than what you promised to the interviewees will likely leave a bad impression of your professionalism. If you need to extend the interview, you may request the interviewee for another interview opportunity.

TIPS FOR INTERVIEWS AND FOCUS GROUPS

When conducting face-to-face interviews:

- **Interview in a private place**: Find an interview place where the interviewee can feel comfortable talking about the topic and there is little noise or interruption.

- **Analyze audio-recorded interview data with team members**: Not all members of your team may have access to the site to conduct face-to-face interviews. Sometimes, only one of your team members can do so, which can be a burden to that team member. Audio-record the interviews and share electronic audio files of the interviews with other team members so that they can contribute to the analysis of the interview data.

When conducting telephone or video-conferencing interviews:

- **Call from a quiet place**: Call your interviewee from a place where there is little noise or interruption.

- **Give all team members an opportunity to interview**: Let's say, your two- or three-member team needs to conduct 10 telephone interviews. All your team members may be present during all 10 interviews by using a telephone-conferencing or video-conferencing system, or each of your team members may conduct three or four interviews alone.

- **Mute the typist's phone or microphone**: Again, when it is not allowed to audio-record interviews, it is helpful to conduct each interview by multiple interviewers. When typing notes, mute the typist's phone or microphone so that the typing sound or other noise does not interfere with interview conversations.

When interviewing minors:

- **Pay special attention to protecting minors' privacy and data confidentiality**: Make sure a parent is present during interviews with minors. If you are external to the organization, ask the organization if the interviews can be part of the organization's official activities (e.g., teachers interviewing students about their learning progress as part of educational activities).

- **Carefully monitor their facial and physical cues**: Even though you assure the interviewees that they can stop the interview anytime if they feel uncomfortable continuing the interview, children may not know how to express their feelings or they may feel they need to follow your direction because you are an adult and they are children. Monitor their facial and physical cues during the interview to see if they show any signs of being nervous or feeling uncomfortable, and adjust your interview procedure as needed.

Use Strategies When Collecting Data From Observations and Tests

Observations and tests usually produce identifiable data; thus, you should use the same/similar strategies that you would use for interviews and focus groups to protect the participants' privacy and to maintain confidentiality of the data.

TIPS FOR OBSERVATIONS OR TESTS

- **Maintain your role as an observer**: You as an observer may actively participate (i.e., interacting with participants) or passively participate (i.e., acting as a bystander) during your observation. You need to decide the type of observation based on the purpose of conducting the observation and maintain your role during your observation.

- **Describe what happened rather than how you felt about it**: For example, instead of recording "a slow performance," describe "it took five attempts to find the correct menu item." You can record both: "It took five attempts to find the correct menu item; it was a slow performance."

- **Store video files in a secure place**: If you are allowed to video-record people's performance, make sure to store the recordings in a secure place. Do not store electronic files in a public domain.

- **Get parental permission to observe or test minors**: If you are observing or testing minors, make sure to get permission from the minors' parents.

Use Strategies to Ensure Anonymity or Confidentiality of Data

You can conduct anonymous surveys, but it is difficult to conduct anonymous interviews or observations because the participants' identities are known to you and are associated with the collected data. However, you can and should still protect their privacy by maintaining confidentiality of the information collected from the interviews as well as surveys or tests. This means you prevent anyone other than the evaluators from being able to identify the participants based on their responses.

Here are several ways to ensure anonymity and confidentiality:

- Use pseudonyms or codes instead of participants' names in your interview or observation notes.

- Replace the survey or test participants' names with codes as soon as data are collected.

- Store the information about the participants' names and the matching codes in a separate document in a secured place.

- Remove any identifiable information from a summary of data to be included in your evaluation report.

- Assign a password to your electronic file that contains identifiable information.

- Destroy the raw script with identifiable information as soon as you prepare a summary of data that does not contain any identifiable information.

- Do not store electronic files of your data in a public domain.

- Set up a password to your computer where the data files are stored.

- Store data collected on printed materials in a locked cabinet/office to which only you and your team members have access.

- Do not share your data with other people who do not need to know.

- Do not gossip about interesting things that you found in your data.

TIPS FOR ENSURING ANONYMITY AND CONFIDENTIALITY

Conduct Formative Meta-Evaluations

You are in Step 8, collecting data. It may take a couple of weeks or more than a month to complete your data collection process, depending on the scope of your project. You hope that your data collection process will go as planned, but you also know that it is not always the case.

You should closely monitor your data collection process and reflect if your plan is indeed working out as planned. If you find difficulty executing your data collection methods, you should discuss right away with your team members and client what the problems are and come up with solutions to the problems.

A solution could be something as simple as sending out a reminder message to survey respondents. Sometimes, you may need to replace a part of your data collection plan with a new plan. You may need to develop a new data collection instrument.

Reflect and discuss with your team members and client any ethical issues that arise during data collection and resolve the issues as quickly as possible.

You may also find out unexpected limitations or barriers to your data collection procedure. Reach out to an expert on program evaluation to get professional advice on handling difficulties and limitations you encountered during data collection.

Chapter Summary

Collect data (Step 8):

- Evaluators should follow professional and ethical guidelines while collecting data.
  - AHRD's standards on ethics and integrity
  - ISPI's code of ethics
  - AEA's guiding principles for evaluators
  - JCSEE's program evaluation standards

- Evaluators should use special care when collecting data from vulnerable populations such as minors, mentally disabled persons, or economically or educationally disadvantaged persons.

- Evaluators may consider using several techniques to increase informants' participation in surveys, interviews, focus groups, observations, or tests.

- Evaluators should pay attention to ensuring anonymity and confidentiality of data.

Chapter Discussion

1. To improve a survey return rate

You are using the SCM to evaluate a training program delivered to call center agents. Based on the results of a survey conducted with the call center agents who completed the training program, you identified five success cases and six nonsuccess cases among them. You completed interviews with the success and nonsuccess case employees and learned quite interesting information from the two groups regarding several unexpected environmental factors that they felt were barriers to their performance. Success and nonsuccess cases both shared common issues while each group reported a different type of problem.

You discussed these interview findings with your client, Sara, who is the manager of the call center agents who completed the training program. Sara was very surprised about the environmental barriers that the call center agents reported during the interviews. She had thought things were going well.

Sara wants to resolve the issues right away, to improve the overall call center performance. She asks you to give her the names of the call center agents you interviewed, so she can contact them and discuss the issues with them.

What would you do? Is it professionally and ethically appropriate to share the names of those you interviewed, so Sara can resolve the issues quickly? Why, or why not?

2. Complying to professional standards and guidelines while collecting data

Review the AEA's guiding principles for evaluators and the JCSEE's program evaluation standards.

Select a couple of categories of the sources that you think you should keep in mind while collecting data during your evaluation project. For example, your situation might fall into the utility category of the JCSEE or the competence category of the AEA guiding principles.

Explain what you as an evaluator (or evaluation team) should do to comply with the selected professional standards or guidelines while collecting data, including specific tips for handling such a situation.

Now, Your Turn—Collect Data

Collecting data is an exciting phase of an evaluation project! Please ensure professional and ethical conduct while collecting data. Good luck!

12

Analyze Data With Rubrics (Step 9)

I t usually takes a few weeks or longer to complete the data collection step. You can start analyzing some of the collected data (e.g., extant data) while collecting other data (e.g., survey or interview data). In some cases, you will have to complete the analysis of a certain type of data before you collect other types of data. For example, when using the Success Case Method (SCM), you need to analyze the survey data in order to select interviewees.

While analyzing data, recall that *measurement* is different from *evaluation*. Measured data do not have values assigned to them. To assign values to data, you

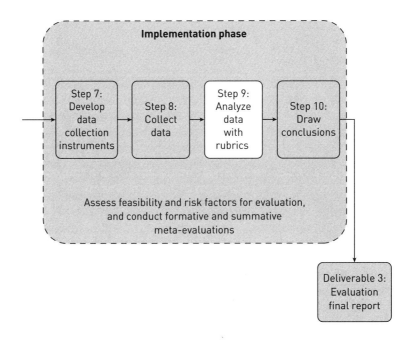

need to use rubrics. Systematic and systemic collection of data and analysis of data against rubrics are part of your evidence-based practice during your evaluation project.

Use Evidence-Based Practice

The term **evidence-based practice** is widely used in various fields, especially the healthcare industry. The fields of management, human performance improvement (HPI), and education also embrace evidence-based practices.

To understand evidence-based practice in the evaluation context, you need to recognize what evidence is, where you find evidence, and how you use the evidence during your evaluation project.

What is evidence, and where do you find evidence?

Evidence is a type of information that supports that something is true or valid. In the evaluation context, you can find two types of evidence:

- One type of evidence comes from professional expertise—that is, the evaluation frameworks, models, procedures, or techniques that evaluation experts have developed and used to show their usefulness (thus, valid in a practical sense). **TWO TYPES OF EVIDENCE**

- Another type of evidence is the data collected from various sources—from the stakeholders or from existing information. The data you collected from surveys, interviews, focus groups, observations, extant data reviews, and tests are all different types of evidence.

During your evaluation project, you use both types of evidence.

How do you use the evidence during your evaluation project? Think for a minute what crime scene investigators do, as their job involves finding and using evidence. They follow certain principles, policies, and procedures on what to do when arriving at a crime scene, collecting data, and documenting the scene. They bring instruments to the crime scene to collect data and connect the dots to draw conclusions about what might have happened at the crime scene.

Similarly, you as an evaluator (or an evaluation team) select and use appropriate evaluation frameworks, models, procedures, and/or techniques that guide you to conduct systematic and systemic evaluations. You also use instruments to collect data from multiple sources. What you do next is to *triangulate* these multiple sources of data against rubrics to determine the quality or value of individual dimensions and draw evidence-based conclusions. **TO MAKE DATA-DRIVEN DECISIONS**

Therefore, evidence-based practice can be described as making *data-driven decisions*. You as an evaluator certainly make a series of data-driven decisions during your evaluation project (e.g., even during the identification and planning phases of your evaluation project, you made decisions about the type of evaluation and dimensions of the evaluation based on the data you collected from the client and other stakeholders). Data-driven decisions involve careful analysis of data.

In this chapter, we will discuss how you analyze data with rubrics when using a descriptive case study type evaluation design. When conducting experimental or quasi-experimental studies to answer dimensional evaluation questions, you need to apply inferential statistical procedures to analyze the quantitative data and rubrics associated with the selected inferential statistical tests such as the Alpha level and effect size. Please see Appendix E. Experimental Studies and Data Analysis With T-Tests Using Excel® for examples.

Keep in Mind: Evaluation = Measurement + Valuation With Rubrics

You collected data by using different data collection methods such as surveys, interviews, observations, extant data reviews, or tests. These are measurement tools, and you completed the measurement step.

Here, you need to keep in mind that measurement is not the same as evaluation. Evaluation involves two steps: measurement and valuation (appraisal). During evaluation, you measure something with an instrument first, and then you analyze the measured result against a **rubric** to assign a value to it.

BMI RUBRICS   As a simple example, think about how you can evaluate your overall health condition. One way is to use the body mass index (BMI). To do so, first, you measure your weight with a weight scale and your height with a measuring tape. Next, you calculate your BMI. Then, you analyze your BMI against a rubric such as the one below with three levels—underweight, normal weight, and overweight. This three-level rubric contains a definition of each level:

1. Underweight: BMI score < 18.5

2. Normal weight: $18.5 \leq$ BMI score < 25.0

3. Overweight: BMI score ≥ 25.0

Your weight being 130 pounds and your height being 5'6" are measurement results, and a BMI score being within a "normal" range is an evaluative conclusion of a dimension called *BMI*.

You may add one more level to the rubric if desirable:

1. Underweight: BMI score < 18.5

2. Normal weight: $18.5 \leq$ BMI score < 25.0

3. Overweight: $25.0 \leq$ BMI score < 30.0

4. Obese: BMI score ≥ 30.0

(see http://www.nhlbi.nih.gov/health/educational/lose_wt/BMI/bmicalc.htm)

A more finely defined rubric contains more levels:

1. Very severely underweight

2. Severely underweight

3. Underweight

4. Normal

5. Overweight

6. Moderately obese

7. Severely obese

8. Very severely obese

As shown in the BMI rubrics above, to develop a rubric, you need to determine three things:

- Number of levels to include in the rubric (e.g., three, four, or eight levels)

- Label for each level (e.g., "underweight" or "normal" or "overweight")

- Definition of each level (e.g., "BMI score < 18.5")

RUBRIC LEVEL = LABEL + DEFINITION

How many levels do you need in your rubric? It largely depends on how you want to use the analyzed results. The eight-level BMI rubric may be used to determine if people's BMI has changed after they complete a 6-month wellness program, whereas the three- or four-level BMI rubric can be used to provide general exercise recommendations to people who have enrolled in a wellness and fitness program.

You may investigate other health-related dimensions such as blood pressure level and cholesterol level, which require different rubrics. Then, your BMI score falling in the normal category along with your blood pressure level and cholesterol level could be combined to indicate how healthy you are overall.

MULTIPLE DIMENSIONS, MULTIPLE RUBRICS

Apply this to your evaluation project. In your evaluation project, you have decided to investigate multiple dimensions of your evaluand. Then, you measured each dimension by using multiple data collection methods such as surveys, interviews/focus groups, observations, extant data reviews, and/or tests. Those data collection methods required you to use measurement instruments such as survey questionnaires, interview protocols, observation checklists, data review checklists, and test questions. Now you need a set of rubrics. You may wait until all data come in before you start analyzing the data with rubrics, or in some cases, you may start analyzing data as they come in.

See Table 50 to compare how two evaluands—Overall Health and Tech Support Ticketing and Tracking System (an example is presented in Table 42 in Chapter 7)—are evaluated with multiple dimensions, multiple data collection methods, and different measurement instruments. Again, multiple rubrics need to be developed.

Evaluand	Dimension	Data Collection Method	Measurement Instrument	Rubric
Overall health	BMI	Weight measure	Weight scale	BMI rubric
		Height measure	Measuring tape	
	Blood pressure level	Blood pressure test	Blood pressure monitor	Blood pressure reading rubric
	Cholesterol level	Blood test	Cholesterol test kit	Cholesterol level rubric
Tech support ticketing and tracking system	User friendliness of system interface	Observation	Observation checklist	Rubric to be developed
		Interview	Interview protocol	Rubric to be developed
	Efficiency in ticketing and tracking process	Observation	Observation checklist	Rubric to be developed
		Interview	Interview protocol	Rubric to be developed
		Interview	Interview protocol	Rubric to be developed
		Extant data review	Review checklist	Rubric to be developed
	User satisfaction	Survey	Survey questionnaire	Rubric to be developed
		Interview	Interview protocol	Rubric to be developed
		Interview	Interview protocol	Rubric to be developed

TABLE 50 ● Evaluating Multiple Dimensions With Multiple Data Collection Methods and Measurement Instruments

Apply the Same or Different Weighting to the Multiple Sets of Data

Earlier, in Chapters 9 and 10, it was suggested that you start developing or at least think about rubrics while developing data collection instruments, because how you want to analyze data with rubrics often shapes the way you develop your data collection instruments, and vice versa.

Whether you have drafted out your rubrics or not, you need to take a look at the collected data and determine whether the data are sufficient enough to be analyzed with rubrics. Even if you have drafted out rubrics before collecting data, you need to revisit your rubrics and may need to adjust them a little bit if data collection did not go as planned. Adjusting rubrics may involve simple changes in criteria, or it may require editing definitions to indicate primary and secondary data sources.

You selected multiple data collection methods for each dimension with the critical multiplism principle in mind, that is, to complement strengths and weaknesses of individual data collection methods. Even though you used a perfect data collection plan, the actual collection of data could go differently than the way you planned. After you obtained data from multiple sources, what do you see in the data? Would you treat them as having the same level of weight, or is one of them more comprehensive than the others?

Let's use this example. You conducted a self-administered survey and interviews with customers to evaluate the *user satisfaction* dimension presented in Chapter 7, Table 42. You invited the entire group of 50 system users to the survey and received a high return rate. You randomly selected 5 people from the 50 stakeholders and invited them to interviews. All of them participated in the interviews. Now you are combining the survey and interview data to evaluate quality of the dimension. Since the survey data and the interview data are both comprehensive and representative, you may treat the survey and interview data equally in terms of significance.

WITH DIFFERENT AMOUNTS OF DATA

However, what if your data collection did not go as planned? What if you had received only five responses from the survey, while all five randomly selected people participated in the interview? In this case, would you assign the same level of weight to both the survey and interview data? Or, would you assign more weight to one of them? The survey return rate is only 10%; you received survey data from only those who were motivated to submit their responses. In contrast, the interview participation rate was 100%, and the interview participants were randomly selected. You also received in-depth information from the interviews.

Based on these contrasting indications of data quality, you may assign more weight to the interview data than the survey data, and treat the interview data as the primary data and the survey data as the secondary data during your triangulation process. This decision would influence how you develop or adjust your rubric and how you analyze the multiple sets of data.

WITH LITTLE TO NO PARTICIPATION OF INFORMANTS

Also consider the possibility of little to no participation of informants in all data collection methods that you planned to use (e.g., a low or zero survey return rate, a low or no participation in interviews). Options are to extend the data collection period to attempt to collect more data, or to seek an alternative data collection method (e.g., review extant data instead of using a survey and interviews) or different data sources (e.g., recruit a different sample of people to the survey or interviews). When there are no other viable options, you may have to report that the quality of the dimension is *inconclusive* due to the lack of data. You may still generate some recommendations for improving the quality of the dimension based on any data available. In doing so, you should clearly indicate that the recommendations are based on limited data.

Therefore, you want to assess significance weighting of each set of data to determine if and how you will develop the rubric to make a judgment about the quality of the dimension. Use Table 51 as general guidelines, and proceed with the following sections if your data warrant the analysis with rubrics.

TABLE 51 ● Guidelines for Using or Not Using Rubrics Based on Significance Weighting of Each Set of Data

#	How significant is each set of data?	Do you have sufficient data to draw a valid conclusion about the quality of the dimension?	Should you use a rubric to make a judgment about the quality of the dimension?	How would you incorporate multiple sources in the rubric?
1	Each set of data is comprehensive, representative, and accurate. Or, each set of data provides a unique, different type of data.	Likely	Use a rubric	Treat each source equally
2	One or two sets of data are comprehensive, representative, and accurate enough while other sets of data are not.	Maybe	Use a rubric	Weigh the primary source(s) more
3	Each set of data severely lacks comprehensiveness, representativeness, and accuracy.	Unlikely	Do not use a rubric	NA. Instead, • Report that quality of the dimension is inconclusive • Generate suggestions for improvement based on available data

Analyze Structured Survey Data With Rubrics

How your rubrics look is largely based on the types of data you collect with your instruments, and vice versa. Let's say you investigated a *job satisfaction* dimension using the following closed-ended survey questions with a 5-point Likert scale:

1. I am recognized for my good performance.

2. My current salary is adequate for my performance.

3. I have a good relationship with my boss.

4. I have a good relationship with my coworkers.

5. I have a secure job.

You collected data from 200 employees, and the data file looks something like the one shown in Table 52.

TABLE 52 ● Hypothetical Data File					
Question Participant	Q1	Q2	Q3	Q4	Q5
1	3	4	5	2	4
2	4	3	3	3	4
3	5	4	4	2	3
199	4	3	3	2	4
200	3	3	4	2	3

The next step is to determine how to analyze the raw survey data. You may generate a group average score or indicate percentages based on the frequency of responses to individual options. If you used a 4-point Likert scale without a midpoint, you want to indicate frequency percentages. Then, you will develop rubric definitions based on either the average score or frequency percentage values.

Using Average Scores

Recall that a 5-point Likert scale with a modifier *Slightly* added to *Disagree* and *Agree* helps it become close to an interval scale. If you decided to treat the 5-point Likert scale as an internal scale and calculate an average score, you need to codify the data by assigning numerical values (1, 2, 3, 4, and 5) to the five points on the Likert scale. If you used another option such as *Don't know* or *Not applicable*, exclude the data that fall into the additional option from the average calculation and report the data separately:

- Strongly disagree (1)

- Slightly disagree (2)

- Neutral (3)

- Slightly agree (4)

- Strongly agree (5)

- Don't know (%)

EXCLUDE *DON'T KNOW* DATA FROM CALCULATING AN AVERAGE SCORE

Let's say that the average score turned out to be 3.89. Now, the question is what does the average score of 3.89 mean in terms of job satisfaction? How would you assign a value to the average score of 3.89? How good or bad is the employees' job satisfaction based on the average score of 3.89? This is where you need a rubric.

To develop a rubric, you also need to decide the number of levels to be used and the labels for individual levels. Compare the following rubrics.

Rubric 1 (Using Four Levels)

You might divide the 5-point scale evenly into four levels, as follows:

- Excellent: Average score is between 4.0 and 5.0

- Good: Average score is between 3.0 and 3.9

- Mediocre: Average score is between 2.0 and 2.9

- Poor: Average score is between 1.0 and 1.9

Then, the average score of 3.89 falls into the *Good* range.

Be aware that the minimum score is 1.0 rather than zero since you assigned one to *Strongly disagree*. Make sure that the ranges defined in different levels are mutually exclusive. In the following example, 2.0, 3.0, and 4.0 overlap between two levels of the rubric:

RUBRIC LEVEL DEFINITIONS SHOULD BE MUTUALLY EXCLUSIVE

- Excellent: Average score is between 4.0 and 5.0

- Good: Average score is between 3.0 and 4.0

- Mediocre: Average score is between 2.0 and 3.0

- Poor: Average score is between 1.0 and 2.0

You can use mathematical symbols to indicate greater than ($>$), equal to or greater than ($\geq$), less than ($<$), and equal to or less than ($\leq$):

- Excellent: $4.0 \leq$ average score ≤ 5.0

- Good: $3.0 \leq$ average score ≤ 3.9

- Mediocre: $2.0 \leq$ average score ≤ 2.9

- Poor: $1.0 \leq$ average score ≤ 1.9

Or

- Excellent: $4.0 \leq$ average score ≤ 5.0

- Good: $3.0 \leq$ average score < 4.0

- Mediocre: $2.0 \leq$ average score < 3.0

- Poor: $1.0 \leq$ average score < 2.0

You may also use different labels for the individual levels of the rubric:

- Superior: $4.0 \leq$ average score ≤ 5.0

- Acceptable: $3.0 \leq$ average score < 4.0

- Improvement needed: $2.0 \leq$ average score < 3.0

- Not acceptable: $1.0 \leq$ average score < 2.0

With the rubric above, the average score of 3.89 falls into the *Acceptable* range.

Rubric 2 (Using Three Levels)

Let's say that the same job satisfaction survey was administered before an intervention was implemented, and the average score at that time was 3.4. So, you decided that as long as the average score of the current job satisfaction (after the intervention was implemented) is above the previous average score of 3.4, it exceeds the organization's expectation. You also decided to use three levels in your rubric. Then, the rubric may look like this:

- Exceeded expectation: Average score is between 3.5 and 5.0

- Improvement needed: Average score is between 2.0 and 3.4

- Serious problems detected: Average score is between 1.0 and 1.9

With this rubric, the average score of 3.89 falls into the *Exceeded expectation* range.

Using Percentages

If you use a 4-point Likert scale without a midpoint, it is an ordinal scale. If you use Yes or No options, it is a nominal scale. When you collect ordinal or nominal data, you may use a percentage of participants who selected a certain point(s) of the response scale in describing the definitions of rubric levels. See Rubric 3 and Rubric 4.

Rubric 3 (Using Four Levels)

- Excellent: 85+% of the participants selected *Strongly agree* or *Slightly agree*

- Good: 70+% of the participants selected *Strongly agree* or *Slightly agree*

- Mediocre: 50+% of the participants selected *Strongly agree* or *Slightly agree*

- Poor: Less than 50% of the participants selected *Strongly agree* or *Slightly agree*

Rubric 4 (Using Three Levels)

- Outstanding: 80+% of the participants selected *Strongly agree* or *Slightly agree*

- Acceptable: 60+% of the participants selected *Strongly agree* or *Slightly agree*

- Unacceptable: Less than 60% of the participants selected *Strongly agree* or *Slightly agree*

Analyze Unstructured Survey or Interview Data With Rubrics

Closed-ended questions in surveys and interviews generate quantitative data. On the other hand, open-ended questions in surveys and interviews generate qualitative data. What would the rubrics for analyzing qualitative data look like? Here are a couple of examples.

Rubric 5 (Using Four Levels)

- Excellent: Overwhelming, consistent positive comments

- Good: Noticeably positive comments with a couple of minor negative comments

- Marginal: Some positive and some negative comments

- Poor: A lot of negative comments

Rubric 6 (Using Three Levels)

- Superb: Mostly positive comments

- Acceptable: Many positive and some minor negative comments

- Poor: Mostly negative comments

Instead of using the words *positive* or *negative*, you can be more specific in describing the definitions of rubric levels, as shown in Rubric 7.

Rubric 7 (Using Three Levels)

- Superb: Most comments indicate users' satisfaction with the system; no comments indicate needs for improvement, and a small number of comments indicate needs for minor changes.

- Acceptable: Many comments indicate users' satisfaction with the system; some comments indicate users' dissatisfaction with the system, but the areas for improvement did not hinder their performance.

- Poor: Many comments indicate users' dissatisfaction with the system, expressing areas that hindered their performance.

While analyzing qualitative data obtained from surveys or interviews, pay attention to the data that informants provided and check if the data are relevant to designated dimensions. Sometimes, you asked a question about Dimension 1, but the informants might have described their experience that is relevant to Dimension 2. Then, you should exclude the information while analyzing Dimension 1 but include it when analyzing Dimension 2.

Analyze Semi-Structured Survey or Interview Data With Rubrics

Semi-structured surveys or interviews generate both quantitative and qualitative data. You can start with two separate rubrics, as shown in Rubric 8.

Rubric 8 (Two Separate Rubrics)

(a) Rubric for quantitative data obtained from closed-ended questions:

- ○ Excellent: $4.0 \leq$ average score ≤ 5.0
- ○ Good: $3.0 \leq$ average score ≤ 3.9
- ○ Mediocre: $2.0 \leq$ average score ≤ 2.9
- ○ Poor: $1.0 \leq$ average score ≤ 1.9

(b) Rubric for qualitative data obtained from open-ended questions:

- ○ Excellent: Overwhelming, consistent positive comments
- ○ Good: Noticeably positive comments with a couple of minor negative comments
- ○ Marginal: Some positive and some negative comments
- ○ Poor: A lot of negative comments

Then, you can consolidate the two rubrics into one that contains criteria for both quantitative and qualitative data, as shown in Rubric 9.

Rubric 9 (One Consolidated Rubric)

- Excellent: $4.0 \leq$ average score ≤ 5.0 and overwhelming, consistent positive comments
- Good: $3.0 \leq$ average score ≤ 3.9 and noticeably positive comments with a couple of minor negative comments
- Marginal: $2.0 \leq$ average score ≤ 2.9 and some positive and some negative comments
- Poor: $1.0 \leq$ average score ≤ 1.9 and a lot of negative comments

PRESENTING QUANTITATIVE AND QUALITATIVE DEFINITIONS IN ONE RUBRIC

In the rubric above, you may set up a rule that both quantitative and qualitative criteria in each definition should be met in order to satisfy the condition. For example, if the average score is 4.1, and all comments are positive, the conclusion would be *Excellent*. However, if the average score is 4.1 and there are some negative comments, then the conclusion could be downgraded to *Good*.

Please also see Appendix D that presents a sample semi-structured survey questionnaire designed to measure two dimensions and sample rubrics for analyzing data for the two dimensions.

Analyze Data Obtained From Observations, Extant Data Reviews, and Tests With Rubrics

If you used observations, extant data reviews, and/or knowledge tests to investigate your dimensions, you would also need to develop rubrics for those data. The definitions of the levels used in each rubric would be different depending on the type of data you obtained.

For example, let's say you obtained data from observations using a checklist with *Did not do it well* (0) and *Did it well* (1), as shown in Chapter 10, Exhibit 16. You observed 10 people. You could decide to use four levels in the rubric, based on the percentage of required behaviors observed in the 10 cases. Then, your rubric may look similar to Rubric 10.

Rubric 10 (for Observations)

- Excellent: 90%–100% of required behaviors observed

- Good: 80%–89% of required behaviors observed

- Marginal: 60%–79% of required behaviors observed

- Poor: Less than 60% of required behaviors observed

You also use checklists when conducting extant data reviews. A sample checklist introduced in Exhibit 18 in Chapter 10 was for analyzing the level of knowledge (knowledge, comprehension, and analysis levels) addressed in 10 lessons. If you want to use four levels in your rubric, your rubric may look similar to Rubric 11.

Rubric 11 (for Extant Data Reviews)

- Excellent: All 10 lessons address application-level skills, and no comments indicate minor improvement needed

- Good: Eight or nine lessons address application-level skills, and a few comments indicate minor improvement needed

- Mediocre: Six or seven lessons address application-level skills, and some comments indicate major improvement needed

- Poor: Between zero and five lessons address application-level skills, and many comments indicate major improvement needed

Here is another example. Let's say that professional reports should be prepared to meet the following three criteria. You may use Rubric 12 to address the content, English, and organization-specific criteria (adapted from D. D. Stevens & Levi, 2005).

Rubric 12 (for Extant Data Reviews)

- Professional: All information is accurate. There are no typos or grammatical errors. Information is logically presented.

- Adequate: Only one piece of information needs to be corrected. There are no more than two typos or grammatical errors. Information is logically presented with a minor change needed.

- Needs work: A couple of pieces of information need to be corrected. There are three to five typos or grammatical errors. Some information needs to be reorganized.

- You'd be fired: Many pieces of information need to be corrected. There are six or more typos or grammatical errors. Information is poorly organized.

Another method is to list the three expected criteria first and describe the rubric, as shown in Rubric 13.

Rubric 13 (for Extant Data Reviews)

Criteria to meet:

- Content: All accurate information

- English: No typos or grammatical errors

- Organization: Logical presentation

Rubric:

- Professional: Met all three criteria

- Adequate: Minor improvement needed on one or two criteria; no major improvement needed

- Needs work: Minor improvement needed on two or three criteria; major improvement needed on only one criterion

- You'd be fired: Major improvement needed on two or three criteria

Knowledge tests containing objective questions generate scores. You may use a rubric similar to Rubric 14 for analyzing test scores, if you are focusing on the group average score.

Rubric 14 (for Knowledge Tests With Objective Questions)

- Excellent: $90 \leq$ average score ≤ 100

- Good: $80 \leq$ average score ≤ 89

- Mediocre: $70 \leq$ average score ≤ 79

- Poor: $0 \leq$ average score ≤ 69

Knowledge tests with essay questions may generate qualitative data, and you can develop rubrics for essays by using techniques similar to developing rubrics for interview data or extant data reviews.

Determine the Number of Levels and Labels for Rubrics

You need to develop multiple rubrics for the individual data collection methods you used. How many levels and which labels should you use in all of your rubrics? There is no one right answer to this question. It largely depends on the purpose of your evaluation (formative or summative), and you may want to choose the one that makes sense for the dimensional questions.

If possible, you want to use a common set of labels and the same number of levels for all rubrics used for individual data collection methods. Mixing different levels and labels of rubrics will make things complicated when you combine the results.

For example, let's say you used the two different sets of rubric labels and levels shown below, to analyze survey and interview data. It would be difficult to combine the survey and interview results to determine quality of the dimension.

DIFFICULT TO COMBINE WHEN DIFFERENT RUBRIC LEVELS AND LABELS ARE USED

Survey rubric:

- Excellent: $4.0 \leq$ average score ≤ 5.0

- Good: $3.0 \leq$ average score ≤ 3.9

- Mediocre: $2.0 \leq$ average score ≤ 2.9

- Poor: $1.0 \leq$ average score ≤ 1.9

Interview rubric:

- Exceeded expectations: Mostly positive comments

- Improvement needed: A mix of positive and negative comments

- Serious problems detected: Mostly negative comments

Conversely, you will find it easy to combine the results if you use the same number of levels and the same labels in both survey and interview rubrics, as shown here:

USE SAME RUBRIC LEVELS AND LABELS

Survey rubric:

- Exceeded expectations: $4.0 \leq$ average score ≤ 5.0

- Met expectations: $3.0 \leq$ average score ≤ 3.9

- Improvement needed: $2.0 \leq$ average score ≤ 2.9

- Serious problems detected: $1.0 \leq$ average score ≤ 1.9

Interview rubric:

- Exceeded expectations: Mostly positive comments

- Met expectations: A mix of positive and negative comments, but more positive comments and no major negative comments

- Improvement needed: A mix of positive and negative comments with more critical negative comments

- Serious problems detected: Mostly negative comments

The following section provides more explanations about how to triangulate results obtained from multiple data sources.

Triangulate Results Obtained From Multiple Sources for Each Dimension

You have developed rubrics for individual data collection methods and analyzed the data against the rubrics. Now, you can determine the quality of each dimension by triangulating the results obtained from the multiple data collection methods. To do so, you have a couple of options: (1) Consolidate multiple rubrics into one, or (2) develop a dimensional triangulation rubric instead.

Consolidate Multiple Rubrics Into One

Take a look at Table 53, which is for the *user satisfaction* dimension presented in Chapter 7, Table 42. You investigated the dimension with three data collection methods, generating three different rubrics. Assuming that three sets of data are equally significant, you can combine three different rubrics into one, as shown in Table 53. The consolidated rubric puts a similar level of emphasis on all three sources of data. After you develop a consolidated rubric, you do not need to refer to the separate rubrics for individual data collection method anymore.

TABLE 53 ● Consolidating Multiple Rubrics Into One Rubric			
Dimension	**Data Collection Method**	**Step 1: Develop separate rubrics for individual data collection methods**	**Step 2: Consolidate the multiple rubrics into one rubric for the dimension**
User Satisfaction	Survey with all users	• Excellent: $4.0 \leq$ average ≤ 5.0 without any *Strongly disagree* or *Slightly disagree* responses • Fair: $3.0 \leq$ average < 4.0 • Poor: $1.0 \leq$ average < 3.0	• Excellent: $4.0 \leq$ survey average ≤ 5.0 without any *Strongly disagree* or *Slightly disagree* responses, and mostly positive interview comments
	Interview with several users	• Excellent: Mostly positive comments • Fair: A mix of positive and negative comments • Poor: Mostly negative comments	• Fair: $3.0 \leq$ survey average < 4.0, and a mix of positive and negative interview comments
	Interview with tech support specialists	• Excellent: Mostly positive comments • Fair: A mix of positive and negative comments • Poor: Mostly negative comments	• Poor: $1.0 \leq$ survey average < 3.0 and mostly negative interview comments

IDENTIFY
PRIMARY AND
SECONDARY
DATA IN RUBRIC
DEFINITIONS,
WHEN NEEDED
However, what if you experience a low survey return rate? Recall the rationale behind the decision to use a combination of multiple data collection methods and sources. It is not to triangulate *any* multiple data sources; it is based on the critical multiplism principle of using a combination of multiple data collection methods and sources to complement their strengths and weaknesses. Surveys have strengths in allowing the collection of data from a large group of people at once. However, this benefit is not achieved when there is a low return rate. Thus, it would be reasonable to take it into account and adjust your rubric accordingly.

If you decide the interview data will be primary data and the survey data will be secondary data because of its low return rate, you may adjust your rubric a little bit differently. For example, in the following rubric example, the criteria for interview data are specifically described and emphasized, whereas the criteria for survey data are more loosely described:

- Excellent: Interview data indicate users' satisfaction with the system and no major dissatisfaction (primary). Most survey responses are *Slightly agree* or *Strongly agree* (secondary).

- Fair: Interview data indicate users' satisfaction with some parts of the system and dissatisfaction with other parts of the system (primary). Most survey responses are *Neutral, Slightly agree*, or *Strongly agree* (secondary).

- Poor: Interview data indicate users' dissatisfaction with the system (primary). Many survey responses are *Strongly disagree* or *Slightly disagree* (secondary).

By using the above rubric, you intend to determine the quality of the dimension mainly based on the interview data (the primary data) first. You apply the survey data (secondary data) with caution, acknowledging its limitations and potentially biased results due to a low return rate.

If you use an experimental design for investigating a dimension, you may also want to develop a rubric for the results of the experimental study, so that all dimensional results can be easily compared and synthesized, especially if you are conducting a summative evaluation. See Table 54.

TABLE 54 ● Dimensional Rubric in an Experimental Study

Dimension	Data Collection Method	Consolidated Dimensional Rubric
User Satisfaction	Survey with randomly selected users (using an experimental design to compare intervention and nonintervention groups) Interview with tech support specialists	• Excellent: Significantly higher satisfaction ($p < .05$) with a large effect size (d) and mostly positive interview comments • Fair: Significantly higher satisfaction ($p < .05$) with a small or medium effect size (d), and a mix of positive and negative interview comments • Poor: Not significantly higher satisfaction ($p \geq .05$), and mostly negative interview comments

TABLE 55 ● Using a Dimensional Triangulation Rubric to Combine Results of Multiple Sources			
Dimension	**Data Collection Method**	**Develop Separate Rubrics for Individual Data Collection Methods**	**Also Develop a Dimensional Triangulation Rubric**
User Satisfaction	Survey with all users	• Excellent: 4.0 ≤ average ≤ 5.0 without any *Strongly disagree* or *Slightly disagree* responses • Fair: 3.0 ≤ average < 4.0 • Poor: 1.0 ≤ average < 3.0	• Excellent: All data sources indicate Excellent • Fair: All data sources indicate either Excellent or Fair • Poor: Any data sources indicate Poor
	Interview with several users	• Excellent: Mostly positive comments • Fair: A mix of positive and negative comments • Poor: Mostly negative comments	
	Interview with tech support specialists	• Excellent: Mostly positive comments • Fair: A mix of positive and negative comments • Poor: Mostly negative comments	

Develop a Dimensional Triangulation Rubric

Instead of consolidating multiple rubrics into one, you can create another rubric to triangulate the results obtained from multiple sources, as shown in Table 55. In this case, you need to use a set of separate rubrics for individual data collection methods as well as the dimensional triangulation rubric.

Determine the Quality of Each Dimension

Whether you consolidate multiple rubrics into one or add a dimensional triangulation rubric, you need to determine the quality of each individual dimension separately. In doing so, you also want to use the same number of levels and the same labels in all dimensional rubrics, if possible.

USE THE SAME RUBRIC LEVELS AND LABELS FOR ALL DIMENSIONS

Table 56 shows a set of consolidated rubrics to be used for the example provided in Chapter 7, Table 42. Table 57 is another example using dimensional triangulation rubrics.

In Table 56, note that when the same data collection instruments are being used to collect data for multiple dimensions, specific question numbers from the instruments have been added in the "Instrument Used" column. The specific question numbers in the table indicate which questions' data are analyzed with the rubrics.

Also, be aware that you may have included some questions in instruments that do not generate evaluative data to be analyzed with rubrics. For example, in a survey questionnaire, you may ask for the respondents' name, their position, number of years in working in the position, or reasons for attending the program. This type of information is not to be analyzed with rubrics.

As a result of analyzing collected data against the consolidated dimensional rubrics, you will be able to determine quality of each dimension. For example,

- Dimension 1: Excellent

- Dimension 2: Fair

- Dimension 3: Fair

This step applies to both formative and summative evaluations. In the next step, formative and summative evaluations diverge. For formative evaluation, you focus on providing evidence-based recommendations for improving individual dimensions. During summative evaluation, you aim at determining the overall quality of the evaluand and its outcomes by synthesizing dimensional results and assisting the stakeholders in making intended summative decisions. In doing so, it is again important to refer to the stakeholders' intended use of the evaluation findings that you initially identified.

TABLE 56 ● Evaluating a New Tech Support Ticketing and Tracking System With Consolidated Dimensional Rubrics

Dimension, PLM, and IW	Data Collection Method	Instrument Used	Rubric Used
1. User-friendliness of system interface— How user-friendly is the system interface? Which parts need clearly written job aids? PLM: Resources IW: Important	1-1. Observe five users while using the system, using a think-aloud method 1-2. Conduct face-to-face interviews with three technical support specialists and a software engineer	1-1. Observation solicitation email message, informed consent form, and observation checklist 1-2. Interview solicitation email message, informed consent form, and semi-structured interview questions: Q3–Q6	• Excellent: Users complete 98+% of tasks without having to ask questions, and mostly positive interview comments • Fair: Users complete 70%–97% of tasks without having to ask questions, and a mix of positive and negative interview comments • Poor: Users complete less than 70% of tasks without having to ask questions, and mostly negative interview comments
2. Efficiency in ticketing and tracking process— How efficiently are the ticketing and tracking process handled? Which steps are delayed, and for what reasons? PLM: Activities IW: Most important	2-1. Observe three technical support specialists while using the system, using a think-aloud method 2-2. Conduct face-to-face interviews with three technical support specialists and a software engineer	2-1. Observation solicitation email message, informed consent form, and observation checklist 2-2. Included in 1-2: Q7–Q9, Q11	• Excellent: Users complete 98+% of tasks without difficulty, all tickets were resolved in a day, and mostly positive interview comments • Fair: Users complete 70%–97% of tasks without difficulty, 70% of tickets were resolved in 2 days, and a mix of positive and negative interview comments

Dimension, PLM, and IW	Data Collection Method	Instrument Used	Rubric Used
	2-3. Conduct face-to-face or telephone interviews with 7 to 10 users	2-3. Interview solicitation email message, informed consent form, and semi-structured interview questions: Q2–Q4	• Poor: Users complete less than 70% of tasks without difficulty, 30% or more tickets were not resolved in 2 days, and mostly negative interview comments
	2-4. Review system logs	2-4. Document review checklist	
3. User satisfaction—How satisfied are the users with the tech support they received via the system? PLM: Outcomes IW: Very important	3-1. Conduct a web-based survey with all users	3-1. Email solicitation message, and an anonymous semi-structured web-based survey instrument: Q4–Q10	• Excellent: 4.0 ≤ survey average ≤ 5.0 without any *Strongly disagree* or *Slightly disagree* responses, and mostly positive interview comments • Fair: 3.0 ≤ survey average < 4, and a mix of positive and negative interview comments • Poor: 1.0 ≤ survey average < 3.0 and mostly negative interview comments
	3-2. Conduct face-to-face or telephone interviews with 7 to 10 users	Included in 2-3: Q6–Q9	
	3-3. Conduct face-to-face interviews with three technical support specialists	Included in 1-2: Q12–13, Q15	

IW, Importance weighting; *PLM*, program logic model.

Conduct Formative Meta-Evaluations

In the previous chapters, we emphasized the importance of performing formative meta-evaluations to check if your data collection instruments and procedures are adequately developed.

You are in Step 9, analyzing the collected data. In this step, it is also critical to conduct internal and external formative meta-evaluations to ensure correct analysis of your data. Here are several techniques you can use:

- Reflect and discuss with your team members and client (also involving other stakeholders if desirable) if the levels and definitions of your rubrics are adequately determined.

- Ask an expert on rubric development to review and provide feedback on your rubrics.

- Ask an expert on program evaluation to review and provide feedback on your dimensional findings.

- If you are using an experimental design, ask an expert on statistics to review and provide feedback on your statistical data analysis.

Formative meta-evaluations during this step help you draw valid conclusions in the next and final step of the 10-step procedure.

TABLE 57 ● **Evaluating a New Tech Support Ticketing and Tracking System With Dimensional Triangulation Rubrics**

Dimension, PLM, and IW	Data Collection Method	Excellent	Fair	Poor	Dimensional Triangulation Rubric
1. User-friendliness of system interface— How user-friendly is the system interface? Which parts need job aids? PLM: Resources IW: Important	1-1. Observe five users while using the system, using a think-aloud method	Users complete 98+% of tasks without having to ask questions	Users complete 70%–97% of tasks without having to ask questions	Users complete less than 70% of tasks without having to ask questions	• Excellent: Both data sources indicate Excellent • Fair: Two data sources indicate either Excellent or Fair • Poor: Any data sources indicate Poor
	1-2. Conduct face-to-face interviews with three technical support specialists and a software engineer	Comments indicate that the system is user-friendly	Comments indicate that the system is user-friendly, with some areas for minor improvement	Comments indicate that the system is not user-friendly	
2. Efficiency in ticketing and tracking process—How efficiently are the ticketing and tracking process handled? Which steps are delayed, and for what reasons? PLM: Activities IW: Most important	2-1. Observe three technical support specialists while using the system, using a think-aloud method	Users complete 98+% of tasks without difficulty	Users complete 70%–97% of tasks without difficulty	Users complete less than 70% of tasks without difficulty	• Excellent: Three or four data sources indicate Excellent, and no data source indicates Poor • Fair: No more than one data source indicates Poor • Poor: More than one data source indicate Poor
	2-2. Conduct face-to-face interviews with three technical support specialists and a software engineer	Comments indicate that all steps are efficiently handled	Comments indicate that a couple of steps should be improved	Comments indicate that many steps should be improved	
	2-3. Conduct face-to-face or telephone interviews with 7 to 10 users	All comments indicate the process being efficient	Some comments indicate needs for minor improvement	Many comments indicate needs for major improvement	
	2-4. Review system logs	All tickets were resolved in a day	70% of tickets were resolved in 2 days	30% or more tickets were not resolved in 2 days	

Dimension, PLM, and IW	Data Collection Method	Excellent	Fair	Poor	Dimensional Triangulation Rubric
3. User satisfaction— How satisfied are the users with the tech support they received via the system? PLM: Outcomes IW: Very important	3-1. Conduct a web-based survey with all users	$4.0 \le$ average ≤ 5.0 without any *Strongly disagree* or *Slightly disagree* responses	$3.0 \le$ average < 4.0	$1.0 \le$ average < 3.0	• Excellent: All data sources indicate Excellent • Fair: All data sources indicate either Excellent or Fair • Poor: Any data sources indicate Poor
	3-2. Conduct face-to-face or telephone interviews with 7 to 10 users	Mostly positive comments	A mix of positive and negative comments	Mostly negative comments	
	3-3. Conduct face-to-face interviews with three technical support specialists	Mostly positive comments	A mix of positive and negative comments	Mostly negative comments	

IW, Importance weighting; *PLM,* program logic model.

Chapter Summary

Analyze data with rubrics (Step 9):

- Evaluators use evidence-based practices during their evaluation by applying relevant frameworks, models, and procedures to the evaluation design, and analyzing multiple sources of data that they collected.

- Evaluation includes measurement and valuation processes. Collecting data is a measurement process. Rubrics are used during the valuation process.

- Evaluators analyze collected data against rubrics to indicate the quality or value of the individual dimensions.

- Evaluators use different rubrics depending on the type of evaluation designs and the type of data collection methods used.

- When using experimental or quasi-experimental studies, evaluators draw conclusions using the rubrics associated with the selected inferential statistical tests (e.g., the Alpha level and effect size).

- When using a descriptive case study type evaluation design, evaluators develop rubrics to be used to analyze the data collected from surveys, interviews, focus groups, observations, extant data reviews, and/or tests.

- After evaluators collect data from multiple sources, they should check if they have sufficient data that warrant the analysis with rubrics.

- During each dimensional analysis, to triangulate the results obtained from multiple sources, evaluators can consolidate separate rubrics developed for individual data collection methods into one or they can develop an additional dimensional triangulation rubric.

- Whether evaluators conduct a formative or summative evaluation, they determine the quality or value of each dimension. Then, the type of evaluation (formative or summative) makes a difference in the next step of analyzing multiple dimensions and drawing conclusions.

Chapter Discussion

1. Quantitative or qualitative rubrics

While developing rubrics, your team member says that quantitative hard data are more valid than qualitative data and that similarly, quantitative rubrics such as Rubric A are better than qualitative rubrics such as Rubric B.

Rubric A:

- Excellent: $4.0 \leq$ average score ≤ 5.0

- Good: $3.0 \leq$ average score ≤ 3.9

- Mediocre: $2.0 \leq$ average score ≤ 2.9

- Poor: $1.0 \leq$ average score ≤ 1.9

Rubric B:

- Excellent: Mostly positive data indicating customer satisfaction

- Good: A mix of positive and negative data, but more positive data and no major negative data

- Mediocre: A mix of positive and negative data with more negative data indicating areas that caused customer dissatisfaction

- Poor: Mostly negative data indicating customer dissatisfaction and significant needs for improvement

Based on that, your team member suggests using only quantitative rubrics. How would you respond to this suggestion? Also, discuss pros and cons of using quantitative rubrics and qualitative rubrics.

2. Evidence-based practice

Sit back and reflect what you have been doing since the beginning of your evaluation project, and recognize different types of evidence that you have been using.

Based on the information, compose a 1-minute elevator speech about how you have been using evidence-based practices during your evaluation project.

Now, Your Turn—Analyze Data With Rubrics

Using Table B-6 Instruments and Rubrics Development Worksheet in Appendix B (Evaluation Development Worksheets), describe the dimensional rubrics you will use to evaluate individual dimensions.

Draw Conclusions (Step 10)

Please recall that evaluation involves *measurement* and *valuation*. In the previous step (Step 9 in Chapter 12), you started working on the valuation part of your evaluation project by developing rubrics and analyzing dimensional results. You are now in the last step of the 10-step evaluation procedure, where you will complete the valuation part by combining dimensional results and drawing conclusions.

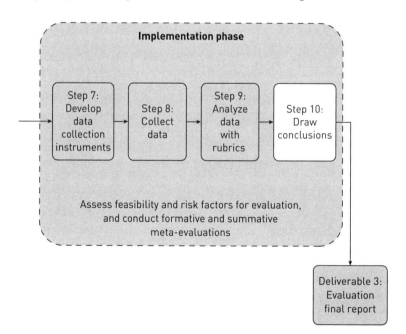

Revisit Formative or Summative Use of Evaluation Findings

After you complete dimensional analyses, the next step is to combine dimensional results and draw conclusions. The way you combine dimensional results and draw conclusions largely depends on the purpose of your evaluation. Therefore, it is important to remind yourself who will use the evaluation findings and how they intend to use the knowledge produced from the evaluation.

During the evaluation identification phase, you characterized your client's evaluation purpose as formative or summative. Formative evaluation results are used to improve the program design and operation to produce desired outcomes. The focus is not to assist stakeholders in determining the overall quality of a program but more to help the stakeholders recognize areas of the program that need to be improved and to recommend ways to make such improvements. Thus, recall that dimensions selected for a formative evaluation will likely address the program's resources, activities, outputs, and some outcomes as shown in the program logic model (see Figure 13 in Chapter 6). You design a formative program evaluation to investigate which parts of the program work and which parts do not. You also investigate environmental factors that facilitate or hinder the program operation and outputs. Although individual dimensional evaluation questions are tailored to each program, most of them would be similar to the following types of questions: **FORMATIVE USE OF EVALUATION FINDINGS**

- How well were the program resources selected, developed, and used?

- How well were the program activities designed and completed?

- How much and how well did the program produce its outputs?

- How close is the program getting to producing desirable outcomes?

- How well have the environmental factors been supporting the success of the program?

- What are the barriers to the success of the program, and how well is the program handling the obstacles? What other supports does the program need?

Looking at internal and external factors (or dimensions) for a program, you have a better understanding of the program implementation status and are able to generate evidence-based (data-driven) conclusions and recommendations for helping stakeholders make improvements on the program design and operation.

Summative evaluation, on the other hand, is designed to focus more on the outputs, outcomes, and impact categories of the program logic model (see Figure 14 in Chapter 6). Therefore, summative evaluation results are used to accomplish the following: **SUMMATIVE USE OF EVALUATION FINDINGS**

- Determine the overall quality of a program.

- Determine the worth of the program (or more specifically, its cost-effectiveness).

- Determine the quality of the performance outcomes needed to be produced (the amount of performance gap closed).

- Determine the program's intended and unintended impact on stakeholders.

- Make administrative decisions such as continuing or discontinuing a program (including funding decisions).

- Implement the knowledge learned from a program to other programs.

With these intentions, you design a summative evaluation to investigate important dimensions of a program that represent the success or failure in accomplishing needed outcomes. Then, you need to synthesize the multiple dimensional results to generate summative conclusions and recommendations to assist stakeholders' future actions (Scriven, 1991b, 2013). Note that the word *synthesize* is used here.

Synthesis is defined as "the combining of separate elements or substances to form a coherent whole" ("Synthesis," n.d.). It is not a synthesis when several blind persons are touching an elephant and each of them is reporting his or her understanding separately. Synthesis is performed when blind persons touch an elephant *and* communicate with each other to figure out what it seems to be as a whole. The spot that each blind person touches and analyzes is analogous to each dimension of a program that you studied. Multiple blind persons can construct the image more accurately when they communicate with each other about their findings. Similarly, when conducting a summative evaluation, each dimension alone may not be sufficient for accurately projecting the overall quality of the program and performance outcomes. It is important to synthesize the results from the multiple dimensions in order to draw credible conclusions about the overall quality.

During formative evaluations, on the other hand, synthesis of multiple dimensional results may or may not be necessary. For a formative evaluation, you and stakeholders likely select dimensions that need to be addressed for improvement rather than dimensions that represent the expected outcomes of the program. Individual dimensions are investigated to show how much the organization has moved toward achieving the performance outcomes, instead of whether the needed performance outcomes have been achieved. Therefore, synthesizing dimensions selected for a formative evaluation may or may not represent the overall quality of the program and performance outcomes. Instead, you need to make sense out of the results obtained from individual dimensions and *prioritize* recommendations based on degrees of importance among the dimensions. You do not always have to provide a separate set of recommendations for each dimension. Some recommendations may intend to handle multiple issues that you uncover across multiple dimensions.

SYSTEMIC APPROACH TO DRAWING CONCLUSIONS

In this sense, whether you are conducting a formative or summative evaluation, you need to use a systemic approach during this 10th step of evaluation where you combine multiple dimensional results, draw conclusions, and generate recommendations. Formative and summative evaluations differ in this way:

- During a formative evaluation, you report dimensional results individually or by triangulating relevant results together, and you present recommendations for improvement. You may synthesize the dimensional results to indicate the quality of ongoing process and outputs of the program, by using a synthesis rubric's levels such as:

  ○ Moving in the right direction

- ○ Need minor improvements
- ○ Need substantial improvements

- In a summative evaluation, you synthesize dimensional results to show the overall quality or worth of the program and make summative recommendations to assist the decisions that the client and stakeholders intend to make. Your synthesis rubric is designed to indicate the overall quality of the program, by using rubric levels such as:

- ○ Outstanding
- ○ Good
- ○ Mediocre
- ○ Unacceptable

Develop a Synthesis Rubric

To synthesize dimensional results, you need a synthesis rubric, which incorporates the degrees of importance weighting among dimensions. You can use a *qualitative rubric* or a *quantitative rubric* to synthesize multiple dimensional results (Davidson, 2005).

However, you should keep in mind that you initially indicated the degrees of importance weighting with an ordinal scale (e.g., *Extremely important, Very important, Somewhat important*). Similarly, the rubrics that you used to triangulate multiple sources of data are ordinal scales as well (e.g., *Excellent, Good, Mediocre,* and *Poor*). Thus, you want to develop a qualitative synthesis rubric first, and think about whether there is a good reason to convert it to a quantitative synthesis rubric.

Qualitative Synthesis

As an example, recall the summative evaluation of an online degree program that was used in Chapter 6 and Chapter 7. In the example, a three-level importance rating scale was used—*Extremely important, Very important,* and *Somewhat important.*

Let's say that the four dimensions' ratings were *Good, Excellent, Mediocre,* and *Good,* as shown in Table 58. To synthesize the results from multiple dimensions in a qualitative way, you may use a qualitative synthesis rubric as shown in Table 59.

In this example, the extremely important dimension (graduation rate) is rated *Good.* The remaining very important dimensions (curriculum design and students' professional accomplishments) and the somewhat important dimension (online learning environment) are rated *Good, Mediocre,* and *Excellent,* respectively. Therefore, overall the online degree program would fall into the *Good* category.

The synthesis rubric does not have to use the same number of levels or labels that were used in dimensional rubrics (*Excellent, Good, Mediocre, Poor*). Table 60 is a synthesis rubric with a different set of labels (*High quality, Good but improvement needed, Significant improvement needed*).

A SYNTHESIS RUBRIC FOR A SUMMATIVE EVALUATION OF AN ONLINE LEARNING PROGRAM

TABLE 58 ● Four Dimensional Results

Dimension and Dimensional Question	Importance Weighting	Raw Result
1. **Curriculum design**—How well is the curriculum designed to support industry expectations and standards?	Very important	Good
2. **Online learning environment**—Does the online delivery technology provide a positive learning environment?	Somewhat important	Excellent
3. **Students' professional accomplishments**—How does the program help students achieve professional accomplishments?	Very important	Mediocre
4. **Graduation rate**—What is the program's 3-year graduation rate?	Extremely important	Good

TABLE 59 ● Qualitative Synthesis Rubric: Example 1

If all extremely important dimensions rated:		If all very important and somewhat important dimensions rated:		The overall quality is:
Excellent		Good or Excellent		Excellent
Good or Excellent	and	Mediocre (up to only one), Good, or Excellent	then	Good
Mediocre or Good		Poor (up to only one), Mediocre, Good, or Excellent		Mediocre
Poor or Mediocre		Poor (more than one), and Mediocre, Good, or Excellent		Poor

TABLE 60 ● Qualitative Synthesis Rubric: Example 2

If all extremely important dimensions rated:		If all very important and somewhat important dimensions rated:		The overall quality is:
Excellent		Good or Excellent		High quality
Good or Excellent	and	Mediocre (up to only one), Good, or Excellent	then	Good but improvement needed
Mediocre or Poor		Poor, Mediocre, Good, or Excellent		Significant improvement needed

Quantitative Synthesis

Qualitative synthesis rubrics with descriptive conditions as described above can be expressed in a quantitative manner, based on the synthesized dimensional results, as shown:

- High quality: $3.5 \leq$ synthesized dimensional results ≤ 4.0

- Good but improvement needed: $2.8 \leq$ synthesized dimensional results < 3.5

- Significant improvement needed: $1.0 \leq$ synthesized dimensional results < 2.8

To use such quantitative synthesis rubrics, first you need to express the dimensional weighting in percentages as shown in two examples in Table 61. In the examples, we used 50%, 20%, 20%, and 10% in Example 1, and 30%, 25%, 25%, and 20% in Example 2, for *Extremely important, Very important, Very important,* and *Somewhat important,* respectively.

Next, you need to assign numerical values to the dimensional results. Here, we assigned 4, 3, 2, and 1, to *Excellent, Good, Mediocre,* and *Poor,* respectively. In doing so, we will have to accept potential errors in this step because the four levels are likely ordinal scale levels rather than interval scale levels.

Depending on the weighted proportion of individual dimensions, the weighted synthesized results may turn out to be slightly different—Example 1 shows 2.9 and Example 2 shows 3.0.

Now, you need to develop the synthesis rubric definitions using numerical criteria. Instead of assigning arbitrary values, you need to think about what makes the *high* quality and what makes the *good-but-improvement-needed* quality. To do so, interestingly enough, you need to go back to qualitative criteria such as the one shown in Table 60.

TABLE 61 ● Two Examples of Incorporating Importance Weighting (%) to Produce Weighted Results				
	Example 1		Example 2	
Dimension	Importance Weighting	Dimensional Result	Importance Weighting	Dimensional Result
1	Very important (20%)	Good (3)	Very important (25%)	Good (3)
2	Somewhat important (10%)	Excellent (4)	Somewhat important (20%)	Excellent (4)
3	Very important (20%)	Mediocre (2)	Very important (25%)	Mediocre (2)
4	Extremely important (50%)	Good (3)	Extremely important (30%)	Good (3)
	Total = 100%	Weighted synthesized result = 2.9	Total = 100%	Weighted synthesized result = 3.0

Let's use Example 1 in Table 61 that uses 50%, 20%, 20%, and 10% as importance weighting levels. It can be considered *High quality* if the following conditions are met:

- The extremely important dimension (50%) is *Excellent* (4).
- The two very important dimensions (20% and 20%) are at least *Good* (3).
- The somewhat important dimension (10%) is also at least *Good* (3).

Then, you would have this formula to calculate the weighted score for the minimum condition for *High quality*: $(0.5 \times 4) + (0.2 \times 3) + (0.2 \times 3) + (0.1 \times 3) = 2.0 + 0.6 + 0.6 + 0.3 = 3.5$. Since the maximum value is 4.0, you would have the following quantitative definition:

- High quality: 3.5 ≤ synthesized dimensional results ≤ 4.0

Similarly, it can be considered *Good but improvement needed* if the following conditions are met:

- The extremely important dimension (50%) is *Good* (3).
- One of the two very important dimensions (20%) is *Mediocre* (2), and the other very important dimension is *Good* (3).
- The somewhat important dimension is also at least *Good* (3).

You would use this calculation: $(0.5 \times 3) + (0.2 \times 2) + (0.2 \times 3) + (0.1 \times 3) = 1.5 + 0.4 + 0.6 + 0.3 = 2.8$. Thus, the minimum value for the *Good but improvement needed* level is 2.8, and you would have the following quantitative definition:

- Good but improvement needed: 2.8 ≤ synthesized dimensional results < 3.5.

That's how you could come up with the following rubric definitions of the three-level quantitative synthesis rubric:

- High quality: 3.5 ≤ synthesized dimensional results ≤ 4.0
- Good but improvement needed: 2.8 ≤ synthesized dimensional results < 3.5
- Significant improvement needed: 1.0 ≤ synthesized dimensional results < 2.8

If you use a different set of importance weighting values such as 30%, 25%, 25%, and 20%, you will have a slightly different set of rubric definitions in the quantitative synthesis rubric:

- High quality: 3.3 ≤ synthesized dimensional results ≤ 4.0
- Good but improvement needed: 2.8 ≤ synthesized dimensional results < 3.3
- Significant improvement needed: 1.0 ≤ synthesized dimensional results < 2.8

Whether you use a qualitative synthesis rubric as shown in Table 60, or a quantitative synthesis rubric using either type of importance weighing values as shown in Table 61, your conclusion will turn out to be the same in this case—*Good but improvement needed.*

These examples illustrate two important points:

1. Development of a quantitative rubric is largely based on a qualitative rubric.

2. A quantitative rubric is not more accurate or more objective than a qualitative rubric.

With that in mind, you may want to consider whether it is worthwhile to go the extra mile to convert a qualitative synthesis rubric to a quantitative one.

Draw Evidence-Based Conclusions and Recommendations

You have decided whether to use a synthesis rubric or not. Now you are ready to draw conclusions and generate recommendations. Whether you are conducting a formative or summative evaluation, you make data-driven decisions, which is part of your evidence-based practice.

DRAW DATA-DRIVEN DECISIONS

The way you draw conclusions differs depending on the intended use of evaluation results. If the stakeholders' intended use of your evaluation is to make necessary changes to the way that the program is designed and delivered so that the program will achieve accreditation in the future, you would focus on providing conclusions on *how close* to or *how far* from meeting accreditation criteria the program is.

You also provide recommendations. For a formative evaluation, you need to explain what needs to be done to make continuous improvement on the quality of the program to be able to achieve accreditation. If the evaluation results will be used to determine whether or not to continue to provide funding for the program, you would need to support your recommendation (as to funding or no funding) with evidence-based explanations.

In making both formative and summative recommendations, not only do you use the data that you collected and analyzed (data-driven decisions), but you can also refer to the literature that supports your recommendations. Here are a few examples.

REFER TO RELEVANT LITERATURE

Example 1. From an evaluation of a mandated annual safety training program, you found out that trainees perceived the presentation to be dull and that examples were irrelevant to their work environment. While recommending the stakeholders to revise the program, you may refer them to instructional strategy development models such as the ARCS model (Keller, 1987) to improve the motivational appeal of the instructional content.

Example 2. From an evaluation of a career development program, you unexpectedly discovered that employees were not satisfied with several aspects of their work environment, including the relationship with their supervisors. The career development program aims at developing employees' capacity, increasing job satisfaction, and improving retention. However, according to Herzberg's (1968) two-factor theory, employees may not feel satisfied with their job even with motivational factors received from the career development program, if there are hygiene factors such as their poor relationship with supervisors. Therefore, you may cite Herzberg's theory to emphasize the importance of including interventions that help improve the employees' relationship with their supervisors.

Example 3. From an evaluation of a project that aimed at facilitating employees to participate in informal learning by using social media apps, you found out that only a small group of the same employees has been using the apps. Using Rogers's (2003) diffusion of innovation, you may identify them as early adopters and generate strategies to help the early and late majority groups engage in five stages of the adoption process (knowledge, persuasion, decision, implementation, and confirmation).

As shown in these examples, using the literature of relevant theories and research findings to support your conclusions and recommendations is also part of your evidence-based practice.

APPLY A SWOT
ANALYSIS

While drawing conclusions and generating recommendations, you can apply a **SWOT analysis** to organize information in a structured manner (Scriven, 2013). SWOT stands for strengths, weaknesses, opportunities, and threats. SWOT questions that you might apply during the concluding step of evaluation include the following:

- **S**trengths—What were the strong aspects of the program? What worked well, and why? (internal, positive)

- **W**eaknesses—What were the weak aspects of the program? What did not work well, and why? (internal, negative)

- **O**pportunities—What environmental factors did the program take advantage of? How did the program do so? (external, positive)

- **T**hreats—What environmental factors jeopardized success of the program? How could the program have avoided them? (external, negative)

Not all four SWOT categories need to be presented. Some projects may present only strengths and weaknesses of the program.

Table 62 lists possible findings of a SWOT analysis based on dimensional results. Most recommendations would be generated based on observed weaknesses of and threats to the program, regarding the design and operation of the program and the program's support systems such as managerial support, organizational culture, or economic trends. Some recommendations could be made based on observed strengths of the program as well (e.g., continue to use the strategy since it is a critical element for the success of the program).

PRIORITIZE
RECOMMENDATIONS
BASED ON
DIMENSIONAL
IMPORTANCE AND
TIMELINESS

You will likely generate multiple recommendations. However, not all recommendations may be equally important. In that case, it would be reasonable to prioritize and document recommendations based on the relative importance of their corresponding dimensions. Take a look at the degrees of importance weighting among your dimensions. Recommendations made for the most important dimension can be indicated as top priorities, compared to the recommendations made for less important dimensions.

TABLE 62 ● Possible SWOT Results		
Results Context	**Positive**	**Negative**
Internal to the program	Strengths • The program selected, developed, and used resources well. • The program designed and completed activities well. • The program produced its outputs as expected. • The program is close to producing, or has produced, desirable outcomes. • The program has produced no or a minimum level of negative side effects and many positive side effects. • The program is cost-effective.	Weaknesses • The program did not properly select, develop, and use resources. • The program did not design and complete activities well. • The program failed to produce its outputs. • The program is having difficulty producing, or has not produced, desirable outcomes. • The program has produced many negative side effects. • The program is not cost-effective.
External to the program	Opportunities • The organization's policies, procedures, and leadership are flexible enough to support the program resources and activities. • External monetary or nonmonetary incentives exist for developing and maintaining a successful program (e.g., job security, bonus, recognition). • The program maintains a long-term relationship with its consumers and earns high-level reputation and trust.	Threats (indicated in italic) • *Consumers' needs are constantly changing*, which the program did not assess and prepare for. • *Competitors may satisfy consumers' needs better*, which the program did not monitor. • The program does not have a plan and capacity to incorporate *technological advancement* in solutions. • *The current funding sources expire soon*, and the program has not found other funding sources.

However, the degree of importance weighting is not the only factor that might influence your decision. Perhaps, it is also important to consider timeliness of the recommended interventions and/or costs for implementing the interventions. Think of the recommendations from both *systematic* and *systemic* perspectives. Which one should be implemented first, and which one next? When one of the recommendations is implemented, how would it affect other recommended interventions? After all, evaluation processes are both systematic and systemic.

Conduct Formative Meta-Evaluations

You are in the last step of the 10-step evaluation procedure, and you need to perform the last set of internal and external formative meta-evaluations on the way you drew conclusions and generated recommendations.

Reflect and discuss with your team members and client (also involving other stakeholders if desirable) if:

- the level and definitions of the synthesis rubric (if used) are adequately determined,

- your recommendations are data-driven and feasible, and

- your conclusions and recommendations support the overall purpose of the evaluation.

Have an expert on program evaluation review and provide feedback on whether the way you combined dimensional results to draw conclusions and generated recommendations is aligned with the overall purpose of the evaluation.

Chapter Summary

Draw conclusions (Step 10):

- After completing the investigation of multiple dimensions of a program, evaluators use the dimensional results to draw conclusions and generate recommendations.

- While drawing conclusions, evaluators should revisit the information about how the stakeholders intend to use evaluation findings.

- Depending on whether it is a summative or formative evaluation, evaluators may use different methods to report multiple dimensional results.

  - For a summative evaluation, evaluators use a synthesis rubric to combine multiple dimensional results to determine the overall quality or worth of the program and performance outcomes achieved. Qualitative synthesis rubrics can be converted to quantitative synthesis rubrics if needed.

  - For a formative evaluation, evaluators may not need to (or cannot) determine the overall quality or worth of the program and performance outcomes achieved. Instead, they report individual dimensional results and generate recommendations for improving the quality of individual dimensions in order to continue to generate the needed performance outcomes.

- Evaluators use evidence-based practices during their evaluation project.

  - Evaluators make data-driven (evidence-based) decisions while drawing conclusions and generating recommendations.

  - Evaluators may use the literature of relevant theories and research findings to support their conclusions and recommendations.

  - Evaluators may use SWOT categories to report strengths, weaknesses, opportunities, and/or threats of the program they found from their data.

- ○ Evaluators prioritize recommendations based on the degrees of importance weighting of individual dimensions to which the recommendations are related. They may apply timeliness and costs for implementing recommendations as well.

- Evaluators should conduct internal and external formative meta-evaluations to ensure evidence-based practices while drawing conclusions and generating recommendations.

Chapter Discussion

1. Evaluation purpose, design, and conclusions

For the past three months, you have been conducting a formative evaluation of a summer youth camp program provided by a nonprofit organization. The formative type of evaluation was determined early in the project after consulting with the client (the camp director) and several other upstream stakeholders and based on the information they said about how they intended to use the evaluation findings.

You are currently in the process of combining dimensional results and providing recommendations for improvement. However, the client called you this morning and asked if you could change the evaluation to a summative evaluation. He explained that to apply for a grant to get additional money to support the program next year, it would be better to have a summative evaluation report in order to include summative information in the grant proposal (i.e., how good overall the program is).

Is it appropriate to change the type of evaluation at this stage of the project? What are the concerns for doing so?

2. Systematic and systemic approaches to evaluation

In the Introduction chapter, we defined program evaluation as:

> the systematic and systemic collection and analysis of information about the process and outcomes of a program in order to make improvements or judgments about the program's quality or value.

Reflect on the micro-level steps and macro-level tasks that you have performed during your evaluation project. Identify systematic and systemic approaches that you used during your project. Discuss what went well as planned and what you could have done differently to conduct your evaluation in a systematic and systemic manner.

Now, Your Turn—Draw Conclusions and Make Recommendations

Draw conclusions based on dimensional results, and make recommendations tailored to the intended use of the evaluation findings. Also, perform internal and external formative meta-evaluations to make improvement and take accountability for the methods that you used to draw conclusions and generate recommendations.

Write a Final Report and Conduct a Summative Meta-Evaluation

You have completed the implementation phase of your evaluation project, and now it is time to write a final report! You will also conduct a summative meta-evaluation.

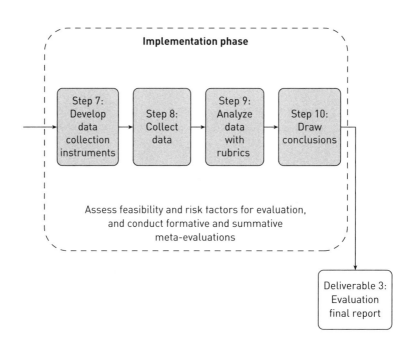

Extend the Evaluation Proposal
to a Final Report

In your evaluation proposal, you presented the following sections describing the organization where the evaluation is conducted, the program and its stakeholders, your evaluation methodology, and your feasibility and risk factors assessment results.

1. Organization

2. Program and Stakeholders

3. Evaluation Methodology

4. Feasibility and Risk Factors

References

Appendices

You will include those sections in your final report by adjusting the verb tense and editing other parts as needed. For example, in your evaluation proposal, you laid out data collection methods as a plan. During the implementation phase, you might have made an adjustment on the initial data collection plan. If so, you should revise the information based on the data collection methods you actually used. Clearly describe the number of informants you recruited and the number of informants who actually participated in your evaluation. The risk factors assessment section should also report how you actually managed risk factors throughout the project.

Then, you will add four new sections, based on the steps you completed during the implementation phase of your evaluation project. You also want to present an executive summary, and you will update References and Appendices as needed:

Executive Summary (new section)

1. Organization (update as needed)

2. Program and Stakeholders (update as needed)

3. Evaluation Methodology (update as needed)

4. Feasibility and Risk Factors (update as needed)

5. Evaluation Results (new section)

6. Conclusions (new section)

7. Meta-Evaluations and Limitations (new section)

8. Reporting (new section)

References (update as needed)

Appendices (update as needed)

Present Dimensional Results in the Evaluation Results Section

The Evaluation Results section is one of the main parts that you need to add to your report. In this section, you will present a summary of the dimensional results—that is, the evidence that you collected and analyzed. You want to present your findings for each dimension in a separate subsection. The content in each subsection should be organized in a structured format, reporting the following items:

CONTENT TO BE PRESENTED IN DIMENSIONAL RESULTS

- Dimensional question investigated and importance weighting assigned

- Data collection methods used (a brief summary)

- Data collected

- Rubrics used

- Dimensional quality determined

- Other observations and discussions

It is important to provide sufficient information about your findings. However, you also need to keep the main body of the report to a reasonable length. To do so, you want to put yourself in the readers' shoes and separate *must-know* information and *nice-to-know* (supporting) information.

In the Evaluation Results section, you should present the must-know information while presenting nice-to-know information in appendices. When you present supporting information in appendices, you should refer to the appendices in the main body of your report—for example,

> About two thirds of the survey respondents perceived the program as an important element for developing their job skills (see Appendix A for a summary of the survey results).

Present Supporting Information in Appendices

Information that you present in appendices are often summaries of data (rather than raw data) you collected from surveys, interviews, focus groups, observations, extant data reviews, and/or tests. Some of the data that you collected are anonymous data, whereas other data are not. While preparing such information to be presented in appendices, please recall what you wrote in the email recruitment messages and the informed consent forms, as well as other relevant guidelines on protecting confidentiality and privacy of informants.

PROTECT CONFIDENTIALITY OF DATA

For example, you might have used statements similar to the following in your email recruitment messages when soliciting survey, interview, and observation participants:

> "This is an anonymous survey, and only a summary of the group responses will be presented in the report."

"We will ask for your name to match your pre-test and post-test data. However, only a summary of data will be presented in a report, and your name will not be used in any written or oral reports."

"The recorded results will be kept anonymous, and only a summary of the results will be presented in the report."

As you promised to them, you should not associate data with the informants' unique characteristics such as names, departments, age, or gender that the readers of your final report can use to identify or be able to guess the informants. See Table 63 for general recommendations.

In addition to the data you collected, you may present other supporting information such as letters or documents you obtained from stakeholders. Before you insert such information in your appendices, you need to check if any information needs to be removed to protect people's privacy. If there are a couple of words, phrases, or lines of statements that need to be removed, you may simply replace the area with a black background (e.g., "According to John Doe" is changed to "According to ▮▮▮▮▮▮ ").

Present Conclusions

You need to draw conclusions tailored to the type of evaluation—that is, the intended use of evaluation results.

TABLE 63 ● General Recommendations on Excluding Identifiable Information From Evaluation Reports		
Data collected from / **OK to present?**	**Definitely no, or usually no**	**Probably yes if there is no identifiable information**
Surveys	Raw survey responses obtained from individual participants, especially hand-written paper-based survey responses	• Quantitative data—a table summarizing group average scores or percentages for individual survey items • Qualitative data—a summary of responses or selected responses
Interviews and focus groups	Entire interview transcripts	A summary of only important information obtained from multiple interviews
Observations	Individual raw observation checklists containing data	A summary of only important information obtained from multiple observations
Extant data reviews	A copy of the extant data itself	A summary of analyzed results
Knowledge tests	Individual raw answer sheets	A table summarizing group average scores for individual test questions

EVIDENCE-BASED
CONCLUSIONS

- If it is a formative evaluation, you describe what needs to be improved, how much it needs to be improved, and how it can be improved. You may list a set of recommendations for each dimension, or some recommendations may apply to multiple dimensions.

- If it is a summative evaluation, you describe the overall quality or worth of the program and performance outcomes based on synthesized dimensional results and present the appropriate decisions (recommendations) made based on the evidence found in the evaluation.

You may present a summary of strengths and weaknesses of the program and opportunities and threats that the program stakeholders need to keep in mind. Use tables and/or figures to provide information in a structured format as needed.

Most importantly, your conclusions and recommendations must be supported by the evidence that you presented in the previous sections of the report.

Report the Findings Ethically

Ethical conduct of evaluation includes not only ethical execution of data collection but also ethical reporting of the findings. Double-check and ensure that the information that you present in the final report does not violate the principles of protecting the rights of human subjects.

While writing a final evaluation report, you may encounter situations that cause ethical dilemmas. Consider the following hypothetical scenario:

ETHICAL REPORT

Sue is a training specialist. She recently conducted an evaluation on the effectiveness of the new sales training program implemented at the company. She has shared a draft of her final report with the training manager, the evaluation client. After reviewing it, the training manager praises her for producing such a comprehensive evaluation report. However, the manager asks her to remove one section that describes that the overall revenue after the new sales training program has not changed and that the lack of change was partially due to factors other than the training program, such as the current high turnover rate and low employee satisfaction level. The manager is concerned that the information could cause readers to overlook other positive outcomes, and even worse, it could create "enemies" who might use the information against them later. Sue understands the manager's concern, but she also knows that without that section, her report would not provide a complete picture of the situation. Sue is trying to decide whether she should be responsive to the manager's concerns and remove the section as suggested or convince the manager why it is important to include the section in the report (Adapted from Scenario 1 on p. 24 in Chyung et al., 2010, with some modifications).

If you were in Sue's situation, what would you do? Would you remove the section as requested? Evaluators may find themselves in similar situations where they are asked, directly or indirectly, to present only positive findings in final reports to make the program "look good."

It is not easy to predict your action based on the brief description of the situation without having a full understanding of the context. However, generally speaking, it would not be justifiable, thus unethical, to remove a section of evaluation results based on the fact that the section presents negative findings. Recall that during the evaluation planning stage, you as an evaluator worked with the stakeholders to select data collection methods necessary to complete the evaluation project. It would be helpful to discuss with your client the importance of providing a comprehensive report as planned and your obligation to follow ethical guidelines and professional standards.

Conduct a Summative Meta-Evaluation

Throughout the evaluation project, you have conducted a series of formative meta-evaluations. Doing so helped you make necessary changes to your evaluation process in a timely manner, which in turn contributed to producing a quality project.

Now that you have completed your evaluation project and written a final report, it is time to conduct a summative meta-evaluation. First, you should meta-evaluate your final report by reflecting on your final report and double-checking if:

EXTERNAL AND INTERNAL META-EVALUATIONS

- all necessary information is presented,

- presented information is accurate, and

- information is ethically reported.

You should also conduct an external meta-evaluation by having an evaluation expert review your evaluation report. The evaluation expert is familiar with systematic, systemic, and ethical conduct of evaluation, and he or she can examine appropriateness of the evaluation purpose, design, implementation procedure, interpretation of results, conclusions, and recommendations described in your evaluation report. In your final report, you can insert a summary of the external meta-evaluator's summative evaluation about the quality of your evaluation report in an appendix.

Report Limitations

Careful planning of an evaluation project leads to successful execution of the evaluation project. However, it is unlikely that things will go as perfectly as planned. You are not conducting an evaluation in a lab where you can control environmental variables. You often have to work with limited resources and handle unanticipated happenings.

Your summative meta-evaluation (internal and external) may also reveal that you should have done things differently during certain steps. You should describe those limitations in the final report to help readers understand the circumstances surrounding the evaluation project and to help readers interpret results properly.

The following are examples of limitations:

- Evaluators' capacity was limited to using a descriptive case study type design when an experimental study was a better option.

EXAMPLES OF LIMITATIONS OF THE EVALUATION PROJECT

- The survey return rate was much lower than expected.

- Evaluators could not solicit enough volunteers among employees for interviews.

- Evaluators could not use the Success Case Model (SCM) as initially planned, because they could not identify distinct success and nonsuccess cases from the survey results.

- Evaluators found that different mentors used different assessment tools, which did not allow them to compare mentees' performance levels.

- The organization did not give external evaluators access to some proprietary data.

- Several stakeholders were laid off during the evaluation process and could not serve as informants anymore.

Write an Executive Summary

In addition to the main body of your evaluation report, you need to provide your stakeholders with an executive summary, which you can insert in front of the main report or prepare in a separate document.

Please be aware that an executive summary is not an introductory section of your final evaluation report. An **executive summary** is a summary of the main report. When writing an executive summary of your evaluation report, you should keep in mind two types of audience:

1. The immediate audience (who are likely familiar with the project and the organizational background)

2. A future audience (who may or may not be familiar with the project and the organizational background)

A CONCISE YET SUFFICIENT SUMMARY Some executive summaries can contain a list of bullet points of the main findings presented in the report. In other cases, executive summaries need to contain concise yet sufficient information about the evaluation process and results for both types of audience. In this book, we will prepare the latter type of executive summary.

An executive summary should help the audience of the evaluation report easily catch the following information without having to review the entire report (recall the 5W1H method and apply it here):

- What program was evaluated and who used the program

- Who requested the evaluation and who conducted the evaluation

- Why it was evaluated

- When and where it was evaluated

- How the evaluation was designed and executed

- What was found and concluded from the evaluation

You also want to present information in the same sequence as the one used in the main report.

To do so, you may organize the content of your executive summary with the following subtitles:

- **Background**: Describing the organizational context, the program, its stakeholders including the evaluation client, and the evaluation team

- **Evaluation methodology**: Describing the purpose and type of evaluation, the dimensions investigated, and the data collection methods used

- **Evaluation results**: Describing the main results found

- **Conclusions**: Describing the conclusions and recommendations generated from the analyzed data

- **Limitations and reporting**: Describing the limitations of the project and the stakeholders to whom you provide the final report

SUGGESTED
SUBSECTIONS OF
AN EXECUTIVE
SUMMARY

The length of an executive summary can be a couple of pages, whereas the main report is around 20 pages in length.

Present the Final Report to Stakeholders

After you write a final report, you submit it to the client and other stakeholders who intend to use the evaluation findings. You may also meet with them to deliver an oral presentation of the evaluation findings. An oral presentation provides the stakeholders with an opportunity to ask you questions about the findings. You might use the meeting to help them engage in discussions about making an action plan based on the evaluation results.

Follow Up With Stakeholders

If you are an internal evaluator (or evaluation team), you may be able to follow up with the stakeholders to continue to assist them to use your evaluation findings. However, if you are an external evaluator (or evaluation team), you may or may not have access to the evaluation context to check up on how the stakeholders are using the evaluation findings. Compared to internal evaluators, external evaluators may have difficulty regaining access to the evaluation context. If you have access to the organization and stakeholders, it is desirable to have a follow-up meeting with the stakeholders to discuss their use of evaluation results.

KEEP IN MIND
THE CYCLICAL
PROCESS OF
PERFORMANCE
IMPROVEMENT

Evaluation is a type of performance improvement strategy, and performance improvement is a cyclical process. An evaluation may lead to changes in the performance improvement practice, which may also lead to a new opportunity to conduct another evaluation.

Present Complete Sections in a Final Report

Table 64 provides a summary of specific information expected in each section of an evaluation final report. You may present some information in a different section if it improves the flow.

TABLE 64 ● Information to Be Presented in an Evaluation Final Report	
Section	**Content**
Title page	• Title of the report, date, and evaluator(s)
Executive summary	• Present a summary of the report in two or three pages. An executive summary is not an introduction to the main report but rather a summary of the main report. • You may include an executive summary in front of the main report, or you may produce an executive summary in a separate document.
1. Organization	• Present the organization's background information, such as its location and history. • Explain the needs that caused the organization to develop and implement the program. When describing time frames, write specific dates (e.g., in 2016), instead of writing "a few years ago." • Present other supporting information, if any, in an appendix.
2. Program and stakeholders	• Provide a detailed description of the program so that readers have a good understanding about how the program operates. Do not assume that your evaluation client is the only reader of the evaluation report. The document can be accessed by others, who may or may not be familiar with the program. • Present any figures or tables that help readers better understand the program (e.g., a room setting, a flowchart of work process, or a workshop procedure). • List different categories of stakeholders (upstream stakeholders, direct impactees, and indirect impactees) with descriptive information to help readers understand how they belong to each category. Describe the size of each stakeholder group, which helps readers understand the scope of the program and the evaluation project. • Present a program logic model or training impact model. • Present other supporting information, if any, in an appendix (e.g., a sample lesson plan).
3. Evaluation methodology	• State the purpose of the evaluation. Clearly describe the intended users and their intended use of evaluation findings. • Describe the type of evaluation (e.g., formative or summative, and goal-based or goal-free) and evaluation frameworks you applied. • Present a list of dimensions along with specific dimensional evaluation questions that you investigated, and explain how you determined the dimensions and their importance weighting values (i.e., whom you involved during the decision and how you facilitated the decision process). • Describe the overall data collection procedure and timeline (that you actually followed). Revise your initial plan if you adjusted it during your actual data collection process. • Present specific data collection methods (that you actually used) in a table format, which can be inserted in the main body of the report or in an appendix. Revise your initial plan if you adjusted it during your actual data collection process. • Describe any other important changes that you made during your evaluation process (especially, any changes made after the data collection step), and clearly explain why you made the changes (e.g., you had to exclude one dimension during your synthesis because you could not collect sufficient data to complete your investigation of the dimension).

Section	Content

4. Feasibility and risk factors	• Describe feasibility of the evaluation project, regarding the following:
	
	  ○ Scope of the project
	  ○ Expected and actual timeline for completion
	  ○ Other relevant factors
	
	• Describe risk factors (that you previously indicated and newly found during data collection and analysis), and describe how you actually managed the risk factors during the project.
	
	• When describing the risk factors that you failed to manage, provide explanations, some of which may be described in the Limitations section.

5. Evaluation results	• Summarize the results of each dimension in a separate subsection, including the following:
	
	  ○ Dimension and its importance weighting
	  ○ Data collection procedure you followed
	  ○ Summary of data collected
	  ○ Rubrics used to analyze the data
	  ○ Quality rating of the dimension
	  ○ Other observations and discussions
	
	• Format text with bulleted or numbered paragraphs when appropriate; use tables and/or figures for effective communication.
	
	• Avoid lengthy descriptions; keep each section concise and refer to appendices for detailed information.
	
	• Present must-know information in this section and nice-to-know information in appendices.

6. Conclusions	• Present conclusions tailored to the stakeholders' intended use of evaluation results:
	
	  ○ Formative evaluation—Provide a succinct summary of the evaluative results obtained from individual dimensions; you may provide the synthesized overall quality of the program and performance outcomes as a means to indicate the level of progress the organization has made in producing the needed outcomes (the amount of performance gap to be closed).
	
	  ○ Summative evaluation—Show the synthesized overall quality or worth of the program and performance outcomes needed to be produced (the amount of performance gap closed), and explain how you arrived at the conclusions.
	
	• Provide a list of recommendations (again, tailored to the stakeholders' intended use of evaluation results), highlighting which ones are more important and why.
	
	• If appropriate, use the SWOT categories to present strengths and weaknesses of the program and opportunities for and threats to the program.

7. Meta-evaluations and limitations	• Describe how you conducted a series of formative meta-evaluations as well as a summative meta-evaluation, what you found out from the meta-evaluations, and how you used the meta-evaluation results. • Explain shortcomings or conditions that you could not control during the evaluation project, which affected the quality of the project; examples include the following:

(Continued)

TABLE 64 ● (Continued)	
Section	**Content**
	○ Lack of access to data sources
	○ Errors in instruments or data collection procedure
	○ Use of indirect measures (e.g., self-reports) rather than direct measures
	○ Organizational culture that hindered execution of some of the planned evaluation activities
	○ Ethical issues that you encountered
	● Based on lessons learned, provide suggestions for future evaluation projects.
8. Reporting	● Describe to whom you will present the evaluation report and in what form (e.g., written, oral, or both; a full report or an executive summary only).
	● Describe if and how you will be able to assist implementation of the recommendations you presented in the report.
References	● List references that you cited in the report.
Appendices	● Present appendices (e.g., instruments and summaries of data).
	● To protect anonymity of informants, do not include identifiable information unless there is a clear reason to do so.

Now, Your Turn—Write a Final Report

Congratulations on completing a full-blown evaluation project!

Now, take the final step and produce an evidence-based and ethical evaluation report. It is also highly recommended that you and your stakeholders share the lessons you learned with other practitioners by making a presentation at a professional conference or publishing a paper in a professional journal.

• Appendix A •

A Summary of the Frameworks Used

Appendix A provides a brief summary of each of the following six frameworks used in this book. For more information, readers should refer to the primary sources cited in each summary.

1. Katzell-based Kirkpatrick's four-level training evaluation framework

2. Kellogg Foundation's guidelines for developing program logic models

3. Michael Quinn Patton's utilization-focused evaluation

4. Michael Scriven's Key Evaluation Checklist

5. Robert Brinkerhoff's Success Case Method

6. Thomas Gilbert's behavior engineering model

1. Katzell-Based Kirkpatrick's Four-Level Training Evaluation Framework

Donald Kirkpatrick started focusing on evaluating training programs in the 1950s. In his early publication in 1956, Kirkpatrick cited the four steps of conducting training evaluation listed by Raymond Katzell, an industrial-organizational psychologist (Kirkpatrick, 1956, 2004), which indicates that the originator of the four steps of training evaluation was Raymond Katzell (Smith, 2008; Thalheimer, 2018). Therefore, in this book, we described the four levels as Katzell-based Kirkpatrick's four-level evaluation framework (Smith, 2008). However, when Kirkpatrick cited Katzell's four steps in his 1956 article, he did not supply a full reference of the actual source where Katzell identified the four steps of training evaluation. Raymond Katzell is well known "for exploring the influence of attitude and leadership on productivity and job satisfaction" in the industrial and organizational psychology field (Coons & Levine, 2004, p. 640), rather than for training evaluation.

Kirkpatrick (1996b) continued to promote the idea of evaluating four aspects of training programs: reaction, learning, behavior, and results. Each step (or level) is designed to elicit different information on the effectiveness of a training program.

1. **Reaction**—How did trainees react to the program?

2. **Learning outcomes**—How much did they learn?

3. **Behavioral change**—How much has their on-the-job behavior changed as a result of the program?

4. **Results on the organization**—To what extent have organizational results occurred because of the program? (Kirkpatrick & Kirkpatrick, 2005a, 2005b)

Kirkpatrick (1996a) explains that while planning a training program, trainers should plan for the organizational results, behavioral change, learning outcomes, and trainees' reaction to the program in that order. Trainers should start by thinking about how a training program can contribute to producing organizational results, and determine what on-the-job behaviors are needed to accomplish the organizational results. Then, they determine what knowledge, skills, and attitudes are necessary to bring about the desired on-the-job behaviors and how to design the program so that trainees will react favorably to the program while completing it. Then, when evaluating training programs, the sequence is reversed—trainers evaluate reaction, learning, behavioral change, and results in that order.

According to Kirkpatrick (1978, 1996b), there are three reasons for evaluating training programs, and his evaluation model can be useful for any of the three reasons:

1. To know how to improve future programs

2. To determine whether to continue or discontinue the program

3. To justify the existence of the training program or department

In other words, the four-level training evaluation framework can be applied to formative or summative evaluations of training programs.

2. Kellogg Foundation's Guidelines for Developing Program Logic Models

Logic models are used to present an idea in a visual and systematic way. Program logic models present how a program should work in a visual way, in a table or a diagram, describing what is planned and what results are expected (Knowlton & Phillips, 2009). Such an illustration of a program serves as a step-by-step road map to its anticipated end results. It also helps explain the overall relationship among elements necessary to run the program and to reach multiple layers of end results. Program logic models can be used to initiate new programs, to communicate about programs, or to evaluate existing programs.

The W. K. Kellogg Foundation is one of the organizations that pioneered in using program logic models in their initiatives (W. K. Kellogg Foundation, 2004). In 1998, the W. K. Kellogg Foundation published *The W. K. Kellogg Foundation Evaluation Handbook*, in which the program logic model was introduced. The W. K. Kellogg Foundation (2004) defines a program logic model as "a picture of how your organization does its work—the theory and assumptions underlying the program. A program logic model links outcomes (both short- and long-term) with program activities/processes and the theoretical assumptions/principles of the program" (p. III). Development and use of a logic model for a program is critical to effective planning and operation of the program.

The W. K. Kellogg Foundation's (2004) program logic model consists of five elements:

1. **Resources/inputs** are what the program uses; that is, "the human, financial, organizational, and community resources a program has available to direct toward doing the work" (p. 2).

2. **Activities** are what the program does with resources/inputs, such as "the processes, tools, events, technology, and actions that are an intentional part of the program implementation" (p. 2). Successful completion of these activities brings about the intended program outputs and outcomes.

3. **Outputs** are what the program delivers as "the direct results of program activities" (p. 8).

4. **Outcomes** are the program participants' "attitudes, behaviors, knowledge, skills, status, or level of functioning" that the program activities intend to change; therefore, outcomes are usually "expressed at an individual level" (p. 8). *Short-term* outcomes are attainable within a couple of years after the program activities are completed, and *longer-term* outcomes are achievable in the following few years.

5. **Impact** refers to "organizational, community, and/or system level changes" that result from program activities (p. 8). Both intended and unintended changes should be recognized.

You use "if–then" statements when reading how multiple elements of a program logic model are connected with each other. You hypothesized that *if* adequate resources are used and *if* necessary activities are successfully completed, *then* expected outputs will be delivered, which will then lead to producing desirable outcomes and positive broad impact down the road.

When you develop a logic model for a program, you determine what outcomes the program is supposed to produce, what outputs need to be delivered to result in such outcomes, and what impact will be produced in the community. Then, you plan for specific activities to be performed and necessary resources to be used.

3. Michael Quinn Patton's Utilization-Focused Evaluation

Michael Quinn Patton, an evaluation consultant, has developed a *utilization-focused evaluation* approach that emphasizes that evaluations should be designed to provide information that the intended audience intends to use. In other words, "the focus in utilization-focused evaluation is on intended use by intended users" (M. Q. Patton, 2012, p. 4). For example, the purpose of an evaluation as well as evaluation methods and timeline should be decided by the primary intended users of the evaluation who are key and diverse evaluation stakeholder constituencies and responsible for helping to put evaluation findings to use (p. 67). The primary intended users are often those who have a high interest in, and can have an influence on, the evaluation project and its use.

Evaluators who use the utilization-focused evaluation approach would need to take the role of not only facilitating the evaluation process but also teaching the intended users about evaluation to help them increase their evaluation capacity (p. 75). Although the number of primary intended users to be involved during the evaluation process would vary depending on the type and scope of evaluation, it would be usually around 6 to 10 and not more than 15 (p. 77).

M. Q. Patton (2012) suggests conducting a utilization-focused evaluation by following 17 steps:

1. Assess and build program and organizational readiness for utilization-focused evaluation.

2. Assess and enhance evaluator readiness and competence to undertake a utilization-focused evaluation.

3. Identify, organize, and engage primary intended users.

4. Conduct situation analysis jointly with primary intended users.

5. Identify and prioritize primary intended uses by determining priority purposes.

6. Consider and build in process uses if and as appropriate.

7. Focus priority evaluation questions.

8. Check that fundamental areas for evaluation inquiry are being adequately addressed.

9. Determine what intervention model or theory of change is being evaluated.

10. Negotiate appropriate methods to generate credible findings that support intended use by intended users.

11. Make sure intended users understand potential methods controversies and their implications.

12. Simulate use of findings.

13. Gather data with ongoing attention to use.

14. Organize and present the data for interpretation and use by primary intended users.

15. Prepare an evaluation report to facilitate use and disseminate significant findings to expand influence.

16. Follow up with primary intended users to facilitate and enhance use.

17. Meta-evaluation of use: Be accountable, learn, and improve. (pp. 13–14)

4. Michael Scriven's Key Evaluation Checklist

Michael Scriven advocates the importance of evaluating a program based on whether it is meeting its consumers' needs rather than whether it has achieved the program developer's objectives. Thus, Scriven's approach to evaluation is characterized as a *consumer-oriented evaluation* (Stufflebeam & Shinkfield, 2007). In Scriven's definition (2015), a program's consumers refer to those who are impacted by the program's success or failure, including direct impactees (recipients or users) and indirect impactees who are impacted via ripple effect (e.g., program recipients' coworkers, customers, or family members).

To guide evaluators to use a systematic approach during the complex professional evaluation process, Scriven (2015) developed the Key Evaluation Checklist, which comprises 18 checkpoints grouped into four parts:

Part A: Preliminaries

   A1. Executive Summary

   A2. Clarifications

   A3. Design and Methods

Part B: Foundations

   B1. Background and Context

   B2. Descriptions and Definitions

   B3. Consumers (Impactees)

   B4. Resources (a.k.a. "Strengths Assessment")

   B5. Values

Part C: Subevaluations

   C1. Process

   C2. Outcomes (a.k.a. Effects)

   C3. Costs

   C4. Comparisons

   C5. Generalizability

Part D: Conclusions & Implications

   D1. Synthesis

   D2. Recommendations, Explanations, Predictions, and Redesigns

   D3. Responsibility and Justification

D4. Report and Support

D5. Meta-evaluation (pp. 1–2)

Scriven (2015) recommends that all checkpoints should be presented in most professional evaluations; however, depending on the budget and timeline, some of the checkpoints may be completed with a light level of coverage.

5. Robert Brinkerhoff's Success Case Method

Robert O. Brinkerhoff, a professor emeritus at Western Michigan University, is the author of several books and many articles on evaluation and training development. In his books *Success Case Method* (2003) and *Telling Training's Story* (2006), Brinkerhoff explains what the Success Case Method (SCM) is and how practitioners can use it to improve learning and performance outcomes.

Brinkerhoff (2005a) starts by sending a clear message that "achieving performance results from training is a whole organization challenge. It cannot be accomplished by the training function alone" (p. 87). Brinkerhoff (2006) asserts that in up to 80% of training programs that failed to produce positive results, the problem was not flawed training interventions but rather factors within the greater performance system that were not aligned well enough to support success. The remaining 20% of failures are caused by the quality of the training programs or the learners' characteristics, including their capacity and motivation. Thus, Brinkerhoff advises practitioners to evaluate not how well a training program (alone) produced expected performance results but how effectively the organization used training.

With that in mind, the SCM is not about simply measuring and documenting the impact of training programs. Application of the SCM provides insights into various factors that influence the success or failure of training programs. Influential factors can be found within the training program or outside the training program, such as managerial commitment or organizational culture. The SCM aims at helping practitioners conduct a systemic investigation of factors that affect the success and failure of training programs.

The SCM procedure consists of five steps:

1. Focus and plan the evaluation.

2. Create an impact model that defines potential results and benefits.

3. Design and conduct a survey to gauge overall success versus nonsuccess rates.

4. Conduct in-depth interviews of selected success and nonsuccess instances.

5. Formulate conclusions and recommendations, values, and return-on-investment. (Brinkerhoff, 2006, p. 30)

The SCM's Step 2 in particular—developing a training impact model—helps evaluators and stakeholders clearly understand the purpose of a training program and its intended impact. A training impact model consists of the following four elements that show a learning-to-performance chain in results:

1. **Program capabilities**—the skills and knowledge that participants gain from a training program

2. **Critical actions**—intended behavioral applications of the program capabilities

3. **Key results**—intended job/team application outcomes

4. **Business goals**—intended highest-level organizational goals (Brinkerhoff, 2006, pp. 77–78)

The SCM Steps 3 and 4 indicate that surveys and interviews are the main data collection methods. Evaluators design a survey to be administered with a sample of performers (using the training impact model as a reference) to reveal which job behaviors led to positive outcomes and which ones did not. Typical survey questions would consist of three to five statements describing critical actions performed, then asking respondents to rate on a response scale the results achieved from the critical actions. For example, if a training program was delivered to teach salespeople to use new sales techniques, a critical action would be to use the new sales techniques when talking with customers. Then, a SCM survey item using that critical action may be designed with a four-level response scale, as shown below:

Q. Using the new sales techniques when talking with customers:

1. I tried this and achieved a concrete and worthwhile result.

2. I tried this, but have not noticed any results.

3. I tried this, but it did not work.

4. I have not tried this yet. (Brinkerhoff, 2006, p. 93)

The SCM's survey method is different from typical survey methods that seek to learn about "average" results (Brinkerhoff, 2005b). The SCM survey method yields information about successful cases and nonsuccessful cases. To identify successful and nonsuccessful cases from the survey data, evaluators cannot use an anonymous survey. The respondents' names must be identified with their data. Evaluators then contact both success cases and nonsuccess cases for follow-up interviews and ask them to tell their stories. The in-depth interviews reveal factors that caused successful and unsuccessful results, which may lie in either the training program, its environment, or both. The evaluation conclusions and recommendations would be determined based on such evidence.

Among several benefits of using the SCM is that it provides the organization with an opportunity to learn the organizational circumstances that facilitated or hindered successful results from success cases (i.e., exemplary cases) and nonsuccessful cases. Then, the organization can use the information to implement appropriate performance improvement interventions.

6. Thomas Gilbert's Behavior Engineering Model

(Adapted from Chyung, 2008)

Thomas Gilbert is known as the father of human performance technology. Gilbert's work was influenced by Frederick Taylor, Kurt Lewin, and B. F. Skinner. He helped to found the National Society for Programmed Instruction in the early 1960s, now known as the International Society for Performance Improvement (Gilbert, 1997; Gilbert, 1996).

As a behaviorist who once worked in Skinner's laboratories, Gilbert applied the principles of behavioral engineering to improving human performance. In his book *Human Competence: Engineering Worthy Performance* (1978), Gilbert describes his principles of engineering human performance and improving human competence in four "leisurely theorems" (p. 15). Gilbert (1996) uses the word *leisurely* "as a synonym for human capital, which is the product of time and opportunity" (p. 15).

In his leisurely theorems, Gilbert (1976) provides foundational concepts of human performance engineering, which help human performance improvement (HPI) practitioners accomplish the following:

1. Understand the meaning of worthy performance.

2. Compare exemplary performance to typical performance, and analyze the gap between the two (i.e., the potential for improving performance).

3. Diagnose areas where performance deficiencies are found, and determine how to produce worthy performance.

4. Develop a systemic perspective on evaluating the values of accomplishments.

The first leisurely theorem is about understanding human competence, which Gilbert (1996) defines as "a function of worthy performance (W), which is a function of the ratio of valuable accomplishment (A) to costly behavior (B)" (p. 18). It is expressed in the following formula: $W = A / B$. In the first leisurely theorem, Gilbert clearly points out that behavior is not the same as accomplishment and that what is valued is *worthy performance*, which is an indicator of human competence.

The second leisurely theorem is about understanding the potential for improving performance (PIP), which is a ratio of exemplary performance to typical performance and thus expressed by the following formula: $PIP = W_{exemplary} / W_{typical}$. The PIP is a conceptual tool that helps uncover the difference between typical performance and worthy performance. It is a measure of opportunity. A high PIP value indicates a lot of opportunity to improve performance.

The third leisurely theorem, also known as the behavior engineering model, is about understanding ways to engineer behaviors to achieve worthy performance. Gilbert (1996) also calls the third theorem the *management theorem*, because from a management viewpoint, it helps to identify the causes of competence and incompetence. Incompetence is ultimately caused by poor management of six factors—data, instruments, incentives, knowledge, capacity, and motives. The first three are environmental factors (E) and the last three are personal factors (P).

Recall the first leisurely theorem expressed in W = A / B. All six factors are necessary to cause a behavior; therefore, B is replaced with (P + E). The behavior engineering model is expressed in the following formula: W = A / (P + E).

The behavior engineering model can be used as a diagnostic tool to investigate the causes of a performance gap and to determine effective and efficient solutions for closing the gap. When diagnosing where the deficiencies in behavior occur, Gilbert suggests investigating the six factors in the following order: Data → Instruments → Incentives → Knowledge → Capacity → Motives. By following his sequence, practitioners would seek to answer questions such as the following:

1. **Data**—Do typical performers know what they are expected to do?

2. **Instruments**—Do they have appropriate tools to do their job?

3. **Incentives**—Are they rewarded for doing a good job?

4. **Knowledge**—Do they have enough knowledge to do their job?

5. **Capacity**—Are they capable of performing, or ready to do, the job?

6. **Motives**—Are they motivated to perform the job?

Practitioners should find a cost-effective way to engineer human behavior. *Worthy performance* is produced when the value of accomplishments exceeds the costs of changing behaviors, as illustrated below:

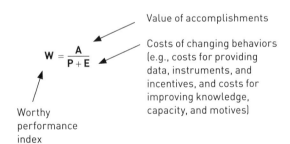

The behavior engineering model helps practitioners diagnose human work behavior in a *systematic* way and develop a set of appropriate interventions to help improve performance. However, "there is no way to alter one condition of behavior without having at least some effect on another aspect—often, a considerable effect. And usually it is difficult, if not impossible, to determine the degree of the diffusion of the effects" (Gilbert, 1996, p. 94). By considering the diffusion of effects, practitioners can also help maximize the overall effects of selected interventions in a *systemic* way.

The fourth leisurely theorem is about understanding systemic layers of valued accomplishments. Gilbert (1996) explains that "we can view human accomplishments at several levels of generality, and the values we assign to these accomplishments at each level will be derived from the level just above them" (p. 112). For example, part of the values we assign to firefighters' work (organizational level) are based on the number of lives that they save (societal level). The values of an individual call center agency's capacity to resolve callers' problems (individual level) are assigned based on the customers' satisfaction level toward the products (organizational level).

• Appendix B •

Evaluation Development Worksheets

Use Table B-1 to complete the following steps during the identification phase of your evaluation project:

- Step 1. Identify an evaluand.
- Step 2. Identify stakeholders.
- Step 3. Identify the purpose of evaluation.
- Macro task: Assess feasibility and risk factors.

Use Table B-2 or B-3, Table B-4, and Table B-5 to complete the following steps during the planning phase of your evaluation project:

- Step 4. Develop a program logic model or a training impact model.
- Step 5. Determine dimensions and importance weighting.
- Step 6. Determine data collection methods.

While completing the following steps, continue to use Table B-5. During Step 9, convert Table B-5 to Table B-6 by replacing the last column with rubrics to be used:

- Step 7. Develop instruments.
- Step 8. Collect data.
- Step 9. Analyze data with rubrics.
- Step 10. Draw conclusions.

All worksheets are available for download at **https://study.sagepub.com/chyung**

Identify an Evaluand, Its Stakeholders, and the Purpose of Evaluation, and Assess Feasibility and Risk Factors

During the initial conversation with your client, you will be able to find information about most of the questions listed in Table B-1. After you write down information for each question, you may need to revisit your client and communicate with other stakeholders to clearly understand the purpose of the evaluation and assess the project feasibility and risk factors.

TABLE B-1 ● For the Identification Phase		
Step	**Question**	**Your Finding**
Identify an evaluand	• What is it?	
	• Where is it implemented?	
	• When was it first implemented?	
	• Why was it implemented? What is the program goal? Was it determined based on a needs assessment?	
	• How does it operate?	
Identify stakeholders	• Who were/are involved in the design, development, implementation, and maintenance of the evaluand (i.e., upstream stakeholders)? • Briefly describe the role that they play as upstream stakeholders. • Indicate the client for the evaluation.	
	• Who are directly impacted by receiving, using, or participating in the evaluand (i.e., downstream direct impactees)? • Describe an approximate number for each category.[1] • Briefly describe how the direct impactees are impacted by the evaluand.	
	• Who are indirectly affected via ripple effect (i.e., downstream indirect impactees)? • Estimate the size of each group of the indirect impactees.[2] • Briefly explain how they are impacted.	
Identify the purpose of evaluation	• Describe the people with whom you talked, to answer the following questions. List other people with whom you plan to talk in the near future to gather more information about the purpose of evaluation.	
	• Who are the intended users of the evaluation findings, and how will they use the evaluation findings?	
	• Based on the "intended use" information above, is it a formative evaluation or a summative evaluation, and how so?	
	• Is it a back-end evaluation, and how so?	
	• Is it a goal-based evaluation, a goal-based evaluation with a goal-free evaluation approach, or a pure goal-free evaluation, and how so?	

Step	Question	Your Finding
	• Combining the above information, write down the evaluation purpose statement for the evaluation. Make sure to include the following: 1. Type of evaluation 2. Focus of evaluation 3. Intended users of evaluation findings 4. Intended use of evaluation findings 5. Organization's and stakeholders' needs	
Assess feasibility and risk factors	• Write down information that you have found about your evaluation project so far in relation to the feasibility categories: 1. Maturity 2. Scope 3. Support 4. Ethical concerns 5. Resources	
	• Make a list of project assumptions.	
	• Write down your risk assessment findings, and describe how you plan to manage the risk factors. • Present a risk assessment matrix.	

---

[1]It is important to estimate the size of the direct impactees in order to gauge the size of direct impact of the evaluand.

[2]It is important to estimate the size of the indirect impactees as much as you can, in order to gauge the size of indirect impact of the evaluand.

Develop a Program Logic Model or a Training Impact Model

In your proposal, you will include either a program logic model or a training impact model. You should select an appropriate one for your evaluand. You may decide to include both, only if each one provides different/helpful information (e.g., the program logic model would provide the overall information about the broad scope of the program, whereas a training impact model would provide information specific to the training aspect of the program).

- If you decide to include a program logic model in your proposal, please use Table B-2.

- If you decide to include a training impact model in your proposal, please use Table B-3.

The original training impact model structure does not include resources and activities categories, but you will add two columns to include the two categories.

TABLE B-2 ● Develop a Program Logic Model				
Resources	**Activities**	**Outputs**	**Outcomes**	**Impact**
What resources should be used to run the program?	What activities should be performed to run the program?	What products should be produced to support the intended outcomes?	What changes in the stakeholders should be made in the next X months (short-term) or X years (long-term)?[3]	What changes in the organization and its society are expected in X–X years due to the outcomes?[4]
• Item • Item • Item	• Item • Item • Item	• Item • Item • Item	• Item • Item • Item	• Item • Item • Item

[3]You may list outcomes with or without the subcategories, short-term and long-term. Either way, please indicate the time frame that is appropriate for your evaluand. If subcategories are not used, what is the time frame for the outcomes category? If used, what are the time frames for the short-term and long-term outcomes? Replace X with appropriate time frames. Write outcomes as specific and measurable as possible.

[4]For some programs (in a fast-changing field), you may expect to see its impact earlier than other programs. Replace X with an appropriate time frame.

TABLE B-3 ● Develop a Training Impact Model					
Resources	**Activities**	**Program Capabilities**	**Critical Actions**	**Key Results**	**Business Goals**
What resources should be used to run the training program?	What activities should be used to run the training program?	What capabilities (i.e., knowledge, skills, and attitudes) should the trainees acquire?	What behaviors should the trainees demonstrate on the job as a result of training?	What job results should the trainees leave behind?	To what organizational goals would the training program contribute?
• Item • Item • Item	• Item • Item • Item	• Item • Item • Item	• Item • Item • Item	• Item • Item • Item	• Item • Item • Item

Determine Dimensions, Dimensional Evaluation Questions, and Importance Weighting Among Dimensions

In Table B-4, describe the process that you went through to make decisions about the list of dimensions and importance weighting.

TABLE B-4 ● Process for Determining Dimensions and Importance Weighting	
Question	**Your Finding**
• How did you determine the dimensions? Briefly describe specific sources you used (among the following four options), the process you followed, and the people whom you involved during the decision: 1. Stakeholders' needs 2. Program logic model 3. Theoretical frameworks 4. Professional and ethical standards	
• How did you determine the relative degree of importance weighting among dimensions? Briefly describe who were involved in the decision and how you involved them during the decision.	
• List dimensions and dimensional questions, and indicate the category of the program logic model or training impact model under which each dimension falls. Also indicate the degree of importance weighting for each dimension.	
• Think about the intended usage of your evaluation findings again. Who among the stakeholders will make use of the evaluation results (directly or indirectly), for what purpose (formative or summative), and in what way? Will the dimensions generate information useful for them?	

Determine Data Collection Methods

Use Table B-5 while determining data collection methods. Follow the step-by-step procedure presented below:

1. Under the first column, in each row:

   a. List a dimension and a dimensional evaluation question.

   b. Identify the category of the program logic model or training impact model with which the dimension is aligned.

   c. Identify the importance weighting for the dimension.

2. In the second column, identify and list feasible data collection methods for each dimension. Clearly describe how you will obtain data, from whom, and how many of them. Please be concise yet specific. Make sure to ask the client and other stakeholders whether those data sources are available. Even if you have a great idea about investigating certain dimensions, it would not be feasible dimensions if no data are available or if you will not be given access to such data.

TABLE B-5 ● Data Collection Methods			
Dimension, PLM/TIM, and IW	**Data Collection Method**	**Instrument to Be Developed**	**Rationale for Using Multiple Sets of Data (Critical Multiplism and Triangulation)**

IW, Importance weighting; *PLM*, program logic model; *TIM*, training impact model.

3. In the third column, identify instruments to be developed and used. In some cases, you may use existing instruments (e.g., you may use the Dimensions of Learning Organization Questionnaire [Marsick & Watkins, 2003] to measure employees' perceptions about their organization as a learning organization). Otherwise, you need to develop all instruments to be used, such as survey questionnaires, interview questions, observation checklists, document review checklists, and test questions. Keep in mind that you also need to develop other supporting materials such as participation solicitation messages and informed consent forms.

4. In the last column, clearly describe the rationale for using such multiple data sets for each dimension in terms of employing critical multiplism and triangulation techniques. For example, if you decided to use a survey and observations for Dimension 1, why? How will they complement each other's strengths and weaknesses?

Develop Instruments and Rubrics

While developing instruments and other materials, continue to use Table B-5 and revise the "Instrument to Be Developed" column with specific information. While completing Step 9 Analyze data, replace the last column with "Rubric to Be Used" as shown in Table B-6.

TABLE B-6 ● Instruments and Rubrics Development Worksheet

Dimension, PLM, and IW	Data Collection Method	Instrument to Be Developed	Rubric to Be Used
1. Curriculum design—How well is the curriculum designed to support industry expectations and standards? PLM: Resources and Activities IW: Extremely important	1-1. Record review of the curriculum by evaluators; all required courses and current elective courses will be reviewed 1-2. Interview with six full-time faculty members in person and 50% of current part-time faculty members (about three members) via telephone	1-1. Document review checklist (see 1-1.Checklist. doc) 1-2. Semi-structured telephone interview instrument for faculty, including the interview solicitation email message, script and questions to be used during interviews (see 1-2.EmailMSG4interview.doc, 1-2.InformedConsentForm. doc, and Q2-Q8 in 1-2. InterviewScript.doc)	• Superior: $9.5 \leq$ checklist scores $\leq$ 10.0 and all interview data indicate high quality content and expertise among faculty • Met expectations: $8.0 \leq$ checklist scores < 9.5 and most interview data indicate high quality content and expertise among faculty and a few minor areas for improvement • Did not meet expectations: $0 \leq$ checklist scores < 8.0
2. Online learning environment—Does the online delivery technology provide a positive learning environment? PLM: Resources and Activities IW: Very important			
3. Dimension—Evaluation question PLM: Category IW: Importance level			

IW, Importance weighting; *PLM*, program logic model.

• Appendix C •

Survey Questionnaire Makeover

Imagine you have been told that in the past the following survey questions were used to evaluate the Effective Mentors program provided to mentors in your organization. Now you are asked to revise the questions based on your knowledge about evidence-based survey design.

Mark the parts that you think need to be changed and explain why. Produce a revised version, and then compare yours with the feedback provided in the following pages.

For each question, please select the option that best represents your opinion about the Effective Mentors program that you completed:

1. The role-play helped the attendees better understand the new mentoring techniques.

   ○ Strongly disagree ○ Somewhat disagree ○ Neutral ○ Somewhat Agree ○ Strongly Agree

2. The video presentation was not interesting.

   ○ Strongly disagree ○ Somewhat disagree ○ Neutral ○ Somewhat Agree ○ Strongly Agree

3. The examples were relevant to my job and helped me understand the mentoring model.

   ○ Strongly disagree ○ Somewhat disagree ○ Neutral ○ Somewhat Agree ○ Strongly Agree

4. The small-group activities helped me understand why it is important to ALF.

   ○ Strongly disagree ○ Somewhat disagree ○ Neutral ○ Somewhat Agree ○ Strongly Agree

5. I will be able to interact with my employees as a more capable mentor.

   ○ Strongly agree ○ Somewhat agree ○ Neutral ○ Somewhat disagree ○ Strongly disagree

6. I feel prepared to use the new mentoring techniques.

   ○ Strongly agree ○ Somewhat agree ○ Somewhat disagree ○ Strongly disagree

7. I would rate the quality of the program as:

   ○ Poor ○ Good ○ Pretty good ○ Very good ○ Excellent

8. I WOULD RECOMMEND THIS PROGRAM TO OTHERS!

   ○ Yes ○ No

---

9. How many times per month do you plan to meet with your mentees?

    O 1–3 times

    O 3–5 times

    O 5–7 times

    O 7 times or more

Feedback: Parts to be changed are marked in bold, and the rationale for the change is described.

1. The role-play helped **the attendees** better understand the new mentoring techniques.

    O Strongly disagree   O Somewhat disagree   O Neutral   O Somewhat Agree   O Strongly Agree

This question is asking survey respondents to represent the entire attendees' opinion. Instead, the question should ask each survey respondent to express their own opinion. Also, if it is possible that some survey respondents did not attend the program while the role-play was used, it is better to provide a "Don't know" option, to prevent them from using Neutral as a dumping ground or having missing data (this applies to several other questions as well), e.g.:

1. The role-play helped me better understand the new mentoring techniques.

    O Strongly disagree   O Somewhat disagree   O Neutral   O Somewhat agree
    O Strongly agree   O Don't know

2. The video presentation **was not interesting**.

    O Strongly disagree   O Somewhat disagree   O Neutral   O Somewhat Agree   O Strongly Agree

This question is negatively worded. Instead, it should be positively worded, e.g.:

2. The video presentation was interesting.

    O Strongly disagree   O Somewhat disagree   O Neutral   O Somewhat agree
    O Strongly agree   O Don't know

3. The examples **were relevant to my job and helped me understand the mentoring model**.

    O Strongly disagree   O Somewhat disagree   O Neutral   O Somewhat Agree   O Strongly Agree

This is a double-barreled question. It should be split into two questions, e.g.:

3-1.   The examples were relevant to my job.

○ Strongly disagree ○ Somewhat disagree ○ Neutral ○ Somewhat agree
○ Strongly agree ○ Don't know

3-2.   The examples helped me understand the mentoring model.

○ Strongly disagree ○ Somewhat disagree ○ Neutral ○ Somewhat agree
○ Strongly agree ○ Don't know

---

4.   The small-group activities helped me understand why it is important to **ALF**.

○ Strongly disagree ○ Somewhat disagree ○ Neutral ○ Somewhat Agree ○ Strongly Agree

---

An acronym used in the question should be spelled out, e.g.:

4.   The small-group activities helped me understand why it is important to always listen first.

○ Strongly disagree ○ Somewhat disagree ○ Neutral ○ Somewhat agree
○ Strongly agree ○ Don't know

---

5.   I will be able to interact with my employees as a more capable mentor.
○ **Strongly agree** ○ **Somewhat agree** ○ **Neutral** ○ **Somewhat disagree** ○ **Strongly disagree**

The Likert scale options in this question are presented in descending order, whereas the Likert scale options used in the previous questions are presented in ascending order. To prevent careless respondents from accidentally selecting a wrong option, it should either provide a clear message about the changed direction in the order of the response options or use the same ascending order of the response options, e.g.:

5.   I will be able to interact with my employees as a more capable mentor.

○ Strongly disagree ○ Somewhat disagree ○ Neutral ○ Somewhat agree
○ Strongly agree

---

6.   I feel prepared to use the new mentoring techniques.
○ **Strongly agree** ○ **Somewhat agree** ○ **Somewhat disagree** ○ **Strongly disagree**

This question uses a 4-point scale without the Neutral point, which will make it difficult to combine the data obtained from multiple questions included in this questionnaire. It is better to use the same response scale by either removing Neutral from other questions or adding Neutral to this question. The Likert scale options should also be presented in the ascending order, e.g.:

6. I feel prepared to use the new mentoring techniques.

    ○ Strongly disagree ○ Somewhat disagree ○ Neutral ○ Somewhat agree
    ○ Strongly agree

---

7. I would rate the quality of the program as:

    ○ **Poor** ○ **Good** ○ **Pretty good** ○ **Very good** ○ **Excellent**

The 5-point response scale used in this question has one negative option (Poor) and four positive options (Good, Pretty good, Very good, and Excellent). Thus, by design, it will generate more positive data than negative data. In some cases, this type of response scale could be used to avoid the ceiling effect (i.e., when most respondents select the most positive option, resulting in little variance in data). Otherwise, the response scale should have balanced options, e.g.:

7. I would rate the quality of the program as:

    ○ Poor ○ Mediocre ○ Average ○ Good ○ Excellent

Another option is to revise the statement to use the Likert scale used in the previous questions, e.g.:

7. I would rate the quality of the program as excellent.

    ○ Strongly disagree ○ Somewhat disagree ○ Neutral ○ Somewhat agree
    ○ Strongly agree

---

8. **I WOULD RECOMMEND THIS PROGRAM TO OTHERS!**

    ○ Yes ○ No

The statement should not be written in all caps.

8. I would recommend this program to others.

    ○ Yes ○ No

---

9. How many times per month do you plan to meet with your mentees?

    ○ **1–3 times**

    ○ **3–5 times**

    ○ **5–7 times**

    ○ **7 times or more**

The response options are not mutually exclusive. They should be revised to:

9. How many times per month do you plan to meet with your mentees?

   O 1–3 times

   O 4–5 times

   O 6–7 times

   O 8 times or more

Another option is to have the respondents write a number:

9. How many times per month do you plan to meet with your mentees?

   _____ times per month

The following is what a revised survey questionnaire would look like:

For each question, please select the option that best represents your opinion about the Effective Mentors program that you completed:

1. The role-play helped me better understand the new mentoring techniques.

   O Strongly disagree O Somewhat disagree O Neutral O Somewhat agree O Strongly agree
   O Don't know

2. The video presentation was interesting.

   O Strongly disagree O Somewhat disagree O Neutral O Somewhat agree O Strongly agree
   O Don't know

3. The examples were relevant to my job.

   O Strongly disagree O Somewhat disagree O Neutral O Somewhat agree O Strongly agree
   O Don't know

4. The examples helped me understand the mentoring model.

   O Strongly disagree O Somewhat disagree O Neutral O Somewhat agree O Strongly agree
   O Don't know

5. The small-group activities helped me understand why it is important to always listen first.

   O Strongly disagree O Somewhat disagree O Neutral O Somewhat agree O Strongly agree
   O Don't know

6. I will be able to interact with my employees as a more capable mentor.

   O Strongly disagree O Somewhat disagree O Neutral O Somewhat agree O Strongly agree

7. I feel prepared to use the new mentoring techniques.

   O Strongly disagree O Somewhat disagree O Neutral O Somewhat agree O Strongly agree

8. I would rate the quality of the program as excellent.

   ○ Strongly disagree ○ Somewhat disagree ○ Neutral ○ Somewhat agree ○ Strongly agree

9. I would recommend this program to others.

   ○ Yes ○ No

10. How many times per month do you plan to meet with your mentees?

    ○ 1–3 times

    ○ 4–5 times

    ○ 6–7 times

    ○ 8 times or more

• Appendix D •

A Sample Survey Questionnaire Measuring Multiple Dimensions, Sample Rubrics, and Reliability Testing With IBM® SPSS® Statistics

Imagine you are evaluating the effectiveness of a team environment implemented in your organization. You plan to use a structured survey instrument designed to measure the following two dimensions:

1. **Perceived value of working in a team environment**: How much do employees value working in a team environment?

2. **Barriers to working in a team**: What difficulties did employees experience while working in a team environment?

You will use an anonymous web-based survey, as shown on the following pages. The survey respondents will open this webpage by clicking a URL inserted in an email message sent to them. An informed consent form will be attached to the email message.

The survey instrument starts by asking the survey respondents to confirm their consent to complete the survey voluntarily. A "Yes" response will take the survey respondent to the next webpage that presents Section I. A "No" response will take the survey respondent to the ending Thank You webpage. Questions in Section 1 measure Dimension 1, and questions in Section 2 measure Dimension 2 (adapted from Chyung, Winiecki, Sevier, & Hunt, 2018).

You may use the following rubrics to analyze the data collected for Dimension 1 and Dimension 2:

Dimension 1:

- Excellent: 5.5 ≤ average score ≤ 7.0 with mostly positive comments

- Good: 4.0 ≤ average score < 5.5 with a lot of positive comments and some minor areas for improvement

- Mediocre: 2.5 ≤ average score < 4.0 with a mix of positive and negative comments

- Poor: 1.0 ≤ average score < 2.5 with many negative comments

SPSS is a registered trademark of International Business Machines Corporation.

WORKING IN A TEAM ENVIRONMENT—VALUES AND BARRIERS

Please select one of the following option buttons to indicate your consent status:

O Yes, I agree to participate in the evaluation study by voluntarily submitting the survey data.

O No, I do not agree to participate in the evaluation study by voluntarily submitting the survey data.

[Click **Next**]

- - - Page Break - - -

Section 1: The following questions ask your opinion about the value of working in a team environment. Please select an option that best represents your opinion.

Q1. Working with others in a team helped me develop project management skills.

Not true O 1 O 2 O 3 O 4 O 5 O 6 O 7 Very true

Q2. Working with others in a team helped me adopt civic values needed to be part of a professional community.

Not true O 1 O 2 O 3 O 4 O 5 O 6 O 7 Very true

Q3. Working with others in a team helped me develop professional skills that are valuable in the workplace.

Not true O 1 O 2 O 3 O 4 O 5 O 6 O 7 Very true

Q4. The more experiences I have working in teams, the better for developing my professional/career capacity.

Not true O 1 O 2 O 3 O 4 O 5 O 6 O 7 Very true

[Click **Next**]

- - - Page Break - - -

Section 2: The following questions ask your opinion about difficulties you may have experienced while working in a team environment. Please select an option that best represents your feelings.

Q5. I often had to take on more than my share of the workload because of low performing teammates.

Not true O 1 O 2 O 3 O 4 O 5 O 6 O 7 Very true

Q6. It was difficult to find teammates who have a work ethic similar to mine.

Not true O 1 O 2 O 3 O 4 O 5 O 6 O 7 Very true

Q7. There was a lot of wasted time handling logistical issues while working in a team.

Not true O 1 O 2 O 3 O 4 O 5 O 6 O 7 Very true

Q8. While working in a team, I felt overworked.

Not true O 1 O 2 O 3 O 4 O 5 O 6 O 7 Very true

[Click **Next**]

- - - Page Break - - -

(Continued)

(Continued)

Q9. What did you like the most about working in a team?

Q10. What did you like the least about working in a team?

Q11. What support, if any, do you need to work effectively in a team environment?

[Click **Next**]

- - - Page Break - - -

Thank you!

Your data has been recorded. You may close your web browser.

Dimension 2:

- Excellent: $1.0 \leq$ average score < 2.5 with little negative comments
- Good: $2.5 \leq$ average score < 4.0 with some minor negative comments
- Mediocre: $4.0 \leq$ average score < 5.5 with some major negative comments
- Poor: $5.5 \leq$ average score ≤ 7.0 with many major negative comments

If you reverse-coded data obtained from Q5 through Q8, the ranges of average scores in your rubric definitions will be the opposite, as shown below:

- Excellent: $5.5 \leq$ average score ≤ 7.0 with little negative comments
- Good: $4.0 \leq$ average score < 5.5 with some minor negative comments
- Mediocre: $2.5 \leq$ average score < 4.0 with some major negative comments
- Poor: $1.0 \leq$ average score < 2.5 with many major negative comments

Before analyzing data against rubrics, you want to know if the multiple survey items are reliably measuring each dimension. You may use a statistical analysis software program such as SPSS to check reliability of the survey items used to measure each dimension. Cronbach's Alpha values of .70 or higher are considered *acceptable* and .80 or higher are considered *good* (Field, 2009).

For example, let's say you administered the survey with 235 employees (Figure D-1). Using SPSS, follow the following steps to produce outputs.

1. In SPSS, select **Analyze** > **Scale** > **Reliability Analysis . . .** from the menu bar.

2. In the Reliability Analysis window (Figure D-2), move Q1, Q2, Q3, and Q4 to the **Items**: box, select **Alpha** as the Model, write Dimension 1 in the **Scale label:** box, and click the **Statistics . . .** button.

FIGURE D-1 ● SPSS Data File

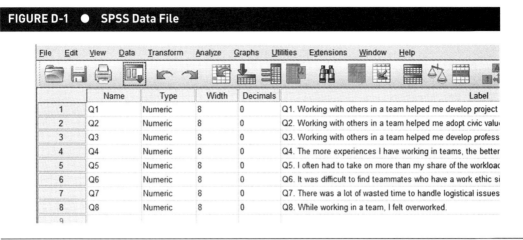

FIGURE D-2 ● Reliability Analysis Window

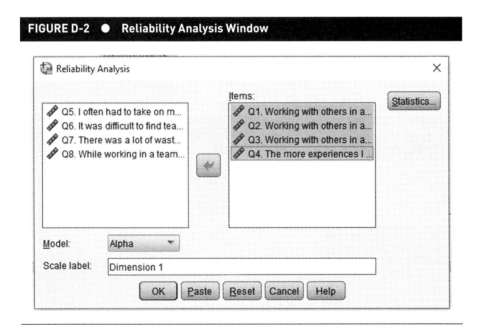

3. Select **Scale if Item Deleted** and click **Continue**. And click **OK**.

4. You have outputs for Dimension 1. **Cronbach's Alpha** is .832, which indicates *good* reliability among items (Figure D-3). The **Cronbach's Alpha if Item Deleted** column of the **Item-Total Statistics** table shows Alpha values lower than .832 (Figure D-4). It means, all four items (Q1 though Q4) are reliable measures of Dimension 1, and none of the four items need to be removed in order to increase the Alpha level.

FIGURE D-3 ● Reliability Output, Showing "Cronbach's Alpha" for Dimension 1

→ **Reliability**

Scale: Dimension 1

Case Processing Summary

		N	%
Cases	Valid	235	100.0
	Excluded[a]	0	.0
	Total	235	100.0

a. Listwise deletion based on all variables in the procedure.

Reliability Statistics

Cronbach's Alpha	N of Items
.832	4

FIGURE D-4 ● Reliability Output, Showing "Cronbach's Alpha if Item Deleted" for Dimension 1

Item-Total Statistics

	Scale Mean if Item Deleted	Scale Variance if Item Deleted	Corrected Item-Total Correlation	Cronbach's Alpha if Item Deleted
Q1. Working with others in a team helped me develop project management skills.	16.81	9.908	.656	.791
Q2. Working with others in a team helped me adopt civic values needed to be part of a professional community.	17.39	8.972	.629	.806
Q3. Working with others in a team helped me develop professional skills that are valuable in the workplace.	16.97	9.628	.692	.775
Q4. The more experiences I have working in teams, the better for developing my professional/career ca...	16.95	9.182	.678	.780

FIGURE D-5 ● Reliability Analysis Window

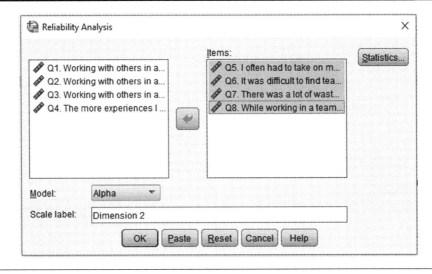

5. Let's repeat the same steps to generate outputs for Dimension 2. Select **Analyze** > **Scale** > **Reliability Analysis . . .** from the menu bar.

6. In the Reliability Analysis window (Figure D-5), remove Q1, Q2, Q3, and Q4 from the **Items**: box, and move Q5 though Q8 to the **Items:** box. Select **Alpha** as the Model, write Dimension 2 in the **Scale label:** box, and click the **Statistics . . .** button.

7. Select **Scale if Item Deleted** and click **Continue**. And click **OK**.

8. You have outputs for Dimension 2. **Cronbach's Alpha** is .802, which indicates *good* reliability among items (Figure D-6). However, in the **Cronbach's Alpha if Item Deleted** column of the **Item-Total Statistics** table, Q8's Alpha value is .824 (Figure D-7), which is higher than .802. It means, removing Q8 will increase the Alpha level from .802 to .824.

Should you remove Q8? Doing so will make only a minor improvement, and even with Q8 data, the overall Cronbach's Alpha value (.802) is within the optimal range.

Then, you want to review the values under the Corrected Item-Total Correlation column—when the values are close to zero, it means the items are not measuring the same thing that other items are measuring. The value for Q8 is .464, which is not close to zero. Therefore, this is not a clear-cut decision.

You have a couple of options. You may decide to use an average score of all four questions (Q5, Q6, Q7, and Q8) for Dimension 2. Or, you may decide to calculate an average score of Q5, Q6, and Q7 for Dimension 2, and report Q8 results separately. It is your call. Next time when you use the survey instrument again, you may remove Q8 or replace it with a different item, and run reliability testing again.

FIGURE D-6 ● Reliability Output, Showing "Cronbach's Alpha" for Dimension 2

→ **Reliability**

Scale: Dimension 2

Case Processing Summary

		N	%
Cases	Valid	235	100.0
	Excluded[a]	0	.0
	Total	235	100.0

a. Listwise deletion based on all variables in the procedure.

Reliability Statistics

Cronbach's Alpha	N of Items
.802	4

FIGURE D-7 ● Reliability Output, Showing "Cronbach's Alpha if Item Deleted" for Dimension 2

Item-Total Statistics

	Scale Mean if Item Deleted	Scale Variance if Item Deleted	Corrected Item-Total Correlation	Cronbach's Alpha if Item Deleted
Q5. I often had to take on more than my share of the workload b...	10.78	19.267	.698	.711
Q6. It was difficult to find teammates who have a work ethic similar to...	11.11	19.615	.665	.728
Q7. There was a lot of wasted time to handle logistical issues.	11.40	20.915	.651	.737
Q8. While working in a team, I felt overworked.	10.83	22.535	.464	.824

• Appendix E •

Experimental Studies and Data Analysis With *t*-Tests Using Excel

An Experimental or Quasi-Experimental Evaluation Design

To determine which evaluation design you need to use for investigating each dimension, you need to think about how the dimensional evaluation question should be answered. You may use an experimental or quasi-experimental design when you need to answer a dimensional question by asserting that a performance intervention program clearly caused production of specific outcomes. This *cause-and-effect* approach is often applied to summative evaluations where you want to show if an implemented program contributed to generating expected outcomes. As examples, consider the following:

- Using job aids (a solution) *caused* the reduction in performance errors (an expected outcome).

- Adding a role-play activity to an existing lecture-based training program (a solution) *caused* improvements in performers' confidence levels and their customers' satisfaction levels (expected outcomes), compared to the results following lecture-based training alone.

The statistics used during experimental or quasi-experimental studies (involving the use of a sample randomly drawn from the population) are called *inferential statistics*. It is not always possible to involve the whole population of the stakeholders in your evaluation. Thus, you study with a sample of the population and use inferential statistics to generalize the sample results to the population.

True experimental studies require not only *random selection* of sample participants from a population but also *random assignment* of sample participants to the intervention and nonintervention groups. When this random assignment is not possible, your study is called a quasi-experimental study.

A Pre–Post Comparison Design or an Intervention-Nonintervension Comparison Design

Two simple experimental/quasi-experimental designs are:

Data collection ＼ Level	2. Learning	3. Behavioral Change	4. Organizational Results
TABLE E-1 ● Comparing Pre- and Post-Measures of a Sample Group on Learning, Behavioral Changes, and Organizational Results			
Method	Test learners' knowledge	Observe learners' work behaviors	Conduct a survey with customers
Instrument	A knowledge test	An observation checklist	A structured survey questionnaire
Time for pre-measure	Before learners participate in the training program	Before learners participate in the training program	Before learners participate in the training program
Time for post-measure	At the end of the training program (to measure knowledge acquisition) A few weeks or months after the training program (to measure knowledge retention)	A few weeks or months after the training program (to allow them to have opportunities to use their new knowledge or skills)	Likely a few months after the training program (to allow enough time for behavioral changes to occur and have impact on changing organizational results)

- to compare pre- and post-measures of the group that received a performance improvement intervention program, or

- to compare the outcomes of an intervention group and a nonintervention group.

For example, when applying the four-level training evaluation framework to your evaluation project, you can set up experimental study designs to compare pre- and post-measures of learning outcomes (Level 2), behavioral changes (Level 3), and organizational results (Level 4) of a training program. See Table E-1.

However, this pre–post comparison design is not always sufficient to indicate that improvement in outcomes was due to the intervention. Other variables, such as changes in the environment, could influence the outcomes. Therefore, a better design is to use an intervention group and a nonintervention group and compare the difference in outcomes between the two groups. If it is safe to assume that the employees who participate in the study do not have prior knowledge about the training topic, you may administer a post-measure only. If you are uncertain about their prior knowledge, you may administer a pre-measure as well. See Table E-2.

Variables, Hypotheses, Sampling, and Inferential Statistical Procedures

To conduct an experimental or quasi-experimental study during your evaluation project, you need sufficient knowledge about using variables, hypotheses, sampling

Level Data collection	2. Learning	3. Behavioral Change	4. Organizational Results
TABLE E-2 ● Comparing Intervention and Nonintervention Sample Groups' Learning, Behavioral Changes, and Organizational Results			
Method	Test learners' knowledge	Observe learners' work behaviors	Conduct a survey with customers
Instrument	A knowledge test	An observation checklist	A structured survey questionnaire
Group conditions	An intervention group completes a training program. A nonintervention group does not complete a training program.		
Time for post-measure	At the end of the training program (to measure the intervention group's knowledge acquisition, compared to the nonintervention group's knowledge) A few weeks or months after the training program (to measure the intervention group's knowledge retention, compared to the nonintervention group's knowledge)	A few weeks or months after the intervention group completed the training program (to allow the intervention group employees to have opportunities to use their new knowledge or skills and to compare the intervention group's changed behavior to the nonintervention group's behavior)	Likely a few months after the intervention group completed the training program (to allow the intervention group to have enough time to make an impact on changing organizational results, compared to the degree of impact that the nonintervention group makes on changing organizational results)

(sample vs. population), and inferential statistics. First, you need to identify variables. The variable that you hypothesize caused an outcome is called an *independent variable*, and the outcome variable based on your hypothesis is a *dependent variable*. When conducting evaluation in the HPI context, the implemented program is often used as an independent variable (e.g., the use of job aids vs. no use of job aids), and the expected learning and performance outcomes are dependent variables (e.g., reduced performance errors, improved confidence levels, or improved customer satisfaction levels).

Your *hypothesis* statement describes a cause-and-effect relationship between the independent variable and the dependent variable. For example, to see if the sales method training program (independent variable) resulted in increased sales (the dependent variable), you may compare the amount of sales *before* the training program to the amount of sales *after* the training program. Your hypothesis would be: *Salespeople, after completing a training program on a new sales method, significantly increased their sales.*

Or you may compare the amount of sales by an intervention group and the amount of sales by a nonintervention group. Your hypothesis would be: The amount of sales that *salespeople who completed a training program on a new sales method is significantly more* than the amount of sales that salespeople who did not complete the training program.

After you collected data to compare pre–post measures of the same group or to compare intervention and nonintervention groups, you need to apply inferential statistical procedures to analyze the data. The typical inferential statistical tests that you use to compare the difference in two groups are *t*-tests. When comparing pre–post measures of the same group, you perform a *paired samples t-test*. When comparing an intervention group and a nonintervention group, you perform an *independent samples t-test*. We will briefly explain how to perform paired samples and independent samples *t*-tests, using Excel. Excel 2016 was used in the following directions.

Paired Samples *t*-Test When Comparing Pre–Post Measures of the Same Group

Let's say you are conducting a Level 2 evaluation of a training program by analyzing if employees who did not have much knowledge on the subject have significantly improved their knowledge as a result of completing the training program. An outline of your research procedure would be as follows.

Hypothesis: *Hypothesis testing* is a test of probability of occurrence. You need to make a *hypothesis statement* that you want to test out. You prepare two types of hypothesis statements:

- Research hypothesis (H_1)—what you expect to happen
- Null hypothesis (H_0)—the opposite of your research hypothesis

In hypothesis testing, you test the probability (likelihood) of a *null hypothesis* (H_0) to be true. For this reason, your research hypothesis (H_1) is also called an *alternative hypothesis*. If your statistical analysis reveals that it is unlikely that a null hypothesis is true, you reject the null hypothesis and accept the alternative (your research) hypothesis to be true, and vice versa.

You may state a hypothesis using a *directional statement* or a *nondirectional statement*. A directional alternative (or null) statement indicates which one of two measures is expected to be better (or not better), whereas a nondirectional alternative (or null) statement simply indicates that two measures will be different (or not different). Here, we will use directional hypothesis statements since the intervention (training) was implemented to improve knowledge. We would use a nondirectional hypothesis statement if the intervention were implemented to see any changes in knowledge.

- H_1: Employees' post-test scores are significantly better than their pre-test scores.
- H_0: Employees' post-test scores are not significantly better than their pre-test scores.

Participants: To conduct an experimental study, you randomly select a sample of employees from the entire employee population. You determine the sample size based on the *confidence level* that you want to use (e.g., a 95% confidence level) and the degree *confidence interval* (a.k.a. *margin of error*) that you are willing to accept when you generalize your sample results to the entire population (Tanner, 2012). To estimate a sample size, you may use a sample size calculator available on the web, using a 95% confidence level and a 5% confidence interval. The larger the sample size, the higher the confidence level and the smaller the confidence interval. For example, if you have a population of 1,000 employees, a sample of 250 employees would give you a smaller margin of error than a sample of 100 employees. In the following directions, we will use a sample of 30 as an example (see Figure E-1).

Data collection: You will administer the same (or a similar) knowledge test twice, once before the sample of employees started the training program (pre-test) and once again after they have completed it (post-test).

Data analysis with paired samples *t*-test using Excel: You will use a paired samples *t*-test to test the null hypothesis. To do so, you may use a statistical analysis software program such as SPSS. Here, we will use Excel's add-in feature called *Data Analysis*, which provides several statistical analysis procedures including paired samples *t*-test and independent samples *t*-test.

First, you may need to activate the **Data Analysis** function in Excel. In Excel,

1. Click the **File** tab, and click **Options**.

2. Click **Add-Ins**, and then in the **Manage** box, select **Excel Add-ins**.

3. Click **Go**.

4. In the **Add-Ins** available box, select the **Analysis ToolPak** checkbox, and click **OK**.

5. After successfully loading the Analysis ToolPak, the **Data Analysis** command appears in the **Analysis** group on the **Data** tab in Excel.

To illustrate the steps for running a paired samples *t*-test, we will use a hypothetical data set.

1. Create a new worksheet and enter the pre-test and post-test scores obtained from 30 participants into two columns as shown in Figure E1. Note that you will likely use a larger sample size for real research projects.

FIGURE E-1 ● An Excel Data File for a Paired Samples *t*-Test

	A	B
1	Pretest	Posttest
2	45	89
3	65	80
4	34	79
5	64	89
6	66	98
7	25	56
8	78	91
9	45	78
10	63	96
11	75	97
12	46	80
13	56	89
14	44	91
15	56	76
16	43	89
17	22	44
18	43	86
19	24	65
20	55	94
21	44	84
22	23	67
23	54	78
24	29	82
25	37	60
26	41	84
27	59	70
28	60	66
29	66	77
30	71	73
31	32	83

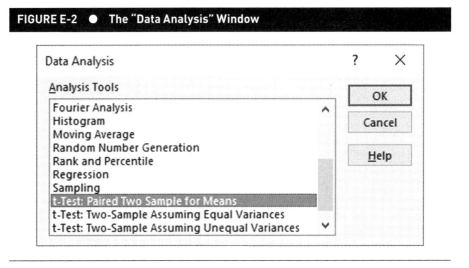

FIGURE E-2 ● The "Data Analysis" Window

2. Select **Data** > **Data Analysis** from the menu bar, select **t-Test: Paired Two Sample for Means**, and click **OK**. See Figure E-2.

3. On the **t-Test Paired Two Sample for Means** window (see Figure E-3),

   - Click the worksheet icon 🔲 next to **Variable 1 Range**, select from **A1** (not A2) to **A31,** and press **Enter**.

   - Click the worksheet icon 🔲 next to **Variable 2 Range**, select from **B1** (not B2) to **B31,** and press **Enter**.

   - Enter **0** in the box next to **Hypothesized Mean Difference** (meaning that you hypothesize that the two sets of data are not going to be different).

   - Checkmark **Labels** (because you included cells **A1** and **B1** in your range and want to indicate that they should be treated as labels rather than a part of the data set).

 - Keep **0.05** as the **Alpha** level.

 - Select **Output Range**, click the worksheet icon next to it to select **D1** (to indicate that this cell will be the upper left corner of the *t*-test output table), and press **Enter**. Click OK.

4. *t*-Test results are presented in your spreadsheet (see Figure E-4). You use the observed *p* value to make your hypothesis-testing decision:

   - If $p < .05$, reject the null hypothesis and accept the alternative hypothesis.

   - If $p \geq .05$, retain the null hypothesis and reject the alternative hypothesis.

You use the *p* value for one tail shown in **E11** because you have a directional hypothesis (if your hypothesis were nondirectional, you would use the *p* value for two

FIGURE E-3   ● The "*t*-Test: Paired Two Sample for Means" Window

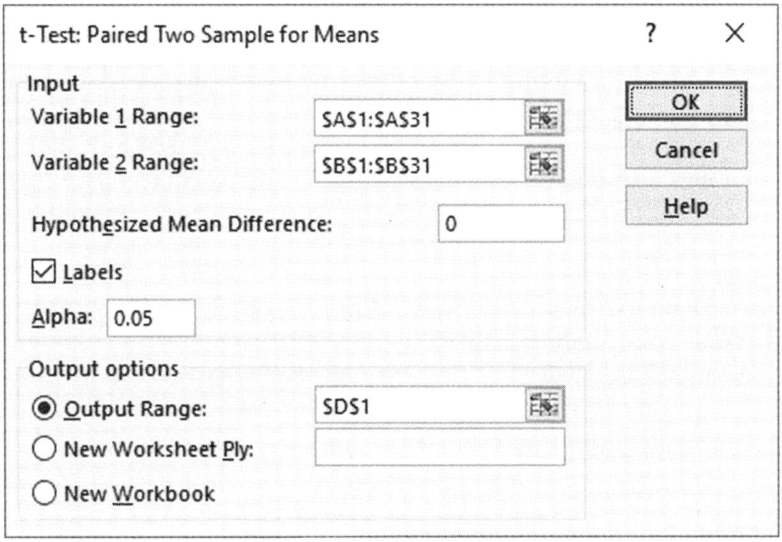

FIGURE E-4   ● Results of a Paired Samples *t*-Test

tails shown in **E13**). Because the *p* value (4.3E-13 = .00000000000043) is smaller than .05, you reject the null hypothesis. The alternative hypothesis is true: Employees' post-test scores are significantly better than their pre-test scores. The post-test's group mean is 79.7 while the pre-test's group mean is 48.8. You can conclude that the training program was effective in helping the trainees learn.

5. The *t*-test results above revealed a statistically significant outcome, indicating that the training program was effective. Statistical significance found in research context does not indicate practical importance in terms of how useful the intervention effect will be in a practical context. The magnitude of the intervention effect is explained with an *effect size*. For paired sample comparisons, you can use a Pearson's *r* value to indicate how strong the intervention effect was. Pearson's *r* can be calculated with SPSS or Excel. The range of *r* values is between -1 and +1. Using an absolute *r* value (|*r*|), the following loose guidelines can be used to classify the degree of effect size (Morgan, Leech, Gloeckner, & Barrett, 2013, p. 102):

- A much larger than typical effect size if |*r*| is around .70
- A large or larger than typical effect size if |*r*| is around .51
- A medium or typical effect size if |*r*| is around .36
- A small or smaller than typical effect size if |*r*| is around .10

The Pearson Correlation *r* value shown in **D7** is .54, which indicates a large effect size. The training program's effectiveness was not only statistically significant but also practically important.

6. It is helpful to show the mean difference in a bar graph. To make a bar graph, select from **D3 to F4** (six cells) as shown in Figure E-5.

Select **Insert** from the menu bar, and select the **Clustered Column** type among the **bar graph** options. Now you have a bar graph showing the mean difference (see Figure E-6). Click on one of the bars; it will select both bars. While both bars are selected, right-click on one of the bars and select **Add Data Label** to show the numerical values above the bars.

FIGURE E-5 ● Selecting Cells to Be Used in a Bar Graph

	A	B	C	D	E	F	G
1	Pretest	Posttest		t-Test: Paired Two Sample for Means			
2	45	89					
3	65	80			*Pretest*	*Posttest*	
4	34	79	Mean		48.83333	79.7	
5	64	89	Variance		259.523	163.9414	
6	56	98			30	30	

FIGURE E-6 ● A Bar Graph Showing Pre-Test and Post-Test Mean Values

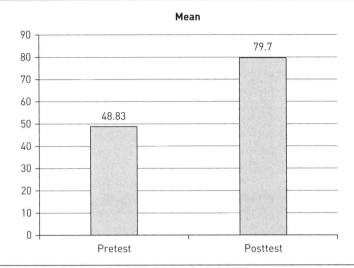

7. Your conclusion and recommendation: Now you may decide to use the research findings as part of your evidence while convincing your management that it would be beneficial to deliver the training program to all other employees as well (i.e., generalizability of inferential statistics). However, you should also point out that factors other than the training program itself could have influenced the improvement from the pre-measure to the post-measure of employee knowledge (e.g., employees also participated in a mentoring program at that time).

Independent Samples *t*-Test When Comparing Intervention and Nonintervention Groups

You can conduct a Level 2 evaluation of a training program to see if employees who completed the training program have a significantly higher level of knowledge on the learned subject than those who did not complete the training program. Then, an outline of your research procedure would be as follows.

Hypothesis: Again, you write down a null hypothesis (H_0) as well as an alternative hypothesis (H_1), and test the probability (likelihood) of a null hypothesis to be true. If your statistical analysis reveals that it is unlikely that a null hypothesis is true, you reject the null hypothesis and accept the alternative (your research) hypothesis to be true, and vice versa. You will use directional hypothesis statements:

-   H_1: The post-test scores of employees who completed the training program are significantly higher than those of employees who did not complete the training program.

- H_0: The post-test scores of employees who completed the training program are not significantly higher than those of employees who did not complete the training program.

Participants: For a true experimental study, you need to use the following two methods:

- Random selection—You randomly select employees from the entire employee population.

- Random assignment—You randomly assign the selected employees to two groups, an intervention group that will receive the training program and a nonintervention group that will not.

The random assignment step—as well as the random selection of participants—ensures that the two groups consist of participants with similar characteristics.

However, in some situations, you may not be able to use a random assignment method. Let's say the organization where you conduct your research (population) has two branches. You randomly selected a sample of employees among those who work in Branch 1 and Branch 2 as your research participants. Instead of randomly assigning the sample of employees to an intervention and nonintervention groups, you assigned employees selected from Branch 1 to an intervention group and employees selected from Branch 2 to a nonintervention group. As shown here, failing to use random assignment makes your research a *quasi-experimental* study.

Data collection: You administer a knowledge test to the employees in the intervention group after they complete the training program, and you administer the same test to the employees in the nonintervention group at the same time.

Data analysis with independent samples *t*-test using Excel: To test the null hypothesis, you use an *independent samples t-test* with SPSS or Excel. As an example, let's say you conducted a quasi-experimental study using data obtained from Branch 1 and Branch 2. You provided a new training program to the employees at Branch 1 (an intervention group), whereas you did not provide it to the employees at Branch 2 (a nonintervention group). After the training program was over, you administered a knowledge test to employees at both branches. Would their test scores be different? If so, how different? Would the difference be statistically significant and practically important?

To illustrate the steps for running an independent samples *t*-test, we will use a hypothetical data set.

1. Enter a set of data into two columns of a new Excel worksheet as shown in Figure E-7. In this example, 60 participants (30 in each group) are used. You may use a larger sample size for real research projects.

2. Select **Data** > **Data Analysis** from the menu bar, and select ***t*-Test: Two-Sample Assuming Unequal Variances** (you can use the ***F*-Test Two-Sample for Variances** test to find out that the variances are unequal). Click **OK**. See Figure E-8.

3. On the *t*-Test Two-Sample Assuming Unequal Variances window (Figure E-9),

    - Click the worksheet icon 🖳 next to **Variable 1 Range**, select from **A1** (not A2) to **A31,** and press **Enter**.

    - Click the icon next to **Variable 2 Range**, select from **B1** (not B2) to **B31,** and press **Enter**.

    - Enter **0** in the box next to **Hypothesized Mean Difference** (meaning that you hypothesize that the two sets of data are not going to be different).

    - Checkmark **Labels** (because you included **A1** and **B1** and want to indicate that they should be treated as labels).

    - Keep **0.05** as the **Alpha** level.

    - Select **Output Range**, click the worksheet icon next to it to select **D1** (to indicate that this cell will be the upper left corner of the *t*-test output table), and press **Enter**.

    - Click **OK**.

4. Detailed *t*-test results are presented (Figure E-10). You use the observed *p* value to make your hypothesis-testing decision:

    - If $p < .05$, then reject the null hypothesis and accept the alternative hypothesis.

    - If $p \geq .05$, then retain the null hypothesis and reject the alternative hypothesis.

Because the *p* value for one tail (**E10** = .004016) is smaller than .05, you decide to reject the null hypothesis, and you conclude that the null hypothesis is not true. The alternative hypothesis is true: The post-test scores of employees who completed the training program (Branch 1) are significantly higher than those of employees who did not complete the training program (Branch 2).The Branch 1 group mean is **80.13** while the Branch 2 group mean is **68.06**. You can conclude that your new instructional strategy is more effective than the previous strategy in helping the trainees learn.

FIGURE E-7 ● **An Excel Data File for an Independent Samples *t*-Test**

	A	B
1	Branch1	Branch2
2	89	75
3	80	77
4	79	92
5	89	96
6	98	66
7	56	47
8	79	88
9	78	91
10	96	54
11	80	88
12	79	46
13	89	56
14	91	91
15	76	76
16	89	89
17	44	44
18	86	43
19	88	24
20	94	94
21	84	84
22	87	87
23	78	54
24	82	70
25	60	66
26	84	41
27	70	59
28	66	89
29	77	57
30	73	66
31	83	32

5. Let's check an effect size. In the previous example for a paired samples *t*-test when *paired samples* were compared, you used a Pearson's *r* value to indicate the effect size. You do not use Pearson's *r* when you compare *independent samples*. A popular method for showing an effect size when comparing

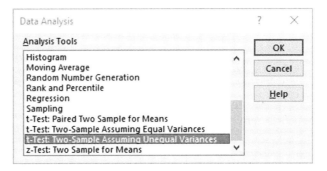

FIGURE E-8 ● The Data Analysis Window

FIGURE E-9 ● The "*t*-Test: Two-Sample Assuming Unequal Variances" Window

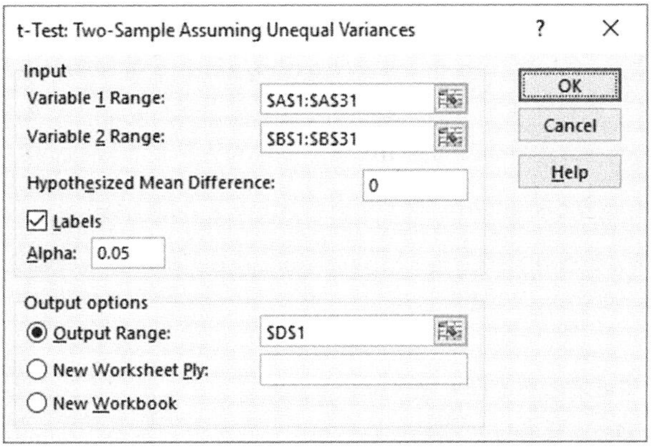

independent samples is Cohen's *d*, the formula of which is: $(M_2 - M_1)/SD_{pooled}$ where:

- M_1 and M_2 = two groups' mean values
- SD_{pooled} = the pooled standard deviation, calculated from

  $\sqrt{(((n_1 - 1) \times SD_1^2 + (n_2 - 1) \times SD_2^2)/(n_1 + n_2 - 2))}$, where:

  ○ n_1 and n_2 = numbers of subjects in two groups
  ○ SD_1 and SD_2 = standard deviations of the two groups (Morgan et al., 2013; Warner, 2008)

To classify the degree of effect size, you can use the following guidelines (Warner, 2008):

- A large effect size if $|d| \geq .80$
- A medium effect size if $.20 < |d| \leq .79$
- A small effect size if $|d| \leq .20$

FIGURE E-10 ● Results of an Independent Samples *t*-Test

	A	B	C	D	E	F	G
1	Branch1	Branch2		t-Test: Two-Sample Assuming Unequal Variances			
2	89	75					
3	80	77			Branch1	Branch2	
4	79	92		Mean	80.13333	68.06667	
5	89	96		Variance	140.2575	428.5471	
6	98	66		Observations	30	30	
7	56	47		Hypothesized Mean Difference	0		
8	79	88		df	46		
9	78	91		t Stat	2.771191		
10	96	54		P(T<=t) one-tail	0.004016		
11	80	88		t Critical one-tail	1.67866		
12	79	46		P(T<=t) two-tail	0.008033		
13	89	56		t Critical two-tail	2.012896		
14	91	91					
15	76	76					

There is no Excel function that generates Cohen's *d* value. You have to manually calculate it. First, you need to calculate the SD_{pooled} value.

$SD_{pooled} = SQRT (((n_1 - 1) \times SD_1^2 + (n_2 - 1) \times SD_2^2) / (n_1 + n_2 - 2))$, where:

- n_1 and n_2 = numbers of subjects in two groups
- SD_1 and SD_2 = standard deviations of the two groups

You already have all values needed to run the formula:

- The number of subjects in two groups is 30, so n_1 is 30 (cell **E6**) and n_2 = 30 (cell **F6**).
- SD^2 is the same as Variance, so SD_1^2 is 140.2575 (cell **E5**) and SD_2^2 is 428.5471 (cell **F5**).

Then, you plug all values into the formula:

$$SD_{pooled} = SQRT (((30 - 1) \times 140.2575 + (30 - 1) \times 428.5471) / (30 + 30 - 2))$$

$$= SQRT (16495.33 / 58) = SQRT (284.40)$$

$$= 16.86$$

Now, Cohen's $d = (M_2 - M_1)/SD_{pooled}$ where M_2 and M_1 = two groups' mean values.

- M_2 is 80.13 (cell **E4**) and M1 is 68.06 (cell **F4**).

Therefore, Cohen's $d = (80.13 - 68.06) / 16.86 = 0.71$, which indicates a high medium effect size.

6. To show the mean difference in a bar graph, select from **D3 to F4** (six cells) as shown in Figure E-11.

Select **Insert** from the menu bar, and select the **Clustered Column** type among the **bar graph** options. Now you have a bar graph showing the mean difference.

Click on one of the bars (it will select both bars). While both bars are selected, right-click on one of the bars and select **Add Data Label** to show the numerical values above the bars.

Let's also change the current vertical axis value range, 62–82, to 0–100. Right-click anywhere on the vertical axis values and select **Format Axis**. On the **Format Axis** pane, change the **Minimum** value (62.0) to 0, and change the **Maximum** value (82.0) to 100. Your bar graph should look as shown in Figure E-12.

7. Your conclusion and recommendation: Now you may decide to use this piece of information as part of your argument while convincing your management that it would be beneficial to use the new training program in all other branches as well (i.e., generalizability of inferential statistics).

FIGURE E-11 ● **Selecting Cells to Be Used in a Bar Graph**

	A	B	C	D	E	F	G
1	Branch1	Branch2		t-Test: Two-Sample Assuming Unequal Variances			
2	89	75					
3	80	77			Branch1	Branch2	
4	79	92		Mean	80.13333	68.06667	
5	89	96		Variance	140.2575	428.5471	
6	98	66		Observations	30	30	
	56	47		Hypothesized Mean Differen		0	

FIGURE E-12 ● **A Bar Graph Showing Two Independent Groups' Mean Values**

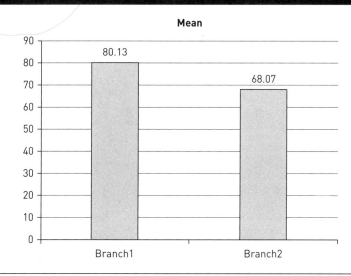

Mean

• Glossary •

This glossary provides brief explanations about how the words and terms are used in this book rather than dictionary definitions. For more information about these words or terms used in the evaluation context, readers are encouraged to refer to the most recent edition of Michael Scriven's *Evaluation Thesaurus*.

Anonymity. With anonymous data, evaluators do not know who submitted the data. Evaluators can ensure anonymity of survey or test data by not asking the informants' names or other identifiable information in the survey or test instruments. Evaluation clients can provide evaluators with anonymous extant data without any identifiable information. It may be difficult to collect anonymous data from interviews, focus groups, or observations because the evaluators have personal contact with the informants during the data collection process. However, evaluators can replace informants' identifiable information with codes while or after collecting data and then use the anonymous data during their data analysis. See also *Confidentiality* and *Informants*.

Assessment. An assessment often refers to an investigation or estimation of the nature, condition, or capacity of something or someone. It may or may not involve the judgment of the quality or value associated with the object or person being assessed. See also *Evaluation*.

Back-end evaluation. A back-end evaluation is conducted after a program has been implemented to assess the quality of the program process and products. Back-end evaluations are compared to front-end evaluations, which are conducted during the front-end stage of program. See also *Front-end evaluation*.

Behavior engineering model. Thomas Gilbert developed the behavior engineering model, a.k.a. the third leisurely theorem, in the 1970s. The behavior engineering model explains six factors that influence performance: three environmental factors (data, instruments, and incentives) and three personal factors (knowledge, capacity, and motives). The model can be used as a cause analysis tool. Evaluators can use the behavior engineering model during the identification phase of an evaluation project, to identify the type of an evaluand. More information about the behavior engineering model is provided in Appendix A. See also *Evaluand*.

Black box evaluation. The concepts of black box, clear box, and gray box evaluations are derived from software testing terminology. When conducting a black box evaluation of a program, evaluators investigate the end results of the program without studying how the program works. See also *Clear box evaluation* and *Gray box evaluation*.

Clear box evaluation. The concepts of black box, clear box, and gray box evaluations are derived from software testing terminology. When conducting a clear box evaluation of a program, evaluators study the inner workings of the program fully, as well as the program outcomes. See also *Black box evaluation* and *Gray box evaluation*.

Confidentiality. When evaluators maintain confidentiality of data, others cannot identify the informants who provided the data. Evaluators must keep confidentiality of data they have obtained. Collecting data anonymously helps evaluators keep confidentiality of the data. See also *Anonymity*.

Construct. A construct—also known as a latent variable—is an abstract concept or idea that cannot be directly measured. To measure a construct, evaluators identify aspects that describe the construct and develop survey items that measure those aspects of the construct. Such survey instruments should be tested for construct validity and reliability. See also *Validity* and *Reliability*.

Critical multiplism. Individual data collection methods are likely imperfect, possessing their own strengths and weaknesses. Thus, evaluators use a multiplist approach to determining data collection methods. By applying the critical multiplism principle, evaluators determine data collection methods first by examining the strengths and weaknesses of each viable data collection method. Then, evaluators select multiple data collection methods that complement the strengths, and compensate for the weaknesses, of individual data collection methods. See also *Triangulation*.

Data collection methods. There are different ways to collect data—self-administered surveys, interviews, focus groups, observations, extant data reviews, and tests. Evaluators should select the data collection methods that are most appropriate for measuring each evaluation dimension. Each type of data collection method has its strengths and weaknesses. Thus, evaluators should also apply a multiplist approach when determining data collection methods and triangulate the data obtained from different sources. See also *Critical multiplism* and *Triangulation.*

Descriptive case study type evaluation design. See *Descriptive evaluation design.*

Descriptive evaluation design. When using a descriptive evaluation design, evaluators study a case without manipulating any variables. The case can be a person, a group of people, or an organization, which is often purposely selected (a.k.a. purposive sampling). By generating descriptive information about the case, evaluators gain an in-depth understanding about the case. To increase credibility of their conclusions, evaluators often triangulate multiple sets of data obtained from multiple sources. See also *Experimental evaluation design* and *Triangulation.*

Dimensional evaluation question. Once a dimension is identified in a word or a short phrase, a dimensional evaluation question is formulated to indicate the focus of the dimensional investigation. Evaluators design their evaluation project to answer dimensional evaluation questions. See also *Dimensions.*

Dimensions. Michael Scriven uses the word *dimensions* to refer to the characteristics of an evaluand. During a system-focused evaluation, evaluators investigate both internal and external dimensions of a program. Each dimension is described by a word or a short phrase (e.g., managerial support) and accompanied with a dimensional evaluation question (e.g., How much support does the management provide for the training program?). See also *Evaluand* and *System-focused evaluation.*

Direct impactees. Direct impactees of a program are the individuals who receive, use, or participate in the program. See also *Indirect impactees.*

Downstream consumers. Downstream consumers of a program are the individuals who are directly or indirectly affected by the program. See also *Direct impactees* and *Indirect impactees.*

Evaluand. Michael Scriven coined the term *evaluand* to refer to an entity that is being evaluated. In the human performance improvement context, performance improvement interventions such as training programs or incentive programs can be evaluands. See also *Evaluee.*

Evaluation. Michael Scriven defines *evaluation* as the process of determining the merit, worth, or significance of something. Evaluation conducted on a performance improvement intervention program in the human performance improvement context can be characterized as a type of program evaluation. In this book, program evaluation is defined as the systematic and systemic collection and analysis of information about the process and outcomes of a program in order to make improvements or judgments about the quality or value of the program.

Evaluation client. An evaluation client is the one who requests and receives service from evaluators. An evaluation client is the one who approves the statement of work and the evaluation proposal and receives the evaluation final report from the evaluators.

Evaluation proposal. During the evaluation planning phase, evaluators work closely with the client and other stakeholders to gather information necessary to develop an evaluation implementation plan and write an evaluation proposal. The evaluation methodology section of an evaluation proposal describes the purpose and type of the evaluation, the program dimensions to be investigated, and the data collection procedure and timeline. The evaluation proposal should be approved by the client before moving on to the implementation phase of the evaluation project.

Evaluator. An evaluator is a person who designs and conducts an evaluation. Evaluators can be internal or external to the organization in which the evaluation is conducted.

Evaluee. An evaluee is a person who is being evaluated.

Evidence-based practice. Evaluators should use evidence-based practices during evaluation. Evidence-based practices involve making expertise-based and data-driven decisions. Evaluators use evaluation frameworks, models, and procedures that evaluation experts developed and have shown the effectiveness through multiple usage (i.e., expertise-based decisions). Evaluators also collect multiple sets of data, triangulate the multiple sets of data, and make decisions supported by the data (i.e., data-driven decisions). See also *Triangulation.*

Executive summary. An executive summary of an evaluation report is a short document that summarizes the main points described in the full report. Evaluators can apply the five Ws and one H (5W1H) method to writing an executive summary. An executive summary should enable readers to have a good understanding of what was evaluated, why it was evaluated, who evaluated it, for whom it was evaluated, when and where it was evaluated, how the evaluation was designed and executed, what the evaluation found, and what the evaluation concluded. See also *Five Ws and one H (5W1H) method.*

Experimental evaluation design. Evaluators can use an experimental evaluation design to show a cause-and-effect relationship between an intervention program and its outcomes. When using an experimental evaluation design, evaluators randomly select a sample of participants from the population and randomly assign them to different conditions (e.g., an intervention program used or no intervention program used) to see if the different conditions produce different outcomes. When it is not practical to use a random assignment method, the study becomes a quasi-experiment. See also *Descriptive evaluation design.*

Extant data review. Existing data and information is a type of data source that evaluators can use. Extant data may exist in print or electronic files. Examples include training materials, data obtained from previously administered surveys, test scores stored on a learning management system, employee performance records, and employee turnover rates and reasons.

Feasibility. Evaluators should assess whether the evaluation can be successfully completed, considering various factors such as the maturity of the evaluand, scope of the evaluation, organizational support for the evaluation, ethical concerns for the evaluation, and resources available for the evaluation. Evaluators' limited knowledge and skills to be able to conduct a certain type of evaluation should be considered as a risk factor during the feasibility assessment. See also *Risk factors.*

Five Ws and one H (5W1H) method. The five Ws and one H are who, when, where, what, why, and how. The 5W1H method is often used by journalists as a way to ask questions and gather information. Evaluators can use the 5W1H method to gather information about the evaluand from its stakeholders, or while writing an executive summary of an evaluation report. See also *Evaluand* and *Executive summary.*

Focus group. Focus groups are guided group interviews. During a focus group, a facilitator guides group discussions among participants with diverse backgrounds to encourage them to express their experiences, opinions, and reactions on a chosen topic, product, or program. The group discussions likely generate a lot of qualitative data and some quantitative data. Focus groups are often administered in a face-to-face setting; however, they can be administered using a video conferencing system. See also *Interview.*

Formative evaluation. Formative evaluations are a type of evaluation, the purpose of which is to help make improvement-related decisions about the evaluand. Traditionally in the context of curriculum development, formative evaluations are conducted during the curriculum development stage in order to make improvements on the quality of the curriculum, whereas summative evaluations are conducted after a curriculum has been developed and implemented. In the human performance improvement context, it is more appropriate to make an intention-driven distinction rather than the time-specific distinction between the two types of evaluation. Formative evaluations are conducted when the stakeholders intend to use the evaluation findings to make improvements on the process and quality of an evaluand during the development stage or even after the evaluand has been developed and implemented. See also *Summative evaluation.*

Four levels of training evaluation. The four-level training evaluation framework—evaluations of reaction, learning, behavioral change, and results—has been widely used in training evaluations. More information about the four-level training evaluation approach is provided in Appendix A.

Front-end evaluation. Programs are initiated and developed based on needs and inputs from various sources. Front-end evaluations are conducted during this front-end stage of the program. Needs assessments are a type of front-end evaluation. See also *Back-end evaluation* and *Needs assessment.*

Gantt chart. A Gantt chart was developed by an American engineer, Henry Gantt, at the turn of the 20th century. It is a type of bar graph used to illustrate a project schedule. Evaluators may use a Gantt chart to develop their evaluation project schedule and communicate it with the client and other stakeholders.

Goal-based evaluation. Evaluators may evaluate a program against the program goals to see how well the program is designed and implemented to achieve the program goals or how well the program has actually achieved the program goals. It is appropriate to conduct a goal-based evaluation if the program goals were determined based on the program stakeholders' needs. Otherwise, using a goal-based approach comes with risk of evaluating the program against goals that may be obsolete, irrelevant, or inappropriate for the stakeholders. In such cases, evaluators should incorporate an assessment of stakeholders' needs during the evaluation process. See also *Goal-free evaluation.*

Goal-free evaluation. Instead of evaluating a program against the program goals, evaluators can conduct a goal-free evaluation without knowledge of the program goals. In goal-free evaluations, evaluators investigate various program outcomes. Some of the investigated outcomes may be related to the program goals (intended) and some of them may not be (unintended). As internal evaluators are likely exposed to the program goals, external evaluators are in a better position to perform goal-free evaluations. See also *Goal-based evaluation.*

Gray box evaluation. The concepts of black box, clear box, and gray box evaluations are derived from software testing terminology. In software testing, gray box testing uses the positive aspects of clear box testing and black box testing. Similarly, when conducting a gray box evaluation of a program, evaluators adopt the positive aspects of clear box investigation of program components (high level, not operation principles in detail) and a black box investigation of program outcomes. See *Black box evaluation* and *Clear box evaluation.*

Human performance improvement (HPI). Also known as human performance technology, human performance improvement is a transdisciplinary field of practice that promotes the use of systematic and systemic approaches to improving work processes and outcomes. HPI practitioners adopt knowledge from various fields, including psychology, instructional technology, management, organizational development, and evaluation, and apply the HPI principles in various industries.

Human subjects. Human subjects are living individuals who serve as informants during any type of research activity, including evaluation. Evaluators recruit human subjects and collect data from them via self-administered surveys, interviews, focus groups, observations, and tests. Evaluators must engage in ethical conduct while handling human subjects and their data. See also *Informants, Informed consent form,* and *Institutional review board.*

Identification phase. During an identification phase, evaluators communicate with the client to identify or understand the program to be evaluated (a.k.a. an evaluand), its stakeholders, and the purpose of the evaluation. Evaluators also assess feasibility and risk factors for the evaluation project. If feasible, evaluators prepare a statement of work. See also *Evaluand, Stakeholders,* and *Statement of work.*

Implementation phase. During an implementation phase, evaluators implement the evaluation plan as proposed. Evaluators develop data collection instruments, collect data with the instruments, analyze data with rubrics, and draw conclusions. Evaluators continue to perform formative meta-evaluations to ensure proper implementation of the evaluation plan. At the end of the implementation phase, evaluators prepare a final evaluation report and conduct a summative meta-evaluation. Evaluators submit a final report to the client and other stakeholders and may assist them in implementing the findings.

Importance weighting. While investigating multiple dimensions of a program, evaluators identify the degrees of importance among the dimensions based on how stakeholders intend to use the evaluation findings. Stakeholders may perceive all dimensions to be equally important. When stakeholders identify dimensions with different degrees of importance, evaluators use the information to determine appropriate data collection methods to be used to investigate individual dimensions or to prioritize a list of recommendations for improving the quality of the program. See also *Dimensions.*

Indirect impactees. Indirect impactees of a program are the individuals who are impacted by the direct impactees of the program by ripple effect. See also *Direct impactees.*

Informants. Informants are the individuals who provide data about different aspects of a program via different data collection methods such as self-administered surveys, interviews, focus groups, observations, and tests. Informants are selected among the stakeholders of a program. Evaluators must engage in ethical conduct while handling informants as human subjects. See also *Human subjects* and *Stakeholders.*

Informed consent form. While recruiting potential informants, evaluators must obtain their consent to participate in an evaluation before collecting data from them. Evaluators must provide informants with sufficient information about the evaluation purpose, procedure, risks, benefits, participants' rights, and methods for protecting confidentiality of data. This information is written in a document, called an informed consent form. Recruited informants should be able to make an informed decision as to whether to participate in the evaluation or not. See also *Informants.*

Institutional review board. An institutional review board is a committee that reviews, approves, and monitors research involving human subjects. The institutional review board ensures that research is designed and executed with human subjects in an ethical manner, protecting their rights and welfare. See also *Human subjects.*

Intention-driven method. When determining whether to conduct a formative or summative evaluation of a program, it is recommended that evaluators use the intention-driven method—that is, evaluators should determine the type of evaluation (formative or summative) based on how the stakeholders intend to use the evaluation findings. See also *Formative evaluation* and *Summative evaluation.*

Intervention-focused evaluation. Intervention-focused evaluation is a way to characterize how evaluators approach their evaluation. When using an intervention-focused evaluation approach, evaluators assume that the intervention (the program itself) is responsible for achieving program goals. Thus, evaluators focus on investigating the program's known needs, internal process, and intended outcomes, without considering other environmental factors that may also have influenced the success or failure of the program. Therefore, evaluators are encouraged to conduct a system-focused evaluation. See also *System-focused evaluation.*

Interview. Interviews are a data collection method. Evaluators conduct interviews with purposively selected informants among stakeholders to solicit information about a topic. Interviews can be conducted in a face-to-face setting, by telephone, or via video conferencing system. Interview questions can be structured, semi-structured, or unstructured. Most interviews are used to obtain in-depth qualitative data, whereas structured interviews may produce quantitative data.

Iterative design approach. While following a step-by-step evaluation procedure, evaluators should use an iterative design approach to revisit previous steps and modify the evaluation plan as they discover new information.

Key Evaluation Checklist. Michael Scriven developed the Key Evaluation Checklist to assist evaluators with designing, managing, monitoring, and executing evaluations. More information about the Key Evaluation Checklist is presented in Appendix A.

Measurement. Measurement is a method of determining the quantity (e.g., in numbers) or quality (e.g., in degrees) of something. Evaluators use different data collection methods such as self-administered surveys, interviews, focus groups, observations, extant data reviews, and tests to measure specific aspects of a program. Measurement is not the same as evaluation. For example, measuring one's weight on a scale is not the same as evaluating the person's overall health. Similarly, measuring participants' reaction to a training program with a self-administered survey is not the same as evaluating the program's overall worth. See also *Evaluation.*

Merit. The evaluand's merit refers to its internal quality, which tends to stay the same regardless of where the evaluand is implemented. See also *worth.*

Meta-evaluation. A meta-evaluation is an evaluation of an evaluation. Evaluators should conduct formative and summative meta-evaluations. Evaluators conduct formative meta-evaluations during the evaluation process to check and improve the quality of the evaluation plan and execution. Then, evaluators conduct a summative meta-evaluation at the end of the evaluation project to reveal the overall quality of the evaluation. Meta-evaluations can be performed by the evaluators themselves and/or external evaluators.

Needs assessment. Needs assessment is the systematic and systemic determination of the gaps between current and desired conditions. Needs assessments can be characterized as a type of evaluation. However, in the human performance improvement context, needs assessments are performed in order to determine what type of interventions need to be designed and implemented, whereas a program evaluation is conducted after a program has been implemented to assess the quality of the program process and outcomes. See also *Evaluation.*

Observation. Observation is a data collection method. Evaluators use their senses to record what is happening in a natural learning and performance setting. Evaluators may use checklists to guide their observation process and recording, producing quantitative and/or qualitative data.

Planning phase. During a planning phase, evaluators work with the client and other stakeholders to develop (or review) a logic model of the program to be evaluated, determine dimensions to be investigated, and determine data collection methods. Evaluators continue to monitor the program feasibility and risk factors, and start conducting formative meta-evaluations to ensure they are developing an appropriate evaluation plan. If the evaluation project is still feasible, evaluators submit an evaluation proposal to the client. See also *Meta-evaluation* and *Evaluation proposal*.

Program evaluation. See *Evaluation*.

Program logic model. A program logic model depicts the if–then relationship among key elements of a program. Common categories used to describe key elements of a program are resources, activities, outputs, outcomes, and impact. Resources and activities are means, and outputs, outcomes, and impact are end results of a program. See also *Training impact model*.

Reliability. A structured survey instrument may contain multiple survey items that measure a construct. Reliability of the structured survey instrument refers to how consistently the multiple survey items measure the construct they were intended to measure. See also *Construct* and *Validity*.

Research. Research is a systematic and systemic investigation of phenomena using randomly or purposively selected samples, which results in new knowledge generalizable to the population or applicable to other similar contexts. Researchers may conduct qualitative or quantitative research.

Response scale. Structured survey questionnaires provide respondents with specific options from which they choose to answer the survey questions. A set of these response options is called a response scale. An example is the Likert scale consisting of *Strongly disagree, Slightly disagree, Neutral, Slightly agree*, and *Strongly agree*.

Risk factors. Risk factors during an evaluation project refer to various factors that may negatively impact successful completion of the evaluation project. To maximize the success of the evaluation project, evaluators

should assess potential risk factors systemically and develop plans for minimizing the damage these risk factors may cause.

Rubric. Rubrics are the standards or criteria that evaluators apply while analyzing the data they have collected. These standards are expressed as a set of levels and definitions. Rubric definitions can be quantitatively or qualitatively stated. Evaluators use rubrics to determine the quality of an evaluand's dimensions or the overall quality of an evaluand.

Stakeholders. Stakeholders of a program are the individuals that hold a stake in the program. Michael Scriven categorizes three types of stakeholders—upstream stakeholders (or upstream impactees), direct impactees, and indirect impactees. Evaluators select informants among stakeholders. See also *Upstream stakeholders, Direct impactees*, and *Indirect impactees*.

Statement of work (SOW). A statement of work is a document that lays out an overall scope of work to be completed. It describes the objectives and deliverables of the work, resources to be used, and timeline to be followed. A statement of work is prepared in the early stage of an evaluation project to get agreement on the scope of the project from both the service requester (the client) and service provider (the evaluator).

Success Case Method. The Success Case Method is an evaluation framework developed by Robert Brinkerhoff that guides evaluators in examining how the organization has used a training program. While using the method, evaluators develop a training impact model. As part of data collection, evaluators conduct a self-administered survey with those who have completed a training program and identify successful and unsuccessful performance cases based on the survey data. Then, evaluators conduct interviews with successful and unsuccessful cases to investigate various factors that contributed to their performance outcomes. In doing so, evaluators likely identify positive and negative environmental factors as well as the training program's effectiveness. More information about the Success Case Method is provided in Appendix A. See also *Training impact model*.

Summative evaluation. Summative evaluation is a type of evaluation, the purpose of which is to help make accountability-related decisions on an evaluand. Traditionally in the context of curriculum development, summative evaluations are conducted after a curriculum has been developed and implemented, whereas formative evaluations are conducted during the curriculum development stage in order to make improvements on the quality of the curriculum. In the human performance improvement context, it is more appropriate to make an intention-driven distinction rather than the time-specific distinction between the two types of evaluation. After an evaluand has been implemented, a summative evaluation is performed when stakeholders intend to use the evaluation findings to make accountability-related decisions on the evaluand. See also *Formative evaluation.*

Survey (self-administered). Self-administered surveys are a data collection method. Evaluators use structured, semi-structured, or unstructured survey instruments to obtain quantitative and/or qualitative data. Self-administered surveys can be conducted on paper (on site or via mail) or online (on the web or via email).

SWOT analysis. SWOT stands for strengths, weaknesses, opportunities, and threats. The SWOT analysis is used to assess the strengths and weaknesses of a program (or an organization), the opportunities it has, and the threats it faces. A SWOT analysis can be used as a strategic planning tool. Evaluators can use a SWOT analysis while summarizing data and generating evidence-based conclusions and recommendations.

Synthesis. Synthesis is used during summative evaluation. After investigating multiple dimensions of a program, evaluators go through a synthesis step to combine the results obtained from the multiple dimensions and draw conclusions about the overall quality of the program and performance outcomes.

Systematic approaches. Systematic approaches to human performance improvement or evaluation refer to following an effective and efficient step-by-step procedure that leads to intended positive outcomes. An analogy is a group of hikers laying out and following a sufficient number of stepping stones to cross a stream. Another analogy is following a recipe to cook a meal. Similarly, following the 10-step procedure presented in this book is a systematic approach to evaluation. To achieve the desired outcomes, systematic approaches often need to be complemented with systemic approaches. See also *Systemic approaches.*

System-focused evaluation. System-focused evaluation is a way to characterize how evaluators approach evaluation. When conducting a system-focused evaluation, evaluators investigate not only the program itself but also environmental factors that may influence the success and failure of the program. When using a system-focused evaluation approach, evaluators investigate the program's known and unknown needs, internal and external processes, and intended and unintended outcomes. See also *Intervention-focused evaluation.*

Systemic approaches. Systemic approaches to human performance improvement or evaluation involve considering various factors within the immediate system and outside the system that may influence the human performance improvement process and outcomes positively and negatively while following a systematic procedure. An analogy is playing tic-tac-toe or Omok (a.k.a. Five in a Row), a game in which a player watches the opponent's moves while trying to place three or five straight marks to win. Each of the opponent's moves (the environmental factor) influences the player's subsequent move, and vice versa. Systemic approaches during an evaluation project involve assessing feasibility and risk factors and conducting meta-evaluations to make necessary changes to the evaluation plan. They also include accounting for the interconnections of various subsystems such as using inputs from different types of stakeholders, investigating multiple dimensions (internal and external to the program), and triangulating multiple sources of data. See also *Systematic approaches.*

Test. Tests are a data collection method. Using written or performance tests, evaluators assess the amount and accuracy of knowledge and skills that participants possess.

Training impact model. The training impact model included in Brinkerhoff's Success Case Model contains four categories of end results that a training program is expected to help produce—program capabilities, critical actions, key results, and business goals. The training impact model is a type of program logic model that depicts the if–then relationship among key elements of a training program. See also *Program logic model.*

Triangulation. Triangulation is to compare multiple sets of data on the same topic to check if one set of data is supported by other sets of data. Evaluators can collect multiple sets of data from different sources (e.g., different groups of stakeholders), by using different data collection methods (e.g., surveys and interviews), or through different time frames.

Data obtained from multiple evaluators (e.g., multiple observers) can be triangulated as well. During triangulation, evaluators may observe consistency, inconsistency, or contradiction among multiple sets of data. When multiple sets of data show consistency, evaluators have a high level of confidence in their conclusions drawn from them. Inconsistency or contradiction among multiple sets of data will lead evaluators to look for explanations through an in-depth analysis of the data or additional data collection. See also *Evidence-based practice*.

Upstream stakeholders (upstream impactees). Upstream stakeholders of a program are individuals who were or are involved in the design, development, implementation, and maintenance of the program.

Utilization-focused evaluation. Michael Quinn Patton developed the utilization-focused evaluation approach, which emphasizes that evaluations should be designed to provide information that the stakeholders intend to use. More information about the utilization-focused evaluation is provided in Appendix A.

Validity. A structured survey instrument may contain multiple survey items that measure a construct. Validity of a survey instrument refers to how accurately the multiple survey items measure the construct. See also *Reliability*.

Worth. An evaluand's worth refers to its external value, which tends to change depending on the external factors surrounding the evaluand. See also *Merit*.

• References •

American Evaluation Association. (2004). *Guiding principles for evaluators* (developed in 1994 and revised in 2004). Retrieved from http://www.eval.org/d/do/32

American Society for Training & Development. (2009). *The value of evaluation: Making training evaluations more effective.* Alexandria, VA: ASTD Research Department.

American Society for Training & Development. (2012). *2012 State of the industry.* Alexandria, VA: ASTD Research Department.

American Society for Training & Development. (2016). *2016 State of the industry.* Alexandria, VA: ASTD Research Department.

Anderson, L. W., & Krathwohl, D. R. (2001). *A taxonomy for learning, teaching, and assessing: A revision of Bloom's taxonomy of educational objectives* (Complete edition). New York, NY: Addison Wesley Longman.

Barkin, J. R., Chyung, S. Y., & Lemke, M. (2017). Following a 10-step procedure to evaluate the administrative services qualification card program. *Performance Improvement, 56*(8), 6–15. doi:10.1002/pfi.21717

Bloom, B. S., Engelhart, M. D., Furst, E. J., Hill, W. H., & Krathwohl, D. R. (1956). *Taxonomy of educational objectives: The classification of educational goals (Handbook I: Cognitive domain).* New York, NY: David McKay.

Boise State University, Office of Research Compliance. (2017). *Informed consent—Basic.* Retrieved from https://research.boisestate.edu/compliance/institutional-review-board-irb-home/irb-applications-forms-and-samples/

Brinkerhoff, R. O. (2003). *Success case method: Find out quickly what's working and what's not.* San Francisco: Berrett-Koehler.

Brinkerhoff, R. O. (2005a). The success case method: A strategic evaluation approach to increasing the value and effect of training. *Advances in Developing Human Resources, 7*(1), 86–101. doi: 10.1177/1523422304272172

Brinkerhoff, R. O. (2005b). Success case method. In S. Mathison (Ed.), *Encyclopedia of evaluation* (pp. 401–402). Thousand Oaks, CA: Sage.

Brinkerhoff, R. O. (2006). *Telling training's story: Evaluation made simple, credible, and effective.* San Francisco, CA: Berrett-Koehler.

Brown, T. A. (2015). *Confirmatory factor analysis for applied research* (2nd ed.). New York, NY: Guilford Press.

Chen, H. T. (1990). *Theory-driven evaluations.* Newbury Park, CA: Sage.

Chen, H. T. (1996). A comprehensive typology for program evaluation. *Evaluation Practice, 17*(2), 121–130. doi:10.1177/109821409601700204

Chyung, S. Y. (2008). *Foundations of instructional and performance technology.* Amherst, MA: HRD Press.

Chyung, S. Y. (2015). Foundational concepts for conducting program evaluations. *Performance Improvement Quarterly, 27*(4), 77–96. doi:10.1002/piq.21181

Chyung, S. Y., Barkin, J., & Shamsy, J. (2018). Evidence-based survey design: The use of negatively-worded items in surveys. *Performance Improvement Journal, 57*(3), 16–25. doi:10.1002/pfi.21749

Chyung, S. Y., & Berg, S. A. (2009). Linking practice and theory. In R. Watkins & D. Leigh (Eds.), *The handbook of improving performance in the workplace: Vol. 2. Selecting and implementing performance interventions* (pp. 27–50). San Francisco, CA: Pfeiffer. doi:10.1002/9780470592663.ch21

Chyung, S. Y., Kennedy, M., & Campbell, I. (in press). Evidence-based survey design: The use of ascending and descending order of Likert-type scale options. *Performance Improvement Journal.*

Chyung, S. Y., Olachea, S., Olson, C., & Davis, B. (2016). A systematic evaluation of a soccer club's college advisory program. In J. Stefaniak (Ed.), *Cases on human performance improvement technologies* (pp. 211–243). Hershey, PA: IGI Global. doi:10.4018/978-1-4666-8330-3

Chyung, S. Y., Roberts, K., Swanson, I., & Hankinson, A. (2017). Evidence-based survey design: The use of a midpoint on the Likert scale. *Performance Improvement Journal, 56*(10), 15–23. doi:10.1002/pfi.21727

Chyung, S. Y., Winiecki, D., & Downing, J. (2010). Training and performance improvement professionals' perspectives on ethical challenges during evaluation practice. *Performance Improvement Quarterly, 23*(1), 7–29. doi:10.1002/piq.20073

Chyung, S. Y., Winiecki, D., Hunt, G., & Sevier, C. (2018). Measuring learners' attitudes toward team projects: Scale development through exploratory and confirmatory factor analyses. *American Journal of Engineering Education, 8*(2), 61–82. doi:10.19030/ajee.v8i2.10065

Chyung, S. Y., Wisniewski, A., Inderbitzen, B., & Campbell, D. (2013). An improvement- and accountability-oriented program evaluation: An evaluation of the Adventure Scouts Program. *Performance Improvement Quarterly, 26*(3), 87–115. doi:10.1002/piq.21155

Cook, T. D. (1985). Postpositivist critical multiplism. In L. Shotland & M. M. Mark (Eds.), *Social science and social policy* (pp. 21–62). Beverly Hills, CA: Sage.

Coons, E. E., & Levine, E. L. (2004). Raymond Abraham Katzell (1919–2003). *American Psychologist, 59*(7), 640.

Davidson, E. J. (2005). *Evaluation methodology basics: The nuts and bolts of sound evaluation.* Thousand Oaks, CA: Sage.

Denton, C., Eisele, A., & Swanson, I. (2015). *Steering e-campers toward STEM and BSU COEN* (Unpublished evaluation class project). Boise State University, Boise, ID.

Denzin, N. K. (2009). *The research act: A theoretical introduction to sociological methods.* New York, NY: Routledge.

DeVellis, R. F. (2012). *Scale development: Theory and applications* (3rd ed.). Thousand Oaks, CA: Sage.

Evaluate. (n.d.). In *Concise Oxford Dictionary of Etymology.* Retrieved from https://www.etymonline.com/word/evaluation

Evaluation. (n.d.). In *Merriam-Webster's online dictionary.* Retrieved from http://www.merriam-webster.com/dictionary/evaluation

Fabrigar, L. R., & Wegener, D. T. (2012). *Exploratory factor analysis.* New York, NY: Oxford University Press.

Fain, J. A. (2005). Is there a difference between evaluation and research? *The Diabetes Educator, 31*(2), 150, 155. doi:10.1177/014572170503100201

Field, A. (2009). *Discovering statistics using SPSS* (3rd ed.). Thousand Oaks, CA: Sage.

Fitzpatrick, J., Christie, C., & Mark, M. (2009). *Evaluation in action: Interviews with expert evaluators.* Thousand Oaks, CA: Sage.

Gagné, R. M., Briggs, L. J., & Wager, W. W. (1992). *Principles of instructional design.* Orlando, FL: Harcourt Brace Jovanovich.

Gantt, H. L. (1919). *Work, wages and profit* (2nd ed.). New York, NY: Engineering Magazine.

Garland, R. (1991). The mid-point on a rating scale: Is it desirable? *Marketing Bulletin, 2,* 66–70. Retrieved from http://marketing-bulletin.massey.ac.nz/V2/MB_V2_N3_Garland.pdf

Gilbert, T. F. (1976, November). Training: The $100 billion opportunity. *Training and Development,* 3–8.

Gilbert, T. F. (1978). *Human competence: Engineering worthy performance.* New York, NY: McGraw-Hill.

Gilbert, T. F. (1996). *Human competence: Engineering worthy performance* (Tribute ed.). Washington, DC: International Society for Performance Improvement.

Gilbert, T. F. (1997). Ph.D. Engineering performance improvement with or without training. In P. J. Dean & D. E. Ripley (Eds.), *Performance improvement pathfinders: Models for organizational learning systems* (pp. 45–64). Silver Spring, MD: International Society for Performance Improvement.

Gilbert, T. F. (2007). *Human competence: Engineering worthy performance* (Tribute ed.). San Francisco, CA: Pfeiffer.

Herzberg, F. (1968). One more time: How do you motivate employees? *Harvard Business Review, 46*(1), 53–63.

Holton, E. F. (1996). The flawed four-level evaluation model. *Human Resource Development Quarterly, 7*(1), 5–21. doi:10.1002/hrdq.3920070103

Houts, A. C., Cook, T. D., & Shadish, W. R. (1986). The person-situation debate: A critical multiplist perspective. *Journal of Personality, 54*(1), 52–104. doi:10.1111/j.1467-6494.1986.tb00390.x

Johns, R. (2005). One size doesn't fit all: Selecting response scales for attitude items. *Journal of Elections, Public Opinion and Parties, 15*(2), 237–264. doi:10.1080/136898805001788

Johnson, C. E. (2012). *Meeting the ethical challenges of leadership: Casting light or shadow* (4th ed.). Thousand Oaks, CA: Sage.

Joint Committee on Standards for Educational Evaluation. (2017). *Program evaluation standards statements.* Retrieved from http://www.jcsee.org/program-evaluation-standards-statements

Kaufman, R. (2000). *Mega planning: Practical tools for organizational success.* Thousand Oaks, CA: Sage.

Keller, J. (1987). The systematic process of motivational design. *Performance and Instruction, 26*(9/10), 1–8. doi:10.1002/pfi.4160260902

Kendrick, T. (2015*). Identifying and managing project risk: Essential tools for failure-proofing your project* (3rd ed.). New York, NY: American Management Association.

Kennedy, P. E., Chyung, S. Y., Winiecki, D. J., & Brinkerhoff, R. O. (2014). Training professionals' usage and understanding of Kirkpatrick's level 3 and level 4 evaluations. *International Journal of Training and Development, 18*(1), 1–21. doi:10.1111/ijtd.12023

Kirkpatrick, D. L. (1956). How to start an objective evaluation of your training program. *Journal of the American Society of Training Directors, 10–11* (May-June), 18–22.

Kirkpatrick, D. L. (1978, September). Evaluating in-house training programs. *Training & Development Journal, 32,* 6–9.

Kirkpatrick, D. L. (1996a). *Evaluating training programs: The four levels.* San Francisco, CA: Berrett-Koehler.

Kirkpatrick, D. L. (1996b). Great ideas revisited. *Training & Development, 50*(1), 54–59.

Kirkpatrick, D. L. (2004). How to start an objective evaluation of your training program. *T+D, 58*(5), 1–3.

Kirkpatrick, D. L., & Kirkpatrick, J. D. (2005a). *Evaluating training programs: The four levels* (3rd ed.). San Francisco, CA: Berrett-Koehler.

Kirkpatrick, D. L., & Kirkpatrick, J. D. (2005b). *Transferring learning to behavior: Using the four levels to improve performance.* San Francisco, CA: Berrett-Koehler.

Knowlton, L., & Phillips, C. (2009). *The logic model guidebook: Better strategies for great results.* Thousand Oaks, CA: Sage.

Kulas, J. T., & Stachowski, A. A. (2013). Respondent rationale for neither agreeing nor disagreeing: Person and item contributors to middle category endorsement intent on Likert personality indicators. *Journal of Research in Personality, 47*(4), 254–262. doi:10.1016/j.jrp.2013.01.014

Lewis, C., & Rieman, J. (1994). *Task-centered user interface design: A practical introduction* (Chapter 5: Testing the design with users). Retrieved from http://hcibib.org/tcuid/chap-5.html#5-5

Likert, R. (1932). A technique for the measurement of attitudes. In R. S. Woodworth (Ed.), *Archives of psychology* (Vol. 22, No. 140, pp. 5–55). New York, NY: Science Press.

Lincoln, Y. S., & Guba, E. G. (1980). The distinction between merit and worth in evaluation. *Educational Evaluation and Policy Analysis, 2*(4), 61–71. doi:10.3102/01623737002004061

Lincoln, Y. S., & Guba, E. G. (1985). *Naturalistic inquiry.* Newbury Park, CA: Sage.

Maeda, H. (2015). Response option configuration of online administered Likert scales. *International Journal of Social Research Methodology, 18*(1), 15–26. doi:10.1080/13645579.2014.885159

Marsick, V. J., & Watkins, K. E. (2003). Demonstrating the value of an organization's learning culture: The dimensions of the learning organization questionnaire. *Advances in Developing Human Resources, 5*(2), 132–151. doi:10.1177/1523422303005002002

Mathison, S. (1988). Why triangulate? *Educational Researcher, 17*(2), 13–17. doi:10.3102/0013189X017002013

Mathison, S. (2008). Chapter 9: What is the difference between evaluation and research and why do we care? In N. L. Smith & P. R. Brandon (Eds.), *Fundamental issues in evaluation* (pp. 183–196). New York, NY: Guilford Press.

Mayer, R. E. (2003). The promise of multimedia learning: Using the same instructional design methods across different media. *Learning and Instruction, 13*(2), 125–139. doi:10.1016/S0959-4752(02)00016-6

McLaughlin, J. A., & Jordan, G. B. (2004). Using logic models. In J. S. Wholey, H. P. Hatry, & K. E. Newcomer (Eds.), *Handbook of practical program evaluation* (2nd ed., pp. 7–32). San Francisco, CA: Jossey-Bass.

Merrill, M. D. (2013). *First principles of instruction.* San Francisco, CA: Pfeiffer.

Merritt, S. M. (2012). The two-factor solution to Allen and Meyer's (1990) Affective Commitment Scale: Effects of negatively worded items. *Journal of Business Psychology, 27,* 421–436. doi:10.1007/s10869-011-9252-3

Microsoft. (2018). *Present your data in a Gantt chart in Excel.* Retrieved from https://support.office.com/en-us/article/present-your-data-in-a-gantt-chart-in-excel-f8910ab4-ceda-4521-8207-f0fb34d9e2b6#OfficeVersion=Mac

Morgan, G. A., Leech, N. L., Gloeckner, G. W., & Barrett, K. C. (2013). *IBM SPSS for introductory statistics: Use and interpretation* (5th ed.). New York, NY: Routledge.

Nadler, J. T., Weston, R., & Voyles, E. C. (2015). Stuck in the middle: The use and interpretation of midpoints in items on questionnaires. *Journal of General Psychology, 142*(2), 71–89. doi:10.1080/00221309.2014.994590

Nicholls, M. E. R., Orr, C. A., Okubo, M., & Loftus, A. (2006). Satisfaction guaranteed: The effect of spatial biases on responses to Likert scales. *Psychological Science, 17*(12), 1027–1028. doi:10.1111/j.1467-9280.2006.01822.x

O'Sullivan, R. G. (2004). *Practicing evaluation: A collaborative approach*. Thousand Oaks, CA: Sage.

Patton, M. Q. (2008). *Utilization-focused evaluation* (4th ed.). Thousand Oaks, CA: Sage.

Patton, M. Q. (2012). *Essential of utilization-focused evaluation*. Thousand Oaks, CA: Sage.

Patton, R. (2006). *Software testing* (2nd ed.). Indianapolis, IN: Sams.

Peeterse, N., Catcott, L., & Yandell, A. (2011). *Best technical consult help desk program* (Unpublished evaluation class project). Boise State University, Boise, ID.

Preskill, H., & Russ-Eft, D. (2005). *Building evaluation capacity: 72 activities for teaching and training*. Thousand Oaks, CA: Sage.

Pulichino, J. P. (2007). *Usage and value of Kirkpatrick's four levels of training evaluation* (Unpublished doctoral dissertation). Pepperdine University, Malibu, CA.

Qarterman, S., & Shaerrer, S. (2011). *Hospital physician and nurse rounding evaluation final report* (Unpublished evaluation class project). Boise State University, Boise, ID.

Raaijmakers, Q. A. W., van Hoof, A., 't Hart, H., Verbogt, T. F. M. A., & Vollebergh, W. A. M. (2000). Adolescents' midpoint responses on Likert-type scale items: Neutral or missing values? *International Journal of Public Opinion Research, 12*(2), 208–216. doi:10.1093/ijpor/12.2.209

Raydugin, Y. (2013). *Project risk management: Essential methods for project teams and decision makers*. Hoboken, NJ: Wiley.

Rogers, E. (2003). *Diffusion of innovation* (5th ed.). New York, NY: Free Press.

Rummler, G. A., & Brache, A. P. (2012). *Improving performance: How to manage the white space on the organization chart* (3rd ed.). San Francisco, CA: Jossey-Bass.

Saks, A. M., & Burke, L. A. (2012). An investigation into the relationship between training evaluation and the transfer of training. *International Journal of Training and Development, 16*(2), 118–127. doi:10.1111/j.1468-2419.2011.00397.x

Scriven, M. (1967). The methodology of evaluation. In O. Smith (Ed.), *Perspectives of curriculum evaluation: AERA monograph series on curriculum evaluation* (No. 1, pp. 39–83). Chicago, IL: Rand McNally.

Scriven, M. (1991a). Beyond formative and summative evaluation. In M. W. McLaughlin & D. C. Phillips (Eds.), *Evaluation and education: At quarter century* (pp. 19–64). Chicago, IL: National Society for the Study of Education.

Scriven, M. (1991b). *Evaluation thesaurus* (4th ed.). Newbury Park, CA: Sage.

Scriven, M. (1991c). Pros and cons about goal-free evaluation. *American Journal of Evaluation, 12*(1), 55–76.

Scriven, M. (1999). The fine line between evaluation and explanation. *Research on Social Work Practice, 9*(4), 521–524. doi:10.1177/104973159900900407

Scriven, M. (2005). Metaevaluation. In S. Mathison (Ed.), *Encyclopedia of evaluation* (pp. 249–251). Thousand Oaks, CA: Sage.

Scriven, M. (2013). *Key Evaluation Checklist*. Retrieved from http://www.michaelscriven.info/images/KEC_3.22.2013.pdf

Scriven, M. (2015). *Key Evaluation Checklist*. Retrieved from http://www.michaelscriven.info/images/MS_KEC_8-15-15.doc

Shadish, W. R. (1993). Critical multiplism: A research strategy and its attendant tactics. *New Directions for Program Evaluation, 60*, 13–57. doi:10.1002/ev.1660

Smith, S. (2008). Why follow levels when you can build bridges? *Training + Development, 62*(9), 58–62.

Stevens, D. D., & Levi, A. J. (2005). *Introduction to rubrics: An assessment tool to save grading time, convey effective feedback and promote student learning*. Sterling, VA: Stylus.

Stevens, S. S. (1946). On the theory of scales of measurement. *Science, 103*, 677–680. doi:10.1126/science.103.2684.677

Stufflebeam, D. L. (2007). *CIPP evaluation model checklist*. Retrieved from http://www.wmich.edu/evalctr/archive_checklists/cippchecklist_mar07.pdf

Stufflebeam, D. L., & Shinkfield, A. J. (2007). *Evaluation theory, models, & applications*. San Francisco, CA: Jossey-Bass.

Synthesis. (n.d.). In *Dictionary.com*. Retrieved from http://www.dictionary.com/browse/synthesis

Tanner, D. (2012). *Using statistics to make educational decisions*. Thousand Oaks, CA: Sage.

Thalheimer, W. (2018). *Donald Kirkpatrick was not the originator of the four-level model of learning evaluation*. Retrieved from https://www.worklearning.com/2018/01/30/donald-kirkpatrick-was-not-the-originator-of-the-four-level-model-of-learning-evaluation/

Trevisan, M. S., & Walser, T. M. (2015). *Evaluability assessment: Improving evaluation quality and use*. Thousand Oaks, CA: Sage.

Tuckman, B. (1994). *Conducting educational research* (4th ed.). Orlando, FL: Harcourt Brace College.

Tyler, R. W. (1986). The five most significant curriculum events in the twentieth century. *Educational Leadership, 44*(4), 36–38.

Tyler, R. W. (1991). General statement on program evaluation. In M. W. McLaughlin & D. C. Phillips (Eds.), *Evaluation and education: At quarter century* (pp. 3–17). Chicago, IL: National Society for the Study of Education.

United Way of America. (1996). *Measuring program outcomes: A practical approach*. Alexandria, VA: Author.

U.S. Department of Health & Human Services, Office for Human Research Protections. (2010). Protection of Human Subjects, 45 C.F.R. pt. 46 (2009). Retrieved from http://www.hhs.gov/ohrp/regulations-and-policy/regulations/45-cfr-46/index.html

Van Tiem, D., Moseley, J., & Dessinger, J. C. (2012). *Fundamentals of performance improvement: Optimizing results through people, process, and organizations* (3rd ed.). San Francisco, CA: Pfeiffer.

W. K. Kellogg Foundation. (1998). *W. K. Kellogg Foundation evaluation handbook*. Retrieved from https://www.wkkf.org/resource-directory/resource/2010/w-k-kellogg-foundation-evaluation-handbook

W. K. Kellogg Foundation. (2004). *W. K. Kellogg Foundation logic model development guide*. Retrieved from https://www.wkkf.org/resource-directory/resource/2006/02/wk-kellogg-foundation-logic-model-development-guide

Wang, G. (2002). Control group methods for HPT program evaluation and measurement. *Performance Improvement Quarterly, 15*(2), 32–46. doi:10.1111/j.1937-8327.2002.tb00248.x

Warner, R. M. (2008). *Applied statistics: From bivariate through multivariate techniques*. Thousand Oaks, CA: Sage.

Weiss, C. H. (1972). *Evaluation research: Methods of assessing program effectiveness*. Englewood Cliffs, NJ: Prentice-Hall.

Weiss, C. H. (1995). Nothing as practical as good theory: Exploring theory-based evaluation for comprehensive community initiatives for children and families. In J. I. Connell, A. C. Kubisch, L. B. Schorr, & C. H. Weiss (Eds.), *New approaches to evaluating community initiatives: Concepts, methods, and contexts* (pp. 64–92). Washington, DC: Aspen Institute.

Wholey, J. S. (1979). *Evaluation: Promise and performance*. Washington, DC: Urban Institute.

Worcester, R. M., & Burns, T. R. (1975). A statistical examination of the relative precision of verbal scales. *Journal of the Market Research Society, 17*(3), 181–197.

Yang, B., Watkins, K. E., & Marsick, V. J. (2004). The construct of the learning organization: Dimensions, measurement, and validation. *Human Resource Development Quarterly, 15*(1), 31–55.

Yarbrough, D. B., Shulha, L. M., Hopson, R. K., & Caruthers, F. A. (2011). *The program evaluation standards: A guide for evaluators and evaluation users* (3rd ed.). Thousand Oaks, CA: Sage.

• Index •